T5-BQA-010

LIBRARY OF NEW TESTAMENT STUDIES

447

Formerly the Journal for the Study of the New Testament Supplement series

THE HEAVENLIES IN EPHESIANS

A LEXICAL, EXEGETICAL, AND CONCEPTUAL ANALYSIS

M. JEFF BRANNON

Published by T&T Clark International
A Continuum Imprint
The Tower Building, 11 York Road, London SE1 7NX
80 Maiden Lane, Suite 704, New York, NY 10038

www.continuumbooks.com

British Library Cataloguing-in-Publication Data
A catalogue record for this book is available from the British Library

ISBN: HB: 978-0-567-57741-2

Typeset by Free Range Book Design & Production
Printed and bound in Great Britain

Contents

Abbreviations

AB	Anchor Bible
AGJU	Arbeiten zur Geschichte des Antiken Judentums und des Urchristentums
ANRW	Hildegard Temporini and Wolfgang (eds), *Aufstieg und Niedergang der Römischen Welt: Geschichte und Kultur Roms im Spiegel der neueren Forschung* (Berlin: W. de Gruyter, 1972–)
ASV	American Standard Version
Bib	*Biblica*
BNTC	Black's New Testament Commentaries
BSac	*Bibliotheca Sacra*
CBQ	*Catholic Biblical Quarterly*
ConBNT	Coniectanea Biblica, New Testament
CRINT	Compendia Rerum Iudaicarum ad Novum Testamentum
DPL	*Dictionary of Paul and His Letters*
EBib	Études bibliques
EDNT	Horst Balz and Gerhard Schneider (eds), *Exegetical Dictionary of the New Testament* (trans. James W. Thompson and John W. Medendorp; 3 vols; Grand Rapids: Eerdmans, 1990–93)
EKKNT	Evangelisch-Katholischer Kommentar zum Neuen Testament
ExpTim	*Expository Times*
FzB	Forschung zur Bibel
HTKNT	Herders theologischer Kommentar zum Neuen Testament
HTR	*Harvard Theological Review*
IBC	Interpretation: A Bible Commentary for Teaching and Preaching
ICC	International Critical Commentary
JJS	*Journal of Jewish Studies*
JSNT	*Journal for the Study of the New Testament*
JSNTSup	*Journal for the Study of the New Testament*, Supplement Series

JSPSup	*Journal for the Study of the Pseudepigrapha*, Supplement Series
LSJ	H. G. Liddell, Robert Scott and H. Stuart Jones, *A Greek–English Lexicon* (Oxford: Clarendon Press, 9th edn, 1996)
LXE	LXX English Translation
NASB	New American Standard Bible
NCB	New Century Bible
Neot	*Neotestamentica*
NICNT	New International Commentary on the New Testament
NIDNTT	*The New International Dictionary of New Testament Theology*
NIGTC	The New International Greek Testament Commentary
NovTSup	*Novum Testamentum*, Supplements
NRSV	New Revised Standard Version
NT	New Testament
NTD	Das Neue Testament Deutsch
NTL	New Testament Library
NTS	*New Testament Studies*
OT	Old Testament
ÖTK NT	Ökumenischer Taschenbuchkommentar zum Neuen Testament
OTP	James Charlesworth (ed.), *Old Testament Pseudepigrapha*
RGG	*Die Religion in Geschichte und Gegenwart*
RSV	Revised Standard Version
SBLSP	*SBL Seminar Papers*
SJLA	Studies in Judaism and Late Antiquity
SNTSMS	Society for New Testament Monograph Series
SP	Sacra Pagina
SUNT	Studien zur Umwelt des Neuen Testaments
TDNT	Gerhard Kittel and Gerhard Friedrich (eds), *Theological Dictionary of the New Testament* (trans. Geoffrey W. Bromiley; 10 vols; Grand Rapids: Eerdmans, 1964–)
TNTC	Tyndale New Testament Commentaries
TTod	*Theology Today*
VC	*Vigiliae christianae*
WBC	Word Biblical Commentary
WUNT	Wissenschaftliche Untersuchungen zum Neuen Testament
ZKT	*Zeitschrift für Katholische Theologie*
ZNW	*Zeitschrift für die Neutestamentamentliche Wissenschaft*

Ancient Sources

Old Testament

Gen. Genesis
Exod. Exodus
Lev. Leviticus
Num. Numbers
Deut. Deuteronomy
Ruth Ruth
1 Sam. 1 Samuel
2 Sam. 2 Samuel
1 Kgs 1 Kings
2 Kgs 2 Kings
1 Chron. 1 Chronicles
2 Chron. 2 Chronicles
Ezra Ezra
Neh. Nehemiah
Job Job
Ps. Psalm
Isa. Isaiah
Ezek. Ezekiel
Dan. Daniel
Hos. Hosea
Jon. Jonah
Zech. Zechariah
Mal. Malachi

New Testament

Mt. Matthew
Mk Mark
Lk. Luke
Jn John
Rom. Romans
1 Cor. 1 Corinthians
2 Cor. 2 Corinthians
Gal. Galatians
Eph. Ephesians
Phil. Philippians
Col. Colossians
1 Thess. 1 Thessalonians
2 Thess. 2 Thessalonians
1 Tim. 1 Timothy
2 Tim. 2 Timothy
Heb. Hebrews
Jas James
1 Pet. 1 Peter
2 Pet. 2 Peter
1 Jn 1 John
Rev. Revelation

Apocrypha

1 Esd. 1 Esdras
Jdt. Judith
Tob. Tobit
1 Macc. 1 Maccabees
2 Macc. 2 Maccabees
3 Macc. 3 Maccabees
Odes Odes

Old Testament Pseudepigrapha

Apoc. Mos. *Apocalypse of Moses*
Apoc. Sedr. *Apocalypse of Sedrach*
Apoc. Zeph. *Apocalypse of Zepheniah*
Aristob. *Aristobulus*
Asc. Isa. *Ascension of Isaiah*
Bar. *Baruch*
3 Bar. *3 Baruch*
1 En. *1 Enoch*
2 En. *2 Enoch*
3 En. *3 Enoch*
4 Ezra *4 Ezra*
Gk. Apoc. Ezra *Greek Apocalypse of Ezra*
Jub. *Jubilees*
LAE *Life of Adam and Eve*
Orph. Orphica
Ques. Ezra *Questions of Ezra*
Sib. Or. *Sibylline Oracles*
T. Abr. *Testament of Abraham*
T. Benj. *Testament of Benjamin*
T. Dan *Testament of Dan*

T. Job	*Testament of Job*
T. Levi	*Testament of Levi*
T. Moses	*Testament of Moses*
T. Sol.	*Testament of Solomon*

Dead Sea Scrolls

1QH	*Hymns/Hodayot*
1QM	*War Scroll*
1QS	*Community Rule/ Manual of Discipline*
1QSb	*Community Rule*
4Q285	*Destruction of the Kittim/Messianic Leader*
4Q317	*Phases of Moon* (cryptic script)
4Q319	*Heavenly Concordances*
4Q320	*Priestly Courses II*
4Q330	*Priestly Courses IV*
4Q405	*Songs of the Sabbath Sacrifice*
4Q491	*War Scroll*
11Q14	*Benedictions* (=4Q285)

Apostolic Fathers

Ignatius, *Eph.*	Ignatius, *To the Ephesians*
Ignatius, *Trall.*	Ignatius, *To the Trallians*
Ignatius, *Smyrn.*	Ignatius, *To the Smyrnaeans*
Polycarp, *Phil.*	Polycarp, *The Letter of Polycarp to the Philippians*
Mart. Pol.	*Martyrdom of Polycarp*
1 Clem.	*1 Clement*
2 Clem.	*2 Clement*

Abstract

In Ephesians, readers of the New Testament encounter one of the most intriguing phrases throughout the whole of Scripture. The expression 'in the heavenlies' appears five times in the letter and is not found in any other place in the New Testament. While there is nothing inherently intriguing about the words ἐν τοῖς ἐπουρανίοις, the phrase proves to be of interest to biblical scholars because of the various contexts in which it is utilized. The two appearances which have caused the most consternation among New Testament scholars are the session of earthly believers ἐν τοῖς ἐπουρανίοις in 2.6 and the presence of the spiritual forces of evil ἐν τοῖς ἐπουρανίοις in 6.12. The seeming implausibility of these two statements has led commentators to interpret this peculiar expression in a variety of ways. The purpose of this book, therefore, is to perform a lexical, exegetical, and conceptual analysis of the expression ἐν τοῖς ἐπουρανίοις in Ephesians. Within this broader purpose, this book: (1) argues against the prevailing interpretation of 'the heavenlies' propagated by Hugo Odeberg and subsequently adopted by Michael Everett McGough in his unpublished ThD dissertation 'An Investigation of Ἐπουρανίοις in Ephesians'; (2) builds upon and augments A. T. Lincoln's research from his article 'A Re-Examination of "the Heavenlies" in Ephesians' and from his monograph *Paradise Now and Not Yet*; (3) provides in-depth examinations of three significant concepts associated with this expression, namely the redeemed on earth having a heavenly status, evil powers in heaven, and the cosmology of Ephesians.

The evidence considered includes an examination of the term ἐπουράνιος from Greek sources, Jewish sources, the Apostolic Fathers, and the Septuagint. In addition, the New Testament uses of ἐπουράνιος outside Ephesians are analysed through a brief exegesis of the passages in which the term appears. The exegetical chapters within the letter of Ephesians itself will include comparisons with the Old Testament, the New Testament, and Second Temple Jewish texts including the Qumran manuscripts and apocalyptic literature. From my examination of the evidence, I conclude (1) that there is no basis for a distinction between the terms οὐρανός and ἐπουράνιος in Ephesians; (2) that the prevailing interpretation of 'the heavenlies' is both flawed and untenable; (3) that Qumran and apocalyptic texts can shed light upon and assist in a proper understanding of the difficult passages in which the expression ἐν τοῖς ἐπουρανίοις appears. The primary contribution to the New Testament field is that this book represents the most comprehensive study of 'the heavenlies' in Ephesians. Throughout the course of the book, other areas of contribution include studies of the term ἐπουράνιος, a heavenly status for the redeemed on earth, evil powers in heaven, the cosmology of Ephesians, and the role of 'the heavenlies' within the thought of Ephesians.

Preface

My initial interest in and exposure to 'the heavenlies' in Ephesians was from a Greek Readings course on Ephesians during my time as a student at Reformed Theological Seminary (Orlando, FL). When we arrived at Eph. 2.6 and read that God has raised up believers and seated them 'in the heavenlies', I recall thinking what an astonishing and perplexing statement that was. No doubt I had probably read this verse dozens of times in prior Bible study, but for some reason, the extraordinary character of this statement had previously eluded me. Though it had certainly captured my interest, I was nevertheless content at the time not to probe any further into the mystery of Eph. 2.6. My interests in the New Testament, and, more specifically, in the areas of eschatology and resurrection, were also cultivated during my time as a seminary student at Reformed Theological Seminary. Consequently, early in my PhD studies at the University of Edinburgh, I had discussions with Professor Larry Hurtado, the supervisor of my PhD studies, about subjects such as resurrection and ascension when I needed to settle on a dissertation topic. After one of those conversations, Professor Hurtado suggested 'the curious notion of a heavenly status for the redeemed on earth' as a dissertation topic. From that suggestion, I began my investigation of 'the heavenlies' in Ephesians. This book is the fruit of that investigation and represents a minor revision of my PhD dissertation submitted to the University of Edinburgh.

When undertaking a project of this magnitude and nature, there are of course a number of people who contribute to its completion. I would like to express my sincerest gratitude and appreciation for the many people who assisted in various ways with the completion of my PhD studies and helped bring this book to its fruition. Dr Richard Seay, my high school Latin teacher, taught me how to study a foreign language, gave me a love for learning languages, and taught me how to develop an argument and write an essay. A number of professors at Reformed Theological Seminary (Orlando, FL) contributed to the development of my theology and helped shape my interest in the New Testament. My courses with Dr Richard Pratt were invaluable for shaping my theology, my understanding of Scripture, and my theological interests.

Additionally, my New Testament professors, Dr Al Mawhinney, Dr Reggie Kidd, and Dr Chuck Hill, gave me a love for the New Testament and shaped my understanding of the New Testament. In particular, Dr Chuck Hill went out of his way to assist me as I considered academic pursuits and applied to PhD programmes.

In Edinburgh, I had numerous friends and colleagues who both enriched my time in Edinburgh and encouraged me as I completed my studies. I would like to thank several colleagues from New College – Dave Allen, David McCabe, Holly Carey, Mike Leary, Judy Diehl, Jeromey Martini, Will Rutherford, Stephen Myers, John Tweeddale, Jason Curtis, Sebastian Moll, Andy O'Neill, Rob Burns, Chris Keith, Dieter Roth, Brandon Crowe, Derek Brown, and Mike Naylor – whose friendships were a source of both fellowship and encouragement as I completed my studies. My family's time and experience at Buccleuch Free Church were a source of friendship, fellowship, spiritual growth, and encouragement. I would like to thank the congregation of Buccleuch Free Church for teaching us the meaning and nature of biblical fellowship and love. In particular, I would like to thank Neil, Mary, Amy, and Neil Montgomery Campbell for their love, friendship, hospitality, and encouragement during our time in Edinburgh. Many others – Donald, Mairi, and Ed Forsyth, Roddy and Christine Macleod, Bob and Heather Ackroyd, John and Angela Tweeddale, Stephen and Lisa Myers, John and Anne Macrae, Richard and Sarah Lytle, Eric and Moira Mackay, Rob and Emma Burns, Warren and Holly Carey, and Willy Lytle – were also a rich source of friendship and fellowship. I would also like to thank Bob Ackroyd for his pastoral care, guidance, and encouragement to me during our time in Edinburgh.

As I completed my dissertation, I received excellent guidance and support from the supervisor of my PhD studies, Professor Larry Hurtado. I would like to thank Professor Hurtado for his suggestion which helped me identify my topic and for his ongoing supervision which helped me refine my topic – the heavenlies in Ephesians. Professor Hurtado's guidance and supervision throughout the course of my studies were invaluable for the completion of my thesis and subsequently this book. Finally, I would like to express my sincere gratitude for Professor Hurtado's incredible patience with me as I completed my studies, often in an untimely manner. In addition, I would also like to thank my examiners, Professor Max Turner and Dr Helen Bond, for their guidance for my revisions and for their thoughtful suggestions on how to improve this book.

The completion of PhD studies almost always requires some form of financial assistance and my case is no exception. I would like to thank St Paul's Presbyterian Church for their support and oversight during my programme. I would also like to thank Effie Neill, Carol Brewer, Kezlon Semanda, and Hal Hadden for their financial contributions. I am appreciative of my parents-in-law, Terry and Fran Neill, who made a number of contributions during my studies to assist with our living expenses. My grandparents George and Catherine Coaker regularly supported us throughout both my studies at Reformed Theological Seminary and the University of Edinburgh. In particular, I would like to thank my parents, Mark and Jo Littlejohn, for their financial support and encouragement during my studies. I could not have completed this project without their overwhelming generosity and support.

Finally, I would like to thank my family for their incredible love, patience, endurance, and encouragement throughout the completion of this project. My life was blessed beyond measure and my studies were greatly enriched with the birth of three children while I completed my PhD studies and this book. My first son Colin, the little comedian in our family, has an insatiable enthusiasm for life and love for others. My second son Drew, the little professor in our family, exudes kindness, thoughtfulness, love, and yet also a sharp, dry wit. My third son Evan, the little adventurer in our family, brings us great joy through his easy-going nature, his wild adventures, and his sense of humour. Colin, Drew, and Evan, I love and cherish each of you and am so grateful to have you in my life. Finally, I would like to express my love and appreciation for my wife Jennifer without whom I could never have completed my studies or this book. Jennifer worked to support us for the majority of my time at Reformed Theological Seminary and for the first year and a half of my PhD studies at the University of Edinburgh. Of greater significance than any financial support, she endured much more than should be asked or expected of any wife as I completed my studies. Jen, your love and encouragement during this adventure were essential for the completion of this book. More than anything, even in the midst of my doubt and unbelief, you never wavered from your belief and confidence that I could do this. I dedicate this book to you.

With great appreciation and sincere gratitude,

M. Jeff Brannon
2011

Chapter 1

Introduction

1. *Introduction to 'the Heavenlies'*

In Ephesians readers of the New Testament encounter one of the most intriguing phrases throughout the whole of Scripture. The phrase ἐν τοῖς ἐπουρανίοις appears five times in the letter and is not found in any other place in all of Scripture. While there is nothing inherently intriguing about the words ἐν τοῖς ἐπουρανίοις, the expression proves to be of interest because of the various contexts in which it appears. In Eph. 1.3 God has blessed believers with every spiritual blessing 'in the heavenlies'[1] in Christ. In Eph. 1.20 God has raised Christ from the dead and seated Christ at his right hand in the heavenlies. In Eph. 2.6 God has also raised believers up with Christ and seated them with Christ in the heavenlies. In Eph. 3.10 the manifold wisdom of God is made known through the church to the rulers and authorities in the heavenlies. Finally, in Eph 6.12 the church's struggle is not against flesh and blood, but rather against the rulers, the authorities, the world forces of darkness, and the spiritual forces of evil in the heavenlies.

While all of the references to 'the heavenlies'[2] in Ephesians are noteworthy, two of the passages have proved quite troublesome for students of the New Testament. Specifically, Eph. 2.6 and Eph. 6.12 have caused the most consternation to scholars. On the one hand, in 2.6 Paul portrays believers as already having attained a heavenly status when he writes that they have been seated with Christ ἐν τοῖς ἐπουρανίοις. On the other hand, in 6.12 Paul writes that the spiritual forces of evil are also ἐν τοῖς ἐπουρανίοις. In these passages, two things

1 Here we utilize quotation marks in order to demonstrate the stereotypical nature of the expression 'in the heavenlies' and to clarify its use here as a translation of the Greek expression ἐν τοῖς ἐπουρανίοις. So as not to belabour the reader, henceforth we will no longer utilize quotation marks to set apart the expression 'in the heavenlies', though its use in this book is always as the English equivalent of ἐν τοῖς ἐπουρανίοις.

2 Once again, the quotation marks for 'the heavenlies' clarify the term's use as the equivalent of the Greek expression τὰ ἐπουράνια, the neuter nominative plural of the Ephesian phrase ἐν τοῖς ἐπουρανίοις. Like we stated above, we will no longer utilize quotation marks for the phrase 'the heavenlies', though its use in this book is always as the English equivalent of τὰ ἐπουράνια.

seem patently out of place. First, it does not seem reasonable that earthly believers should be depicted as already in heaven. Second, the fact that the forces of evil are ἐν τοῖς ἐπουρανίοις is difficult to reconcile with many conceptions of heaven. These two statements have proved to be enigmatic for New Testament scholars and their seeming implausibility has led commentators to interpret this peculiar expression in a variety of ways. Therefore, the purpose of this book is to perform a lexical, exegetical, and conceptual analysis of the heavenlies in Ephesians.

2. *Justification for the Study*

While most commentaries include a few pages devoted to the heavenlies, few scholars have written at any length on the subject. Two of the more thorough and influential treatments are Hugo Odeberg's *The View of the Universe in the Epistle to the Ephesians*[3] and Andrew T. Lincoln's treatment found principally in 'A Re-Examination of "The Heavenlies" in Ephesians'[4] but also in *Paradise Now and Not Yet*.[5] In *The View of the Universe in the Epistle to the Ephesians*, Odeberg argues that the heavenlies describe 'the whole of the Spiritual Reality ... including not only the heavens but also the spiritual life, in which the Church partakes in its earthly conditions'.[6] Andrew T. Lincoln, on the other hand, disagrees with Odeberg's central thesis and argues that the heavenlies are properly understood 'within the context of Pauline eschatology'.[7] In his monograph *Paradise Now and Not Yet*, Lincoln also devotes a chapter to understanding the references to heaven in Ephesians within the context of Pauline eschatology. The brevity alone of these works suggests that a more thorough treatment could contribute to a proper understanding of the heavenlies in Ephesians. Moreover, the fact that these two highly influential commentators are in disagreement also suggests that there is no consensus within New Testament scholarship on the proper interpretation of the heavenlies as of yet.

The only study of greater length is Michael Everett McGough's unpublished dissertation, 'An Investigation of Ἐπουράνιος in Ephesians'.[8]

3 Hugo Odeberg, *The View of the Universe in the Epistle to the Ephesians* (Lund: Gleerup, 1934).

4 Andrew T. Lincoln, 'A Re-Examination of "The Heavenlies" in Ephesians', *NTS* 19 (1973), pp. 468–83.

5 Andrew T Lincoln, *Paradise Now and Not Yet: Studies in the Role of the Heavenly Dimension in Paul's Thought with Special Reference to his Eschatology* (SNTSMS 43; Cambridge: Cambridge University Press, 1981).

6 Odeberg, *View*, p. 12. We will discuss Odeberg's treatment in detail in chapter 2.

7 Lincoln, 'Re-Examination', p. 469; cf. also pp. 479–83. We will discuss Lincoln's view in detail in chapter 2.

8 Michael Everett McGough, 'An Investigation of Ἐπουράνιος in Ephesians' (unpublished doctoral dissertation; New Orleans Baptist Theological Seminary, 1987).

In his dissertation, McGough seems to follow closely Odeberg's interpretation and defines the heavenlies as 'a sphere of existence that embraces earthly and spiritual realities in which believers participate in their earthly, historical existence'.[9] McGough attempts to strengthen his interpretation by appealing to the use of the term ἐπουράνιος within extant Greek literature. At this point, we could detail a host of problems and inadequacies with McGough's dissertation; however, we will reserve our interaction with McGough and our critiques of his interpretation for the body of this book (in particular chapters 3 and 4). For now, it will suffice to note that we consider McGough's dissertation to be full of errors and problems which need to be corrected and addressed. Finally, though his dissertation is of greater length than other treatments, McGough makes no substantive contribution to the subject of the heavenlies in Ephesians.

3. *Approach to the Study*

Our examination of the heavenlies in Ephesians will be lexical, exegetical, and conceptual. We will begin our analysis with a review of the primary ways in which the heavenlies have been interpreted (chapter 2). The focus of chapters 3 and 4 will be primarily lexical through an examination of the meaning and usage of the term ἐπουράνιος in both biblical and extra-biblical literature. Our survey of ἐπουράνιος will include evidence from Greek sources, Jewish sources, the Apostolic Fathers, the Septuagint, and the New Testament. This analysis will inform our understanding and interpretation of the expression ἐν τοῖς ἐπουρανίοις in Ephesians. Chapters 5 through 9 will consist of an exegetical and conceptual analysis of the heavenlies in all of its appearances in Ephesians (1.3; 1.20; 2.6; 3.10; 6.12). The conceptual aspect of our examination will include studies of heavenly blessing (1.3), Christ's heavenly reign (1.20), heavenly ascent in Second Temple Jewish literature (2.6), a heavenly status for the redeemed on earth (2.6), the revelation of divine mysteries in apocalyptic literature and in Paul (3.10), and the presence of evil powers in heaven (6.12). These conceptual analyses will draw upon a wide range of sources including the Old Testament, the New Testament, and Second Temple Jewish literature including the Qumran manuscripts. In addition to the conceptual studies of the heavenlies in Ephesians, we will also interact with various exegetical issues in the passages which contain the expression ἐν τοῖς ἐπουρανίοις (1.3-14; 1.15-23; 2.1-10; 3.1-13;

9 McGough, 'Investigation', pp. 95–96. McGough's conclusions are very similar to Odeberg's and, though he does not acknowledge so, it seems that McGough is greatly indebted to Odeberg's interpretation. We will interact with McGough's dissertation in detail in relevant places in our examination.

6.10-20), which will in turn allow us to understand the meaning and use of the heavenlies within the thought and flow of Ephesians.

4. Assumptions of the Study

a. Authorship

The question of authorship for Ephesians is most complex. The letter's authorship is perhaps debated more than any other book's in the New Testament, as scholars appear quite divided over the issue. Some of the more recent commentators who defend Pauline authorship include Markus Barth,[10] Luke Timothy Johnson,[11] F. F. Bruce,[12] G. B. Caird,[13] Michael D. Goulder,[14] Clinton E. Arnold,[15] Ernst Percy,[16] Peter T. O'Brien,[17] Max Turner,[18] Harold W. Hoehner,[19] Francis Foulkes,[20] Klyne Snodgrass,[21] Ben Witherington III,[22] John R. W. Stott,[23] John Paul

10 Markus Barth, *Ephesians* (AB 34–34A; 2 vols; Garden City: Doubleday, 1974), p. 49.

11 Luke Timothy Johnson, *The Writings of the New Testament: An Interpretation* (Minneapolis: Fortress Press, rev. edn, 1999), p. 412. Johnson is inclined to accept Pauline authorship but expresses some hesitancy when he writes that if Paul did not write the letter, then it was written by his best disciple.

12 F. F. Bruce, *The Epistles to the Colossians, to Philemon, and to the Ephesians* (NICNT; Grand Rapids: Eerdmans, 1984), pp. 229–33. Bruce refers to Ephesians as 'the quintessence of Paulinism' in *Paul: Apostle of the Free Spirit* (Exeter, Paternoster, 1977), p. 424.

13 G. B. Caird, *Paul's Letters From Prison* (The New Clarendon Bible, New Testament; Oxford: Oxford University Press, 1976), pp. 11–29.

14 Michael D. Goulder, 'The Visionaries of Laodicea', *JSNT* 43 (1991), pp. 15–39.

15 Clinton E. Arnold, 'Ephesians, Letter to the', *DPL*, pp. 238–49 (240–42).

16 Ernst Percy, *Die Probleme der Kolosser-und Epheserbriefe* (Acta Regiae Societatis Humaniorum Litterarum Lundensis 39; Lund: Gleerup, 1946).

17 Peter T. O'Brien, *The Letter to the Ephesians* (The Pillar New Testament Commentary; Grand Rapids: Eerdmans, 1999), pp. 1–47.

18 Max Turner, 'Ephesians', *New Bible Commentary* (ed. D. A. Carson, R. T. France, J. A. Motyer, and G. J. Wenham; Leicester: InterVarsity, 4th edn, 1994), pp. 1222–44 (1222).

19 Harold W. Hoehner, *Ephesians: An Exegetical Commentary* (Grand Rapids: Baker, 2002), pp. 2–61.

20 Francis Foulkes, *The Letter of Paul to the Ephesians: An Introduction and Commentary* (TNTC; Leicester: InterVarsity, 1989), pp. 44–48.

21 Klyne Snodgrass, *Ephesians* (The NIV Application Commentary; Grand Rapids: Zondervan, 1996), pp. 23–30.

22 Ben Witherington III, *The Letters to Philemon, the Colossians, and the Ephesians: A Socio-Rhetorical Commentary on the Captivity Epistles* (Grand Rapids: Eerdmans, 2007), pp. 19, 223–24.

23 John R. W. Stott, *The Message of Ephesians: God's New Society* (The Bible Speaks Today; Leicester: InterVarsity, 1979), pp. 16–22.

Heil,[24] and A. van Roon.[25] On the other hand, those who argue against Pauline authorship and contend that Ephesians is 'deuteropauline' include Ernest Best,[26] Andrew T. Lincoln,[27] Rudolf Schnackenburg,[28] Franz Mussner,[29] Edgar J. Goodspeed,[30] Horacio E. Lona,[31] Larry J. Kreitzer,[32] Jean-Noël Aletti,[33] Joachim Gnilka,[34] Bonnie B. Thurston,[35] Margaret Y. MacDonald,[36] C. Leslie Mitton,[37] Ralph P. Martin,[38] and Werner Georg Kümmel.[39] In addition, John Muddiman[40] and M.-É. Boismard[41] represent a 'middle' position and argue that Ephesians is the result of a later follower of Paul who has edited and expanded a genuine

24 John Paul Heil, *Ephesians: Empowerment to Walk in Love for the Unity of All in Christ* (Studies in Biblical Literature 13; Atlanta: Society of Biblical Literature, 2007), pp. 4–6.

25 A. van Roon, *The Authenticity of Ephesians* (NovTSup 39; Leiden: Brill, 1974). A. van Roon argues for the authenticity of Ephesians but also postulates that a secretary wrote the letter from a draft by the apostle Paul, pp. 413–40.

26 Ernest Best, *A Critical and Exegetical Commentary on Ephesians* (The New International Critical Commentary; London: T & T Clark, 1998), pp. 6–36.

27 Andrew T. Lincoln, *Ephesians* (WBC 42; Nashville: Thomas Nelson, 1990), pp. lix–lxxiii.

28 Rudolf Schnackenburg, *Ephesians: A Commentary* (trans. Helen Heron; Edinburgh: T & T Clark, 1991), pp. 24–28.

29 Franz Mussner, *Der Brief an die Epheser* (ÖTK NT,10; Gütersloh: Gütersloher Verlagshaus, 1982), pp. 17–18, 33–34.

30 Edgar J. Goodspeed, *The Meaning of Ephesians* (Chicago: The University of Chicago Press, 1933), p. 10.

31 Horacio E. Lona, *Die Eschatologie im Kolosser- und Epheserbrief* (FzB 48; Würzburg: Echter, 1984), p. 427.

32 Larry J. Kreitzer, 'The Plutonium of Hierapolis and the Descent of Christ into the "Lowermost Parts of the Earth" (Ephesians 4,9)', *Bib* 79 (1998), pp. 381–93; Larry J. Kreitzer, '"Crude Language" and "Shameful Things Done in Secret" (Ephesians 5.4, 12): Allusions to the Cult of Demeter/Cybele in Hierapolis?', *JSNT* 71 (1998), pp. 51–77.

33 Jean-Noël Aletti, *Saint Paul Épître aux Éphésiens: Introduction, traduction et commentaire* (*EBib* new series 42; Paris: J. Gabalda, 2001), pp. 17–32.

34 Joachim Gnilka, *Der Epheserbrief* (HTKNT 10:2; Freiburg: Herder, 1971), pp. 13–21.

35 Bonnie B. Thurston, *Reading Colossians, Ephesians, and 2 Thessalonians: A Literary and Theological Commentary* (Reading the New Testament Series; New York: Crossroad, 1995), pp. 84–87.

36 Margaret Y. MacDonald, *Colossians and Ephesians* (SP 17; Collegeville, MN: The Liturgical Press, 2000), pp. 15–17.

37 C. Leslie Mitton, *Ephesians* (NCB; London: Marshall, Morgan & Scott, 1976), pp. 2–11.

38 Ralph P. Martin, *Ephesians, Colossians, and Philemon* (IBC; Atlanta: John Knox Press, 1991), pp. 2, 4.

39 Werner Georg Kümmel, *Introduction to the New Testament* (trans. Howard Clark Kee; Nashville: Abingdon, 17th edn, 1975), pp. 357–63.

40 John Muddiman, *A Commentary on the Epistle to the Ephesians* (BNTC; London: Continuum, 2001), pp. 2–47.

41 M.-É. Boismard, *L' Énigme de la lettre aux Éphésiens* (*EBib* new series 39; Paris: J. Gabalda, 1999), pp. 9–16, 163–75.

Pauline letter. When we consider the evidence for and against Pauline authorship, what is immediately apparent is that scholars are almost equally divided.[42] In his commentary on Ephesians, Harold Hoehner refutes the prevailing but misguided notion that the great majority of New Testament scholars argue against Pauline authorship.[43] Through a thorough examination of the evidence, Hoehner demonstrates that scholars, including those in the twentieth century, have been equally divided on the issue of authorship for Ephesians.[44] As a result of his analysis, we can agree with Hoehner that 'acceptance of the Pauline authorship of Ephesians has had a long tradition'.[45]

In our examination of the heavenlies in Ephesians, we will proceed on the assumption that the apostle Paul was the author of Ephesians. There is indeed a long tradition of acceptance and we remain unpersuaded by the arguments against Pauline authorship. However, we should make clear that the purpose of this book is patently not to argue for a particular position on the authorship of Ephesians.[46] Practically, for the aims of this book, the issue of whether or not Paul penned Ephesians is of little consequence. The reason for this is because the great majority of scholars who argue for deuteropauline authorship still maintain that Ephesians was written in and stands in the Pauline tradition.

Excursus on Pseudonymous Authorship of Ephesians

In 'The Problem of Pseudonymity', James D. G. Dunn defines pseudonymity 'as an acceptable practice, *not* intended to deceive, but a means of affirming the continuity of God's purpose between the circumstances of the named author and the circumstances of the actual author'.[47] As a general rule, those who argue against Pauline authorship of Ephesians understand the letter in this manner – as continuing in the Pauline tradition and without intent to deceive.[48] In his commentary

42 For a more comprehensive analysis, see especially Hoehner's chart which chronologically tracks scholars on both sides of the issue (in addition to those who have changed or are uncertain), *Ephesians*, pp. 9–18.

43 Hoehner, *Ephesians*, pp. 6–20. Hoehner cites Raymond E. Brown who contends that 'a fair estimate might be that at the present moment about 80 percent of critical scholarship holds that Paul did not write Eph', *The Churches the Apostles Left Behind* (New York: Paulist; London: Geoffrey Chapman, 1984), p. 47. As cited in Hoehner, *Ephesians*, p. 7, note 5.

44 Hoehner, *Ephesians*, pp. 6–20. See especially Hoehner's chart, pp. 9–18.

45 Hoehner, *Ephesians*, p. 20.

46 For more detailed and thorough treatments which defend the Pauline authorship of Ephesians, see Hoehner, *Ephesians*, pp. 2–61; O'Brien, *Ephesians*, pp. 1–47; van Roon, *Authenticity*; Percy, *Probleme*.

47 James D. G. Dunn, 'The Problem of Pseudonymity', *The Living Word* (Philadelphia: Fortress Press, 1987), pp. 65–85 (68). Emphasis Dunn's.

48 Any attempt to deceive would be completely at odds with the author's ethical teaching in Eph. 4.25 which reads, 'Therefore, laying aside falsehood, speak truth each

> on Ephesians, Lincoln attributes the letter to a later follower of Paul who wrote to guide the churches in Asia Minor after the death of the apostle.[49] In such a scenario, it is almost certain that these churches would have heard about the apostle's martyrdom and would have recognized Ephesians as instruction from a trusted teacher within the Pauline tradition.[50] Ernest Best emphasizes that the author of Ephesians had no intent to deceive, but simply desired to instruct Christians in the same manner as Paul if he had still been alive.[51] Similarly, Schnackenburg writes that the author 'understands himself as "only" a communicator and interpreter of the Pauline tradition'.[52] In his study of eschatology in Colossians and Ephesians, Horacio E. Lona regards Ephesians as deuteropauline but yet contends that 'der Verfasser [bleibt] auf der Linie der paulinischen Theologie und bewahrt den eschatologischen Ausblick'.[53] Finally, in reference to mystical thought in Colossians and Ephesians, Alan F. Segal writes, 'If contemporary scholars were not convinced of the Pauline authorship of these letters, one can nonetheless say that they give irrefutable evidence about the popularity of Paul's mystical teaching among his earliest disciples and the direction in which these mystical teachings were interpreted'.[54] The significance of this understanding of pseudonymity for Ephesians is that regardless of one's particular position on the letter's authorship, it is evident that the letter stands in the Pauline tradition and can justifiably be referred to as 'Pauline'.

Throughout this book, we will in various places compare the terminology, theology, eschatology, and cosmology of Ephesians with the rest of the Pauline corpus. Of course, our position on the authorship of Ephesians allows for this and indeed demands it; however, as we observed in the above excursus, since those who argue for pseudonymous authorship of Ephesians still maintain that the letter was written in and stands in the Pauline tradition, the task of comparing the thought of Ephesians with the rest of the Pauline corpus would be of value regardless of our particular position on authorship. For this reason, we can confidently assert that the authorship of Ephesians is of little consequence for the purposes of this book.

one of you with his neighbor, for we are members of one another.' However, an open fiction where the recipients understood that the pseudonymous letter stood in the Pauline tradition would not be at odds with this instruction. Unless otherwise noted, all Scripture citations are from NASB.

49 Lincoln, *Ephesians*, pp. lix–lxxiii. Lincoln even contends that the writer was a member of a Pauline 'school', p. lxxii.

50 Lincoln, *Ephesians*, p. lxxii.

51 Best, *Ephesians*, p. 13.

52 Schnackenburg, *Ephesians*, p. 37.

53 Lona, *Eschatologie*, p. 427.

54 Alan F. Segal, *Paul the Convert* (New Haven: Yale University Press, 1990), p. 69.

b. The destination of Ephesians

Like the question of authorship, the destination of Ephesians is also one of the most complex issues associated with the letter. Matters are complicated by a significant textual matter in Eph. 1.1 which makes it impossible to know with any certainty the specific addressees of the letter. To be specific, the words ἐν Ἐφέσῳ are omitted in a number of early manuscripts including P^{46}, ℵ, B, 6, and 1739. Though scholars often disagree about the particulars of the letter's destination,[55] there is almost universal agreement that Ephesians was addressed to a church or group of churches in Asia Minor.[56] While the original text of 1.1 remains in doubt,[57] the overwhelming amount of evidence points to a destination in Asia Minor.[58] As a result, we agree with and will proceed upon the general scholarly consensus that Ephesians was addressed to a group of churches in Asia Minor, perhaps the churches along the road from Ephesus to Colossae.[59]

c. Relationship to Colossians

New Testament scholars have long observed a close connection between Colossians and Ephesians.[60] Indeed, Francis Foulkes writes, 'Without fear of contradiction it may be said that there are more numerous and

55 For example, Lincoln hypothesizes, on the basis of Col. 4.13 and the awkward syntax of Eph. 1.1, that the original addressees were Hierapolis and Laodicea, *Ephesians*, pp. 1–4. Turner writes that while Ephesians might have been a circular letter for all of the churches in Asia Minor, it is even more likely that 'it was written for the churches along or near the road Tychicus would have taken from Ephesus to Colossae, including Magnesia, Tralles, Hierapolis, and Laodicea', Turner, 'Ephesians', p. 1222. Similarly to Turner, O'Brien writes that the addressees were churches in Asia Minor, 'perhaps in and around Ephesus, or on the road to Colossae', O'Brien, *Ephesians*, p. 49.

56 See, e.g., Lincoln, *Ephesians*, pp. lxxxi–lxxxiii, 1–4; Turner, 'Ephesians', pp. 1222, 1225; O'Brien, *Ephesians*, pp. 47–49; Schnackenburg, *Ephesians*, p. 29; Hoehner, *Ephesians*, pp. 78–79; Foulkes, *Ephesians*, pp. 19–47; Clinton E. Arnold, *Ephesians: Power and Magic: The Concept of Power in Ephesians in Light of Its Historical Setting* (Cambridge: Cambridge University Press, 1989), p. 5; Kreitzer, '"Crude Language"'; Kreitzer, 'Plutonium'; Best, *Ephesians*, pp. 4–6; Goulder, 'Visionaries', p. 16; Martin, *Ephesians*, pp. 3–6; MacDonald, *Colossians and Ephesians*, pp. 17–18; Snodgrass, *Ephesians*, p. 21; Heil, *Ephesians*, pp. 6–9; Bruce, *Colossians, Philemon, Ephesians*, p. 245.

57 For detailed discussions of the textual issues in Eph. 1.1 and the difficulties of reconstructing the verse, see Ernest Best, 'Ephesians 1.1', *Essays on Ephesians* (Edinburgh: T & T Clark, 1997), pp. 1–16; Ernest Best, 'Ephesians 1.1 Again', *Essays on Ephesians* (Edinburgh: T & T Clark, 1997), pp. 17–24.

58 For discussions of and justification for an Asia Minor destination, see the references listed above.

59 See Turner, 'Ephesians', pp. 1222–25.

60 For discussions, see Lincoln, *Ephesians*, pp. xlvii–lviii; O'Brien, *Ephesians*, pp. 8–21; Best, *Ephesians*, pp. 20–25; Turner, 'Ephesians', pp. 1222–24; Hoehner, *Ephesians*, pp. 30–38; Muddiman, *Ephesians*, pp. 7–11; Schnackenburg, *Ephesians*, pp. 30–33; Foulkes, *Ephesians*, pp. 19–47.

more sustained similarities between Ephesians and Colossians than between any other two New Testament letters.'[61] Though there is not universal agreement,[62] the great majority of scholars contend that Paul (or a later disciple of Paul) wrote Colossians for a specific purpose and then wrote Ephesians later (either immediately after or some time after) with more general purposes and for a larger readership.[63] In this book, in accordance with the general academic consensus, we will operate under the assumption that Ephesians was dependent upon Colossians. Indeed, it is our view that Paul wrote Colossians in order to address the specific needs and challenges of the church in Colossae, and then wrote Ephesians, with many of the same themes, for a wider and more general readership, namely the churches along the road from Ephesus to Colossae.[64] On his journey, Tychicus would have taken Colossians, Philemon, and Ephesians to their intended addressees and destinations (cf. Eph. 6.21-22; Col. 4.7-9).

5. *Contribution of the Study*

The primary contribution to the field of New Testament studies is that this book represents the most comprehensive study of the heavenlies in Ephesians. As we documented above, while commentaries often devote two or three pages to the heavenlies, there are very few examinations of greater length and depth. Those examinations that are more fully developed are so far still only journal articles which can be expanded upon. It is our hope and expectation that this book serves as a thorough lexical, exegetical, and conceptual analysis of the heavenlies in Ephesians. Specifically, in our examination, we will demonstrate that there is no basis for a distinction between the terms οὐρανός and ἐπουράνιος in Ephesians. As a result, the prevailing interpretation of the heavenlies, originally put forth by Hugo Odeberg but subsequently adopted by the majority of commentators,[65] including Michael E. McGough in his unpublished dissertation 'An Investigation of 'Επουράνιος in Ephesians', is both flawed and untenable. In this

61 Foulkes, *Ephesians*, p. 25. Turner notes that one-third of the wording of Colossians is taken up in Ephesians, 'Ephesians', p. 1222.

62 Of primary significance is Ernest Best's view that neither the priority of Colossians nor Ephesians can be established with any certainty. For his discussions, see Best, *Ephesians*, pp. 20–25; Ernest Best, 'Who Used Whom? The Relationship of Ephesians and Colossians', *NTS* 43 (1997), pp. 72–96.

63 See, e.g., Schnackenburg, *Ephesians*, pp. 30–33; Foulkes, *Ephesians*, pp. 19–47; Turner, 'Ephesians', pp. 1222–24; Lincoln, *Ephesians*, pp. xlvii–lviii.

64 So Turner, 'Ephesians', pp. 1222–25.

65 See history of interpretation (chapter 2) for a detailed discussion of Odeberg's view and for a discussion of the numerous scholars who have subsequently been influenced by or adopted it.

way, our book will also serve as a corrective to the work of McGough. Furthermore, it is our hope that this book, though we will not agree with him on all points, will build upon and augment the work of A. T. Lincoln in his article 'A Re-Examination of the "the Heavenlies" in Ephesians' and his monograph *Paradise Now and Not Yet*. Throughout the course of this book, other areas of contribution include studies of the term ἐπουράνιος, a heavenly status for the redeemed on earth, evil powers in heaven, the cosmology of Ephesians, and the role of the heavenlies within the thought of Ephesians. In our examinations of a heavenly status for the redeemed on earth and evil powers in heaven, we hope to shed light on these issues that have proved to be 'stumbling blocks' for New Testament scholars. Finally, we will address the issue of why Paul utilized this realized eschatological language in Eph. 2.6, a subject by and large overlooked in studies of Ephesians.[66]

66 So Arnold who writes that apart from the work of Lona (and now Arnold), there has not been a significant effort to discern Paul's motivation for the realized eschatological emphasis in Eph. 2.4-10, *Power and Magic*, p. 147.

Chapter 2

The History of Interpretation of 'the Heavenlies'

1. *Purpose*

The expression ἐν τοῖς ἐπουρανίοις has proved to be both one of the most interesting and perplexing expressions in the New Testament. As we noted in the introduction, Eph. 2.6 and Eph. 6.12 have caused the most consternation to scholars who seek to understand the heavenlies in Ephesians. Specifically, the heavenly status granted to earthly believers in 2.6 and the presence of the spiritual forces of evil in the heavenlies in 6.12 have led commentators to understand these verses in a variety of ways. The purpose of this chapter is to review the ways in which the expression ἐν τοῖς ἐπουρανίοις has been understood in recent history and to interact critically with the various interpretations.[1] At the conclusion of our review, we will offer some final comments and a preliminary conclusion on how the heavenlies in Ephesians are to be understood.

2. *Origin of the Expression*

While the adjective ἐπουράνιος can be found elsewhere in the New Testament,[2] the phrase ἐν τοῖς ἐπουρανίοις occurs five times and is unique to Ephesians (1.3; 1.20; 2.6; 3.10; 6.12). Though hypotheses have been set forth, the origin of the expression remains uncertain. Perhaps it was a traditional formula used in the worship of the early church.[3] Many commentators recognize an extended *berakah* or

1 We should note here that Lincoln's 'Re-Examination' provides an excellent review of scholarship until the time of its publication (1973). As a result, we will interact only briefly with the majority of the scholarship Lincoln reviews in his article. We will, however, provide our own thorough review of Hugo Odeberg's treatment of the heavenlies since it has been so influential and since, though we agree with Lincoln's general conclusion, we disagree with his primary critique of Odeberg.

2 The adjective ἐπουράνιος outside of its usage in Ephesians appears once in John (3.12), five times in 1 Corinthians (15.40; 15.48; 15.49), once in Philippians (2.10), once in 2 Timothy (4.18), and six times in Hebrews (3.1; 6.4; 8.5; 9.23; 11.16; 12.22). The term is also a sparsely attested textual variant for οὐράνιος in Mt. 18.35.

3 Lincoln, *Ephesians*, p. 20. Lincoln suggests a possible analogy with other expressions such as ἐν ὑψίστοις (Mk 11.10) or ἐν ὑψηλοῖς (Heb. 1.3).

blessing in Eph. 1.3-14 which has characteristics of a hymn.[4] If the author of Ephesians incorporated an already existing hymn, then the first occurrence of ἐν τοῖς ἐπουρανίοις would have originated from an earlier source.[5] Paul might have liked the phrase and continued to use it throughout the remainder of the letter. This theory is doubtful, however, as attempts at discovering the structure of the hymn have proved unsuccessful. Furthermore, it seems more likely that the opening *berakah* is the author's original composition.[6] That the phrase was not part of a hymn does not rule out the possibility that it was a fixed liturgical formulation from the worship of the church which Paul chose to utilize for his own particular purpose.[7] In addition, recent rhetorical analysis has allowed for the possibility that Paul utilized Asiatic epideictic rhetoric in his composition of Ephesians so the choice of the more impressive and ornamented ἐπουράνιος or ἐν τοῖς ἐπουρανίοις (as opposed to οὐρανός or ἐν (τοῖς) οὐρανοῖς) would be expected.[8] There is also an appearance of the term ἐπουράνιος in LXX Psalm 67 (v. 15), a psalm which Paul later draws upon in order to emphasize Christ's role as the giver of gifts to the church in his ascension (Eph. 4.7-13).[9] Suggestions that the popularity of the term ἐπουράνιος in Asia Minor might have accounted for its initial appearance in Ephesians cannot be proved and so remain only hypotheses.[10]

3. Local Meaning

A much debated question is whether Paul intended a masculine or neuter nominative for the phrase, the masculine being οἱ ἐπουράνιοι and the neuter being τὰ ἐπουράνια.[11] Most interpreters, without much

4 Lincoln, *Ephesians*, pp. 10–12; Best, *Ephesians*, pp. 105–10; Chrys C. Caragounis, *The Ephesian Mysterion: Meaning and Content* (ConBNT 8; Lund: Gleerup, 1977), pp. 41–45; Barth, *Ephesians*, pp. 97–101. For the most thoroughgoing analysis of hymnic elements in Eph. 1.3-14, see Jack T. Sanders, 'Hymnic Elements in Ephesians 1–3', *ZNW* 56 (1965), pp. 214–32, especially pp. 223–32.

5 W. Hall Harris III, '"The Heavenlies" Reconsidered: *Οὐρανός* and *Ἐπουράνιος* in Ephesians', *BSac* 148:589 (1991), pp. 72–89 (73).

6 Lincoln, *Ephesians*, pp. 13–14; Best, *Ephesians*, pp. 109–10; Harris, 'Reconsidered', p. 73.

7 Best, *Ephesians*, p. 118; Lincoln, *Paradise*, p. 140.

8 See Witherington III, *Letters*, p. 232. See also Witherington III's general discussion of Asiatic rhetoric in Ephesians (*Letters*, pp. 1–10, 219–23) and his analysis of Eph. 1.3-14 in the light of rhetorical analysis (*Letters*, pp. 227–37).

9 Since in LXX Ps. 67.15, τὸν ἐπουράνιον is a substantive for God as 'the Heavenly One' and represents the translation of the Hebrew שַׁדַּי, there is no explicit connection between the Ephesian expression ἐν τοῖς ἐπουρανίοις and LXX Psalm 67.

10 See, e.g., Arnold, *Power and Magic*, p. 152.

11 Odeberg, *View*, p. 7.

certainty, express a slight preference for the neuter.[12] A second and more important question is the precise meaning of the phrase, namely whether or not it should be understood as local. The gender of the adjective does not bear upon the decision as both οἱ ἐπουράνιοι (to be completed by τόποι in a local sense) and τὰ ἐπουράνια can have either local or non-local meanings. A non-local meaning would render the translation 'among the heavenly beings' for the masculine or 'in/with/by the heavenly things' for the neuter.[13]

While most commentators agree that the phrase carries a local meaning in certain occurrences, some disagree about its significance in all of the instances. Some early commentators, such as Chrysostom, Theodoret, and Luther, regarded the expression as a reference to 'heavenly things' and so a further description of the spiritual blessings granted to believers in Eph. 1.3.[14] T. K. Abbott also seemed to be hesitant to ascribe to the phrase a local meaning in all of its occurrences in the epistle. Abbott wrote that Eph. 6.12 is not certainly local and concluded that 'it is not correct to say, with some expositors, that everywhere else in this Epistle the signification is local'.[15] Abbott's hesitancy to grant a local meaning in 6.12 quite possibly arose from a desire to keep the spiritual forces of evil out of heaven. Interestingly, several church fathers (including the above-mentioned Chrysostom and Theodore) had the same problem and interpreted the expression in 6.12 in a referential sense.[16] Ulrich Simon grants both a personal and local connotation when he writes that the heavenlies refer both to the location of Christ's work of salvation and to the partakers of that salvation.[17]

Although the question of gender remains open and cannot be determined with certainty, the appearances of ἐν τοῖς ἐπουρανίοις in Ephesians demand a local translation. Hugo Odeberg correctly identifies the stereotypical nature of the phrase and concludes that it must retain

12 Odeberg, *View*, p. 7; Lincoln, *Ephesians*, p. 20; Best, *Ephesians*, p. 116; Barth, *Ephesians*, p. 78; van Roon, *Authenticity*, p. 214; Wesley Carr, *Angels and Principalities: The Background, Meaning and Development of the Pauline Phrase hai Archai kai hai Exousiai* (SNTSMS 42; Cambridge: Cambridge University Press, 1981), pp. 93–94; Aletti, *Éphésiens*, p. 56.

13 Odeberg, *View*, p. 7. Compare Jn 3.12 for the neuter and Phil. 2.10 as a debated example of the masculine.

14 Lincoln, 'Re-Examination', p. 469.

15 T. K. Abbott, *The Epistles to the Ephesians, and to the Colossians* (ICC; Edinburgh: T & T Clark, 1897), p. 5. Abbott also seemed to waver on whether to interpret the expression in 1.3 as local or as a further description of the spiritual blessings.

16 See Christopher J. A. Lash, 'Where Do Devils Live?: A Problem in the Textual Criticism of Ephesians 6,12', *VC* 30 (1976), pp. 161–74 (163). Chrysostom and Theodore take ἐν as equivalent to ὑπέρ and περί correspondingly so that believers' struggle with the spiritual forces of evil is *about* heavenly things (as opposed to earthly ones). My emphasis.

17 Ulrich Simon, *Heaven in the Christian Tradition* (London: Wyman and Sons, 1958), p. 189; cf. Lincoln, 'Re-Examination', p. 476.

the same meaning in all of the passages.[18] Though some commentators have questioned the meaning in 1.3 and 6.12, the phrase clearly refers to a locality in 1.20, 2.6, and 3.10.[19] Since the phrase is used as a formula and the majority of the references will not allow for a non-local interpretation, the most appropriate meaning for the five occurrences of the expression is a local one.[20] Consequently, views which interpret the expression in a personal or descriptive sense must be rejected.[21]

4. Major Schools of Thought

New Testament scholars have tended to understand the heavenlies along one of three basic lines of thought.[22] First, many commentators assert that the heavenlies are correctly understood by way of analogy with certain philosophical frameworks such as Hellenistic mystery religions, Platonism, or Gnosticism; thus these philosophical frameworks become the proper interpretive grid for discerning the meaning of the expression. Second, others have followed Hugo Odeberg's highly influential treatment in *The View of the Universe in the Epistle to the Ephesians*, where Odeberg contends that the heavenlies ought to be understood not only as 'the heavens' but also as the spiritual life of the church on earth.[23] Third, some commentators have followed Andrew T. Lincoln's influential suggestion that the heavenlies are properly understood within the context of Pauline eschatology.[24] In our analysis, we will first review these three significant schools of thought and then proceed to review some of the more recent contributions to the heavenlies.

18 Odeberg, *View*, p. 7; Lincoln, 'Re-Examination', p. 469; Harris, 'Reconsidered', p. 74.

19 Odeberg, *View*, pp. 7–8; Lincoln, 'Re-Examination', p. 469. Lincoln writes that an understanding of the phrase as referring to 'heavenly things' in 1.3 must be rejected because the other four references (1.20; 2.6; 3.10; 6.12) will not bear a non-local interpretation.

20 Lincoln, 'Re-Examination', p. 476; Odeberg, *View*, pp. 7–8; Caragounis, *Mysterion*, p. 147; Harris, 'Reconsidered', p. 74; Barth, *Ephesians*, pp. 78–79; van Roon, *Authenticity*, pp. 213–15; Bruce, *Colossians, Philemon, Ephesians*, p. 254; Schnackenburg, *Ephesians*, p. 51; O'Brien, *Ephesians*, pp. 96–97; Aletti, *Éphésiens*, p. 56. See also Carr, *Angels*, p. 96, and John G. Gibbs, *Creation and Redemption: A Study in Pauline Theology* (Leiden: Brill, 1971), pp. 130–31, who both ascribe to the phrase 'a figuratively local meaning'.

21 Odeberg, *View*, p. 7. See also Lincoln's rejection of Simon in 'Re-Examination', p. 476.

22 The categories above are general and we only utilize them as an introduction to various trends in interpretation.

23 Odeberg, *View*, p. 12.

24 Lincoln, 'Re-Examination', p. 469.

5. *Hellenistic Mystery Religions, Gnosticism, and Platonism as Philosophical Frameworks*[25]

Finding affinities with Hellenistic religions, Wilfred L. Knox believes that the author's use of the word 'mystery' served as an apologetic against the mystery religions. The Hellenistic readers were less concerned with the relationship between Jews and Gentiles, but instead desired a 'mystery' which would prove attractive to other religions.[26] The centre of the mystery 'is concerned with the ascent of the church to heaven and its consequent triumph over the powers that rule the heavenly spheres'.[27] In Ephesians, not only is the ascent of the soul to heaven depicted, but also the rulers and authorities learn the manifold wisdom of God from the church as it passes through the heavenly spheres.[28] Thus the author of Ephesians 'has ... established Christianity as a "mystery" as against other "mysteries" which threatened to prove more attractive'.[29] This 'mystery' which explains the Christian message in the terms of the Hellenistic religions would serve to validate the cause of the church and would prove effective in attracting others to the Christian community. We agree with Knox that the heavenly status granted to believers in 2.6 was likely motivated by a particular circumstance in the lives of Paul or his readers;[30] however, the links to Hellenistic mystery religions prove tenuous. Moreover, Knox seems to downplay both the influence of Jewish thought on Paul and the Jew-Gentile teaching in Ephesians.

In his article 'Seated in the Heavenlies: Cosmic Mediators in the Mysteries of Mithras and the Letter to the Ephesians', Timothy B. Cargal draws parallels between Eph. 2.6, Mithraism, and Hellenistic mystery religions.[31] Cargal believes that part of Christianity's success should be attributed to its adoption of a Hellenistic worldview through its 'presentation of Christ as a cosmic mediator'.[32] However, Cargal writes that the success of Christianity can also be attributed to the fact that it was not as tied to the details of the Hellenistic worldview as was

25 Since Lincoln's 'Re-Examination' serves as a good review of many of these commentators and schools of thought, our comments here will be brief.

26 Wilfred L. Knox, *St. Paul and the Church of the Gentiles* (Cambridge: Cambridge University Press, 1939), p. 190.

27 Knox, *St. Paul*, p. 190. Although he does not explicitly mention Eph. 2.6, it seems evident that Knox has this reference in mind when writing this material.

28 Knox, *St. Paul*, p. 190.

29 Knox, *St. Paul*, p. 190.

30 We will investigate more fully the possible motivation for Paul's remarkable statement in Eph. 2.6 that believers are seated ἐν τοῖς ἐπουρανίοις in chapter 7, the exegetical and conceptual analysis of Eph. 2.6.

31 Timothy B. Cargal, 'Seated in the Heavenlies: Cosmic Mediators in the Mysteries of Mithras and the Letter to the Ephesians', *SBLSP* 33 (1994), pp. 804–21.

32 Cargal, 'Seated', p. 820.

Mithraism.[33] Finally, Cargal raises the possibility that this identification with and yet separation from the Hellenistic mystery religions was a 'strategy' of Christianity.[34] As we noted in our critique of Knox, Cargal does not emphasize the influence of Jewish thought in Paul's worldview, nor does Cargal recognize the significance of Christology and union with Christ for Paul in the formation of Eph. 2.6.

Among other commentators, Heinrich Schlier interprets the heavenly status granted to believers in Eph. 2.6 against a Gnostic background.[35] Schlier recognizes that the term ἐπουράνιος is not different from οὐράνιος and that as an adjective or a noun, it means that which belongs to heaven, that which is in heaven, or heavenly.[36] After he asks the questions, 'welche Wirklichkeit ist mit der Formel ἐν τοῖς ἐπουρανίοις begriffen, was sind die ἐπουράνια?', he goes on to describe the heavenlies as 'die Himmel des Daseins'.[37] In his understanding, man is challenged to choose for one or the other heavens of 'existence', either for the reign of Christ above all the heavens or for the heaven of the evil powers.[38] Schlier writes:

> Die Herausforderung der Transzendenz, jener übermächtigen Tiefe des menschlichen Daseins, ist eine solche zur Entscheidung. Der Mensch und die Erde sind stets angerufen, sich für den einen oder anderen 'Himmel' ihres Daseins zu entscheiden. Seit Christi Jesu Erhöhung 'über alle Himmel', 4, 10, aber ist der Mensch gefragt, ob er sich für die 'Herrschaft' Christi, die in sich allen Himmeln 'überlegen' ist, oder für einen der Lebensträume, die ihm diese oder jene Mächte einräumen, entscheiden will.[39]

Thus man is faced with an existential decision – to choose for the reign of Christ who is above all the heavens and to live under his authority or to choose for the realm of the evil powers. Though Schlier is correct in recognizing the antithesis between the reign of Christ and the forces of evil in the heavenlies, he also reduces the Pauline gospel and its cosmic

33 Cargal, 'Seated', p. 820.

34 Cargal, 'Seated', p. 820.

35 See also H. Traub, 'Οὐρανός, Οὐράνιος, 'Επουράνιος, Οὐρανόθεν', *TDNT* 5, pp. 497–543 (539–40). For a brief discussion of additional scholars who interpret the heavenlies in Ephesians by way of analogy with Gnosticism, see Lincoln, 'Re-Examination', pp. 473, 477. Lincoln interacts with E. Kasemann, 'Epheserbrief', *RGG* 2, pp. 518–19 and H. Conzelmann, *Der Brief an die Epheser* (NTD; Göttingen: Vandenhoeck and Ruprecht, 11th edn, 1968), pp. 56–57.

36 Heinrich Schlier, *Der Brief an die Epheser* (Düsseldorf: Patmos-Verlag, 1957), p. 45. Schlier writes, 'Der Begriff ἐπουράνιος, der sich an sich von οὐράνιος nicht unterscheidet, meint als Adjektiv oder Substantiv das, was zum "Himmel" gehört, was am oder im Himmel ist, was "himmlisch" ist.'

37 Schlier, *Epheser*, p. 46.

38 Schlier, *Epheser*, p. 47.

39 Schlier, *Epheser*, p. 47.

dimensions to an existential personal decision.[40] Moreover, interpretations within a Gnostic framework such as Schlier's most likely represent attempts to demythologize heaven.[41]

That Ephesians should be interpreted along Gnostic lines or that Gnostic thought served as the backdrop for some of the concepts in the letter is highly doubtful. If, as we have assumed, Paul was indeed the author of Ephesians, then he probably wrote Ephesians some time between 60 and 62 AD;[42] however; regardless of their position on authorship, most commentators agree that the letter was written some time between 60 and 90 AD.[43] Thus, chronologically, the link with a fully developed Gnosticism is problematic. In addition, several scholars have proposed that a more appropriate background for Ephesians and its realized eschatology is found in the Qumran manuscripts.[44]

In his study of the heavenlies, R. Martin Pope argues for both a Jewish and Platonic background.[45] He believes that Eph. 3.10 and 6.12 are related to the Jewish conception of angelology and the understanding that the unseen world was inhabited by both good and evil spirits.[46] In these verses, 'the Apostle reveals no divergence from the current Jewish views of the spiritual world'.[47] Pope goes on to write, however, that 1.3, 1.20, and 2.6 are better understood in the light of Hellenistic thought. In Pope's understanding, since Christ is a spiritual person and the focus of the unseen world is on Christ, Christ is not to be understood through sense perception. Consequently, the heavenly places are the home of the exalted Christ, and the saints are lifted into the noumenal world where the spiritual Christ is exalted (2.6). On account of sharing Christ's life and having access to Christ's home, believers are fittingly portrayed as blessed 'with every spiritual blessing' (1.3).[48]

40 Lincoln, 'Re-Examination', p. 477.

41 Best, *Ephesians*, p. 116.

42 So O'Brien, *Ephesians*, p. 57; Hoehner, *Ephesians*, pp. 92–97.

43 Best, *Ephesians*, p. 45; Lincoln, *Ephesians*, pp. lxxii–lxxiii; O'Brien, *Ephesians*, p. 57; Schnackenburg, *Ephesians*, p. 33.

44 Lincoln, 'Re-Examination', p. 477. Lincoln also cites Karl Georg Kuhn's, 'Der Epheserbrief im Lichte der Qumrantexte', *NTS* VII (1960–61), pp. 334–46. Kuhn writes, 'Heute kann man nun nicht mehr davon reden, wie Schlier ... doch recht vage sagt, die Sprache des Epheserbriefes stehe unter dem Einfluß der judenchristlichen "Gnosis". Angesichts der umfangreichen Texte von Qumran muß man nun sagen, daß die Sprache des Epheserbriefes unter dem Einfluß dieses Schrifttums steht', p. 335. As cited in Lincoln, 'Re-Examination', p. 477, note 5. We will discuss more fully the relationship between various Qumran texts and Ephesians later in the book.

45 R. Martin Pope, 'Studies in Pauline Vocabulary: Of the Heavenly Places', *ExpTim* 23 (1912), pp. 365–68.

46 Pope, 'Studies', p. 366.

47 Pope, 'Studies', p. 366.

48 Pope, 'Studies', p. 366.

While it remains a possibility that Paul in Ephesians implicitly addresses a heresy of a Hellenistic cosmological nature, it is misguided to suggest that the proper background for understanding the heavenlies is a Platonic or Hellenistic framework. In his article 'A Re-Examination of "The Heavenlies" in Ephesians', Lincoln emphasizes that the Old Testament and Jewish view of heaven is the proper background for Paul's conception of the heavenlies.[49] For this reason, Pope errs by abandoning his Jewish conception of heaven in 3.10 and 6.12 in favour of a Hellenistic background.[50]

6. *Hugo Odeberg*

Hugo Odeberg's treatment of the heavenlies in *The View of the Universe in the Epistle to the Ephesians* remains one of the most significant and influential.[51] For this reason, it merits a lengthy review and analysis. In his study, Odeberg first recognizes that in Ephesians the church participates in the 'Divine Reality' in its earthly life.[52] For this reason, when commenting on Eph. 2.6, he presents his central thesis by interpreting the ἐπουράνια 'as a term designating the whole of the Spiritual Reality, the Divine World, including not only the heavens but also the spiritual life, in which the Church partakes in its earthly conditions'.[53] With this understanding, Odeberg draws a distinction between the meaning and usage of οὐρανοί and ἐπουράνια in Ephesians.[54]

In arriving at his conclusion, Odeberg first considers all that is included within the ἐπουράνια in Ephesians. He reasons that the expression cannot refer to one single segment of the universe because the heavenlies include God, Christ, the spiritual powers, the cosmic powers, and the evil agencies.[55] That the highest and the lowest celestial regions are incorporated ἐν τοῖς ἐπουρανίοις perhaps leads to the conclusion that the phrase in question is identical in meaning to ἐν τοῖς οὐρανοῖς, and would thus stand in opposition to the ἐπίγειος.[56] However, upon closer inspection, Odeberg believes that this interpretation is doubtful since the author of Ephesians makes use of the expression ἐν τοῖς ἐπουρανίοις in a stereotypical manner, thereby setting it apart from the familiar use of οὐρανοί. Furthermore, Odeberg contends that in Ephesians, the author does not directly contrast

49 Lincoln, 'Re-Examination', pp. 469, 474, 477.

50 So Lincoln, 'Re-Examination', p. 477.

51 See excursus below.

52 Odeberg, *View*, p. 12.

53 Odeberg, *View*, p. 12.

54 So Odeberg who writes, 'Hereby a distinction has been found between the use of the two similar terms οὐρανοί and ἐπουράνια', *View*, p. 12.

55 Odeberg, *View*, p. 8.

56 Odeberg, *View*, p. 8.

the ἐπουράνια with the ἐπίγεια, but rather solicits the use of οὐρανός to provide that distinction.[57] The absence of a contrast with ἐπίγειος and the fact that earthly man is explicitly not ἐν οὐρανοῖς lead Odeberg to conclude that the heavenlies include not only all of the celestial regions, but also the spiritual life of the church in its earthly condition.[58]

While Odeberg's work has proved highly influential, it has nonetheless found an array of critics in recent studies. In his article, 'A Re-Examination of "The Heavenlies" in Ephesians', Andrew T. Lincoln disagrees with Odeberg's thesis and attempts to illuminate the expression by interpreting it within the context of Pauline eschatology.[59] Lincoln recognizes a parallel between 1.20, where Christ is said to be ἐν τοῖς ἐπουράνιοις and 6.9, where Christ is described as ἐν οὐρανοῖς, and thus concludes that there is a close relationship between οὐρανός and ἐπουράνιος in Ephesians.[60] Lincoln's most compelling critique is that 'Odeberg allows 2.6 to inform his definition falsely so that the heavenlies become assimilated into the experience of the Church instead of the Church being seen to have its existence in the heavenly realm because it is in Christ.'[61] Thus the heavenlies should not be defined by the experience of the church, but upon Christ's resurrection, ascension, and exaltation (1.20). Moreover, believers can be described as in the heavenlies because of their union with Christ.[62]

Lincoln continues his critique of Odeberg by writing that his view is not able to do justice to the extreme poles of blessing in 1.3 and the forces of evil in 6.12. He writes,

> Most telling against Odeberg's interpretation is the fact that his summary of the 'Weltbild' of Ephesians which is frequently quoted by others – ἐν τῷ

57 Odeberg, *View*, pp. 8–9. Οὐρανός appears four times in the epistle with all of the instances providing some sort of contrast to the earth. Ephesians 1.10 contrasts ἐπὶ τοῖς οὐρανοῖς with ἐπὶ τῆς γῆς. Ephesians 3.15 contrasts ἐν ουρανοῖς and ἐπὶ γῆς. Ephesians 4.9-10 records that the one who descended εἰς τὰ κατώτερα (μέρη) τῆς γῆς is also the one who ascended ὑπεράνω πάντων τῶν οὐρανῶν. Ephesians 6.9 exhorts masters (κύριοι) (earthly masters who are described as κατὰ σάρκα in 6.5) to do good to their servants because both the servants' and the masters' lord (κύριός) is ἐν οὐρανοῖς.

58 Odeberg, *View*, pp. 9, 12.

59 Lincoln, 'Re-Examination', p. 469.

60 Lincoln, 'Re-Examination', pp. 478–79. Lincoln reiterates the same point in *Paradise*, p. 140, and *Ephesians*, p. 20. For others who contend that οὐρανός and ἐπουράνιος are closely related, see Caragounis, *Mysterion*, pp. 146, 150; Best, *Ephesians*, pp. 116–17; Percy, *Probleme*, pp. 181–82, note 7; Hans Bietenhard, *Die himmlische Welt im Urchristentum und Spätjudentum* (Tübingen: J. C. B. Mohr, 1951), p. 211, note 1. In his article 'Οὐρανός, Οὐράνιος,'Ἐπουράνιος, Οὐρανόθεν', Traub writes that 'ἐν τοῖς ἐπουρανίοις is materially a full equivalent of the simple ἐν τοῖς οὐρανοῖς', p. 539.

61 Lincoln, 'Re-Examination', p. 478.

62 Lincoln, 'Re-Examination', p. 478. The author of Ephesians highlights the importance of union with Christ when he writes συνήγειρεν καὶ συνεκάθισεν ἐν τοῖς ἐπουρανίοις ἐν Χριστῷ Ἰησοῦ.

> κόσμῳ χωρὶς Χριστοῦ, ἐν τοῖς ἐπουρανίοις ἐν Χριστῷ, Χριστὸς ὁ τὰ πάντα ἐν πᾶσιν πληρούμενος – just does not fit, for it completely ignores the fact that according to 3.10 and 6.12, there are some in the heavenlies without Christ.[63]

At first glace, Lincoln's 'most telling' critique appears to be quite compelling; however, upon closer inspection, perhaps Lincoln pronounces judgement too hastily in this instance. One clue that this might be the case is that in his own treatment, Odeberg also recognizes the presence of those without Christ ἐν τοῖς ἐπουρανίοις. He notes that τὰ ἐπουράνια are not the exact equivalent of the spiritual realm of the church when he writes,

> For with Spiritual Realm we are wont to associate the idea of a life wholly in accordance with the Divine Will. But we have already found that the ἐπουράνια include even the cosmical powers, and also that the author speaks of evil *spiritual* agencies, which latter likewise are located in the ἐπουράνια. The ἐπουράνια are decidedly not identical with the realm of Life, Light and Truth of Johannine terminology. Neither is the expression ἐν τοῖς ἐπουρανίοις synonymical with 'in Christ Jesus'.[64]

Since Odeberg clearly makes this concession, it seems likely that his worldview refers *only* to human beings and not to the forces of evil when he writes, 'ἐν τῷ κόσμῳ χωρὶς Χριστοῦ, ἐν τοῖς ἐπουρανίοις ἐν Χριστῷ ...'.[65] In actuality, though they disagree on the meaning and location of ἐν τοῖς ἐπουρανίοις, Odeberg's worldview of Ephesians here is essentially the same as Lincoln's view since Lincoln also associates believers' experience in the heavenlies with their union with Christ. Lincoln makes this connection explicit when he writes,

> For it is only because believers are ἐν Χριστῷ Ἰησοῦ that it can be said that God has done for them what he has already done for Christ. The σύν-compounds together with the phrase ἐν Χριστῷ Ἰησοῦ underline this intimate union between Christ and believers and the statement that believers have been made to sit with Christ in the heavenlies spells out the implications of this relationship of incorporation in Christ in their most developed form in the Pauline corpus.[66]

In Lincoln's view, whereas those without Christ are in the world, believers are in the heavenlies because they are in Christ. Lincoln's critique fails

63 Lincoln, 'Re-Examination', p. 479. In this quote Lincoln refers to Odeberg's 'Weltbild' of Ephesians found in *View*, p. 20. Lincoln repeats this same critique in *Paradise*, p. 140, and *Ephesians*, p. 20.

64 Odeberg, *View*, p. 12.

65 Odeberg, *View*, p. 20. My emphasis.

66 Lincoln, *Paradise*, p. 148.

because Odeberg's 'weltbild' refers *only to humans* and not to the spiritual forces of evil. Thus both Odeberg's view and Lincoln's view allow for the presence of spiritual forces of evil ἐν τοῖς ἐπουρανίοις. The true point of disagreement between Odeberg and Lincoln is in the meaning they ascribe to the expression ἐν τοῖς ἐπουρανίοις, specifically the location which it describes.[67] We should note here that we agree with Lincoln that ἐν τοῖς ἐπουρανίοις is closely related to ἐν (τοῖς) οὐρανοῖς[68] and that Pauline eschatology can help illumine some of the statements regarding the heavenlies. Our disagreement is with Lincoln's primary critique of Odeberg, which we regard as a flawed means to Lincoln's conclusion.

Other commentators have also disagreed with Odeberg's central thesis that the heavenlies should be defined as the spiritual atmosphere of the church on earth, but on somewhat different grounds. For example, Chrys Caragounis argues that the term ἐπουράνιος 'always (refers) to that which is spatially distinct from the earth' and that Odeberg's understanding is flawed because it is misplaced to include the ἐπίγεια in the ἐπουράνια.[69] In a similar vein, Ernest Best argues that five appearances of ἐπουράνιος and four of οὐρανός do not provide enough evidence to posit a major distinction between the terms if their normal meaning is the same 'unless a clear and undisputed difference can be discerned in their use'.[70] For Best, this is not the case in Ephesians.[71] Rather, a more cohesive interpretation would be in accord with the lexical usage outside of Ephesians.[72]

Of no minor significance is Odeberg's motivation for positing a major distinction in meaning between the terms ἐπουράνιος and οὐρανός. He writes,

> The seemingly absurd hypothesis that in Ephesians ἐπουράνιος includes that which elsewhere is expressed by that term and the term signifying its opposite viz. ἐπίγειος actually seems to find its support in the fact that earthly man, *scilicet* the believer, whereas expressly not in heaven (6.9) already in his earthly life is in the midst of τὰ ἐπουράνια (2.6).[73]

67 We should note here that our disagreement with Lincoln's analysis of the heavenlies in 'Re-Examination' and *Paradise* is neither with his central argument nor his primary conclusion. Rather, we disagree with Lincoln's principal critique of Odeberg and so one of the ways in which he arrives at his conclusion.

68 Lincoln, 'Re-Examination', pp. 469, 479. Later we will argue that the above expressions are not merely closely related but synonymous.

69 Caragounis, *Mysterion*, pp. 147–50. See also Caragounis's brief analysis of the term ἐπουράνιος from a variety of Greek sources by which he arrives at his definition for ἐπουράνιος, pp. 147–50.

70 Best, *Ephesians*, pp. 116–17.

71 Best, *Ephesians*, pp. 116–17; cf. Caragounis, *Mysterion*, pp. 147–50.

72 So Best, *Ephesians*, pp. 116–17, and Caragounis, *Mysterion*, p. 150. We find this critique – that there is no lexical basis for Odeberg's understanding of ἐν τοῖς ἐπουρανίοις – to be the most compelling. We will explore this argument in detail in chapters 3 and 4.

73 Odeberg, *View*, p. 9.

Here we see that the paradox of believers already having attained heavenly status is unintelligible to Odeberg and so he allows this presupposition to be determinative for his understanding of the heavenlies. Ernest Best also discerns this motivation and writes, 'Odeberg is concerned, as it were, to keep believers on earth ...'[74] It is our contention that the difficult statements concerning the heavenlies in Ephesians – namely that believers are seated ἐν τοῖς ἐπουρανίοις and that the spiritual forces of evil are ἐν τοῖς ἐπουρανίοις – are what lead commentators such as Odeberg to spiritualize the heavenlies. The questions that remain then are whether the term ἐπουράνιος is 'flexible' enough to carry this meaning and whether there is sufficient evidence to support this view.[75] We will later argue that the answer to both of these questions is 'no'.

Excursus on the influence of Hugo Odeberg

In 'A Re-Examination of "The Heavenlies" in Ephesians', Andrew Lincoln notes that the bulk of Odeberg's thesis is followed by Bruce Metzger and J. G. Gibbs.[76] In 'Paul's Vision of the Church', Metzger defines the heavenlies as 'the unseen spiritual region which lies behind and above the world of sense' and also concludes that the phrase ἐν τοῖς ἐπουρανίοις is not identical with the phrase ἐν οὐρανῷ.[77] Gibbs writes that the expression does not refer to a place in the universe apart from the earth. Rather, he ascribes to the phrase a 'figuratively local meaning' and concludes that it describes 'the realm where Christ is, wherever his lordship is exercised'.[78] In *Paul's Letters from Prison*, G. B. Caird writes that the heavenlies are not a remote region separate from the earth but rather the spiritual environment where unseen forces contend for man's allegiance.[79] Similarly, Foulkes follows Caird and defines the heavenlies as 'an invisible spiritual environment ... the realm of all the unseen forces, good and evil, which struggle to dominate the individual and corporate life of humanity'.[80] Bonnie Thurston defines the heavenlies as 'the realm of unseen forces that exert their influence on human beings'.[81] In *A Translator's Handbook on Paul's Letter to the Ephesians*, Robert G. Bratcher and Eugene A. Nida seem to adopt Odeberg's interpretation when they write that, though the usual

74 Best, *Ephesians*, p. 117.

75 In 'Investigation' McGough argues that there is indeed evidence to posit a distinction between the terms within Greek literature.

76 Lincoln, 'Re-Examination', p. 477.

77 Bruce Metzger, 'Paul's Vision of the Church', *TTod* 6.1 (1949), pp. 49–63 (54). In his interpretation Metzger cites and follows Odeberg.

78 John G. Gibbs, *Creation and Redemption: A Study in Pauline Theology* (Leiden: Brill, 1971), p. 130.

79 Caird, *Paul's Letters*, p. 66.

80 Foulkes, *Ephesians*, p. 54.

81 Thurston, *Colossians, Ephesians*, p. 94.

meaning of ἐπουράνιος refers to a spatial distinction with the earth, such is not always the case in Ephesians.[82] Indeed, the presence of believers (2.6) and the spiritual forces of evil (6.12) ἐν τοῖς ἐπουρανίοις leads Bratcher and Nida to conclude that the phrase refers to 'the spiritual world, the timeless, supramaterial realm where those spiritual events referred to take place'.[83] John R. W. Stott writes that the heavenlies are not 'any literal spatial abode, but rather the unseen world of spiritual reality'.[84] Leon Morris adopts Stott's definition and also defines the heavenlies as 'the unseen world of spiritual reality'.[85] Snodgrass writes that the term 'heavenly realms' is not a synonym for heaven and that it 'does not refer to a physical location but to a spiritual reality – God's world, in which believers have a share and which evil forces still seek to attack. It includes all of the believer's relation to God and the church's experience. It is a way of saying that this world is not the only reality.'[86] Charles H. Talbert writes that the heavenlies refer 'to the realm of transcendence, the spiritual dimension beyond the world of sense'.[87] Arthur G. Patzia concludes that the heavenlies '(signify) the spiritual world, that is, the unseen world of spiritual reality and activity'.[88] Erwin Penner defines the heavenlies as 'a sphere of spiritual reality in which believers come to partake even while they still live on earth'.[89] Finally, we should also mention McGough who defines the heavenlies as 'a sphere of existence that embraces earthly and spiritual realities in which believers participate in their earthy, historical existence'.[90] Additionally, though their commentaries preceded Odeberg's treatise, similar sentiments can be found from J. Armitage Robinson, J. B. Lightfoot, and John S. Clemens. Robinson defines the heavenlies as 'the sphere of spiritual activities: that immaterial region, the "unseen

82 Robert G. Bratcher and Eugene A. Nida, *A Translator's Handbook on Paul's Letter to the Ephesians* (New York: United Bible Societies, 1982), pp. 10–11.

83 Bratcher and Nida, *Handbook*, pp. 10–11. Bratcher and Nida even advise translators not to use the words 'heaven' or 'heavens' in their translation.

84 Stott, *Message*, p. 35.

85 Leon Morris, *Expository Reflections on the Letter to the Ephesians* (Grand Rapids: Baker Books, 1994), p. 15.

86 Snodgrass, *Ephesians*, pp. 46–47; see also Snodgrass's similar conclusions in his exegesis of 2.6, 3.10, and 6.12, *Ephesians*, pp. 102, 163, 340.

87 Charles H. Talbert, *Ephesians and Colossians* (Paideia Commentaries on the New Testament; Grand Rapids: Baker Academic, 2007), p. 44.

88 Arthur G. Patzia, *Ephesians, Colossians, and Philemon* (New International Biblical Commentary 10; Peabody, MA: Hendrickson, 1990), p. 150; see also Patzia's description of the heavenlies in 2.6 as 'the invisible world of spiritual reality where Christ reigns supreme', p. 180.

89 Erwin Penner, 'The Enthronement of Christ in Ephesians', *Direction* 12.3 (1983), pp. 12–19 (14).

90 McGough, 'Investigation', pp. 95–96. We will interact with McGough's treatment in detail below and in chapters 3 and 4 of this book.

universe", which lies behind the world of sense'.[91] Lightfoot writes, 'The heaven, of which the Apostle here speaks, is not some *remote locality*, some *future abode*. It is the heaven which lies within and about the true Christian.'[92] Clemens regards the heavenlies as 'having special reference to *conditions* of life and being' and writes that an acceptable interpretation of ἐν τοῖς ἐπουρανίοις would be 'in the spiritual world'.[93] From this brief excursus, we note two significant points. First, all of these interpretations involve on various levels a spiritualization of the heavenlies, demonstrate affinities with Odeberg's interpretation and principal conclusion, and prove to be either directly or indirectly influenced by the interpretation popularized by Odeberg. Second, the spiritualization of the heavenlies developed and popularized by Odeberg seems at present to be the dominant interpretation of the heavenlies in Ephesians.

7. Andrew T. Lincoln

After our review of Hugo Odeberg, we now turn our attention to A. T. Lincoln's treatment of the heavenlies. Lincoln's view, which is found predominantly in his article, 'A Re-Examination of "The Heavenlies" in Ephesians', but also in *Paradise Now and Not Yet* and in his commentary on Ephesians, has also proved to be influential among an array of New Testament scholars. As previously noted, Lincoln's basic thesis is that the expression ἐν τοῖς ἐπουρανίοις is correctly understood within the context of Pauline eschatology.[94]

Though Lincoln has been referenced at times in our interaction with other commentators, we will here highlight some of the principal concerns in his interpretation. In contrast to Odeberg, Lincoln understands the phrases ἐν τοῖς ἐπουρανίοις and ἐν τοῖς οὐρανοῖς to be closely related.[95] Furthermore, he believes the proper background for understanding the heavenlies is the Old Testament and Jewish conception of heaven. In this view, creation consists of two major parts – the heavens and the earth.[96] The Old Testament's unsophisticated doctrine of heaven could refer to the

91 J. Armitage Robinson, *St. Paul's Epistle to the Ephesians* (London: James Clarke, 1904), p. 21. Robinson writes that the heavenlies are a region of ideas with great forces at work, yet Christ is enthroned over all of them, pp. 20–21.

92 Joseph Barber Lightfoot, *Notes on Epistles of St. Paul from Unpublished Commentaries* (London: MacMillan, 1895), p. 312. Emphasis Lightfoot's.

93 John S. Clemens, 'Note on the Phrase ἐν τοῖς ἐπουρανίοις', *ExpTim* 2 (1891), p. 140.

94 Lincoln, 'Re-Examination', p. 469.

95 Lincoln, 'Re-Examination', p. 479.

96 Lincoln, 'Re-Examination', p. 479. Lincoln writes that Paul's view can ultimately be traced back to the opening statement of all of Scripture, 'In the beginning God created the heavens and the earth' (Gen. 1.1).

atmospheric heaven, the firmament, or the abode of God.[97] Within the Old Testament structure, heaven 'had a priority as the upper and controlling part of the universe', yet also is now involved in God's eschatological plan.[98] It is primarily to this latter aspect that ἐν τοῖς ἐπουρανίοις refers. Lincoln writes,

> The reference is to this heaven as it takes its place in the cosmic drama of redemption, that is, in that act of the drama which Christ has inaugurated by his death, resurrection and ascension. In Ephesians heaven still has a controlling function but now in a redemptive sense, for the significance of the ascension of Christ, integral to this letter and its formula, is that it involved initial and terminal points, both considered as definite localities, the one where Christ was – on earth; the other where he now is – in heaven. Because Christ is central in God's plan for heaven, the Church 'in Christ' must also play its part in this realm. An interpretation of the formula from this perspective fits without difficulty each of the Ephesian references.[99]

Lincoln finds the references to Christ's ascension (1.20), believers' participation in Christ's reign (2.6), and spiritual blessing (1.3) to be representative of the 'already' aspect of Pauline eschatology.[100] Although Paul continues to refer to this age as the 'present age', he also conveys that the 'age to come' was inaugurated with Christ.[101] Since these two ages presently coexist with both horizontal and vertical dimensions, the believer participates in two worlds at the same time – the earthly and the heavenly – and so can appropriately be described as ἐν τοῖς ἐπουρανίοις.[102] Similarly, though the blessings for those 'in Christ' will only be fully realized in the coming age, they are nonetheless a present reality for believers.[103] For Lincoln, the presence of the evil powers in the heavenlies (3.10, 6.12) can also be understood within this eschatological perspective and the overlap of the two ages. Because the 'age to come' has not been fully realized, heaven remains involved in the present evil age until the final victory of Christ ushers in the consumma-

97 Lincoln, 'Re-Examination', p. 479.

98 Lincoln, 'Re-Examination', p. 480.

99 Lincoln, 'Re-Examination', p. 480. Additionally, Lincoln writes 'ἐν τοῖς ἐπουρανίοις in this letter particularly places heaven in a Pauline eschatological perspective', p. 479.

100 Lincoln, 'Re-Examination', p. 482.

101 Lincoln notes that Eph. 1.21 contains the only explicit reference in the Pauline corpus to the two ages (ἐν τῷ αἰῶνι τούτῳ ἀλλὰ καὶ ἐν τῷ μέλλοντι), 'Re-Examination', p. 481; cf Lincoln, *Ephesians*, p. lxxxix.

102 Lincoln, 'Re-Examination', p. 481. Incorporation into Christ is also integral for Lincoln's understanding of the heavenly status granted to believers in Eph. 2.6, 'Re-Examination', pp. 472–74. Lincoln writes, 'Christ has been raised and exalted, and nothing less is involved than the believer by virtue of his existential union with this Christ actually sharing His life and reign in heaven where he is', 'Re-Examination', p. 474.

103 Lincoln, Re-Examination', pp. 471, 481.

tion of the new age.[104] In 3.10 'ἐν τοῖς ἐπουρανίοις has reference to a realm where spiritual powers exist who in God's cosmic redemptive plan are being subjected to his final purpose of summing up all things, including τὰ ἐπὶ τοῖς οὐρανοῖς, in Christ (cf. 1.10)'.[105] Ephesians 6.12 also takes on eschatological significance since believers are depicted as already involved in a cosmic battle, but with Christ having won the decisive victory.[106]

We must here acknowledge our debt to Lincoln's noteworthy study of the heavenlies which provided a much-needed corrective to the prevailing view which spiritualized the heavenlies in Ephesians. His treatment of the expression ἐν τοῖς ἐπουρανίοις has proved to be influential among a number of New Testament scholars[107] and has likewise incited others to re-examine the meaning of the phrase.[108] While we agree with the great bulk of Lincoln's study, we can nonetheless identify one point of disagreement which we have already discussed above – that Lincoln's primary critique of Odeberg is flawed.[109] In order both to arrive at Lincoln's conclusions and to disprove Odeberg's view, we agree with Best and Caragounis that the primary issue is the question of the lexical usage and flexibility of the term ἐπουράνιος. We will examine this question in detail in chapters 3 and 4.[110]

Though not strictly a point of disagreement, we might also question Lincoln's assertion that 'ἐν τοῖς ἐπουρανίοις in this letter particularly places heaven in a Pauline eschatological perspective'.[111] First, we should note that there is nothing inherently eschatological about the words or expression ἐν τοῖς ἐπουρανίοις. This seems to be what Best has in mind in his critique of Lincoln when he writes, '"In the heavenlies" does not then by itself provide a realized eschatological slant.'[112] To be fair, Lincoln does not actually write that the expression carries a *realized* eschatological slant.[113] However, Best appropriately critiques Lincoln when he writes

104 Lincoln, 'Re-Examination', p. 480.

105 Lincoln, 'Re-Examination', p. 475.

106 Lincoln, 'Re-Examination', p. 475.

107 See, e.g., O'Brien, *Ephesians*, pp. 96–97, and to a somewhat lesser degree Harris, 'Reconsidered'; Best, *Ephesians*, pp. 115–19; Hoehner, *Ephesians*, pp. 168–70.

108 In 'Reconsidered', Harris both acknowledges a debt to Lincoln and yet also perceives a need to re-examine the subject whereby Harris arrives at somewhat different conclusions. Though McGough in some places acknowledges his debt to Lincoln, he arrives at very different conclusions in his dissertation.

109 See our discussion above wherein we conclude that Lincoln's 'most telling' critique of Odeberg is flawed.

110 Though our disagreements with Lincoln are not great, we will nonetheless proceed in a somewhat different direction when attempting to understand correctly the heavenlies in Ephesians and will also disagree with Lincoln on a couple of more minor points. Moreover, as we detailed in the Introduction, we also believe that Lincoln's work can be expanded upon.

111 Lincoln, 'Re-Examination', p. 479; cf. pp. 469, 480.

112 Best, *Ephesians*, p. 117.

113 Contra Best, *Ephesians*, p. 117. Emphasis mine.

that the reference to spiritual blessing in 1.3 does indeed represent a form of realized eschatology but that this blessing does not 'necessarily apply to "in the heavenlies"'.[114] In this sense, as we noted above, there is nothing inherently eschatological about the expression ἐν τοῖς ἐπουρανίοις.

The question still remains, however, whether in Ephesians 'ἐν τοῖς ἐπουρανίοις ... places heaven in a Pauline eschatological perspective'.[115] It is our contention that the answer to this question and its various issues is rather complex. On the one hand, we could answer with a resounding 'yes'. It is certainly clear that spiritual blessing (1.3), Christ's reign over his enemies (1.20), a heavenly status for those in Christ (2.6), and the revelation of divine mysteries (3.1-13) all entail some sort of realized eschatology whereas the location of the spiritual forces of evil in the heavenlies (3.10; 6.12) and believers' current conflict with these spiritual forces of evil (6.12) depict a future or 'not yet' eschatology. In this sense, the expression in the heavenlies is utilized in contexts which provide a 'snapshot' of sorts of Paul's already/not yet eschatological paradigm.

Furthermore, we can also agree with Lincoln that in Ephesians 'heaven ... takes its places in the cosmic drama of redemption, that is, in that act of the drama which Christ has inaugurated by his death, resurrection, and ascension'.[116] There is no doubt that Paul depicts heaven as both involved in the drama of Christ's redemption and yet as also involved in the present evil age. What is not as clear, however, is whether this has specific reference to the expression ἐν τοῖς ἐπουρανίοις. This seems to be Lincoln's implication when he writes,

> It will have become clear that ἐν τοῖς ἐπουρανίοις is closely related to ἐν τοῖς οὐρανοῖς. But whereas ὁ οὐρανός can be used in various contexts and with varying shades of meaning, including the eschatological, ἐν τοῖς ἐπουρανίοις in this letter particularly places heaven in a Pauline eschatological perspective.[117]

Here, it seems that Lincoln draws a literary distinction in Ephesians between ἐν τοῖς ἐπουρανίοις and ἐν (τοῖς) οὐρανοῖς. This distinction is loose though, since, as Lincoln admits, οὐρανός can also be utilized in eschatological contexts. It is our opinion that Lincoln's argument loses some of its force since οὐρανός is also clearly utilized in an eschatological perspective in 1.10 and 4.10. Whether there is such a literary distinction in Ephesians where ἐν τοῖς ἐπουρανίοις (as opposed to ἐν [τοῖς] οὐρανοῖς) depicts the location of Christ's cosmic work of salvation,[118] we cannot

114 Best, *Ephesians*, p. 117.

115 Lincoln, 'Re-Examination', p. 479.

116 Lincoln, 'Re-Examination', p. 480.

117 Lincoln, 'Re-Examination', p. 479.

118 About the expression ἐν τοῖς ἐπουρανίοις Lincoln writes, 'The reference is to this heaven as it takes its place in the cosmic drama of redemption, that is, in that act

be certain. The ascension of Christ in 4.10 ὑπεράνω πάντων τῶν οὐρανῶν, which also depicts Christ's reign, seems to have a similar force to Christ's ascension ἐν τοῖς ἐπουρανίοις in 1.20. Consequently, while we agree with Lincoln that heaven is involved in the cosmic drama of Christ's redemption and that this understanding is true of the expression ἐν τοῖς ἐπουρανίοις, it is much less clear whether this bears any significance for its relation to the usage of ἐν (τοῖς) οὐρανοῖς in Ephesians.[119]

8. *Chrys C. Caragounis*

In his excursus on the heavenlies in *The Ephesian Mysterion*, Chrys C. Caragounis arrives at conclusions which are on the whole similar to Lincoln's, though the means to Caragounis's conclusions are somewhat different from Lincoln's. Essential to Caragounis's interpretation is the notion that the meaning of ἐπουράνιος is not different from the meaning of οὐράνιος.[120] Recalling the places where ἐπουράνιος occurs in Greek literature, Caragounis notes that the word has a diverse range of meanings, but that it always refers to 'that which is spatially distinct from the earth'.[121] In an effort to clarify the meaning of ἐν τοῖς ἐπουρανίοις, Caragounis describes the heavenlies as a local reference to that which is above the earth.[122] The heavenlies, therefore, represent both the location of God's throne and the realm of the spiritual world under God's throne.[123]

Of particular interest is Caragounis's application of his understanding of the heavenlies to some of the particular passages in Ephesians. Regarding Ephesians 2.6, whereas Odeberg draws a distinction between οὐρανός and ἐπουράνιος in Ephesians, Caragounis regards man as living

of the drama which Christ has inaugurated by his death, resurrection and ascension', 'Re-Examination', p. 480.

119 We should clarify that the reference here is merely to a literary distinction between the two expressions for heaven and not a distinction in meaning. We will later argue that there is no distinction in meaning between the two expressions.

120 Caragounis, *Mysterion*, p. 146. Here Caragounis lists the adjectival forms though the adjective οὐράνιος does not appear in Ephesians. Similarly, he also writes that οὐρανός is not different in meaning from the ἐπουράνια, *Mysterion*, p. 150.

121 Caragounis, *Mysterion*, p. 147. See Caragounis's very brief study of the term ἐπουράνιος, pp. 147–50. Curiously, after stating this, Caragounis considers that this data, including both biblical and non-biblical examples, may not be helpful in ascertaining the meaning of the expression ἐν τοῖς ἐπουρανίοις because of its use as a formula in Ephesians. That the normal lexical usage of the term ἐπουράνιος may not apply to its use in Ephesians is almost identical to Odeberg's claims in *View*, pp. 8–12, especially 9; however, we should note here that Caragounis's final conclusion regarding τὰ ἐπουράνια is indeed in accordance with the lexical usage of ἐπουράνιος outside Ephesians.

122 Caragounis, *Mysterion*, p. 150.

123 Caragounis, *Mysterion*, p. 150.

on two planes at the same time – the earthly and the heavenly.[124] The earthly plane is physical and according to sight while the heavenly plane is a higher, spiritual one.[125] In his attempt to explain this paradox, he writes that 'believers are seated ἐν τοῖς ἐπουρανίοις not in any real sense as yet, but in anticipation by virtue of their being the Body of Christ, Who is Himself seated there'.[126] While we agree that this proleptic sense of believers as already seated with Christ ἐν τοῖς ἐπουρανίοις is an important aspect, we also find this interpretation by itself insufficient for a proper understanding of Eph. 2.6.[127] Additionally, this understanding does not seem to cohere completely with Caragounis's statement which views man as *living on two planes at the same time*.[128] If, as Caragounis suggests, believers are indeed living on a heavenly plane in addition to an earthly one, then it seems that there is more than merely a sense of 'anticipation' for the heavenly status granted to believers in Eph. 2.6.

After his brief analysis of the references to ἐν τοῖς ἐπουρανίοις and οὐρανός in Ephesians, Caragounis ends his excursus with an attempt to harmonize these passages into a cosmology of sorts for the letter. What is of great surprise is that, though Caragounis had previously written that οὐρανός is not different in meaning from the ἐπουράνια,[129] he now concludes that τὰ ἐπουράνια overlap with οὐρανός but yet are not completely identical with it.[130] While οὐρανός comprises the layers from the air all the way up to God's throne, τὰ ἐπουράνια is made up of only the higher levels from God's throne to the realm of the cosmic forces.[131] Caragounis provides no justification for this distinction other than his remark that τὰ ἐπουράνια are bound up with the salvation events.[132] That the heavenlies are bound up with the salvation events is similar to Lincoln's argument that the heavenlies are a reference to the cosmic

124 Caragounis, *Mysterion*, p. 150. Cf. Lincoln's statement that believers participate in two worlds at the same time – the earthly and the heavenly, 'Re-Examination', p. 481.

125 Caragounis, *Mysterion*, p. 150.

126 Caragounis, *Mysterion*, p. 150. Bruce seems to interpret this reference similarly when he writes, 'It can best be understood as a statement of God's purpose for his people – a purpose which is so sure of fulfillment that it can be spoken of as having already taken place', *Colossians, Philemon, Ephesians*, p. 287.

127 This will be discussed in greater detail in our study of Eph. 2.6. For now, we will simply note that we believe there are also mystical (i.e. Spiritual, of the Spirit), eschatological, and historical components to this aspect of believers and their union with Christ.

128 My emphasis.

129 Caragounis, *Mysterion*, p. 150.

130 Caragounis, *Mysterion*, p. 152.

131 Caragounis, *Mysterion*, p. 152. This also seems odd given the reference to Satan in Eph. 2.2 as τὸν ἄρχοντα τῆς ἐξουσίας τοῦ ἀέρος. Since the spiritual forces of evil are ἐν τοῖς ἐπουρανίοις in 6.12 and since Satan is located in 'the air' in 2.2, then it would seem to follow that the heavenlies also include whatever region Paul intends in his reference to 'the air'. It is our contention that the references to ἐν τοῖς ἐπουρανίοις and ἐν (τοῖς) οὐρανοῖς in Ephesians are synonymous.

132 Caragounis, *Mysterion*, p. 152.

drama of redemption.[133] While such arguments are difficult wholly to dismiss, as we detailed above, they are also not without their difficulties.

9. Michael Everett McGough

Michael Everett McGough's unpublished dissertation 'An Investigation of 'Επουράνιος in Ephesians' proves to have a number of affinities with Odeberg's treatment. Although McGough does not acknowledge this, it seems almost certain that he has been highly influenced by Hugo Odeberg's *The View of the Universe in the Epistle to the Ephesians.*[134] In his dissertation, McGough writes that his purpose is to investigate the meaning of ἐν τοῖς ἐπουρανίοις in order to establish its significance for understanding Ephesians.[135] He begins his task by conducting a study of the term ἐπουράνιος in Greek literature. In his analysis, McGough argues for a distinction in meaning between the terms οὐρανός and ἐπουράνιος[136] which he later applies to his interpretation of the heavenlies in Ephesians. Whereas the term οὐρανός or the expression ἐν τοῖς οὐρανοῖς 'refers either to a part of created reality or to the abode of God',[137] the term ἐπουράνιος or the expression ἐν τοῖς ἐπουρανίοις represents either a heavenly or earthly interaction[138] or 'a realm of existence (which) is not to be located in some region or territory above the earth ... a sphere of existence that embraces earthly and spiritual realities in which believers participate in their earthly, historical existence'.[139]

With these definitions, we can observe that McGough's conclusions for the meaning of the term ἐπουράνιος and the expression ἐν τοῖς

133 Lincoln, 'Re-Examination', p. 480.

134 While much of Odeberg's argument pervades McGough's dissertation, it is interesting that McGough cites him on only one occasion – when referencing Odeberg's critique for a Gnostic interpretation of the heavenlies, McGough, 'Investigation', p. 61.

135 McGough, 'Investigation', p. 2.

136 McGough, 'Investigation', pp. 8–9, 13–14, 28–29. With this argument, McGough deviates from Odeberg in that Odeberg never writes that οὐρανός and ἐπουράνιος are to be distinguished in their normal usage, but rather only in Ephesians. In fact, Odeberg readily admits that his argument that ἐπουράνιος in Ephesians includes both its normal meaning and its opposite is a 'seemingly absurd hypothesis', Odeberg, *View*, p. 9.

137 McGough, 'Investigation', p. 102; cf. p. 171. Similar to Odeberg, McGough also notes that in Ephesians οὐρανός is used to contrast the transcendent realm of the upper heavens with the earth, 'Investigation', p. 99.

138 McGough, 'Investigation', p. 102. In his word study, McGough argues that ἐπουράνιος communicates earthly and heavenly interaction in numerous places, e.g. pp. 8, 10, 12–13, 15, 22, 25–26, 28–30, 39, 48–49. He also contends that the expression ἐν τοῖς ἐπουρανίοις contains an element of earthly interaction with heavenly things, p. 100. Additionally, of particular interest is McGough's assertion that the term οὐρανός in Ephesians does not contain an element of interaction since it represents a part of created reality or the abode of God, p. 159.

139 McGough, 'Investigation', pp. 95–96.

ἐπουρανίοις are somewhat inconsistent. In regard to his first claim, we certainly do not need to conduct a word study in order to demonstrate earthly and heavenly interaction. We need to look no further than an Old Testament theophany, the appearance of the angel Gabriel to Mary in the New Testament, or the very incarnation of Christ himself to demonstrate the reality of earthly and heavenly interaction. Though in Ephesians there is ample evidence of heavenly and earthly interaction, we dispute McGough's argument that this notion is inherent to the term ἐπουράνιος.[140] Furthermore, the complexity in Ephesians is not that there is earthly and heavenly interaction. We have already demonstrated that this is a principle throughout the whole of Scripture. What is striking is the nature of this interaction – namely that believers are blessed with every spiritual blessing in the heavenlies and that believers (on earth) are already seated with Christ in the heavenlies.

Regarding McGough's second claim, that the expression ἐν τοῖς ἐπουρανίοις refers to 'a realm of existence (which) is not to be located in some region or territory above the earth ... a sphere of existence that embraces earthly and spiritual realities in which believers participate in their earthly, historical existence',[141] we notice a marked similarity to Odeberg's interpretation that the heavenlies should be understood as 'designating the whole of the Spiritual Reality, the Divine World, including not only the heavens but also that spiritual life, in which the Church partakes in its earthly conditions'.[142] It is important to remember here that McGough reaches this conclusion from his analysis of Ephesians *and* from his examination of the term ἐπουράνιος in Greek literature. Our response to these claims, as Best has argued, is that the term ἐπουράνιος cannot carry the meaning which Odeberg and McGough argue for in Ephesians. Finally, we will address McGough's claim that there is a distinction in meaning between οὐρανός and ἐπουράνιος throughout wider Greek literature in chapters 3 and 4 of this book. Suffice it to say now that we regard McGough's interaction with the primary material to be erroneous and problematic.

140 Similarly, we also reject McGough's claim that the term οὐρανός or the expression ἐν (τοῖς) οὐρανοῖς inherently cannot contain an element of interaction with the earth. Indeed, this idea is preposterous. We need to look no further than Eph. 1.10 and the ἀνακεφαλαιώσασθαι of all things in Christ, things in the heavens and things on the earth (τὰ ἐπὶ τοῖς οὐρανοῖς καὶ τὰ ἐπὶ τῆς γῆς).

141 McGough, 'Investigation', pp. 95–96.

142 Odeberg, *View*, p. 12. We have already stated that though McGough does not credit him, much of Odeberg's interpretation pervades McGough's dissertation.

10. Horacio E. Lona

In *Die Eschatologie im Kolosser- und Epheserbrief*, Horacio E. Lona seeks to explain the emphasis on realized eschatology in Colossians and Ephesians. In light of his task, he devotes some of his attention to the heavenlies in Ephesians. Lona first disagrees with the distinction Odeberg draws between οὐρανός and ἐν τοῖς ἐπουρανίοις and contends that the terms have the same meaning.[143] Nevertheless, Lona does argue for a literary distinction in their usage in Ephesians when he writes, 'Im Unterschied zum Sprachgebrauch von οὐρανός verbinden sich mit ἐν τοῖς ἐπουρανίοις wesentliche Aussagen über die Gemeinde.'[144] With this statement, Lona also reveals one of the key tenets in his understanding of the heavenlies in Ephesians. Whereas Lincoln and Caragounis understand the heavenlies from eschatological and soteriological perspectives accordingly, Lona contends that the expression ἐν τοῖς ἐπουρανίοις is utilized in statements about the church or the community of believers.[145]

For Lona, the keys to understanding the realized eschatology in Ephesians are found in ecclesiology and Christology. Since the author of Ephesians writes the letter during a time of religious and cultural crisis, he reflects on the church and its need to be legitimized as an institution.[146] Lona writes, 'Die Analyse der Texte hat nämlich ergeben, daß die Eschatologie von Eph eine ekklesiologische Eschatologie ist.'[147] Consequently, for Lona, the motivation for the realized eschatological emphasis in Ephesians is the establishment of the church. In his understanding of the heavenlies in 1.3 and 2.6, Lona writes that the distance between heaven and earth remains but that 'Himmel und Erde (verbinden) sich in der Gestalt der Kirche geheimnisvoll'.[148] While we regard Lona's claim that the heavenlies should be understood primarily within the context of ecclesiology as doubtful, we do find his argument that heaven and earth are united in the form of the church to have both theological and textual support within Ephesians. In the Old Testament, the Temple represented the location of God's presence on earth. Since in Ephesians Paul describes the church with the image of the Temple (2.19-22), the church can appropriately be understood as the locus of

143 Lona, *Eschatologie*, pp. 297–98. Lona argues against Odeberg's interpretation when he writes, 'Damit ist nicht gesagt, daß ἐν τοῖς ἐπουρανίοις auch τὰ ἐπίγεια umfaßt', p. 298.

144 Lona, *Eschatologie*, p. 298.

145 As in the case of Lincoln and Caragounis, such a literary distinction between the expressions ἐν τοῖς ἐπουρανίοις and ἐν (τοῖς) οὐρανοῖς in Ephesians is possible but not without its difficulties.

146 See Lona, *Eschatologie*, pp. 428–48.

147 Lona, *Eschatologie*, p. 442. Emphasis Lona's.

148 Lona, *Eschatologie*, p. 298.

God's presence on earth. Such an idea informs our understanding of the heavenlies but yet still is not identical with the heavenly status granted to believers in 2.6. We will turn our attention to these texts and themes in greater detail in our discussion of Eph. 2.6.

As we have noted, Lona regards the motivation for the eschatological emphasis in Ephesians to be the establishment of the church. However, for Lona, the reason that the church in Eph. 2.6 can be described as in the heavenlies and so have a spatial component is because of Christology, namely because believers are 'in Christ'.[149] Lona writes, ''Εν Χριστῷ bezeichnet nämlich die Situation der Gläubigen auf Erden in ihrer Bezogenheit auf den erhöhten Herrn. Nur in dieser Bezogenheit sind sie ἐν τοῖς ἐπουρανίοις.'[150] Since believers are identified and united with Christ, they can appropriately be described as ἐν τοῖς ἐπουρανίοις.[151] Lona also notes the connection between the description of believers in Eph. 2.5-6 and the description of Christ in Eph. 1.20 when he writes, 'So wie Christus nach 1,20 durch die Kraft Gottes von den Toten auferweckt und in den Himmel zur Rechten Gottes versetzt wurde, so wurde der Christ von Gott mit Christus auferweckt und in den Himmel versetzt.'[152] Thus there is a connection between Christology, i.e. the exaltation of Christ, and soteriology, i.e. the salvation benefits which are subsequently granted to those 'in Christ'.[153] We agree with Lona that union with Christ is a significant interpretive key for understanding the heavenly status granted to believers in Eph. 2.6, and we will explore this notion in greater detail in our discussion of this passage.[154]

149 Lona, *Eschatologie*, p. 298. Lona notes that the eschatology in Ephesians is more spatial than temporal and writes that the author of Ephesians utilizes ἐν τοῖς ἐπουρανίοις to highlight this spatial dimension to eschatology, pp. 363–64.

150 Lona, *Eschatologie*, p. 298. Emphasis Lona's.

151 Though Lona notes that 'im Eph wird die Taufe nicht erwähnt', p. 361, he also seems at times to connect baptism with believers' experience of the heavenly world. He writes, 'Die Beheimatung in der Kirche schlägt nicht nur eine Wurzel in der Geschichte. Sie verbindet zugleich die Gläubigen mit der himmlischen Welt, zu der sie durch die Taufe gehören (1,3; 2,6)', *Eschatologie*, p. 444.

152 Lona, *Eschatologie*, p. 363. Lona also recognizes that connection between Col. 2.12-13 and Eph. 2.5-6 and writes that the author of Ephesians reorganizes the statements of Col. 2.12-13, p. 361.

153 Lona, *Escahtologie*, pp. 362–63.

154 We should point out here that the notion of union with Christ as an interpretive key for understanding believers' heavenly status in Eph. 2.6 has also been significant for a number of other commentators. See, e.g., Lincoln, 'Re-Examination', pp. 472–74, 481–82; Lincoln, *Paradise*, p. 148; Lincoln, *Ephesians*, pp. 100–09; Best, *Ephesians*, pp. 117, 214–23; Bietenhard, *Die himmlische Welt*, p. 211, note 1; Thomas G. Allen, 'Exaltation and Solidarity with Christ: Ephesians 1.20 and 2.6', *JSNT* 28, (1986), pp. 103–20.

11. W. Hall Harris III

In his article '"The Heavenlies" Reconsidered: Οὐρανός and Ἐπουράνιος in Ephesians', W. Hall Harris III investigates the much-disputed assertion that οὐρανός and ἐπουράνιος are used interchangeably in Ephesians.[155] In his analysis, Harris examines all of the occurrences of the terms οὐρανός and ἐπουράνιος in Ephesians. On the majority of the fundamental issues, Harris agrees with the findings of recent scholars.[156] He also acknowledges the importance of Lincoln's observations, namely that Paul's concept of heaven was generally derived from the unsophisticated Old Testament view of heaven, and that the author was not concerned about the number of heavens.[157] However, Harris warns that these observations must not be pressed too far, and he allows for the possibility that the use of the plural οὐρανοῖς may indeed be of some significance.[158]

Though Harris provides some helpful comments on all of the passages he examines, it is our view that his article makes very little contribution to a proper understanding of the heavenlies in Ephesians. His conclusions for the relationship between the terms οὐρανός and ἐπουράνιος are at best ambiguous and at worst inconsistent. At times, Harris seems to imply that there should be a distinction between these terms. He writes, 'This raises the possibility that ἐπουράνιος is a more comprehensive term than commonly thought. It is possible that it bridges the extremes of both ἡ γῆ and ὁ οὐρανός in some sense. According to Hanson, it is "more like a dimension than a place."'[159] Such a definition would indeed be similar to that of commentators such as Odeberg and McGough who argue for a major distinction in meaning between οὐρανός and ἐπουράνιος in Ephesians. In other places, Harris seems to imply that the expressions ἐν τοῖς ἐπουρανίοις and ἐν (τοῖς) οὐρανοῖς are interchangeable.[160]

155 Harris, 'Reconsidered', p. 73. Harris also mentions specifically the question of whether the expressions ἐν τοῖς ἐπουρανίοις and ἐν (τοῖς) οὐρανοῖς in Ephesians are used interchangeably. Cf. Jean-Noël Aletti who more or less follows Harris's view in Aletti, *Éphésiens*, pp. 56–57.

156 For example, Harris recognizes that the expression ἐν τοῖς ἐπουρανίοις is properly understood in a local sense, 'Reconsidered', p. 74. Additionally, he emphasizes the importance of being 'in Christ' for receiving spiritual blessing and for participating in Christ's reign, pp. 74, 78.

157 Harris, 'Reconsidered', p. 75. Thus the use of the plural οὐρανοῖς would best be understood as a reflection of the Hebrew שָׁמַיִם.

158 Harris, 'Reconsidered', pp. 75–76. Since only the plural form appears in Ephesians, Harris is open to the idea of a universe consisting of three or four stories; however, later in his article, Harris agrees that a two-storied cosmology best fits the references to heaven in Ephesians, 'Reconsidered', pp. 83–84, 89.

159 Harris, 'Reconsidered', p. 86. Harris cites A. T. Hanson, *The New Testament Interpretation of Scripture* (London: SPCK, 1980), p. 139. As cited in Harris.

160 See Harris's discussions of 1.20 and 2.6 where this is seemingly the case,

In his analysis of Eph. 6.9, Harris believes there are two primary reasons for Paul's preference for οὐρανός (ἐν οὐρανοῖς) on this occasion. First, this usage is consistent with the contrastive relationship of ἡ γῆ and ὁ οὐρανός in Ephesians.[161] Second, Harris suggests that the author utilized this term to emphasize the spatial and positional contrast between the exalted Christ (in heaven) and believers (on earth).[162] Whereas the term ἐπουράνιος depicts both the locus of Christ and believers who are in him, οὐρανός refers to Christ in contrast with those on earth.[163] With this argument, Harris again seems to imply some sort of distinction between οὐρανός and ἐπουράνιος in Ephesians, though he does not clearly define what this distinction actually is.[164]

In his conclusion, Harris once again affirms the notion that οὐρανός is the preferred term to emphasize the contrastive relationship between heaven and earth. At no point in his article does Harris attempt to answer why this might be the case or what the implications are for this conclusion. In his conclusion for the term ἐπουράνιος, Harris writes,

> Ἐν τοῖς ἐπουρανίοις is the location of the current conflict in which believers participate through their presence there 'in' Christ. But οἱ ἐπουράνιοι in Ephesians is primarily viewed as the location of the exalted Christ, the place where He now is and from which He exercises His universal sovereignty in the present age.[165]

This conclusion seems a valid one if what Harris argues for here is some sort of literary distinction between οὐρανός and ἐπουράνιος in Ephesians. If this is the case, then his conclusions would actually be very similar to Lincoln's but consequently would not advance the conversation of the heavenlies. The major difficulty is that Harris is not at all clear in his arguments or conclusions. Therefore, we believe Harris falls short of his goal to determine whether οὐρανός and ἐπουράνιος are used interchangeably in Ephesians. In our view, Harris's article actually demonstrates that there is still no consensus on how readers of Ephesians should understand the heavenlies. The great amount of

'Reconsidered', pp. 76–78. See also Harris's concluding section where he seems to imply an element of interchangeability, though 'not ... complete interchangeability', 'Reconsidered', p. 89.

161 Harris, 'Reconsidered', p. 85. We have previously noted this contrastive relationship between ἡ γῆ and ὁ οὐρανός in Ephesians.

162 Harris, 'Reconsidered', p. 85.

163 Harris, 'Reconsidered', p. 85.

164 Cf. Aletti who more or less follows Harris and also seems to draw a minor distinction between οὐρανός and ἐπουράνιος in Ephesians. Whereas the terms οὐρανοί and γῆ refer to created reality in its totality, the term ἐπουράνιος, as suggested by the prefix ἐπί, refers to 'un au-delà des cieux physiques, un 'lieu' réservé pour les êtres spirituels, qui sont soustraits à l'influence de ce monde-ci,' Aletti, *Éphésiens*, p. 57.

165 Harris, 'Reconsidered', p. 89.

confusion which surrounds the expression ἐν τοῖς ἐπουρανίοις demonstrates once again the need for additional study.

12. Conclusions

Our review of the major ways in which the heavenlies have been interpreted has yielded some interesting results. First, we can conclude that there still remains no consensus on how the heavenlies in Ephesians should be understood. We have noted the influence of both Hugo Odeberg and Andrew T. Lincoln in how New Testament scholars have interpreted the expression ἐν τοῖς ἐπουρανίοις. Odeberg and those who follow him have drawn a distinction between ἐν (τοῖς) οὐρανοῖς and ἐν τοῖς ἐπουρανίοις in Ephesians and have tended to spiritualize the heavenlies in order to make sense of difficult passages such as Eph. 2.6 and 6.12. Other commentators such as Lincoln, Caragounis, and Lona have argued that the two expressions are generally synonymous but have interpreted the usage of ἐν τοῖς ἐπουρανίοις along eschatological, soteriological, or ecclesiological lines.

While we have agreed with the majority of Lincoln's conclusions, we have disagreed primarily with how he arrives at his conclusions, namely his principal critique of Odeberg. Rather, we have found Best's critique – that it is improper to posit a major distinction in meaning between ἐν (τοῖς) οὐρανοῖς and ἐν τοῖς ἐπουρανίοις when their normal usage is the same – quite salient. If Best is correct, then it is indeed improper to 'spiritualize' the heavenlies as many commentators have done. What is of particular interest here is McGough's study of the term ἐπουράνιος within wider Greek usage in which McGough in fact argues for a major distinction in meaning between οὐρανός and ἐπουράνιος.

As a result of the various meanings assigned to ἐπουράνιος, it is our contention that the lexical range and usage of this term are of great significance for properly interpreting the heavenlies in Ephesians. We will turn our attention to this task in chapters 3 and 4 through an extensive examination of the term ἐπουράνιος in both biblical and non-biblical texts. Though it seems quite lofty, it is our goal to demonstrate that there is no lexical basis for Odeberg's interpretation of the heavenlies whereby he defines them 'as a term designating the whole of the Spiritual Reality, the Divine World, including not only the heavens but also that spiritual life, in which the Church partakes in its earthly conditions'.[166] Additionally, we will provide evidence that McGough's study is erroneous and that the expressions ἐν τοῖς ἐπουρανίοις and ἐν (τοῖς) οὐρανοῖς should indeed be understood as synonymous. It is our view that these tasks are of primary significance, since, as we demonstrated

166 Odeberg, *View*, p. 12.

in our excursus on the influence of Odeberg's interpretation, we regard Odeberg's interpretation of the heavenlies as the prevailing view among New Testament scholars. After our study of the usage of ἐπουράνιος, we will focus our attention on exegetical and conceptual issues which have often been overlooked in studies of the heavenlies.

Chapter 3

Study of 'Επουράνιος in Greek Literature outside the New Testament

1. *Purpose of and Justification for an Examination of* 'Επουράνιος

The purpose of this chapter is to investigate the meaning and usage of ἐπουράνιος in a variety of Greek sources so as to inform our understanding of the heavenlies in Ephesians. In our review of the major ways the heavenlies have been interpreted, we concluded that the meaning, usage, and 'flexibility' of the term ἐπουράνιος are of great significance for a proper understanding of the expression ἐν τοῖς ἐπουρανίοις in Ephesians. As we noted, Odeberg and those who have been influenced by him have 'spiritualized' the heavenlies by defining them as the spiritual atmosphere of the church on earth.[1] In this chapter, we will explore whether there is any justification within other Greek literature for Odeberg's interpretation and for the distinction he draws between οὐρανός and ἐπουράνιος. Of particular interest is McGough's argument that there is indeed evidence for a major distinction in meaning between οὐρανός and ἐπουράνιος within wider Greek usage.[2] In our examination of ἐπουράνιος, however,

1 In a sense, our study of ἐπουράνιος in chapters 3 and 4 is the foundation for the exegetical and conceptual portion of this book. If, as Odeberg, McGough, and others contend, the heavenlies describe the spiritual atmosphere of the church on earth, then there would be no reason to examine the notion of heavenly ascent or a heavenly status granted to the redeemed on earth precisely because the expression ἐν τοῖς ἐπουρανίοις would not actually signify 'heaven' but merely a spiritual reality. The same is true for the spiritual forces of evil which reside ἐν τοῖς ἐπουρανίοις. If this only refers to a spiritual reality rather than the equivalent of ἐν (τοῖς) οὐρανοῖς, then there is no reason to explore the notion of evil powers in heaven.

2 Not only does McGough draw this distinction, but he also critiques Lincoln for not properly recognizing this distinction in Ephesians and for not observing the usage of ἐπουράνιος in wider Greek literature, 'Investigation', p. 62. While we will primarily interact with McGough's examination in the footnotes below, we can appropriately summarize the conclusions of his study of ἐπουράνιος with three principal tenets. First, McGough argues for a major distinction in meaning between the terms οὐρανός (or the adjectival οὐράνιος) and ἐπουράνιος, 'Investigation', pp. 8–9, 13–14, 28–29, 48–49, 95–96, 99–100, 102, 159, 171. Second, McGough believes that, in contrast to a location or spatial referent, the meaning communicated by the term ἐπουράνιος is that of 'spiritual reality', 'Investigation', pp. 95–96. Third, McGough regards the notion of heavenly and earthly interaction as

we will insist that there is no basis for Odeberg's interpretation and that McGough's study is severely flawed. In contrast to those who 'spiritualize' the heavenlies in Ephesians, we will demonstrate that the term ἐπουράνιος always refers to that which is spatially distinct from the earth.[3] Additionally, in contrast to Odeberg's understanding and McGough's analysis, we will demonstrate that the usage of the terms οὐρανός/οὐράνιος and ἐπουράνιος within wider Greek literature actually provides evidence that the expressions ἐν (τοῖς) οὐρανοῖς and ἐν τοῖς ἐπουρανίοις are synonymous. Finally, it is our hope that this extensive study of ἐπουράνιος will also serve as a contribution to the field of New Testament scholarship.

2. Methodology

A search in the Thesaurus Lingua Graecae reveals over 4,000 appearances of the term ἐπουράνιος within extant Greek literature. Though the most accurate method would be to consult all of these sources, such a task would in actuality be both impractical and inappropriate for our purposes in this book.[4] As a result, we must be selective in our choice of passages to examine. Since one of our objectives is to compare and contrast our conclusions with the findings of McGough in his study, it is essential to provide a fresh examination of all of the passages within his study.[5] The sources in McGough's study, outside the New

inherent to the term ἐπουράνιος; see e.g. 'Investigation', pp. 8, 10, 12–13, 15, 22, 25–26, 28–30, 39, 48–49, 100. McGough writes 'The pervading idea suggested by ἐπουράνιος is that of interaction. In the majority of the references cited in this section, the expression of reality implied by ἐπουράνιος concerns the interaction of the heavenly dimension with the earthly dimension', 'Investigation', p. 48. See our history of interpretation for a brief critique of this argument.

3 See also Caragounis, *Mysterion*, p. 147. Here we should also acknowledge that we agree with the general exegetical principle that the meaning or usage of a word is often determined by context; however, it is also true that a word has a semantic range with a variety of meanings and nuances which are then clarified by the context. This exegetical principle is significant for our purposes if we maintain that the term ἐπουράνιος does not ever carry the meaning 'spiritual reality'. If there is no basis or precedent for this definition or for the distinction between ἐπουράνιος and οὐρανός outside Ephesians, then it is improper to draw such conclusions within the letter itself. This is essentially the argument which Best employs in his rejection of Odeberg's interpretation of the heavenlies when he writes that 'five instances of one Greek word and four of the other are statistically too few to enforce a major distinction between them if their normal meaning is the same', Best, *Ephesians*, pp. 116–17.

4 Such a task is inappropriate since our purpose in this book is not only a lexical examination but also an exegetical and a conceptual one.

5 It seems that McGough primarily selected a number of passages from those listed in BDAG and LSJ and supplemented those with a few additional passages.

Testament examples,[6] are as follows: *Odyssey* 17.484; *Iliad* 6.129-31; *Iliad* 6.527; Plato, *Phaedrus* 256d; Theocritus 25.5; Moschus, *Europa* 2.21; Sextus Empiricus, *Against the Astrologers* 5.44; Lucian, *Dialogues of the Gods* 4.3; *Corpus Hermeticum*, *Stobaei Hermetica* 12.1, *Stobaei Hermetica* 21.12, *Fragment* 26.9, *Abammonis Ad Porphyrium* 8.C; second century papyri; Paris Papyri 574.3042; Quintus Smyrnaeus, *The Fall of Troy* 2.429; LXX Ps. 67.15; 2 Macc. 3.39; 3 Macc. 6.28; 3 Macc. 7.6; *Sibylline Oracles* 4.51; *Sibylline Oracles* 4.135; Philo, *Legum Allegoria* 3.168, *De Gigantibus* 62, *De Virtutibus* 3.12. Moreover, we have also selected twelve additional texts which prove to be significant for a proper understanding of the heavenlies in Ephesians. From Jewish writings, two passages in *Testament of Job* (36.3 and 38.5) and one in *Testament of Abraham* (chapter 4) are noteworthy not only because of their proximity in date to the New Testament documents, but also because of the usage of ἐπουράνιος in these passages. Finally, several passages in the Apostolic Fathers (Ignatius, *Eph.* 13.2; Ignatius, *Trall.* 5.1-2; Ignatius, *Trall.* 9.1; Ignatius, *Smyrn.* 6.1a; Polycarp, *Phil.* 2.1; *Mart. Pol.* 14.3; *Mart. Pol.* 20.2; *1 Clem.* 61.2; *2 Clem.* 20.5) are also essential to consult since they quite possibly represent the church's earliest understanding of the term ἐπουράνιος subsequent to its usage in 'the heavenlies' passages of Ephesians. These passages prove to be an appropriate sample since they by and large reflect the texts listed by BDAG and LSJ.[7] Moreover, since many of these passages contain not only an appearance of ἐπουράνιος, but also an appearance of οὐρανός or the adjectival οὐράνιος, they are particularly significant for our understanding of the heavenlies in Ephesians.

In this list of passages, we find texts from a variety of genres and from many different time periods. For any study of this nature, some sources are inevitably more important than others. The New Testament documents, and even more specifically the letters within the Pauline corpus, are considerably more significant for our purposes than, for example, Homer's eighth-century Greek. What is particularly striking though, whether we trace ἐπουράνιος diachronically or synchronically, is the relative uniformity and consistency of how the term is used – as a reference to that which is spatially distinct from the earth. Though we regard the sources which are synchronous with Ephesians as of greater significance,[8] it is nevertheless beneficial also to examine the

6 We will examine the NT usage of ἐπουράνιος in chapter 4.

7 With this sample, we examine the great majority of the passages listed in both BDAG and LSJ.

8 For a discussion of diachronic and synchronic word analysis, the dangers of diachronic analysis for determining word meaning, and the significance and priority of synchronic analysis for determining the meaning of a word, see Peter Cotterell and Max Turner, *Linguistics and Biblical Interpretation* (Downers Grove, IL: InterVarsity, 1989), pp. 131–35.

meaning and usage of the term ἐπουράνιος in a wide variety of sources to demonstrate our claim that the terms οὐρανός/οὐράνιος and ἐπουράνιος within wider Greek literature are synonymous.

Before we begin our examination, we should point out one final methodological issue. One obvious difference between the terms ἐπουράνιος and οὐρανός is that the former is an adjective while the latter is a noun. In this sense, we would not assert that they are synonymous since one means 'heavenly' and the other means 'heaven'. When we make the claim throughout this chapter that the terms ἐπουράνιος and οὐρανός are in fact synonymous, what we mean is that they are synonymous in respect to the locations they represent. The implication of this is that the expressions ἐν (τοῖς) οὐρανοῖς and ἐν τοῖς ἐπουρανίοις, when both are local as in Ephesians, are synonymous. Within our examination, however, we will often state that the terms ἐπουράνιος and οὐρανός are synonymous for ease of communication.[9]

3. *Various Greek Sources*

a. Homer, Odyssey *17.484 (483–84)*[10]

'Αντίνο', οὐ μὲν κάλ' ἔβαλες δύστηνον ἀλήτην,
οὐλόμεν', εἰ δή πού τις ἐπουράνιος θεός ἐστιν.
καί τε θεοὶ ξείνοισιν ἐοικότες ἀλλοδαποῖσι,
παντοῖοι τελέθοντες, ἐπιστρωφῶσι πόληας,
ἀνθρώπων ὕβριν τε καὶ εὐνομίην ἐφορῶντες.

Antinous, thou didst not well to strike the wretched wanderer. Doomed man that thou art, what if haply he be some god come down from heaven! Aye, and the gods in the guise of strangers from afar put on all manner of shapes, and visit the cities, beholding the violence and the righteousness of men. (Murray)

From the larger context of *Odyssey* 17.483–84, we learn that Odysseus disguises himself and asks for help from Antinous. Antinous responds in contempt to Odysseus's request for help and throws a footstool at Odysseus. After Antinous's foolish decision, one of the youths speaks

9 For further clarification and elaboration of our claim that the terms ἐπουράνιος and οὐρανός/οὐράνιος are synonymous, see the appendix which details our definition and clarification of synonymy.

10 The first reference listed is the one with the appearance(s) of ἐπουράνιος. The portion in parentheses is the entire passage recorded in our analysis for the purpose of providing a larger context. Throughout this examination, we will not provide the full bibliographic information for primary sources in the text or the footnotes. The reader can locate this information in the bibliography. We will, however, identify the translator after each translation.

the words recorded above to Antinous. In BDAG, this appearance of ἐπουράνιος is listed as an adjective describing God and 'pertaining to being associated with a locale for transcendent things and beings, *heavenly, in heaven*'.[11] The fact that Odysseus is described as a possible heavenly (ἐπουράνιος) god is consistent with the term's definition as a reference to that which is spatially distinct from the earth.[12]

b. Homer, Iliad *6.129, 131 (128–31)*

> εἰ δέ τις ἀθανάτων γε κατ' οὐρανοῦ εἰλήλουθας,
> οὐκ ἂν ἔγωγε θεοῖσιν ἐπουρανίοισι μαχοίμην.
> οὐδὲ γὰρ οὐδὲ Δρύαντος υἱός, κρατερὸς Λυκόοργος,
> δὴν ἦν, ὅς ῥα θεοῖσιν ἐπουρανίοισι ἔριζεν·
>
> But if you are one of the immortals come down from heaven, I will not fight with the heavenly gods. No, for not even the son of Dryas, mighty Lycurgus, lived long, he who strove with heavenly gods. (Murray)

In this passage, Diomedes inquires about the nature of Glaukos by asking him if he is one of the immortals who has come down from heaven (κατ' οὐρανοῦ). Diomedes next acknowledges that he would not fight with the heavenly gods (θεοῖσιν ἐπουρανίοισι) because not even mighty Lycurgus lived long after striving with the heavenly gods (θεοῖσιν ἐπουρανίοισι). The significance of this passage from the *Iliad* is that both ἐπουράνιος and οὐρανός appear in the same context. The natural reading is to understand the prior location of the immortals who have come down from heaven (κατ' οὐρανοῦ) as the same as that which is represented by 'θεοῖσιν ἐπουρανίοισι'. Though these gods are actually encountered on earth, the fact that they are 'ἐπουρανίοισι' gods communicates either their prior location or their abode.[13] The usage of these two terms in this passage clearly demonstrates that they are synonymous in reference to the location they represent. Moreover, there is nothing in this passage to suggest that there is a major distinction between ἐπουράνιος and οὐρανός.[14]

11 BDAG, p. 388. Italics in BDAG.

12 Contra McGough who uses this passage merely to demonstrate the interaction of the heavenly with the earthly, 'Investigation', pp. 7–8. Again, our disagreement is not with McGough's argument for heavenly and earthly interaction but with the notion that this idea is inherent to the term ἐπουράνιος.

13 This would in effect be the equivalent of saying, 'The Italian man works in Paris.' Though the Italian man is currently in Paris, the adjective 'Italian' does not lose its local quality since he is originally from Italy or identifies Italy as his home.

14 Contra McGough who seemingly in an effort to force this text to conform to his presuppositions draws a major distinction between these terms. He concludes that οὐρανός was the prior location of the immortal while the term ἐπουράνιος was employed when the immortal was encountered on earth, 'Investigation', pp. 8–9. With this conclusion,

c. *Homer,* Iliad *6.527 (526–29)*

ἀλλ' ἴομεν· τὰ δ' ὄπισθεν ἀρεσσόμεθ', αἴ κέ ποθι Ζεὺς
δώῃ ἐπουρανίοισι θεοῖς αἰειγενέτῃσι
κρητῆρα στήσασθαι ἐλεύθερον ἐν μεγάροισιν,
ἐκ Τροίης ἐλάσαντας ἐυκνήμιδας Ἀχαιούς.

But let us go; these things we will make good later on, if Zeus will grant us to set for the heavenly gods who are for ever a bowl of freedom in our halls, when we have driven from the land of Troy the well-greaved Achaeans. (Murray)

This passage, which is not listed either in BDAG or LSJ, is of little value for a proper understanding of ἐπουράνιος or its relation to οὐρανός. There is nothing here to suggest that the term ἐπουράνιος does not retain its usual meaning – as a reference to that which is spatially distinct from the earth. The reference to 'ἐπουρανίοισι θεοῖς' is the same as *Iliad* 6.128–31 discussed above. The fact that ἐπουράνιος is utilized to describe the gods should make it clear that the reference is to heaven or that which is distinct from the earth. Similarly, though the 'ἐπουρανίοισι θεοῖς' are encountered on earth, their description as ἐπουράνιος suggests a quality about them which is distinct from the earth. Consequently, nothing in *Iliad* 6.526–29 would lead us either to reject the normal understanding of ἐπουράνιος or to substantiate a distinction between the various terms for heaven under consideration.[15]

d. *Plato,* Phaedrus *256d*

εἰς γὰρ σκότον καὶ τὴν ὑπὸ γῆς πορείαν οὐ νόμος ἐστὶν ἔτι ἐλθεῖν τοῖς κατηργμένοις ἤδη τῆς ἐπουρανίου πορείας, ἀλλὰ φανὸν βίον διάγοντας εὐδαιμονεῖν μετ' αλλήλων πορευομένους, καὶ ὁμοπτέρους ἔρωτος χάριν, ὅταν γένωνται, γενέσθαι.

for it is the law that those who have once begun their upward progress shall never again pass into darkness and the journey under the earth, but shall live a happy life in the light as they journey together, and because of their love shall be alike in their plumage when they receive their wings. (Fowler)

McGough implies that the term ἐπουράνιος is utilized to refer to that which is on the earth. Here it seems that McGough fails to differentiate between the basic functions of an adjective and a noun.

15 Contra McGough who once again implies that ἐπουράνιος was utilized because the gods were to attend an earthly celebration, 'Investigation', pp. 9–10. McGough also uses this passage to argue for the interaction of the earthly with the heavenly as an essential component of the term ἐπουράνιος, pp. 9–10.

In this passage, Plato writes of the heavenly journey (τῆς ἐπουρανίου πορείας) when the soul leaves the body. Those who have begun this heavenly journey will never again journey under the earth (τὴν ὑπὸ γῆς πορείαν). The only point of significance to note here is the contrast between the heavenly journey (τῆς ἐπουρανίου πορείας) and the earthly journey (τὴν ὑπὸ γῆς πορείαν). This contrast provides a clear distinction between the terms ἐπουράνιος and γῆ and the locations they represent.[16] This is significant since some commentators such as Odeberg and McGough have argued that the lack of contrast between ἐπουράνιος and γῆ in Ephesians is evidence for a distinction between ἐπουράνιος and οὐρανός in Ephesians. From our analysis of other Greek literature, however, we can establish that the normal usage of ἐπουράνιος is in contrast to the earth.

e. Theocritus 25.5 (3–6)

> ἔκ τοι ξεῖνε πρόφρων μυθήσομαι ὅσσ' ἐρεείνεις,
> Ἑρμέω ἁζόμενος δεινὴν ὄπιν εἰνοδίοιο·
> τὸν γάρ φασι μέγιστον ἐπουρανίων κεχολῶσθαι
> εἴ κεν ὁδου ζαχρεῖον ἀνήνηταί τις ὁδίτην.

> Sir, I will gladly tell you all you ask of me. Trust me, I hold the vengeance of Hermes o' the Ways in mickle awe and dread; for they say he be the wrathfullest God in Heaven an you deny a traveller guidance that hath true need of it. (Edmonds)

f. Moschus, Europa *2.21*

> ὀψὲ δὲ δειμαλέην ἀνενείκατο παρθένον αὐδήν·
> 'τίς μοι τοιάδε φάσματ' ἐπουρανίων προΐηλεν;

> At last she raised her maiden voice in accents of terror saying: 'Who of the People of Heaven did send me forth such phantoms as these?' (Edmonds)

We will evaluate together the two passages listed above since their use of ἐπουράνιος is the same and since there is little contribution from these passages for our purposes. According to BDAG, ἐπουρανίων is a designation of the gods in both passages.[17] In Theocritus 25.5 the old

16 Contra McGough who writes that ἐπουράνιος 'is understood here as referring to a realm of existence or manner of living beyond physical life', 'Investigation', p. 11. With this understanding, McGough once again spiritualizes the meaning of ἐπουράνιος rather than understanding the term as spatially distinct from the earth. For McGough, the primary contrast between ἐπουράνιος and the earth is spiritual rather than spatial.

17 BDAG, p. 388. BDAG lists the function of the term in these passages as a designation of the gods under the larger definition of 'pertaining to being associated with a locale for transcendent things and beings, *heavenly, in heaven*'. Italics original.

ploughman speaks of Hermes and says literally that he is the greatest of the heavenly ones (ἐπουρανίων) to be angered. In *Europa* 2.21 Europa has a dream about a struggle between two continents for possession of her. In response to the dream, she says, 'Who of the People of Heaven (literally of the heavenly ones) (ἐπουρανίων) did send me forth such phantoms as these?' The 'heavenly ones' is thus a term for the gods and this substantival use of ἐπουράνιος is frequently employed to refer to a deity. These references here to 'the heavenly ones' or to gods should be understood as a contrast to those on the earth.[18]

g. *Sextus Empiricus,* Against the Astrologers *5.44 (43–45a)*

Ὁ μὲν οὖν χαρακτὴρ τῆς Χαλδαϊκῆς μεθόδου τοιοῦτος ἔοικεν εἶναι· ῥᾴδιον δ' ἔστι λοιπὸν ἐπὶ παραδοθέντι τούτῳ συμπεριφέρεσθαι ταῖς κομιζομέναις ἀντιρρήσεσιν. καὶ δὴ ἔνιοι μὲν ἀγροικότερον πειρῶνται διδάσκειν ὡς οὐ πάντως συμπάσχει τοῖς οὐρανίοις τὰ ἐπίγεια· οὐδὲ γὰρ οὕτως ἥνωται τὸ περιέχον ὡς τὸ ἀνθρώπινον σῶμα, ἵνα ὃν τρόπον τῇ κεφαλῇ τὰ ὑποκείμενα μέρη συμπάσχει καὶ τοῖς ὑποκειμένοις ἡ κεφαλή, οὕτω καὶ τοῖς ἐπουρανίοις τὰ ἐπίγεια, ἀλλά τις ἔστι τούτων διαπορὰ καὶ ἀσυμπάθεια ὡς ἂν μὴ μίαν καὶ τὴν αὐτὴν ἐχόντων ἕνωσιν.

Such then, it seems, is the main outline of the Chaldean doctrine; and now that this has been expounded it is easy to follow intelligently the counter-arguments which are brought forward. Some people, indeed, try to argue quite bluntly that terrestrial things do not 'sympathize' altogether with things celestial; for the surrounding vault is not unified in the same way as the human body, so that things on earth should 'sympathize' with things in the heavens in the same way as the lower parts of the body sympathize with the head, and the head with the lower parts, but in respect of the former there exists a difference and want of sympathy, as they have not one and the same unification. (Bury)

This passage from Sextus Empiricus proves to be of great significance for a proper understanding of ἐπουράνιος and its relationship with οὐράνιος. After Sextus Empiricus had outlined the Chaldean doctrine, he listed some popular counter-arguments to the Chaldean doctrine. The first counter-argument is that 'terrestrial things (τὰ ἐπίγεια) do not "sympathize" (συμπάσχει) altogether with things celestial (τοῖς οὐρανίοις)'. He then explains that the surrounding vault (τὸ περιέχον) is different from the human body. Therefore, things on earth (τὰ ἐπίγεια) should not sympathize (συμπάσχει) with heavenly things (τοῖς ἐπουρανίοις) in the same way as the head with the lower parts of the body.

18 Contra McGough who once again maintains that the usage of ἐπουράνιος in these passages demonstrates the interaction of the earthly and heavenly dimensions, 'Investigation', pp. 12–13.

The significance of this passage is that it suggests the complete interchangeability of the terms ἐπουράνιος and οὐράνιος. Sextus Empiricus utilized the adjectives ἐπουράνιος and οὐράνιος in the same way and to communicate the same idea. In this text, both adjectives appear in the dative case (ἐπουρανίοις and οὐρανίοις) preceded by the definite article also in the dative case (τοῖς). Sextus Empiricus contrasted both of these adjectives for 'heavenly' with the exact same phrase for the earthly – τὰ ἐπίγεια. He also used the same verb in the same form (συμπάσχει) for both examples of the contrast between the earthly and the heavenly. The only plausible explanation for the different terms is that Sextus Empiricus simply chose to vary his word choice for 'heavenly'. In this instance, it is clear that the phrases τοῖς οὐρανίοις and τοῖς ἐπουρανίοις are synonymous and refer to that which is spatially distinct from the earth.[19]

h. Lucian, Dialogues of the Gods *10 (4).3*

> σὺ δὲ – ἤδη γὰρ ἐπουράνιος εἶ – πολλὰ εὖ ποιήσεις ἐντεῦθεν καὶ τὸν πατέρα καὶ πατρίδα, καὶ ἀντὶ μὲν τυποῦ καὶ γάλακτος ἀμβροσίαν ἔδῃ καὶ νέκταρ πίῃ·
>
> You're one of heaven's company now, and can do a lot of good to your father and country from here. Instead of your cheese and milk, you'll have ambrosia to eat and nectar to drink ... (Macleod)

The context of this passage is a conversation between Zeus and Ganymede wherein Zeus tells Ganymede that he is immortal now and one of heaven's company (ἤδη γὰρ ἐπουράνιος εἶ) (literally 'for now you are heavenly' or 'for now you are a heavenly one'). There is a clear contrast with earthly things when Zeus later tells Ganymede to 'stop longing for things below' (τῶν κάτω). The contrast with the 'things below' (τῶν κάτω) and the location of the conversation in heaven both confirm the normal usage and understanding communicated by the term ἐπουράνιος – as a reference to that which is spatially distinct from the earth.[20] Additionally, an appearance of οὐρανός in the larger

19 Contra McGough who in spite of the obvious similarity in the way these two terms are used arrives at a different conclusion and suggests a possible distinction between ἐπουράνιος and οὐράνιος. He writes, 'Even though this counter argument to the Chaldean doctrine denies interaction of the celestial with the terrestrial, it nonetheless recognizes a distinction between τοῖς οὐρανίοις and τοῖς ἐπουρανίοις,' 'Investigation', p. 14. Though McGough makes this surprising claim, he makes no attempt whatsoever to support it and does not appeal to the text, context, or author's word choice in arriving at this conclusion. It seems as though McGough simply cannot allow for the two terms to be synonymous here because that would not support his misguided understanding of the heavenlies in Ephesians and, as a result, the conclusions from his flawed word study.

20 Contra McGough who once again misses the significance of the passage and merely writes that the dialogue between Zeus and Ganymede implies future interaction of

context of this passage is also significant. Later in the dialogue, Zeus corrects Ganymede when Ganymede states that he knows how to pour milk. Zeus says, ‘This is heaven (ὁ οὐρανός ἐστι), let me tell you, and, as I said just now, our drink is nectar’ (10 [4].4). Zeus’s description of Ganymede as ἐπουράνιος and the description of their present location as οὐρανός clearly demonstrate that these two ‘heaven’ terms refer to the same location.[21]

i. Corpus Hermeticum

In our examination of ἐπουράνιος, we will now interact very briefly with four texts from the *Corpus Hermeticum* – *Stobaei Hermetica Excerpt* 12.1, *Stobaei Hermetica Excerpt* 21.2, *Fragment* 26.9, and *Abammonis Ad Porphyrium Responsum* 8.2c. Our analysis of these passages will be brief since these particular texts are not of great significance for our purposes. In *Stobaei Hermetica Excerpt* 12.1 the author writes that providence is the sovereign design of the heavenly God (τοῦ ἐπουρανίου θεοῦ). In this instance, ἐπουράνιος is employed as an adjective to describe God. This usage of ἐπουράνιος is common and in accord with the definition we have argued for throughout this chapter – as a reference to that which is spatially distinct from the earth.[22] Similarly, in *Stobaei Hermetica Excerpt* 21.2, Hermes writes that the sun is an image of the heavenly Maker (τοῦ ἐπουρανίου δημιουργοῦ [θεοῦ]). The term is again utilized here as an adjective to describe the Maker or Creator. This title is undoubtedly a reference to God as the text later reveals that he is the one who made the entire universe. The interjection of θεοῦ as an interpolation only serves to confirm that this is indeed a reference to God. As noted above, this use of ἐπουράνιος is common and in agreement with its normal understanding.[23]

Fragment 26.9 begins with a discussion of God’s omnipotence. Later in the passage, the author contrasts earthly things with heavenly things (τῶν ἐπιγείων πρὸς τὰ ἐπουράνια).[24] In addition to earthly and heavenly

the heavenly and earthly dimensions, ‘Investigation’, p. 15. BDAG lists this passage from Lucian ‘as a designation of the gods’, p. 388. This usage is listed under the wider definition of ‘pertaining to being associated with a locale for transcendent things and beings, *heavenly, in heaven*’, BDAG, p. 382.

21 McGough either misses or simply chooses not to interact with the appearance of οὐρανός a few lines later; as a result, he cannot comment on the relationship between οὐρανός and ἐπουράνιος.

22 McGough merely summarizes this passage and provides no analysis, ‘Investigation’, p. 16.

23 McGough once again merely summarizes this passage and then writes that the context is difficult to ascertain since a portion of the text is missing, ‘Investigation’, p. 16.

24 Though, in his notes to *Hermetica* (ed. and trans. Walter Scott; vol. 1; Oxford: Oxford University Press), Walter Scott regards this portion of the text to be an interpolation, pp. 542–45, the passage is nevertheless of value since the interpolation still represents how the term ἐπουράνιος was understood and utilized.

things, the author also contrasts the corporeal with the incorporeal, the perishable with the eternal, things with beginning with things without beginning, and things which are all-powerful with things which have need. The contrast between τῶν ἐπιγείων and τὰ ἐπουράνια demonstrates once again that ἐπουράνιος refers to that which is spatially distinct from the earth.[25] The other contrasts in the passage only serve to reinforce the idea that there is a fundamental distinction between τὰ ἐπίγεια and τὰ ἐπουράνια. Finally, in *Abammonis Ad Porphyrium Responsum* 8.2c, τῶν ἐπουρανίων is used substantivally as a designation of the gods. There is nothing in any of these passages which would suggest a different understanding of ἐπουράνιος than as a reference to that which is spatially distinct from the earth.

j. Second Century Papyri

> κεῖται μὲν γαίῃ φθίμενον δέμας, ἡ δὲ δοθεῖσα ψυχή μοι ναίει δώματ' ἐπουράνια.[26]
>
> On the one hand, the body, after it has decayed, is destined for the earth, but on the other hand, the soul, having been given to me, dwells in heavenly houses.[27]

This fragment contrasts the body (δέμας) which is destined for the earth (γαίῃ) with the soul (ψυχή) which dwells in heavenly houses (δώματ' ἐπουράνια).[28] It is implausible that δώματ' ἐπουράνια here could refer to some sort of spiritual atmosphere on earth. The usage of ἐπουράνιος is straightforward and the term here is correctly understood within its normal meaning as referring to that which is spatially distinct from the earth.[29]

25 Contra McGough who writes that the contrast between the earthly and heavenly in this passage demonstrates the distinction between two expressions of reality that have different natures, 'Investigation', p. 17. Though this conclusion is not completely inadequate, McGough is still forced to spiritualize the heavenlies here because he cannot allow for τὰ ἐπουράνια and τὰ ἐπίγεια to refer to different locations since this would be detrimental to his thesis.

26 Fragment from James Hopes Moulton and George Milliagan, *The Vocabulary of the Greek Testament: Illustrated from the Papyri and Other Non-Literary Sources* (London: Hodder and Stoughton, rev. edn, 1952), p. 252.

27 My translation.

28 Note the use of the contrastive expression μὲν ... δέ.

29 Contra McGough who once spiritualizes ἐπουράνιος when he writes that it '(refers) to a realm of existence beyond physical life', 'Investigation', p. 18. While McGough's assessment here is not entirely incorrect, his reluctance to assign any spatial significance to δώματ' ἐπουράνια is still lacking.

k. Paris Papyri 574.3042 (3037–44)

ὁρκίζω σε, πᾶν πνεῦμα δαιμόνιον, λαλῆσαι ὁποῖον καὶ ἂν ἧς, ὅτι ορκίζω σε κατὰ τῆς σφραγῖδος ἧς, ἔθετο Σολομὼν ἐπὶ τὴν γλῶσσαν τοῦ'Ιηρεμίου καὶ ἐλάλησεν. καὶ σὺ λάλησον ὁποῖον ἐὰν ἧς ἐπεουράνιον ἢ ἀέριον εἴτε ἐπίγειον εἴτε ὑπόγειον ἢ καταχθόνιον ἢ'Εβουσαῖον ἢ Χερσαῖον ἢ Φαρισαῖον.[30]

I adjure thee, every daemonic spirit, say whatsoever thou art. For I adjure thee by the seal which Solomon laid upon the tongue of Jeremiah and he spake. And say thou whatsoever thou art, in heaven, or of the air, or on earth, or under the earth or below the ground, or an Ebusaean, or a Chersaean, or a Pharisee. (Strachan)

In his analysis of this papyri, Adolf Deissmann writes, 'In spite of the resemblance to Philippians 2.10, Ephesians 2.2, 3.10, (and) 6.12, this is not a quotation from St. Paul. The papyrus and St. Paul are both using familiar Jewish categories.'[31] Three of the terms from this text – ἐπουράνιος, ἐπίγειος, and καταχθόνιος – also appear in Phil. 2.10.[32] In addition, the adjective ἀέριος in Paris Papyri 574.3042 is reminiscent of the appearance of the noun ἀήρ in Eph. 2.2 when Paul writes that believers formerly walked κατὰ τὸν ἄρχοντα τῆς ἐξουσίας τοῦ ἀέρος. The term ὑπόγειος appears only once in all of Scripture in LXX Jer. 45.11. Though, as Deissmann noted, these are familiar Jewish categories, it is nonetheless difficult to identify with any certainty precisely what these terms represent. It is possible that the author of this text intended the terms ἐπεουράνιος and ἀέριος to be understood as synonymous; however, it also remains possible that ἐπεουράνιος and ἀέριος refer to different heavenly regions. The same is also true for the terms ὑπόγειος and καταχθόνιος; they could be synonymous or καταχθόνιος could refer specifically to the abode of the dead while ὑπόγειος would be a more general term for 'under the earth'. For our purposes, what is significant is the clear contrast between ἐπίγειος, which refers to the earth, and ἐπουράνιος, which refers to that which is spatially distinct from the earth.[33]

30 Text from Adolf Deissmann, *Light from the Ancient Near East: The New Testament Illustrated by Recently Discovered Texts of the Graeco-Roman World* (trans. R. M. Strachan; London: Hodder and Stoughton, 1910), p. 257.

31 Deissmann, *Light*, p. 261, note 10.

32 Both ἐπουράνιος and ἐπίγειος appear elsewhere in Scripture including other Pauline passages. The term καταχθόνιος is a hapax legomena.

33 Contra McGough who writes that this passage demonstrates the spiritual quality inherent in the term ἐπουράνιος, 'Investigation', p. 19. McGough also believes this text demonstrates the possibility that evil is associated with ἐπουράνιος. McGough's conclusion here is interesting since it quite possibly reveals part of his motivation for 'spiritualizing' the heavenlies. Just as it does not make sense that believers should be granted a heavenly status while on earth (Eph. 2.6), so also it does not follow that evil should be associated with the heavenlies (Eph. 6.12). As we have previously noted, these two perplexing

l. Quintus Smyrnaeus, The Fall of Troy *2.429*

ἐγὼ δέ μιν οὐκ ἀλεγίζω οὐδέ μιν ἀθανάτῃσιν ἐπουρανίῃσιν εἴσκω.

Nothing I reck of her, nor rank her with the immortal Heavenly Ones. (Way)

In the larger context of this passage, Memnon strikes Achilles's arm with his spear and subsequently boasts to Achilles of his divine birth. Memnon then insults Achilles's mother and questions her divinity by saying that she is not one of the immortal Heavenly Ones (ἀθανάτῃσιν ἐπουρανίῃσιν). Here we see that ἐπουράνιος is once again employed as a substantival designation of the gods. This usage is in accordance with the definition argued for throughout this chapter – as a reference to that which is spatially distinct from the earth.[34]

4. *Philo*

a. Philo, Legum Allegoria *Book III LVIII.168*

τοὺς οὖν ἀσκητὰς ὥσπερ νόμισμα δοκιμάζει ὁ ὀρθὸς λόγος, πότερα κεκηλίδωνται ἐπί τι τῶν ἐκτὸς ἀναφέροντες τὸ τῆς ψυχῆς ἀγαθὸν ἢ ὡς δόκιμοι διαστέλλουσιν ἐν διανοίᾳ μόνῃ τοῦτο διαφυλάττοντες. τούτοις συμβέβηκε μὴ τοῖς γηίνοις ἀλλὰ ταῖς ἐπουρανίοις ἐπιστήμαις τρέφεσθαι.

The right principle, therefore, tests all aspirants as one does a coin, to see whether they have been debased in that they refer the soul's good to something external, or whether, as tried and approved men, they distinguish and guard this treasure as belonging to thought and mind alone. Such men have the privilege of being fed not with earthly things but with the heavenly forms of knowledge. (Colson and Whitaker)

In Philo's Book III of *Legum Allegoria*, we find appearances of ἐπουράνιος, οὐρανός, and οὐράνιος. The meanings of and relationship between these various 'heaven' words are of considerable importance for our purposes in this chapter. The fact that Ephesians and *Legum Allegoria* are both first-century-AD compositions only serves to heighten the significance of this passage for understanding the heavenlies in

statements have provided the impetus for commentators such as Odeberg and McGough to spiritualize the heavenlies in Ephesians.

34 McGough mistakenly interacts with the wrong passage here when he argues that the significance of ἐπουράνιος is the heavenly ones' ability to see all things including earthly events, 'Investigation', p. 20. In this instance, McGough examines 2.443 where the term ἐπουράνιος does not even appear. The all-seeing heavenly ones in this passage are described as πανδερκέες Οὐρανίωνες.

Ephesians. In his allegory of Exod. 16.4 in Book III, Philo compares the food which comes from heaven to heavenly forms of knowledge which feed the soul. He writes,

> That the food of the soul is not earthly (γήινοι) but heavenly (οὐράνιοι), we shall find abundant evidence in the Sacred Word. 'Behold I rain upon you bread out of heaven (‹ἐκ› τοῦ οὐρανοῦ) ... The soul is fed (τρέφεται) not with things of earth (γηίνοις) that decay, but with such words as God shall have poured like rain out of that lofty and pure region of life to which the prophet has given the title of "heaven"' (οὐρανόν) (III.162). (Colson and Whitaker)

A few verses later in III.168, Philo continues his commentary on Exod. 16.4 and writes that those who live by the divine law 'have the privilege of being fed (τρέφεσθαι) not with earthly (γηίνοις) things but with the heavenly (ἐπουρανίοις) forms of knowledge'.

Once more, in a passage in which οὐρανός, οὐράνιος, and ἐπουράνιος all appear, we observe that these three terms are used with no distinction in meaning and refer to the same location. It would be preposterous to conclude that the food which is heavenly (οὐράνιοι) and which comes from heaven (‹ἐκ› τοῦ οὐρανοῦ) in III.162 describes a different location than the heavenly (ἐπουρανίοις) forms of knowledge in III.168. We find additional support for this conclusion when we note that Philo contrasts the food which is of 'heaven' (οὐρανόν) to the things of earth (γηίνοις) which decay (III.162) just as he contrasts the heavenly (ἐπουρανίοις) forms of knowledge with the earthly things (τοῖς γηίνοις) (III.168). Similarly, the fact that Philo employs the same verb (τρέφω) for both metaphors is striking. The soul is fed (τρέφεται) with things from heaven (οὐρανόν) in III.162 while those who live by the divine law are fed (τρέφεσθαι) with heavenly (ἐπουρανίοις) forms of knowledge in III.168. Consequently, we must conclude that Philo here uses the terms οὐρανός, οὐράνιος, and ἐπουράνιος synonymously and to refer to that which is spatially distinct from the earth.[35] It is quite possible that Philo in this passage alternates between the adjectives οὐράνιος and ἐπουράνιος merely for stylistic purposes.

Not only does this passage from *Legum Allegoria* demonstrate the synonymous usage of οὐρανός, οὐράνιος, and ἐπουράνιος, it also serves as attestation for a link between the Old Testament שָׁמַיִם and ἐπουράνιος. In the Greek Old Testament, there is only one appearance of ἐπουράνιος (LXX Ps. 67.15) since οὐρανός is used almost universally

35 Contra McGough who once again spiritualizes the meaning of ἐπουράνιος, 'Investigation', p. 31. McGough does not interact with the appearances of οὐρανός and οὐράνιος in this passage and so cannot comment on the relationship Philo perceived between these various 'heaven' terms. Once again, in light of McGough's argument that there is a major distinction in meaning between ἐπουράνιος and οὐρανός in Greek literature, such an oversight is evidence of the considerable deficiencies in his examination.

for the translation of the Hebrew שָׁמַיִם. As we noted above, in his commentary on the bread ἐκ τοῦ οὐρανοῦ (מִן־הַשָּׁמַיִם, Hebrew Bible) in Exod. 16.4, Philo writes that those who live by the divine law are fed with heavenly (ἐπουρανίοις) forms of knowledge (III.168). With this metaphor, Philo associates this heavenly (ἐπουράνιος) knowledge with οὐρανός in LXX Exod. 16.4 and so also the שָׁמַיִם in the Hebrew Scriptures' Exod. 16.4. Such an association, especially within the Jewish framework of Philo, serves as further attestation that the expressions ἐν (τοῖς) οὐρανοῖς and ἐν τοῖς ἐπουρανίοις are synonymous and refer to that which is spatially distinct from the earth.

b. Philo, De Gigantibus *XIV.62*

> Ὁ γοῦν Ἀβραὰμ μέρχι μὲν διατρίβων ἦν ἐν τῇ τε καὶ δόξῃ, πρὶν μετονομασθῆναι, καλούμενος Ἀβρὰμ [ἦν] ἄνθρωπος οὐρανοῦ τήν τε μετάρσιον καὶ τὴν αἰθέριον φύσιν ἐρευνῶν καὶ τά τε συμβαίνοντα καὶ τὰς αἰτίας καὶ εἴ τι ἄλλο ὁμοιότροπον φιλοσοφῶν -- οὗ χάριν καὶ προσρήσεως οἷς ἐπετήδευσεν ἔτυχεν οἰκείας· Ἀβρὰμ γὰρ ἑρμηνευθεὶς πατήρ ἐστι μετέωρος, ὄνομα τοῦ τὰ μετέωρα καὶ ἐπουράνια περισκοπουμένου πάντα πάντῃ νοῦ πατρός, πατὴρ δὲ τοῦ συγκρίματος ὁ νοῦς ἐστιν ὁ ἄχρις αἰθέρος καὶ ἔτι περαιτέρω μηκυνόμενος --·
>
> Thus Abraham, while he sojourned in the land of the Chaldeans – sojourned, that is, in mere opinion – and with his name as yet unchanged from Abram, was a 'man of heaven'. He searched into the nature of the supra-terrestrial and ethereal region, and his philosophy studied the events and changes which there occur, and their causes and the like. And therefore he received a name suitable to the studies which he pursued. For 'Abram' being interpreted is the uplifted father, a name which signifies that mind which surveys on every side the whole compass of the upper world of heaven, called father-mind because this mind which reaches out to the ether and further still is the father of our compound being. (Colson and Whitaker)

In this passage from Philo's *De Gigantibus*, we find further confirmation that the terms οὐρανός, ἐπουράνιος, and οὐράνιος are utilized synonymously. In the wider context of this passage, we read that 'some men are earth-born (οἱ γῆς), some heaven-born (οἱ οὐρανοῦ), and some God-born (οἱ θεοῦ γεγόνασιν ἄνθρωποι)' (*De Gigantibus* 60). Philo continues and writes that 'the heavenly (οὐράνιον) in us is the mind, as the heavenly beings (τῶν κατ' οὐρανόν) are each of them a mind'. In *De Gigantibus* 62, we read that Abram is a 'man of heaven' (ἄνθρωπος οὐρανοῦ) and that his name 'signifies that mind which surveys on every side the whole compass of the upper world of heaven (τὰ μετέωρα καὶ ἐπουράνια)'.[36] The proper understanding of this passage and the natural

36 Here the translation 'of the upper world of heaven' is a genitive of apposition.

conclusion is that τὰ μετέωρα καὶ ἐπουράνια, which Abram surveys, describes the same location as the reference to Abram as a ἄνθρωπος οὐρανοῦ.[37] The previous references to 'the heaven-born' (οἱ οὐρανοῦ) and 'the heavenly' (οὐράνιον) only serve to reinforce this argument.

c. *Philo,* De Virtutibus *3.12*

> οἱ μὲν γὰρ τὰς ἐπιφανείας τῶν ὁρατῶν καταθεῶνται, ἅμα δεόμενοι φωτὸς ἔξωθεν, ἡ δὲ καὶ διὰ βάθους χωρεῖ τῶν σωμάτων, ὅλα δι' ὅλων καθ' ἕκαστα τῶν μερῶν ἀκριβοῦσα καὶ περιαθροῦσα καὶ τὰς τῶν ἀσωμάτων φύσεις, ἃ σ ἐπισκοπεῖν αἴσθησις ἀδυνατεῖ· σχεδὸν γὰρ πᾶσαν ὀξυωπίαν ὀφθαλμοῦ καταλαμβάνει, μὴ προσδεομένη νόθου φωτός, ἀστὴρ οὖσα αὐτὴ καὶ σχεδόν τι τῶν ἐπουρανίων ἀπεικόνισμα καὶ μίμημα.
>
> The body's eyes observe the surfaces of things visible and need the external help of light, but the mind penetrates through the depth of material things, accurately observing their whole contents and their several parts, surveying also the nature of things immaterial, which sense is unable to decry. For we may say that it achieves all the keenness of vision, which an eye can have, without needing any adventitious light, itself a star and, we may say, a copy and likeness of the heavenly company. (Colson and Whitaker)

In *De Virtutibus* 3.12 Philo compares the eyes of a person which observe the things visible with the mind which 'penetrates through the depth of material things' and can also discern the nature of immaterial things, inaccessible to the senses. He continues and also writes that the mind is 'a copy and likeness of the heavenly company (τῶν ἐπουρανίων)'. Here we find an implicit contrast between ἐπουράνιος and the earth when Philo writes that the eyes observe visible things, i.e. things on the earth which eyes can see. The fact that the mind, however, can also discern immaterial things makes it 'a copy and likeness of the heavenly company (τῶν ἐπουρανίων)'. The usage of ἐπουράνιος in this passage is consistent with our argument that the term always refers to that which is spatially distinct from the earth.[38]

37 Contra McGough who implies that the usage of ἐπουράνιος here merely represents a spiritual reality and earthly and heavenly interaction, 'Investigation', pp. 31–32. McGough once again does not interact with the appearances of οὐρανός and οὐράνιος in this passage. Consequently, he cannot comment on whether there is a major distinction in meaning between the terms or whether they are utilized synonymously.

38 McGough provides no real analysis of the reference to τῶν ἐπουρανίων when he writes that 'one usage of ἐπουράνιος in *De Virtutibus* suggests a realm of body of reality that is immaterial and not observable by the natural eye', 'Investigation', p. 32.

5. Old Testament Pseudepigrapha

a. Sibylline Oracles *4.51 (49–53)*

πρῶτα μὲν Ἀσσύριοι θνητῶν ἄρξουσιν ἁπάντων
ἓξ γενεὰς κόσμοιο διακρατέοντες ἐν ἀρχῇ,
ἐξ οὗ μηνίσαντος ἐπουρανίοιο θεοῖο
αὐτῇσιν πολίεσσι καὶ ἀνθρώποισιν ἅπασιν
γῆν ἐκάλυψε θάλασσα κατακλυσμοῖο ῥαγέντος.

First, the Assyrians will rule over all mortals,
holding the world in their dominion for six generations
from the time when the heavenly God was in wrath
with the cities themselves and all men,
and the sea covered the earth when the Flood burst forth. (Collins)[39]

The usage of ἐπουράνιος in *Sibylline Oracles* 4.51 as an adjective to describe God (ἐπουρανίοιο θεοῖο) is straightforward.[40] We have documented this usage numerous times in our examination and it is in agreement with our argument that ἐπουράνιος always refers to that which is spatially distinct from the earth.[41] Additionally, in 4.57, we read that the stars will fall from heaven (ἀπ' οὐρανόθεν). Although it is not one of the words under primary consideration for this study, οὐρανόθεν is an adverb meaning 'from heaven' and is obviously a cognate of οὐρανός/οὐράνιος. This appearance of οὐρανόθεν with ἐπουράνιος only serves to reinforce our argument that ἐπουράνιος is synonymous with these related terms for heaven.

b. Sibylline Oracles *4.135 (130–36)*

ἀλλ' ὁπότ' ἂν χθονίης ἀπὸ ῥωγάδος Ἰταλίδος γῆς
πυρσὸς ἀπαστράψας εἰς οὐρανὸν εὐρὺν ἵκηται,
πολλὰς δὲ φλέξῃ πόλιας καὶ ἄνδρας ὀλέσσῃ,
πολλὴ δ' αἰθαλόεσσα τέφρη μέγαν αἰθέρα πλήσῃ,
καὶ ψεκάδες πίπτωσιν απ' οὐρανοῦ οἷά τε μίλτος,
γινώσκειν τότε μῆνιν ἐπουρανίοιο θεοῖο,
εὐσεβέων ὅτι φῦλον ἀναίτιον ἐξολέσουσιν.

But when a firebrand, turned away from a cleft in the earth

39 Translation by J. J. Collins from *OTP* (ed. James H. Charlesworth; 2 vols; London: Darton, Longman & Todd, 1983–85). All further translations from *Sibylline Oracles* are also from Collins in *OTP*.

40 See again BDAG, p. 388. This use is listed as an adjective of God 'pertaining to being associated with a locale for transcendent things and beings ...'.

41 Contra McGough who again states that ἐπουράνιος here communicates earthly and heavenly interaction, 'Investigation', p. 29.

in the land of Italy, reaches to broad heaven,
it will burn many cities and destroy men.
Much smoking ashes will fill the great sky,
and showers will fall from heaven like red earth.
Know then the wrath of the heavenly God,
because they will destroy the blameless tribe of the pious. (Collins)

Similarly to many of the passages in our examination, *Sib. Or.* 4.130–36 contains appearances of both ἐπουράνιος and οὐρανός and, as a result, is of primary significance for a proper understanding of these terms and their relationship. The *Sibylline Oracles*' close proximity in composition to Ephesians is also of no minor significance for additional attestation of the relationship between these two terms in the late first century AD.[42] In this passage, the author issues a warning when he writes, 'But when a firebrand reaches to broad heaven' (εἰς οὐρανὸν εὐρύν) (4.131) and 'showers (fall) from heaven (απ' οὐρανοῦ) like red earth' (4.134), then the readers should 'know then the wrath of the heavenly God' (ἐπουρανίοιο θεοῖο) (4.135). The natural reading of this passage leads to the conclusion that the location described by εἰς οὐρανὸν εὐρύν and απ' οὐρανοῦ is the same as the location of the reference to the heavenly God (ἐπουρανίοιο θεοῖο). Since that which symbolizes God's wrath comes from the same place where God is located, it follows that ἐπουράνιος and οὐρανός here are synonymous and refer to that which is spatially distinct from the earth.[43]

42 In his introduction to *The Sibylline Oracles: Books III–V* (New York: MacMillan, 1918), H. N. Bate writes that scholars generally date Book IV shortly after the eruption of Mount Vesuvius in 79 AD, p. 24. This date is of course close to the range of dates proposed by NT scholars for the composition of Ephesians (c. 60–80 AD).

43 Contra McGough who, following a different text, draws a distinction in meaning between the smoking ashes which fall from οὐρανίους and the wrath of the heavenly (ἐπουρανίου) (sic) God, 'Investigation', pp. 29–30. It is unclear which Greek text McGough follows here since he provides no citation with a Greek text. Rzach's *Oracula Sibyllina* contains a textual apparatus and does not list McGough's variants in either case; however, Rzach does list ἀπουρανίοιο (ἀπ' οὐρανίοιο *F*) as a variant for ἐπουρανίοιο (line 135), p. 99. Nevertheless, whether we follow the text recorded and referenced above or McGough's variants, our conclusion is still the same. The location communicated by ἐπουράνιος should be understood as the same as that which is communicated by οὐρανός/οὐράνιος.

c. Testament of Job[44]

Though there is some disagreement over the date and background of *Testament of Job*, we regard the document as a first-century-BC or AD Jewish composition written in Greek with possible Christian editing.[45] The book's proximity to the dating of the New Testament and its Judaeo-Christian theology make *Testament of Job* an important source for our examination. Within *Testament of Job*, there are numerous appearances of both ἐπουράνιος and οὐρανός with important implications for a proper understanding of these terms and their relationship.

In a discussion between Elious and Job, on account of Job's misfortunes, Elious tells Job that he has become a joke and asks him, 'Where now is the splendor of your throne?' (32.11). Job responds, 'My throne is in the super-terrestrial realm, and its splendor and majesty are from the right hand of ‹the Father›[46] in the heavens (ἐν οὐρανοῖς)' (33.2). Baldas later questions Job and asks him, 'Is your heart in a stable condition?' (36.2). Job answers,

> ‹ἐν› μὲν τοῖς γηίνοις οὐ συνέστηκεν, ἐπειδὴ ἀκατάστατος ἡ γῆ καὶ οἱ κατοικοῦντες ἐν αὐτῇ· ἐν δὲ τοῖς ἐπουρανίοις συνέστηκεν ἡ καρδία μου διότι οὐχ ὑπάρχει ἐν οὐρανῷ ταραχή (36.3).[47]
>
> It is not involved with earthly things since the earth and those who dwell in it are unstable. But my heart is involved with heavenly things for there is no upheaval in heaven (36.3).

This particular passage is significant for two reasons. First, the exact expression which appears in Ephesians (ἐν τοῖς ἐπουρανίοις) also appears here but with the postpositive δέ after the preposition ἐν. There is little evidence to suggest any sort of dependence in either direction between Ephesians and *Testament of Job*.[48] However, the appearance

44 BDAG records two references for ἐπουράνιος in *Testament of Job* (36.3 and 38.5). According to BDAG, these examples refer to heavenly things under the larger definition of 'pertaining to being associated with a locale for transcendent things and beings, *heavenly, in heaven*', p. 388 (italics original). Since a large portion of *Testament of Job* is significant for our examination of ἐπουράνιος, the entire text from 32.11–40.4 will be examined. Consequently, we will cite the Greek texts and English translations when appropriate within the body of our examination. Unless otherwise noted, the texts and translations cited are from Kraft. Significant textual variants are from Brock.

45 R. P. Spittler, 'Introduction to *Testament of Job*', *OTP* 1, pp. 829–38 (830–33).

46 ‹ › encloses material absent from S but supplied from another source. As cited in Robert A. Kraft et al. (eds), *The Testament of Job: According to the SV Text* (Pseudepigrapha Series, Society of Biblical Literature, 4/Texts and Translations, Society of Biblical Literature, 5; Missoula, MT: Society of Biblical Literature and Scholars Press, 1974), p. 15.

47 Brock lists οὐρανοῖς (V text) as a variant for ἐπουρανίοις.

48 Spittler does, however, draw a comparison between *T. Job* 36.3-5 and Col. 3.1-4, p. 857, note 36a. We will later argue and demonstrate that Col. 3.1-4 is both conceptually and linguistically related to Eph. 2.5-6.

of the same expression within Jewish literature might support the notion that ἐν τοῖς ἐπουρανίοις was a fixed liturgical formula utilized in Jewish and/or Christian circles. Regardless of whether or not we arrive at this conclusion, the usage of ἐν τοῖς ἐπουρανίοις here should inform our understanding of the heavenlies in Ephesians. Second, this passage clearly demonstrates the synonymous usage of οὐρανός and ἐπουράνιος. For our purposes, it is significant that the appearance of ἐν τοῖς ἐπουρανίοις occurs between two appearances of οὐρανός. It is evident that the reference to Job's heart as involved with heavenly things ἐν τοῖς ἐπουρανίοις refers to the same location as the location of Job's throne ἐν οὐρανοῖς and the place where there is no upheaval ἐν οὐρανῷ. We find a clear contrast with the earth when we read that Job's heart is not involved with earthly things (‹ἐν› τοῖς γηίνοις) since those who dwell on the earth (ἐν αὐτῇ) are unstable.[49] It is crucial that we recognize the connection between ‹ἐν› τοῖς γηίνοις, ἡ γῆ, and ἐν αὐτῇ as well as the connection between ἐν δὲ τοῖς ἐπουρανίοις and ἐν οὐρανῷ. The usage of οὐρανός and ἐπουράνιος in this context makes it clear that these terms are synonymous and refer to that which is spatially distinct from the earth.

Though Kraft's translation cited above translates ‹ἐν› τοῖς γηίνοις and ἐν τοῖς ἐπουρανίοις in a descriptive sense,[50] it is also possible that these expressions could be translated as local if συνέστηκεν is taken in an intransitive sense.[51] This would render the translation, 'It (Job's heart) is not held together in the earthly places since the earth and those who dwell in it are unstable. But my heart is held together in the heavenly places for there is no upheaval in heaven.'[52] With this translation, there is continuity with the other prepositional phrases ἐν αὐτῇ and ἐν οὐρανῷ since they are all translated in a local sense.[53] Regardless of whether we interpret these phrases in a local or a descriptive sense, it is nonetheless clear that the usage of both οὐρανός and ἐπουράνιος is consistent with our argument that these terms always refer to that which is spatially distinct from the earth.

As Job's accusers continue to question him in *Testament of Job*, we find other appearances of ἐπουράνιος. In response to Baldas's questions, Job retorts, 'For who are we to be busying ourselves with heavenly matters (τῶν ἐπουρανίων), seeing that we are fleshly (σάρκινοι) and have our lot in dust and ashes (ἐν γῇ καὶ σποδῷ)?' (38.2-3). Job next asks Baldas, 'If you do not understand the function of the body (τὴν τοῦ σώματος πορείαν),

49 The ἐν αὐτῇ refers back to ἡ γῆ.

50 BDAG also cites *T. Job* 36.3 as a reference to heavenly things and thus not as local, p. 388.

51 Cf. Col. 1.17 where all things hold together/are held together (συνέστηκεν) in Christ.

52 My translation.

53 But see e.g. Eph. 1.3 where ἐν τοῖς ἐπουρανίοις is best translated as local and ἐν πάσῃ εὐλογίᾳ πνευματικῇ is best understood in a descriptive sense.

how will you understand the heavenly matters (τὰ ἐπουράνια)?' (38.5). In this passage, we see that 'heavenly things' (τῶν ἐπουρανίων) is contrasted with the earth as those who are fleshly have their lot in dust and ashes (ἐν γῇ καὶ σποδῷ). The contrast between the heavenly (ἐπουρανίων, ἐπουράνια) and the body or flesh is also best understood as a spatial contrast between heaven and earth. Job's point in these contrasts is that people cannot expect to understand heavenly matters or the ways of God if they cannot even comprehend earthly matters fully. Thus the usage of ἐπουράνιος here is consistent with our argument that the term always refers to that which is spatially distinct from the earth.

There is one final passage from *Testament of Job* which is significant for our purposes. In chapter 39, when the kings began to search for the remains of Job's children at the request of his wife, Job told them not to labour in vain and said, 'For you will not find my children, since they were taken up into the heavens (εἰς τοὺς οὐρανούς) by the creator, their king' (39.11-12). The kings responded by implying that Job was out of his mind for saying, 'My children have been taken up into heaven (εἰς τὸν οὐρανόν)!' (39.13). When the kings once more ask Job for the truth concerning his children, he stands up, gives thanks to the Lord, and tells them to look up to the east. Upon looking up, the kings 'saw (Job's) children crowned alongside the splendor of the heavenly one (ἐπουρανίου)' (39.13–40.4). This passage from *Testament of Job* 39 also clearly demonstrates that οὐρανός and ἐπουράνιος refer to the same location. Job's claim that his children have been taken εἰς τοὺς οὐρανούς is substantiated by the appearance of his children alongside the heavenly one (ἐπουρανίου). As previously noted, this usage of ἐπουράνιος as a substantival designation of God is common and has been attested numerous times in this examination.

d. Testament of Abraham *IV (Recension A)*[54]

> καὶ ὁ ἀρχιστράτηγος εἶπεν· Κύριε, πάντα τὰ ἐπουράνια πνεύματα ὑπάρχουσιν ἀσώματα, καὶ οὔτε ἐσθίουσιν οὔτε πίνουσιν· καὶ οὗτος δὲ ἐμοὶ τράπεζαν παρέθετο ἐν ἀφθονίᾳ πάντων ἀγαθῶν τῶν ἐπιγείων καὶ φθαρτῶν·
>
> Then the Archistrategos said, 'Lord, all the heavenly spirits are incorporeal and neither eat nor drink and he has set before me a table with an abundance of all good earthly and corruptible things.' (Stone)

In *Testament of Abraham*, the Lord sends his archangel Michael (also referred to as Archistrategos) to inform Abraham of his impending death. After he visits Abraham, Michael ascends to heaven (εἰς τὸν οὐρανόν) and expresses to the Lord his hesitancy to pronounce death

54 A portion of Section IV is recorded.

on such a righteous man. As a result, the Lord tells Michael that he will communicate the news of Abraham's impending death to Isaac in a dream. Finally, the Lord also instructs Michael to visit Abraham again, to do whatever he says, and to eat whatever he eats. In response to these instructions from the Lord, Michael says that the heavenly spirits (τὰ ἐπουράνια πνεύματα) are incorporeal and neither eat nor drink.

In this passage, we find a contrast between ἐπουράνιος and the earth when Michael states that τὰ ἐπουράνια πνεύματα are incapable of eating and drinking from the earthly and corruptible things (τῶν ἐπιγείων καὶ φθαρτῶν).[55] Of perhaps greater significance is the appearance of οὐρανός in the wider context of this passage from *Testament of Abraham*. Michael's ascent εἰς τὸν οὐρανόν and his subsequent description of himself as one of τὰ ἐπουράνια πνεύματα clearly communicate that the locations represented by ἐπουράνιος and οὐρανός are synonymous.[56] It is only natural to conclude that the locations of 'heaven' (τὸν οὐρανόν) and its inhabitants (τὰ ἐπουράνια πνεύματα) are the same. The usage of ἐπουράνιος in *Testament of Abraham* is consistent with our argument that the term always refers to that which is spatially distinct from the earth and that it is synonymous with οὐρανός.[57]

6. *Septuagint*

a. *LXX Psalm 67.15*

> ἐν τῷ διαστέλλειν τὸν ἐπουράνιον βασιλεῖς ἐπ' αὐτῆς χιονωθήσονται ἐν Σελμων
>
> When the heavenly One scatters kings upon it, they shall be made snow-white in Selmon. (LXE; Brenton)

In LXX Ps. 67.15, τὸν ἐπουράνιον, as the translation of the Hebrew שַׁדַּי, is a substantive describing God. The fact that ἐπουράνιος is utilized here as a translation for שַׁדַּי does not indicate that the term loses its basic meaning as a reference to that which is spatially distinct from the earth.[58] Rather, it is likely that the translator of this psalm employed the idea of the 'Heavenly One' (τὸν ἐπουράνιον) to communicate the Hebrew

55 This contrast between τὰ ἐπουράνια πνεύματα and τῶν ἐπιγείων is evident, though there is also a clear contrast between the corporeal and incorporeal.

56 There is also a reference to the stars of heaven (ἀστέρας τοῦ οὐρανοῦ) in *Testament of Abraham* IV.

57 For additional examples and evidence from *Testament of Abraham*, see the uses of οὐρανός and ἐπουράνιος in sections VI–VII. See also *T. Abr.* 2.3, where τοῦ ἐπουρανίου is a substantive for God, *T. Abr.* 6.4, where ἐπουρανίους describes the three heavenly angels, and *T. Abr.* 17.11, where τοῦ ἐπουρανίου is an adjective describing God.

58 Contra McGough who once again writes that the significance of this verse is the interaction of the heavenly with the earthly, 'Investigation', p. 25.

Bible's description of God as the Almighty (שַׁדַּי). Since LXX Ps. 67.15 is the only place where ἐπουράνιος appears in the Greek Old Testament, this translation for שַׁדַּי does not appear to be common; however, we do find that the expression τοῦ θεοῦ τοῦ οὐρανοῦ is also employed as a translation for שַׁדַּי in LXX Ps. 90.1.[59] The usage of τὸν ἐπουράνιον in Ps. 67.15 and τοῦ θεοῦ τοῦ οὐρανοῦ in Ps. 90.1 is highly significant since it strongly suggests that these two expressions are interchangeable and provides further evidence that it is mistaken to posit a major distinction in meaning between ἐπουράνιος and οὐρανός.[60]

b. 2 Maccabees 3.39

> αὐτὸς γὰρ ὁ τὴν κατοικίαν ἐπουράνιον ἔχων ἐπόπτης ἐστὶν καὶ βοηθὸς ἐκείνου τοῦ τόπου καὶ τοὺς παραγινομένους ἐπὶ κακώσει τύπτων ἀπολλύει
>
> For he who has his dwelling in heaven watches over that place himself and brings it aid, and he strikes and destroys those who come to do it injury. (NRSV)[61]

In the larger context of this verse, Heliodorus, a servant of the king, attempted to confiscate money from the temple without just cause. In response, 'the priests prostrated themselves before the altar ... and called toward heaven' (εἰς οὐρανόν) for the protection of the Lord (v. 15). The women of the city also held up their hands to heaven (εἰς τὸν οὐρανόν) and made supplication (v. 20). As Heliodorus continued his plan and arrived at the treasury, a rider on a horse appeared, rushed Heliodorus, and struck him with its front hooves (v. 25). Two other young men of great strength and beauty also appeared and flogged him continuously. After the high priest offered a sacrifice for Heliodorus's recovery, the same young men appeared again to Heliodorus and said, 'Be very grateful to the high priest Onias, since for his sake the Lord has granted you your life. And see that you, who have been flogged by heaven (ἐξ οὐρανοῦ), report to all people the majestic power of God' (v. 34). Later, Heliodorus recognized the power of God and uttered the words from the present passage, 'For he who has his dwelling in heaven (αὐτὸς γὰρ ὁ

59 Similarly to our evaluation of τὸν ἐπουράνιον in LXX Ps. 67.15, concerning τοῦ θεοῦ τοῦ οὐρανοῦ in LXX Ps. 90.1, Traub writes, 'Finally, the OT belief that God, as Creator of heaven and Ruler of heaven, is linked with heaven, is itself the occasion for the adding of οὐρανός to the original text. Thus שַׁדַּי is rendered ὁ θεὸς τοῦ οὐρανοῦ in Ps. 91:1', Traub, *TDNT* 5:510. This same explanation is equally applicable for the decision to render שַׁדַּי as τὸν ἐπουράνιον in LXX Ps. 67.15.

60 McGough does not examine LXX Ps. 90.1 and so cannot comment on the relationship between ἐπουράνιος in 67.15 and οὐρανός in 90.1.

61 All further quotations and translations from 2 and 3 Maccabees are from the NRSV.

τὴν κατοικίαν ἐπουράνιον) watches over that place and brings it aid, and he strikes and destroys those who come to do it injury.'

The context, flow, and word choice of this passage from 2 Maccabees all support the notion that ἐπουράνιος and οὐρανός are synonymous and refer to the same location. The priests called towards heaven (εἰς οὐρανόν), the women raised their hands to heaven (εἰς τὸν οὐρανόν), and Heliodorus was flogged by heaven (ἐξ οὐρανοῦ). It is inconceivable to suppose that God's description as having a heavenly dwelling (αὐτὸς γὰρ ὁ τὴν κατοικίαν ἐπουράνιον) would refer to some other location or idea than that communicated by οὐρανός. Both the context and the diction of the passage clearly support our argument that ἐπουράνιος refers to that which is spatially distinct from the earth and is used to describe the same location as οὐρανός.[62]

c. 3 Maccabees 6.28

> ἀπολύσατε τοὺς υἱοὺς τοῦ παντοκράτορος ἐπουρανίου θεοῦ ζῶντος ὃς ἀφ' ἡμετέρων μέχρι τοῦ νῦν προγόνων ἀπαραπόδιστον μετὰ δόξης εὐστάθειαν παρέχει τοῖς ἡμετέροις πράγμασιν
>
> Release the children of the almighty and living God of heaven, who from the time of our ancestors until now has granted an unimpeded and notable stability to our government.

In the larger context of this passage, Ptolemy IV Philopator, the king of Egypt, attempted to have the Jews killed by crushing them with elephants. Eleazar, a Jewish priest, prayed to the Lord for deliverance. When the animals arrived, the Jews also 'raised great cries to heaven' (μέγα εἰς οὐρανὸν ἀνέκραξαν) (6.17). In response to their prayers, God 'opened the heavenly gates' (ἠνέῳξεν τὰς οὐρανίους πύλας) (6.18) and two angels descended to thwart the plans of the king. When Ptolemy's plan was

62 Contra McGough who merely summarizes the larger passage and then concludes that the divine intervention of the heavenly God to protect the temple implies earthly and heavenly interaction, 'Investigation', pp. 25–26. In his assessment, McGough does not address the three appearances of οὐρανός earlier in the passage and so he cannot comment on the relation between οὐρανός and ἐπουράνιος in this text. We consider this omission to be inexcusable in light of McGough's argument that there is a major distinction in meaning between οὐρανός and ἐπουράνιος since passages in which both terms appear are of obvious significance for a proper understanding of their meaning and relationship. Second Maccabees 3.34, which states that Heliodorus is flogged by heaven (ἐξ οὐρανοῦ), also militates against McGough's assertion that οὐρανός does not contain an element of interaction with the earth, 'Investigation', pp. 48–50, 96–101. As stated previously, the presence or absence of heavenly and earthly interaction is not inherent to a word's lexical meaning but rather is part of specific belief systems or worldviews. In Judaeo-Christian theology, heavenly and earthly interaction is at the heart of its beliefs, so it should come as no surprise that, such as in this passage, an angel or representative from heaven is employed by God to accomplish a particular purpose on earth.

hindered, his anger turned to compassion (6.22) and he commanded, 'Release the children of the almighty and living God of heaven' (ἀπολύσατε τοὺς υἱοὺς τοῦ παντοκράτορος ἐπουρανίου θεοῦ ζῶντος) (6.28). Subsequently, the king gave thanks to heaven (εἰς οὐρανόν) for his own deliverance (6.33).

This passage from 3 Maccabees also proves to be significant for a proper understanding of ἐπουράνιος and its relationship to οὐρανός/οὐράνιος. The Jews cried to heaven (εἰς οὐρανόν), God opened the heavenly (οὐρανίους) gates, Ptolemy commanded that the children of the heavenly (ἐπουρανίου) God be released, and the king gave thanks to heaven (εἰς οὐρανόν). It is interesting that the author here employed three different words which refer to heaven – the noun οὐρανός, the adjective οὐράνιος, and the adjective ἐπουράνιος – without any discernible difference in meaning. The natural reading of this passage is to understand all three terms as referring to the same location and as spatially distinct from the earth.[63] It is quite possible that the author here employed both the adjectival οὐράνιος and ἐπουράνιος simply for stylistic variation.

d. 3 Maccabees 7.6

> ἡμεῖς δὲ ἐπὶ τούτοις σκληρότερον διαπειλησάμενοι καθ' ἣν ἔχομεν πρὸς ἅπαντας ἀνθρώπους ἐπιείκειαν μόγις τὸ ζῆν αὐτοῖς χαρισάμενοι καὶ τὸν ἐπουράνιον θεὸν ἐγνωκότες ἀσφαλῶς ὑπερησπικότα τῶν Ιουδαίων ὡς πατέρα ὑπὲρ υἱῶν διὰ παντὸς συμμαχοῦντα
>
> But we very severely threatened them for these acts, and in accordance with the clemency that we have toward all people we barely spared their lives. Since we have come to realize that the God of heaven surely defends the Jews, always taking their part as a father does for his children ...

The larger context of 3 Macc. 7.6 is generally the same as the passage examined immediately above (3 Macc. 6.28) since it continues the story of God's deliverance of the Jews from Ptolemy IV Philopator. After their deliverance, the Jews feasted with the king and subsequently asked for dismissal to their homes. Ptolemy granted this request and wrote a letter to the generals in the cities about his concern for the Jews. In this letter, Ptolemy wrote that the heavenly God (τὸν ἐπουράνιον θεόν) surely defends the Jews (7.6). Here we observe again the common usage of ἐπουράνιος as an adjective to describe God.[64] This usage is in agreement

63 Contra McGough who maintains that there is a distinction in meaning between οὐρανίους and ἐπουρανίου in this passage and concludes that the usage of ἐπουράνιος here implies earthly and heavenly interaction, 'Investigation', p. 27. The implication of McGough's conclusion is that οὐράνιος in this passage does not contain an element of heavenly and earthly interaction. See our analysis of 2 Macc. 3.39 for a critique of McGough and this conclusion.

64 BDAG also lists 3 Macc. 6.28 and 7.6 as modifying God and under the larger defi-

with our argument that ἐπουράνιος always refers to that which is spatially distinct from the earth.[65]

7. *Apostolic Fathers*[66]

a. Ignatius, To the Ephesians *13.2 (1-2)*

> 13.1 Σπουδάζετε οὖν πυκνότερον συνέρχεσθαι εἰς εὐχαριστίαν θεοῦ καὶ εἰς δόξαν. ὅταν γὰρ πυκνῶς ἐπὶ τὸ αὐτὸ γίνεσθε, καθαιροῦνται αἱ δυνάμεις τοῦ σατανᾶ, καὶ λύεται ὁ ὄλεθρος αὐτοῦ ἐν τῇ ὁμονοίᾳ ὑμῶν τῆς πίστεως. (2) οὐδέν ἐστιν ἄμεινον εἰρήνης, ἐν ᾗ πᾶς πόλεμος καταργεῖται ἐπουρανίων καὶ ἐπιγείων.
>
> Therefore make every effort to come together more frequently to give thanks and glory to God. For when you meet together frequently, the powers of Satan are overthrown and his destructiveness is nullified by the unanimity of your faith. (2) There is nothing better than peace, by which all warfare among those in heaven and those on earth is abolished. (Holmes; Lightfoot)

The Apostolic Fathers are significant for New Testament studies since they represent some of the earliest Christian literature coinciding with or shortly after the New Testament documents. Though it is possible that Ignatius had access to a number of New Testament documents, the strongest cases for literary dependence are from 1 Corinthians and Ephesians.[67] Consequently, for our purposes, it is of no minor significance that the writings of Ignatius represent one of the earliest interpretations of Ephesians.

In Ignatius, *Eph.* 13.1-2, Ignatius exhorts his readers to meet together frequently so that through their unanimity of faith the powers of Satan will be overthrown, and there will be peace which abolishes all warfare among the heavenly and earthly ones (ἐπουρανίων καὶ ἐπιγείων). Of particular significance is the contrast Ignatius draws between 'the heavenly' (ἐπουρανίων) and 'the earthly' (ἐπιγείων). Though it is possible, we cannot establish with certainty any dependence of this passage on the Pauline letter of Ephesians. There are some similarities in vocabulary and themes with the Pauline Ephesians, but these similarities are also present in other

nition of 'pertaining to being associated with a locale for transcendent things and beings ...', p. 388.

65 Contra McGough who concludes that the usage of ἐπουράνιος here implies earthly and heavenly interaction, 'Investigation', pp. 27–28.

66 Our examination of the Apostolic Fathers includes all of the references to ἐπουράνιος in the Apostolic Fathers, though the passage from the Moscow manuscript of *Mart. Pol.* 22.3 will be only very briefly discussed in our discussion of *Mart. Pol.* 20.2.

67 Michael E. Holmes (ed.), *The Apostolic Fathers: Greek Texts and English Translations* (Grand Rapids: Baker Books, 3rd edn, 1999), p. 133.

Pauline writings.[68] It is possible that Ignatius here draws upon the themes of spiritual warfare with the evil spiritual powers in the heavenlies (Eph. 6.10-20) and unity of faith for the promotion of peace (Eph. 4.3-5, 13) in order to apply these themes to the specific circumstances of his readers.

If the usage of ἐπουράνιος in this passage does indeed reflect Ignatius's interpretation of the heavenlies, then Ignatius's contrast between 'ἐπουρανίων' and 'ἐπιγείων' is of particular importance. As part of their evidence for a distinction between ἐπουράνιος and οὐρανός in Ephesians, commentators such as Odeberg and McGough point out that ἐπουράνιος is never contrasted with the earth in Ephesians while οὐρανός always is. The contrast between ἐπουράνιος and ἐπίγειος in Ignatius, *Eph.* 13.2 would thus imply that Ignatius understands the expressions ἐν τοῖς ἐπουρανίοις and ἐν τοῖς οὐρανοῖς as synonymous.[69] Regardless of whether or not there is direct dependence of this passage on Ephesians, it is nonetheless significant that Ignatius contrasts the terms ἐπουράνιος and ἐπίγειος. Finally, the usage of ἐπουράνιος here is consistent with our definition that the term always refers to that which is spatially distinct from the earth.

b. Ignatius, To the Trallians *5.1-2*

> 5.1 Μὴ οὐ δύναμαι ὑμιν τὰ ἐπουράνια γράψαι; ἀλλὰ φοβοῦμαι μὴ νηπίοις οὖσιν ὑμῖν βλάβην παραθῶ. καὶ συγγνωμονεῖτέ μοι, μήποτε οὐ δυνηθέντες χωρῆσαι στραγγαλωθῆτε. (2) καὶ γὰρ ἐγώ, οὐ καθότι δέδεμαι καὶ δύναμαι νοεῖν τὰ ἐπουράνια καὶ τὰς τοποθεσίας τὰς ἀγγελικὰς καὶ τὰς συστάσεις τὰς ἀρχοντικάς, ὁρατά τε καὶ ἀόρατα, παρὰ τοῦτο ἤδη καὶ μαθητής εἰμι. πολλὰ γὰρ ἡμῖν λείπει, ἵνα θεοῦ μὴ λειπώμεθα.
>
> Am I not able to write to you about heavenly things? But I am afraid to, lest I should cause harm to you who are mere babes. So bear with me, lest you be choked by what you are unable to swallow. (2) For I myself, though I am in chains and can comprehend heavenly things, the ranks of the angels and the hierarchy of principalities, things visible and invisible, for all this I am not yet a disciple. For we still lack many things, that we might not lack God. (Holmes; Lightfoot)

68 The following words and themes from Ignatius, *Eph.* 13.1-2 also appear in the Pauline Ephesians: σπουδάζω (4.3); unity (4.3, ἑνότης in Ephesians rather than ὁμονοίᾳ in Ignatius); εἰρήνη (1.2; 2.14; 2.15; 2.17; 4.3 6.15; 6.23); εὐχαριστία (5.4); δύναμις (1.19, 1.21, 3.7; 3.16; 3.20); διάβολος (4.27; 6.11 but σατανᾶ in Ignatius); λύω (2.14); unity of faith (τὴν ἑνότητα τῆς πίστεως in Eph. 4.13 but ἐν τῇ ὁμονοίᾳ ὑμῶν τῆς πίστεως in Ignatius); καταργέω (2.15); ἐπουράνιος (1.3; 1.20; 2.6; 3.10; 6.12); ἐπὶ τῆς γῆς (1.10; 6.3), ἐπὶ γῆς (3.15), γῆς (4.9 but ἐπιγείων in Ignatius, *Eph.* 13.1-2); theme of heavenly warfare. Many of the similarities in vocabulary between Ignatius, *Eph.* 13.1-2 and the NT letter of Ephesians are found in Eph. 2.14-15 and Eph. 4.13.

69 As previously noted, the phrase ἐν οὐρανοῖς is found in Eph. 3.15 and 6.9 whereas ἐπὶ τοῖς οὐρανοῖς is found in 1.10 and τῶν οὐρανῶν in 4.10.

In v. 1, Ignatius seems to draw primarily upon 1 Cor. 3.1-3a where Paul writes, 'And I, brethren, could not speak to you as to spiritual (πνευματικοῖς) men, but as to men of flesh (σαρκίνοις,), as to infants (νηπίοις) in Christ. I gave you milk to drink, not solid food; for you were not yet able *to receive it.* Indeed, even now you are not yet able, for you are still fleshly.' Of particular interest is Ignatius's substitution of ἐπουράνιος (τὰ ἐπουράνια) for Paul's use of πνευματικός in 1 Cor. 3.1. There is precedent for a close relationship between ἐπουράνιος and πνευματικός in 1 Cor. 10.1-4 and 1 Cor. 15.40-50.[70] In this sense, πνευματικός or Spiritual (i.e. of the Spirit) is closely related to ἐπουράνιος since they both represent a quality which is distinct either from natural life or the earth. The τὰ ἐπουράνια of verse 2 are associated with other transcendent concepts such as the ranks of the angels, the hierarchy of principalities, and things invisible (ἀόρατα).[71] The usage of τὰ ἐπουράνια here is consistent with our argument that the term always refers to that which is spatially distinct from the earth.

c. Ignatius, To the Trallians *9.1*

> Κωπώθητε οὖν, ὅταν ὑμῖν χωρὶς Ἰησοῦ Χριστοῦ λαλῇ τις, τοῦ ἐκ γένους Δαυίδ, τοῦ ἐκ Μαρίας, ὃς ἀληθῶς ἐγεννήθη, ἔφαγέν τε καὶ ἔπιεν, ἀληθῶς ἐδιώχθη ἐπὶ Ποντίου Πιλάτου, ἀληθῶς ἐσταυρώθη καὶ ἀπέθανεν, βλεπόντων τῶν ἐπουρανίων καὶ ἐπιγείων καὶ ὑποχθονίων·
>
> Be deaf, therefore, whenever anyone speaks to you apart from Jesus Christ, who was of the family of David, who was the son of Mary; who really was born, who both ate and drank; who really was persecuted under Pontius Pilate, who really was crucified and died while those in heaven and on earth and under the earth looked on. (Holmes; Lightfoot)

In this passage, which was almost certainly a polemic against docetism, it is possible that Ignatius drew upon Philippians 2.[72] The three-fold division of the universe[73] as well as the emphasis on Christ's incarnation

70 See also Lincoln, 'Re-Examination', p. 470. In order to understand the relationship between ἐπουράνιος and πνευματικός in 1 Cor. 10.1-4, we must also refer to Exod. 16.4 where manna came down from heaven (ἐκ τοῦ οὐρανοῦ). This is referred to as πνευματικὸν βρῶμα in 1 Cor. 10.1-4. As cited by Lincoln, 'Re-Examination', p. 470. We will examine 1 Cor. 15.40-50 in our NT study of ἐπουράνιος.

71 Here we find some similarities with Col. 1.15-17, though we cannot be certain whether Ignatius knew this passage or purposely alluded to it.

72 Throughout Ignatius's writings, there are numerous echoes of Pauline letters. Holmes notes that within his collection might have been 1 Corinthians, Ephesians, Romans, Galatians, Philippians, Colossians, and 1 Thessalonians but it is often difficult to determine whether Ignatius's letters are dependent upon the Pauline letters or traditional material, Holmes, *Apostolic Fathers*, p. 133.

73 But note the use of ὑποχθονίων in Ignatius, *Trall.* 9.1 rather than καταχθονίων in

and suffering are all reminiscent of the Christ hymn in Phil. 2.5-11. We cannot with certainty establish any dependence on Phil. 2.5-11, however, and it is just as likely that Ignatius drew upon Christian traditional or confessional material.[74] For our purposes, it significant that we once again find a contrast between the ἐπουράνια and the ἐπίγεια. Consequently, the usage of ἐπουράνιος in Ignatius, *Trall.* 9.1 is consistent with our argument that the term always refers to that which is spatially distinct from the earth.

d. Ignatius, To the Smyrnaeans *6.1a*

Μηδεὶς πλανάσθω καὶ τὰ ἐπουράνια καὶ ἡ δόξα τῶν ἀγγέλων καὶ οἱ ἄρχοντες ὁρατοί τε καὶ ἀόρατοι, ἐὰν μὴ πιστεύσωσιν εἰς τὸ αἷμα Χριστοῦ.

Let no one be misled. Even the heavenly beings and the glory of angels and the rulers, both visible and invisible, are also subject to judgment, if they do not believe in the blood of Christ. (Holmes; Lightfoot)

The primary significance of Ignatius, *Smyrn.* 6.1a is that it reveals the identity of some of the heavenly beings (τὰ ἐπουράνια), the angels and the rulers. The reference here is fairly straightforward. The heavenly beings (or possibly heavenly things) are a reference to the spiritual powers which reside in heaven and their description as ἐπουράνια refers to that which is spatially distinct from the earth. Whether Ignatius conceived of these spiritual powers as wholly good or as in need of some sort of reconciliation, we cannot be certain.

e. Polycarp, The Letter of Polycarp to the Philippians *2.1*

Διὸ ἀναζωσάμενοι τὰς ὀσφύας δουλεύσατε τῷ θεῷ ἐν φόβῳ καὶ ἀληθείᾳ, ἀπολιπόντες τὴν κενὴν ματαιολογίαν καὶ τὴν τῶν πολλῶν πλάνην, πιστεύσαντες εἰς τὸν ἐγείραντα τὸν κύριον ἡμῶν Ἰησοῦν Χριστὸν ἐκ νεκρῶν καὶ δόντα αὐτῷ δόξαν καὶ θρόνον ἐκ δεξιῶν αὐτοῦ· ᾧ ὑπετάγη τὰ πάντα ἐπουράνια καὶ ἐπίγεια, ᾧ πᾶσα πνοὴ λατρεύει, ὃς ἔρχεται κριτὴς ζώντων καὶ νεκρῶν, οὗ τὸ αἷμα ἐκζητήσει ὁ θεὸς ἀπὸ τῶν ἀπειθούντων αὐτῷ.

'Therefore prepare for action and serve God in fear' and truth, leaving behind the empty and meaningless talk and the error of the crowd, and 'believing in him who raised' our Lord Jesus Christ 'from the dead and gave him glory' and a throne at his right hand; to whom all things in heaven and on earth were subjected, whom every breathing creature serves, who is coming as

Phil. 2.10. For the divisions of 'heaven' and 'earth', both passages employ ἐπουρανίων and ἐπιγείων. We will examine Phil. 2.5-11 in our NT study of ἐπουράνιος.

74 As noted above, the use of ὑποχθονίων in Ignatius, *Trall.* 9.1 rather than καταχθονίων would also weaken the argument for direct dependence.

'Judge of the living and the dead,' for whose blood God will hold responsible those who disobey him. (Holmes; Lightfoot)

Polycarp's letter to the Philippians is his only surviving document and it displays great dependence on the Septuagint and early Christian writings.[75] The general academic consensus seems to be that in his letter, Polycarp cited the New Testament documents as authoritative but not necessarily as Scripture.[76] However, one possible significant exception to this is Polycarp's reference to Eph. 4.26 in *The Letter of Polycarp to the Philippians* 12.1 which reads, 'Only, as it is said in these Scriptures, "be angry but do not sin", and "do not let the sun set on your anger".'[77] Only the Latin manuscript of this text survives, which reads, 'Modo, ut his scripturis dictum est, irascimini et nolite peccare, et sol non occidat super iracundiam vestram.'[78] Here the reference is almost certainly to Eph. 4.26 since LXX Ps. 4.5 only contains the first portion of this quotation. For our purposes, it is significant that Polycarp both knew the Pauline letter of Ephesians and also quite possibly regarded the letter as Scripture.[79]

The reference to the subjection of all things – the heavenly things (ἐπουράνια) and the earthly things (ἐπίγεια) – is obviously intended as a comprehensive description of Christ's reign. All things, both those on earth and those in heaven, have been subjected to Christ. In his commentary on this passage, Holmes notes possible connections with 1 Cor. 15.28 and Phil. 3.21.[80] We also note similarities with the ascension text in Eph. 1.20-23 where Christ is at the right hand of God ἐν τοῖς ἐπουρανίοις with all powers and all things in subjection to him. Whether there is direct dependence on any of these specific New Testament texts is difficult to establish and not of great significance for our examination.[81] What is significant is that Polycarp's use of ἐπουράνια is clearly in contrast to the ἐπίγεια. As a result, we see once again that, though it can have various nuances in meaning, the term ἐπουράνιος always refers to that which is spatially distinct from the earth.

75 Holmes, *Apostolic Fathers*, p. 202.

76 Holmes, *Apostolic Fathers*, p. 203.

77 Holmes, *Apostolic Fathers*, pp. 203, 219.

78 As cited in Holmes, *Apostolic Fathers*, p. 218.

79 The 'empty and meaningless talk' (τὴν κενὴν ματαιολογίαν) also represents a possible connection between this passage and Eph. 5.6 where Paul exhorts his readers not to be deceived by empty words (κενοῖς λόγοις).

80 Holmes, *Apostolic Fathers*, p. 207.

81 It is interesting to note the use of ἐπουράνια in Polycarp's ascension text. As we stated above, it is possible that Polycarp drew upon a number of NT texts in this passage. If he had in mind the usage of ἐπουράνιος in Ephesians, then this would only strengthen our argument that the term was understood as synonymous with οὐρανός.

f. Martyrdom of Polycarp *14.3*

> διὰ τοῦτο καὶ περὶ πάντων σὲ αἰνῶ, σὲ εὐλογῶ, σὲ δοξάζω, διὰ τοῦ αἰωνίου καὶ ἐπουρανίου ἀρχιερέως Ἰησοῦ Χριστοῦ, ἀγαπητοῦ σου παιδός, δι' οὗ σοὶ σὺν αὐτῷ καὶ πνεύματι ἁγίῳ δόξα καὶ νῦν καὶ εἰς τοὺς μέλλοντας αἰῶνας, ἀμήν.
>
> For this reason, indeed for all things, I praise you, I bless you, I glorify you, through the eternal and heavenly High Priest, Jesus Christ, your beloved Son, through whom to you with him and the Holy Spirit be glory both now and for the ages to come. Amen. (Holmes; Lightfoot)

This quotation is a portion of Polycarp's last words as recorded in *Martyrdom of Polycarp*. The usage of ἐπουράνιος here is consistent with our argument that the term always refers to that which is spatially distinct from the earth.[82] Jesus, who in this passage is referred to as the eternal and heavenly (ἐπουρανίου) high priest, is described as ἐπουράνιος precisely because the New Testament and other Christian writings present the location of Christ after his death and resurrection to be at the right hand of God in 'heaven' (i.e. οὐρανός).[83]

g. Martyrdom of Polycarp *20.2*

> τῷ δὲ δυναμένῳ πάντας ἡμᾶς εἰσαγαγεῖν ἐν τῇ αὐτοῦ χάριτι καὶ δωρεᾷ εἰς τὴν ἐπουράνιον (m; αἰώνιον, bpsa) αὐτοῦ βασιλείαν διὰ τοῦ παιδὸς αὐτοῦ, τοῦ μονογενοῦς Ἰησοῦ Χριστοῦ, δόξα, τιμή, κράτος, μεγαλωσύνη, εἰς τοὺς αἰῶνας.
>
> Now to him who is able to bring us all by his grace and bounty into his eternal (heavenly) kingdom, through his only begotten Son, Jesus Christ, be glory, honor, power, and majesty forever. (Holmes; Lightfoot)

The appearance of ἐπουράνιος in this verse from *Martyrdom of Polycarp* brings with it a text critical issue. The most reliable valuable manuscript (m) has ἐπουράνιον while bpsa have αἰώνιον.[84] Although ἐπουράνιον was the reading adopted by Lightfoot and Holmes, the translation follows the textual tradition which adopted αἰώνιον. Second Timothy 4.18 contains a similar use of ἐπουράνιος and reads, 'The Lord will rescue me from every evil deed, and will bring me safely to His heavenly (ἐπουράνιον) kingdom; to Him *be* the glory forever and ever. Amen.' This verse from 2 Timothy actually contains the same words for entering

82 BDAG lists the usage of ἐπουράνιος in *Mart. Pol.* 14.3 as an adjective describing Christ and as 'pertaining to being associated with a locale for transcendent things and beings', p. 388.

83 Cf. e.g. Acts 1.11; 2.34; 7.55-56; Eph. 4.10; 6.9; Phil. 3.20; Col. 4.1; 1 Thess. 1.10; 4.16; 2 Thess. 1.7; Heb. 4.14; 7.26; 8.1; 1 Pet. 3.21-22; Rev. 4.2.

84 Holmes, *Apostolic Fathers*, p. 224. B and p are the most valuable after m.

into God's heavenly kingdom as *Martyrdom of Polycarp* although in a different order (εἰς τὴν βασιλείαν αὐτοῦ τὴν ἐπουράνιον in 2 Tim. 4.18 while εἰς τὴν ἐπουράνιον αὐτοῦ βασιλείαν in *Mart. Pol.* 20.2). On the other hand, αἰώνιον seems to fit well with the doxological character of the verse and bears some resemblance to Rom. 16.25-26 and 1 Tim. 6.15-16. Whether or not ἐπουράνιον represents the original reading, this verse is still valuable for discerning the usage and meaning of the term ἐπουράνιος. The use and meaning of ἐπουράνιος in *Mart. Pol.* 20.2 is consistent with our argument throughout this chapter. Jesus's reign and session at the right hand of God take place in heaven.[85] This description of God's kingdom as heavenly (ἐπουράνιος) implies a contrast with that which is associated with the earth. There is also a contrast between the heavenly kingdom and the people on earth who will one day be brought into the heavenly kingdom through Jesus Christ.

We find further confirmation for our interpretation when we compare *Mart. Pol.* 20.2 with *Mart. Pol.* 22.3, which has almost identical wording but with the substitution of οὐράνιον for ἐπουράνιον. *Martyrdom of Polycarp* 22.3b reads 'I gathered it together when it was nearly worn out by age, that the Lord Jesus Christ might also gather me together with his elect into his heavenly kingdom'[86] (εἰς τὴν οὐράνιον βασιλείαν αὐτοῦ). The implication from our comparison of *Mart. Pol.* 20.2 and 22.3 is that there is no distinction in meaning between the adjectives ἐπουράνιος and οὐράνιος. On the contrary, the author(s) seemingly utilized the terms interchangeably and as complete synonyms, perhaps varying the terms merely for stylistic purposes.[87]

h. 1 Clement *61.2*

> σὺ γάρ, δέσποτα ἐπουράνιε, βασιλεῦ τῶν αἰώνων, δίδως τοῖς υἱοῖς τῶν ἀνθρώπων δόξαν καὶ τιμὴν καὶ ἐξουσίαν τῶν ἐπὶ τῆς γῆς ὑπαρχόντων·
>
> For you, heavenly Master, King of the ages, give to the sons of men glory and honor and authority over those upon the earth. (Holmes; Lightfoot)

In *1 Clem.* 61.2 the heavenly Master (δέσποτα ἐπουράνιε) gives glory, honour and authority to those on the earth (ἐπὶ τῆς γῆς). Once again, we find a contrast between ἐπουράνιος and the earth. Additionally, we have noted on numerous occasions that the use of ἐπουράνιος as an adjective

85 Cf. for example Acts 2.34; 7.56; Eph. 1.20; Col. 3.1; Heb. 8.1; 1 Pet. 3.21-22. See above for a more complete list.

86 Translation from Holmes and Lightfoot.

87 Interestingly, the Moscow manuscript of *Mart. Pol.* 22.3 contains ἐπουράνιον rather than οὐράνιον and reads εἰς τὴν ἐπουράνιον αὐτοῦ βασιλείαν, the exact same wording as *Mart. Pol.* 20.2. For the Moscow manuscript of *Mart. Pol.* 22.3, our analysis and conclusion would be the same as our examination of *Mart. Pol.* 20.2.

describing God is common.[88] Since God is in heaven, it is appropriate that he be addressed as ἐπουράνιε.[89] The usage of ἐπουράνιος in *1 Clem.* 61.2 is consistent with our argument that the term should be understood as synonymous with οὐρανός and as a reference to that which is spatially distinct from the earth.

i. 2 Clement *20.5*

> Τῷ μόνῳ θεῷ ἀοράτῳ πατρὶ τῆς ἀληθείας, τῷ ἐξαποστείλαντι ἡμῖν τὸν σωτῆρα καὶ ἀρχηγὸν τῆς ἀφθαρσίας, δι' οὗ καὶ ἐφανέρωσεν ἡμῖν τὴν ἀλήθειαν καὶ τὴν ἐπουράνιον ζωήν, αὐτῷ ἡ δόξα εἰς τοὺς αἰῶνας τῶν αἰώνων. ἀμήν.
>
> 'To the only God, invisible,' the Father of truth, who sent forth to us the Savior and Founder of immortality, through whom he also revealed to us the truth and the heavenly life, to him be the glory forever and ever. Amen. (Holmes; Lightfoot)

The notion that the Saviour revealed 'the heavenly life' (τὴν ἐπουράνιον ζωήν) to those on earth might suggest an interpretation of this reference to ἐπουράνιος as an earthly one; however, it is not uncommon to describe the believer's life on earth as exhibiting heavenly characteristics,[90] nor is it out of the ordinary for an author to encourage believers to a certain lifestyle by employing a heavenly component to an ethical ideal.[91] The difference between *2 Clem.* 20.5 and the appearances of the expression ἐν τοῖς ἐπουρανίοις in Ephesians is found in the function of the adjective ἐπουράνιος. The 'heavenly life' in *2 Clem.* 20.5 describes a lifestyle which is associated with a particular location whereas the function of ἐν τοῖς ἐπουρανίοις in Ephesians is purely local. Thus the 'heavenly life' in *2 Clem.* 20.5 does not lose its spatial component. The heavenly life which Jesus revealed, though it can be experienced on earth, is still associated with heaven and consequently that which is in contrast to the earth.

8. Conclusions

The results from our examination of the lexical usage of ἐπουράνιος are conclusive. The term ἐπουράνιος appears in six passages with the

88 BDAG also identifies the use of ἐπουράνιος in *1 Clem.* 61.2 as an adjective describing God and 'pertaining to being associated with a locale for transcendent things and beings', p. 388.

89 See our analyses of *Mart. Pol.* 14.3 and 20.2.

90 For examples, see Heb. 3.1 where the holy brethren (ἀδελφοὶ ἅγιοι) are partakers (μέτοχοι) of a heavenly calling (κλήσεως ἐπουρανίου) and Heb. 6.4 for those who have tasted of the heavenly gift (τῆς δωρεᾶς τῆς ἐπουρανίου).

91 See, e.g., Col. 3.1-4.

term οὐρανός with no distinction in the locations they represent (*Iliad* 6.129, 131; Lucian, *Dialogues of the Gods* 10 (4).3; 2 Maccabees 3; *Sib. Or.* 4.130-36; *T. Job* 32.11–40.4; *Testament of Abraham* IV). The terms ἐπουράνιος and οὐράνιος appear in Sextus Empiricus, *Against the Astrologers* 5.43-45a as synonyms and with no discernible difference as to their meanings. Three passages contain appearances of ἐπουράνιος, οὐράνιος, and οὐρανός without any distinction in the locations they represent (3 Maccabees 6; Philo, *Legum Allegoria* 3.162-68; Philo, *De Gigantibus* 62). Of particular interest and significance is our observation that in a number of passages, the authors chose to alternate between the various 'heaven' terms (ἐπουράνιος, οὐράνιος, and οὐρανός) merely for stylistic purposes (Sextus Empiricus, *Against the Astrologers* 5.43-45a; Philo, *Legum Allegoria* Book III LVIII.162-68; *T. Job* 32-36). In fourteen of the passages examined, there is a direct contrast between ἐπουράνιος and the earth.[92] These findings demonstrate that there is no precedent for a major distinction in meaning between ἐπουράνιος and οὐρανός/οὐράνιος within extant Greek literature.[93] Furthermore, our findings demonstrate that though the term ἐπουράνιος can have various meanings and nuances, it always refers to that which is spatially distinct from the earth.[94] As a result, from our examination of ἐπουράνιος in extant Greek literature outside the New Testament,[95] we conclude that there is no precedent or basis for a spiritualization of the heavenlies in Ephesians or an interpretation such as Odeberg's wherein he defines the heavenlies as the spiritual environment of the church on earth.[96] The obvious task that remains is to determine the meaning and usage of the term ἐπουράνιος in the New Testament. We now turn our attention to this endeavour in chapter 4.

92 These passages are: Plato, *Phaedrus* 256d; Sextus Empiricus, *Against the Astrologers* 5.43-45a; Lucian, *Dialogues of the Gods* 10 (4).3; *Fragment* 26.9 from *Corpus Hermeticum*; Second Century Papyri; Paris Papyri 574.3037-44; Philo, *Legum Allegoria* III.168; Philo, *De Virtutibus* 3.12; *T. Job* 32.11-40.4; *T. Abr.* IV; Ignatius, *Eph.* 13.1-2; Ignatius, *Trall.* 9.1; Polycarp, *Phil.* 2.1; *1 Clem.* 61.2.

93 Contra McGough, 'Investigation', pp. 8–9, 13–14, 27–30, 48–49, 95–96, 99–100, 102, 159, 171. It seems obvious that McGough arrived at his conclusions beforehand and subsequently forced the primary material to fit with those conclusions.

94 See also Caragounis, *Mysterion*, p. 147.

95 For additional evidence for our arguments and conclusions from other Jewish and Christian literature, see the table below which lists additional appearances of ἐπουράνιος from the Apocrypha, the Old Testament Pseudepigrapha, the Apologists, the Apocryphal Gospels, and Eusebius. In this table, we list only the references and a very brief description of the usage of ἐπουράνιος.

96 This of course is the interpretation of Odeberg, *View*, p. 12. See history of interpretation for a list of NT scholars who have followed or been influenced by his interpretation. That there is no lexical precedent or basis for Odeberg's understanding is detrimental to his thesis. Similarly, our findings are also a direct refutation of McGough who similarly spiritualizes the heavenlies in 'Investigation', pp. 95–96, 102–103.

9. Table of Additional Jewish and Christian Texts with ᾿Επουράνιος

Apocrypha

Odes 14.11	ἐπουράνιε as substantive for God (the heavenly one)

Old Testament Pseudepigrapha

***Sib. Or.* 1.216**	ἐπουρανίοιο as an adjective describing God
***Sib. Or.* 2.222**	ἐπουράνιος as a substantive for God (the heavenly one)
***Sib. Or.* 2.284**	ἐπουρανίοιο as an adjective describing God
***Sib. Or.* 8.66**	ἐπουρανίοιο as an adjective describing God
***Sib. Or.* 21.10**	ἐπουράνιον as an adjective describing God
***Apoc. Sedr.* 7.2**	τὰ ἐπουράνια as the heavenly realms
***3 Bar.* 11.9**	ἐπουρανίου as an adjective describing God
***T. Sol.* A 6.10**	τῶν ἐπουρανίων as a substantive for the heavenly places or the heavenly things and ἐπουρανίους as an adjective describing the heavenly dragons
Orph. 1.34	ἐπουράνιος as an adjective of God or Moses (appearance of ouranos in 1:29)
***Aristob.* 4.3**	ἐπουράνιος as an adjective describing God

Apologists

1 Irenaeus 10.1	ἐπουρανίων in citation of Phil. 2.10
Athenagoras, Plea for Christians 1.18	ἐπουράνιον as an adjective of (God's) heavenly kingdom
Athenagoras, Plea for Christians 1.24	ἐπουρανίου as an adjective for heavenly wisdom in contrast to earthly (ἐπιγείου) wisdom
Athenagoras, Plea for Christians 1.31	ἐπουράνιον as an adjective for heavenly life in contrast to earthly (ἐπίγειον) life
2 Theophilus 1.36	ἐπουράνιον as an adjective of God

Apoc. Gospels

Agrapha 1.10	τὰ ἐπουράνια as a substantive for 'heavenly things' in contrast to earthly things (τὰ ἐπίγεια)

Eusebius

2 Eusebius 22.4	ἐπουράνιον in citation of 2 Tim. 4.18
3 Eusebius 20.3	ἐπουράνιος as an adjective for 'heavenly kingdom' in contrast to an earthly (ἐπίγειος) kingdom

Chapter 4

NEW TESTAMENT STUDY OF 'Επουράνιος

1. *Introduction*

The purpose of this chapter is to examine the meaning and usage of the term ἐπουράνιος in the New Testament outside Ephesians. Outside Ephesians, the term ἐπουράνιος appears fourteen times (Jn 3.12; 1 Cor. 15.40 [2x]; 1 Cor. 15.48 [2x]; 1 Cor. 15.49; Phil. 2.10; 2 Tim. 4.18; Heb. 3.1; Heb. 6.4; Heb. 8.5; Heb. 9.23; Heb. 11.16; Heb. 12.22).[1] For scholars of the New Testament, it will be obvious upon a quick glace at these verses that some of the passages in which the term ἐπουράνιος appears are among the most examined within New Testament scholarship.[2] As a result, we should clarify here that our goal in this chapter is neither to provide an overview of scholarship nor to conduct a detailed exegesis of these passages which would serve merely to rehash commentaries or the primary scholarly interests. We will touch upon many of these scholarly interests and concerns briefly within the body of this chapter but primarily within the footnotes. It is beyond the scope of this chapter to examine these passages in great detail or to provide a detailed exegesis of each text. Such a task would be far too lengthy and impractical and would not serve to advance the principal argument of this chapter. As we stated above, the purpose of this chapter is to examine the meaning and usage of the term ἐπουράνιος in the New Testament. We will also give special attention to the relationship between ἐπουράνιος and οὐρανός in our examinations of these texts.

2. *John 3.12*

John 3.12 is the only place in the Johannine literature where ἐπουράνιος appears.[3] The use of ἐπουράνιος in Jn 3.12 and within

1 The term ἐπουράνιος is also a sparsely attested textual variant for οὐράνιος in Mt. 18.35. The overwhelming textual evidence is for οὐράνιος with support from א B C[2] D K L 33 565 579 892 1241 1424. Support for ἐπουράνιος includes C (probable) W θ f [(1) 13].

2 E.g. John 3; 1 Corinthians 15; Phil. 2.5-11. The passages in Hebrews, for various reasons, have also been the subject of much scholarly interest.

3 Οὐρανός appears seventy times in sixty-six verses in the Johannine literature

the larger context of Jn 3.1-13 support the understanding argued for throughout this book – namely that ἐπουράνιος and οὐρανός refer to the same location. The overarching theme of Jn 3.1-36 is that Jesus is the Son from above.[4] In Jn 3.1-13 Jesus tells Nicodemus that he must be born ἄνωθεν to see the kingdom of God. The Greek term ἄνωθεν can mean 'from above', 'anew', or 'again'.[5] Though Nicodemus understands it as 'again' (v. 4), John's readers will realize that he has missed the point.[6] The most frequent use of the term in John's gospel will lead his readers to understand it as 'from above'.[7] This use of ἄνωθεν fits the theme and tenor of the passage – the Son from above. Nicodemus's misunderstanding leads Jesus to give further explanation when Jesus says, 'Truly, truly, I say to you, unless one is born of water and the Spirit he cannot enter the kingdom of God' (3.5). Though there is no shortage of interpretations for what it means to be born of water and the Spirit,[8] we understand the phrase as the equivalent of being born from above in v. 3[9] and contend that the two terms (water and Spirit) are 'functional equivalents, with water serving as a symbol of the Spirit'.[10]

(eighteen times in sixteen verses in the Gospel of John and fifty-two times in fifty verses in Revelation). Οὐράνιος does not appear in the Johannine corpus.

4 Craig S. Keener, *The Gospel of John: A Commentary* (vol. 1; Peabody, MA: Hendrickson, 2003), pp. 533–83.

5 Keener, *John*, pp. 538–39. See also Andrew T. Lincoln, *The Gospel According to Saint John* (BNTC; London: Hendrickson, 2005), p. 150, and D. A. Carson, *The Gospel According to John* (The Pillar New Testament Commentary; Leicester: InterVarsity, 1991), p. 189.

6 Keener, *John*, pp. 538–39. Keener notes that the narrative has a number of plays on words with such terms as ἄνωθεν, φωνή, and πνεῦμα, p. 537. Concerning Nicodemus's misunderstanding, Keener also notes that secondary characters often served as foils for primary characters in ancient Mediterranean stories. In Jn 3.1-13, Nicodemus serves as a foil who provides Jesus with the opportunity to clarify his statement for John's readers, Keener, *John*, p. 539; see also Lincoln, *John*, p. 150.

7 Keener, *John*, pp. 538–39. See also Carson, *John*, p. 189. Though C. K. Barrett is more sympathetic to Nicodemus's understanding when he notes that it is not completely wrong since it does denote a type of second birth, Barrett nevertheless writes that 'a begetting from above ... must be regarded as the primary meaning', *The Gospel According to St. John* (London: SPCK, 2nd edn, 1978), p. 206.

8 For more detailed discussions, see Keener, *John*, pp. 544–52; Carson, *John*, pp. 191–96; Barrett, *John*, pp. 208–209; George R. Beasley-Murray, *John* (WBC 36; Nashville: Thomas Nelson, 2nd edn, 1999), pp. 48–49.

9 Keener, *John*, p. 547; Lincoln, *John*, p. 150; Carson, *John*, p. 194; Barrett, *John*, p. 208; Beasley-Murray, *John*, p. 48. We regard the context, specifically the idea of being born ἄνωθεν, which appears directly before (v. 3) and after (v. 7) Jesus's statements about being born of the Spirit (vv. 5–6), as clear support of this understanding.

10 Lincoln, *John*, p. 150. For the conceptual basis of water as a symbol of the Spirit, see Lincoln's examples of Ezek. 36.25-27 in the OT, 1QS 4.19-21 in the Qumran literature, and most importantly Jn 7.38-39, Lincoln, *John*, 150. For a grammatical

Within the narrative, after Jesus reiterates the need to be born of the Spirit (v. 6) and to be born ἄνωθεν (v. 7), he says, 'The wind blows where it wishes and you hear the sound of it, but do not know where it comes from and where it is going; so is everyone who is born of the Spirit' (Jn 3.8). Jesus's reference to hearing (ἀκούεις) the sound (φωνή) of the wind (πνεῦμα) is an obvious play on words for the double entendre of listening to (or hearing) the voice of the Spirit.[11] When Nicodemus again exhibits a lack of understanding, Jesus speaks the words found in Jn 3.12-13:[12]

> If I told you earthly things (τὰ ἐπίγεια) and you do not believe, how will you believe if I tell you heavenly things (τὰ ἐπουράνια)? [13] No one has ascended into heaven (εἰς τὸν οὐρανόν), but He who descended from heaven (ἐκ τοῦ οὐρανοῦ): the Son of Man.

To reiterate Nicodemus's failure to understand, Jesus uses a *qal vaomer* argument, whereby he questions Nicodemus that if he does not believe τὰ ἐπίγεια, then how can he believe τὰ ἐπουράνια?[12] Though the precise meanings of the earthly things and the heavenly things are difficult to establish,[13] for our purposes, what is evident is that there is a distinction

explanation, Keener writes, 'John's explicit explanation of "water" as the Spirit in 7.39 invites us to read the more ambiguous 3.5 as a hendiadys', *John*, p. 550. For further discussion of the grammatical basis for this view, see Keener, *John*, pp. 550–51. Carson also regards the phrase 'as a conceptual unity', though he believes that πνεύματος in v. 5 refers not to the Holy Spirit but rather to 'the impartation of God's nature as "spirit" [cf. 4.24]', *John*, pp. 194–95.

11 For further discussion, see Keener, *John*, pp. 555–58; Lincoln, *John*, p. 151; Barrett, *John*, pp. 210–11. As Keener notes, this wordplay also works in Hebrew as קול רוח 'can refer either to the sound of the wind or to the voice of the Spirit', *John*, p. 558.

12 Keener, *John*, p. 559. For a brief discussion of the *qal vaomer* argument and for examples in ancient rhetoric, see pp. 559–60.

13 The difficulty here is the precise meaning of the references to τὰ ἐπίγεια and τὰ ἐπουράνια. While Keener identifies the earthly things as 'probably such analogies as wind and the "water" of proselyte baptism', he does not specifically identify the heavenly things from this passage but rather writes that 'in John, things above are simply the things of God which Jesus shares with the disciples (cf. 16.13-15; Col. 3.1-3)', *John*, pp. 559–60. Lincoln argues that the earthly things represent Jesus's attempt to move from the earthly realities of physical birth and the blowing of the wind to heavenly realities. In this interpretation, Jesus has not actually spoken of 'heavenly things' in vv. 3–8. As a result, Nicodemus's lack of faith precludes Jesus from speaking of 'heavenly things' directly (v. 12), Lincoln, *John*, p. 152; cf. Barrett, *John*, p. 212. Carson contends that 'earthly things' is the new birth referenced by Jesus from the beginning of his conversation with Nicodemus and argues that it is earthly simply because such a new birth takes place on earth. On the other hand, 'the "heavenly things" are then the splendours of the consummated kingdom, and what it means to live under such glorious, ineffable rule', Carson, *John*, p. 199; cf. Beasley-Murray, *John*, pp. 49–50. Part of Carson's justification for these decisions is that 'no-one disbelieves in "earthly things" such as wind and physical birth', Carson, *John*, p. 199; however, it seems that Carson here gets unnecessarily caught up in the terminology which Jesus uses in v. 12, namely the verb πιστεύσετε. For example, it is evident in the NT

between the two. Jesus emphasizes that Nicodemus's misunderstanding or lack of belief of earthly things either precludes Jesus from speaking plainly of heavenly things or reiterates Nicodemus's certain misunderstanding of heavenly things. Of perhaps even greater importance is the appearance of οὐρανός in this passage. Immediately after Jesus rebukes Nicodemus for his inability to understand and/or believe τὰ ἐπουράνια, Jesus states that he is the one who has descended ἐκ τοῦ οὐρανοῦ. Though one term is a noun and the other an adjective, it is obvious that they both represent the same location. Keener recognizes this when he writes, 'Only one born from above (3.3) could "see" God's kingdom, and only [one] who came from above (3.13) could testify firsthand about heavenly realities (3.11) and so reveal heavenly things (3.12).'[14] Therefore, from our analysis of Jn 3.1-13, we once again arrive at the conclusion that it is erroneous to posit a distinction between οὐρανός and ἐπουράνιος in the locations they denote. Rather, our analysis of Jn 3.12-13 supports and confirms our argument that the two terms signify the same location and always refer to that which is spatially distinct from the earth.[15]

and in koine Greek that there is a strong connection between seeing (ὁράω) and knowing (οἶδα among other words for 'see'). This connection is even historically a lexical one as οἶδα (I know; I have seen) is the perfect of εἴδω (I see) which was no longer in use. Also of significance is the frequency with which 'seeing' and 'believing' are associated in John. A cursory scan of the gospel reveals such a connection in at least ten places in the gospel (2.23; 4.48; 6.30; 6.36; 6.40; 9.35-38; 11.45; 20.25; 20.8; 20.29). At other places, there is a strong association between 'knowing' (γινώσκω) and 'believing' (πιστεύω) (1.7-12; 4.53; 6.69; 10.37-38; 1 Jn 4.16). Of even greater interest is the frequency in the gospel where all three of the concepts are associated, the specific terms being πιστεύω, νοέω, οἶδα, ὁράω, and θεάομαι (4.42; 12.39-40; 16.30; 19.35; and 1.29-36 though the specific term πιστεύω is not used in 1.29-36). Interestingly enough, in Jn 3.10-12, all three concepts seem to be associated with the use of γινώσκεις in v. 10, ἑωράκαμεν in v. 11, and πιστεύετε, πιστεύσετε in v. 12. Is there any significance from this cursory study of this terminology and these concepts? The significance is that we believe it is misguided to posit a major distinction between γινώσκεις and πιστεύετε, πιστεύσετε in Jn 3.10-12. In other words, when Jesus questions Nicodemus and rebukes him for not believing (πιστεύετε) 'earthly things', the word usage in this context is actually closely related to knowing, understanding, or perceiving (as in the usage of γινώσκω in v. 10). As a result, we reject Carson's interpretation in which he claims that 'no-one disbelieves in "earthly things" such as wind and physical birth', Carson, *John*, p. 199. We contend that a proper understanding should at least reflect Lincoln's interpretation that Jesus, in his conversation with Nicodemus speaks of 'heavenly things' by analogy to the earthly, Lincoln, *John*, p. 152. We find it even more compelling to understand τὰ ἐπίγεια as the analogy of the wind and to understand τὰ ἐπουράνια as the birth from above which is precisely what Jesus attempted to explain to Nicodemus in a variety of ways including the analogy with earthly things, i.e. the wind. This interpretation fits well with Jesus's description that Nicodemus must be born ἄνωθεν and ἐξ ὕδατος καὶ πνεύματος. Such a new birth would thus be easily identifiable with τὰ ἐπουράνια.

14 Keener, *John*, p. 558. See also Lincoln, *John*, p. 152; Carson, *John*, p. 201; and Barrett, *John*, pp. 212–13.

15 Contra McGough who argues for a distinction between οὐρανός and ἐπουράνιος in Jn 3.12-13, 'Investigation', p. 50. McGough regards the reference to ἐπουράνιος in Jn 3.12

3. 1 Corinthians 15.40 (2x), 48 (2x), 49

First Corinthians 15.39-49 continues Paul's lengthy argument about Christ's resurrection and its implications for those who are in Christ. In 1 Corinthians 15 Paul writes that those who are in Christ will be raised with him (vv. 22, 35) and with a resurrection body (vv. 35-57). Towards the beginning of the passage in 15.40, Paul writes that there are earthly (ἐπίγεια) and heavenly (ἐπουράνια) bodies and that there is different glory ascribed to each. While there is disagreement over the meaning and nature of σώματα ἐπουράνια (v. 40),[16] the description of the glory of the sun, moon, and stars in v. 41 leads us to conclude that the primary reference of σώματα ἐπουράνια is the heavenly bodies in the sky such as the stars and planets.[17] The crux of Paul's argument in vv. 39-41 is that, just as there is a distinction between different types of earthly life, so there is also a distinction between earthly and heavenly bodies, and even a further distinction between various heavenly bodies such as the sun, moon, and the stars.[18] For our purposes, it is important to note once again the distinction between the heavenly (σώματα ἐπουράνια) and the earthly (σώματα ἐπίγεια). Thiselton also recognizes this fundamental distinction and contrast between earthly and heavenly bodies when he writes, 'What Paul aims to set before his readers is the conceivability, on the basis of a theology of God as creator of diverse orders of being, of a "sort of body ... entirely outside our present experience."'[19]

as merely indicative of earthly and heavenly interaction or as evidence of earthly participation in heavenly things, 'Investigation', pp. 39, 50.

16 For a short discussion of the different viewpoints, see Anthony C. Thiselton, *The First Epistle to the Corinthians: A Commentary on the Greek Text* (NIGTC; Grand Rapids: Eerdmans, 2000), pp. 1268–69.

17 Thiselton, *1 Corinthians*, p. 1269. Within this view, however, Thiselton does not rule out entirely an allusion to angelic beings, p. 1269; cf. Wolfgang Schrage, *Der erste Brief an die Korinther* (EKKNT 7/4; 4 vols; Düsseldorf, Benziger, 2001), pp. 4: 290–93. On the other hand, Lincoln writes that ἐπουράνιος is utilized here in a 'purely cosmological sense' and as 'a straightforward reference to the heavenly bodies visible in the sky and not to angels or spiritual beings', Lincoln, *Paradise*, p. 39. Interestingly, McGough also recognizes here that the σώματα ἐπουράνια in 15.40 refer to the sun, moon, and stars, 'Investigation', p. 39. This conclusion seems problematic for McGough's argument since this usage of ἐπουράνιος is clearly spatially distinct from the earth and since McGough argues for no earthly and heavenly interaction in this instance. McGough seemingly attempts to address this quandary by emphasizing the visible nature of the σώματα ἐπουράνια, 'Investigation', p. 39.

18 Lincoln, *Paradise*, p. 38. In addition, Lincoln notes that Paul's purpose in this analogy is to demonstrate the rich variety of God's creation and to emphasize that there is an appropriate glory or body for every type of life, *Paradise*, pp. 38–39. See also Thiselton, *1 Corinthians*, p. 1270.

19 Thiselton, *1 Corinthians*, p. 1268. Thiselton here quotes Richard B. Hays, *First Corinthians* (IBC; Louisville: John Knox Press, 1997), p. 271. As cited in Thiselton, *1 Corinthians*, p. 1268. Italics original.

As he continues his argument, Paul uses the examples of earthly and heavenly bodies with differing glory to illustrate that there is also a distinction between the earthly body and the resurrection body. The earthly body is sown in decay, in dishonour, in weakness, and as a natural body. On the other hand, the resurrection body is raised in immortality, in glory, in power, and as a spiritual body. Paul then continues his excursus by contrasting the first Adam with the last Adam. The first man, Adam, became a living soul (v. 45) and is from the earth (ἐκ γῆς), earthy (χοϊκός) (v. 47).[20] The last Adam became a life-giving spirit (v. 45) and is from heaven (ἐξ οὐρανοῦ) (v. 47). The NASB translation of v. 48, 'As is the earthy, so also are those who are earthy; and as is the heavenly, so also are those who are heavenly,' does not accurately portray the sense of the Greek text as it obscures the close connection between v. 47 and v. 48. In a proper understanding, ὁ πρῶτος ἄνθρωπος ἐκ γῆς χοϊκός from v. 47 should be connected with ὁ χοϊκός from v. 48, and ὁ δεύτερος ἄνθρωπος ἐξ οὐρανοῦ from v. 47 should be connected with ὁ ἐπουράνιος from v. 48. Consequently, a better translation of v. 48 would be, 'As is the earthy one (ὁ χοϊκός),[21] so also are those who are earthy (οἱ χοϊκοί); and as is the heavenly one (ὁ ἐπουράνιος),[22] so also are those who are heavenly (οἱ ἐπουράνιοι).'[23] The first and last Adams are therefore representatives of two distinct groups of people, the earthly and the heavenly.[24]

The next verse in this passage (v. 49) proves to be somewhat problematic because of a highly debated text-critical issue. Depending on whether one reads the future φορέσομεν or the subjunctive φορέσωμεν, the sense of the passage varies to a significant extent. If Paul penned the future, then his message is didactic and he communicates simply that those who belong to the second man from heaven

20 Paul's use of the adjective χοϊκός (vv. 47–49), especially when coupled with ἐκ γῆς (v. 47), is a clear allusion to Gen. 2.7 (χοῦν ἀπὸ τῆς γῆς) even though it is the noun χοῦς which appears in the creation account. For further discussions of χοϊκός and its allusion to Gen. 2.7, see Raymond F. Collins, *First Corinthians* (SP 7; Collegeville, MN: The Liturgical Press, 1999), p. 570; Thiselton, *1 Corinthians*, pp. 1286–87; Lincoln, *Paradise*, p. 45; Schrage, *Korinther*, pp. 308–309.

21 Ὁ χοϊκός is a clear reference to Adam who is explicitly identified as ὁ πρῶτος ἄνθρωπος in v. 45 (cf. v. 47).

22 Though never explicitly identified, ὁ ἔσχατος Ἀδάμ in v. 45, ὁ δεύτερος ἄνθρωπος ἐξ οὐρανοῦ in v. 47, and ὁ ἐπουράνιος in v. 48 all refer to Jesus. See also Rom. 5.12-21 and 1 Cor. 15.20-24 for similar examples of Pauline Adam-Christ eschatological paradigms which explicitly mention Adam and Christ. See further Thiselton, *1 Corinthians*, p. 1282; Collins, *1 Corinthians*, pp. 568–69; Schrage, *Korinther*, pp. 302–306.

23 My translation.

24 Thiselton, *1 Corinthians*, pp. 1281–85; Collins, *1 Corinthians*, pp. 568–70; Lincoln, *Paradise*, pp. 42–50. For Paul's conceptual background of the heavenly man in 1 Cor. 15.39-49, see Lincoln, *Paradise*, pp. 46–50.

(ὁ δεύτερος ἄνθρωπος ἐξ οὐρανοῦ), though they have borne the image of the earthy one (τοῦ χοϊκοῦ), will one day also bear the image of the heavenly one (τοῦ ἐπουρανίου). However, if Paul employed the subjunctive, then the tenor of the passage is more ethical as he exhorts the Corinthians, though they have borne the image of the earthy one (τοῦ χοϊκοῦ), also now to bear the image of the heavenly one (τοῦ ἐπουρανίου).

The manuscript evidence strongly supports the subjunctive reading with a wide variety of attestation including P[46], ℵ, A, C, D, F, G, Ψ, Clement, Origen, Latin Irenaeus, and Gregory of Nyssa. Though the indicative reading has less attestation with B, I, Gregory of Nazianzus, and Didymus as the most important texts, the context of the passage seems to warrant the indicative reading. The tenor of 1 Cor. 15.35-57 is thoroughly didactic rather than ethical.[25] For this reason, though with great hesitancy, we regard the future indicative as the preferred reading.[26] C. K. Barrett appropriately summarizes the main point of v. 49 when he writes that since the creation 'human beings have continued to have the same kind of body, made in the

25 First Corinthians 15.58 follows Paul's discourse with an ethical exhortation but this seems to be more of a segue into his next line of thought rather than a direct application from his previous reasoning.

26 As indicated above, though there is less attestation, this reading does have the support of some reliable sources including Codex Vaticanus. UBS[4] and NA[27] both opt for the future indicative. In *A Textual Commentary on the Greek New Testament* (Stuttgart: Deutsche Bibelgesellschaft, 2nd edn, 1994), Bruce Metzger writes that 'exegetical considerations (i.e., the context is didactic, not hortatory) led the Committee to prefer the future indicative, despite its rather slender external support', p. 502. Others in support of the future indicative include: Thiselton, *1 Corinthians*, pp. 1288–89; C. K. Barrett, *A Commentary on the First Epistle to the Corinthians* (BNTC; London: A & C Black, 2nd edn, 1971), pp. 369, 377; Leon Morris, *The First Epistle of Paul to the Corinthians: An Introduction and Commentary* (TNTC 7; Leicester: InterVarsity, 2nd edn, 1985), p. 226; Schrage, *Korinther*, pp. 312–13. Critical to Barrett's argument is that since the future φορέσομεν and the subjunctive φορέσωμεν would have been pronounced similarly, if not identically, then 'only exegesis can determine the original sense and reading', Barrett, *1 Corinthians*, p. 369, note 2. Those who support the hortatory subjunctive reading include Collins, *1 Corinthians*, p. 572, and Lincoln who writes that it 'brings out more satisfactorily both the eschatological tension of Paul's perspective and the force of his argument', *Paradise*, pp. 50–51. Further support for the subjunctive can be found with Gordon D. Fee who writes that there is nearly universal attestation for the subjunctive and criticizes the UBS committee for '(abandoning) its better text-critical sense', *The First Epistle to the Corinthians* (NICNT; Grand Rapids: Eerdmans, 1987), p. 787. Similar to Lincoln, Fee believes that this ethical exhortation is 'another expression of Paul's "already/not yet" eschatological framework' and that Paul is urging the Corinthians 'to become what they are by grace', Fee, *1 Corinthians*, p. 795. We should point out here that this particular text-critical decision is not integral for our central argument in this chapter – namely a proper understanding of ἐπουράνιος and its relation to οὐρανός/οὐράνιος. In fact, a decision for the subjunctive φορέσωμεν would lend even greater support to the realized aspect in Pauline eschatology as those on earth would be granted a heavenly status of sorts.

image of Adam's. We continue to have this kind of body, living on in a state of corruption, up to the time of the resurrection. But then, in the future, *we shall bear* a different image, that of the heavenly Man whose body is spiritual.'[27]

From our analysis of 1 Cor. 15.39-49, there are a few significant points which should inform our understanding of the term ἐπουράνιος. First, since heavenly (ἐπουράνια) bodies are contrasted with earthly (ἐπίγεια) bodies, we once again find a distinction between the heavenly (ἐπουράνιος) and the earthly (v. 40), though in this case the heavenly bodies are a clear reference to the sun, moon, and stars. The fact that there is a major emphasis on opposites and contrasts throughout this entire passage (1 Cor. 15.39-49) should be even more evidence for a fundamental distinction between the ἐπουράνια and the ἐπίγεια in these verses. Such a distinction should naturally lead to the conclusion that it is severely misguided to include 'the earthly' within the definition of 'the heavenly' (ἐπουράνιος). Second, and perhaps of even greater importance, we observe once again that there is no distinction between the location signified by the terms ἐπουράνιος and οὐρανός.[28] The connection between the second man from heaven (ἐξ οὐρανοῦ) in v. 47 and the heavenly one (ὁ ἐπουράνιος) in v. 48 is evident. Raymond Collins also shares this view when he writes, 'To describe the heavenly one Paul employs the adjective *epouranios* rather than the prepositional phrase "from heaven" (*ex ouranou*) employed in v. 47.'[29] In this instance, as Collins implies, perhaps Paul chooses to alternate between these terms and expressions simply for stylistic purposes. What is evident, however, is that these two 'heaven' words (ἐπουράνιος and οὐρανός) refer to the same location and are references to that which is spatially distinct from the earth.

For our purposes, we should also address one other matter of possible significance. Since Paul writes in v. 48, 'As is the heavenly one, so also are those who are heavenly (οἱ ἐπουράνιοι)',[30] it is important, for our purposes, to determine the reference of οἱ ἐπουράνιοι. Of significance is whether Paul has in mind the redeemed on earth or rather the redeemed when they receive their resurrection bodies at the final resurrection (1 Cor. 15.20-24; 15.50-54). If Paul considers the Corinthians at present

27 Barrett, *1 Corinthians*, p. 377.

28 In his discussion of 1 Cor. 15.40-49, McGough makes no attempt to discern the relationship between ἐπουράνιος and οὐρανός, 'Investigation', pp. 39–40. Such an oversight is unacceptable in light of McGough's argument that there is a major distinction in meaning between these terms. McGough merely writes that the usage of ἐπουράνιος in 15.48-49 is Christological, 'Investigation', pp. 39–40.

29 Collins, *1 Corinthians*, pp. 571–72. Others who support the synonymous use of these terms in this passage include Morris, *1 Corinthians*, pp. 224–25, and Lincoln, *Paradise*, pp. 45–46. See also Morris who notes that the use of the adjectival ἐπουράνιος, rather than ἐξ οὐρανοῦ, points to Christ's heavenly nature as opposed to his heavenly origin, *1 Corinthians*, p. 225.

30 My translation.

to be οἱ ἐπουράνιοι, then, somewhat similarly to Eph. 2.6, the redeemed on earth would be granted a heavenly status.[31] In support of this view, Lincon writes:

> The first man's descendants share his characteristics and are designated *οἱ χοϊκοί*. Likewise those who belong to the second man can be called *οἱ ἐπουράνιοι* by virtue of their relationship to the one who is *ὁ ἐπουράνιος* par excellence. They are heavenly not because they came from heaven or are going to heaven, but because they are 'in Christ' (cf. verse 22) and share his resurrection life ... Despite the Corinthians' ever-realized eschatology Paul is not afraid to grant that those who belong to Christ are *οἱ ἐπουράνιοι*. This quality of heavenliness is not something entirely of the future.[32]

While the arguments of Lincoln, Fee, and Morris are compelling, the theme and context of this particular passage in 1 Corinthians still seem to be consistent with a future eschatological fulfilment. Even the statement concerning those in Christ (ἐν τῷ Χριστῷ) in v. 22 has a completely future fulfilment for believers who will in the future be made alive (ζῳοποιηθήσονται). As a result, though with some hesitancy, it is our conclusion that the point of vv. 48-49 is that believers will in the future be like the heavenly one (ὁ ἐπουράνιος) (v. 48) and so will bear the image of the heavenly one (v. 49) when Christ returns and the final resurrection occurs (vv. 22-23; 51-54).[33]

4. Philippians 2.10

Within the New Testament, the next appearance of the term ἐπουράνιος is located in the famous Christ hymn of Phil. 2.6-11. The amount of research conducted on this passage is enormous[34] and any attempt to

31 Those who argue for such an understanding include: Fee, *1 Corinthians*, pp. 794–95; Lincoln, *Paradise*, pp. 50–52; Morris, *1 Corinthians*, p. 225. Not surprisingly, Lincoln and Fee also argue for the subjunctive reading of v. 49 which seems to correspond well with this interpretation. Interestingly, Morris opts for the future indicative variant in v. 49 but also, in his explanation of v. 48, maintains that Christians are '"heavenly" because of their relationship to Christ', *1 Corinthians*, p. 225.

32 Lincoln, *Paradise*, p. 50. Italics original.

33 Barrett captures the sense of these verses well when he writes, 'All Adam's descendants, being made of dust as he was, have natural bodies, made of dust and animated by *soul (ψυχή)*. But the existence of another Adam with a spiritual body carries with it the existence of a race of men with spiritual bodies. These are received (in the case of Christ as well as in that of the rest of humanity) at the resurrection, only for Christ this has already happened, whereas for men it still lies in the future,' *1 Corinthians*, p. 377.

34 For an introduction to some of the scholarly interests such as, among others, the hymn's authorship, literary form, origin, structure, meaning, and use in Philippians, see Ralph P. Martin, *The Epistle of Paul to the Philippians: An Introduction and Commentary* (TNTC 11; Leicester: InterVarsity, 2nd edn, 1987), pp. 99–114; Peter T. O'Brien, *The*

provide a detailed exegesis or to wade through the vast literature on this subject would be well beyond the scope of this study and yet also would not serve to advance the principal argument of this chapter. As a result, in our analysis, we must paint with a broad brush on subsidiary matters and must also be selective in the matters we investigate. In 2.1-4, Paul encourages the Philippians, as a result of their relationship with Christ (v. 1), to live lives of selflessness and humility. In v. 5, which serves as the segue between Paul's exhortation in vv. 1-4 and the Christ hymn in vv. 6-11, Paul writes, 'Have this attitude in yourselves which was also in Christ Jesus' (Τοῦτο φρονεῖτε ἐν ὑμῖν ὃ καὶ ἐν Χριστῷ Ἰησοῦ). Though there has been considerable discussion over the precise references of some of the words and the proper interpretation of this seemingly simple verse,[35] we take τοῦτο to refer to the attitude described in vv. 1-4 and ἐν ὑμῖν to mean 'among yourselves' and thus to refer to the proper attitude the Philippians are to have towards one another. The phrase ὃ καὶ ἐν Χριστῷ Ἰησοῦ illustrates that Jesus is the one who truly embodied the attitude which Paul describes in vv. 1-4, the ὃ referring back to τοῦτο (and subsequently the attitude depicted by Paul in vv. 1-4) and ἐν Χριστῷ Ἰησοῦ describing Jesus as the one in whom this humility is found.[36] Therefore, we consider the NASB translation above, though certainly not without its difficulties, to be consistent with Paul's thought in this passage. This translation also makes the most sense of v. 5 as a transition from Paul's exhortation to the example of Christ's own humiliation and exaltation in the hymn.[37]

Epistle to the Philippians: A Commentary on the Greek Text (NIGTC; Grand Rapids: Eerdmans, 1991), pp. 186–271; Gerald F. Hawthorne, *Philippians* (WBC 43; Waco: Word Books, 1983), pp. 71–96; Bonnie B. Thurston and Judith M. Ryan, *Philippians and Philemon* (SP 10; Collegeville, MN: Liturgical Press, 2005), pp. 77–92; Stephen E. Fowl, *Philippians* (The Two Horizons New Testament Commentary; Grand Rapids: Eerdmans, 2005), pp. 88–117; Moisés Silva, *Philippians* (Baker Exegetical Commentary on the New Testament; Grand Rapids: Baker Academic, 2nd edn, 2005), pp. 92–116; Jean-Noël Aletti, *Saint Paul Épître aux Philippiens: Introduction, traduction et commentaire* (EBib new series 55; Paris: J. Gabalda, 2005), pp. 137–76; Markus Bockmuehl, *The Epistle to the Philippians* (BNTC; London: Hendrickson, 1998), pp. 114–48. For additional study, see Ralph P. Martin, *Carmen Christi: Philippians ii. 5-11 in Recent Interpretation and in the Setting of Early Christian Worship* (Grand Rapids: Eerdmans, rev. edn, 1983) and consult the lengthy bibliographies in O'Brien, *Philippians*, pp. 186–88, and Hawthorne, *Philippians*, pp. 71–75.

35 For further discussion of the references of τοῦτο and ὃ in addition to interpretations of ἐν ὑμῖν and ἐν Χριστῷ Ἰησοῦ, see O'Brien, *Philippians*, pp. 203–205; Hawthorne, *Philippians*, pp. 79–81; Martin, *Philippians*, pp. 99–100; Silva, *Philippians*, pp. 95–98.

36 So also O'Brien, *Philippians*, p. 205; Thurston, *Philippians*, p. 80; Fowl, *Philippians*, pp. 89–90. Inherent in this understanding is that the verb 'to be' should be supplied in the second half of v. 5.

37 Consistent with the translation/interpretation above is the idea that Paul inserts the Christ-hymn here for ethical purposes. Hawthorne writes, 'Hence, although this hymn is unquestionably a christological gem unparalleled in the NT, although it may be

After Paul's exhortation in vv. 1-4 and his command to have the same attitude as Christ Jesus (v. 5), we arrive at the Christ hymn in vv. 6-11. Though there has been little agreement over its precise structure,[38] we regard the hymn as containing two major divisions – Christ's humiliation in vv. 6-8 and Christ's exaltation in vv. 9-11.[39] Verse 10, which contains the appearance of ἐπουράνιος, is located in the midst of the hymn's description of Christ's exaltation. In v. 9, as a result of Christ's humiliation and obedience, God highly exalts Christ and bestows on him the name which is above every name. Verses 10-11 make clear both the purpose and result of this exaltation[40] – that at the name of Jesus every knee will bow (κάμψῃ) and every tongue will confess (ἐξομολογήσηται)[41] that Jesus Christ is Lord (κύριος).[42]

In v. 10 Paul illustrates the universal scope of the worship attributed to Jesus with three adjectives which function as nouns – ἐπουρανίων καὶ ἐπιγείων καὶ καταχθονίων.[43] In regard to this particular phrase, commentators usually concern themselves with at least three significant

considered soteriological in character, and although it may have been originally composed for christological or soteriological reasons, Paul's motive in using it here is not theological but ethical ... The hymn, therefore, presents Christ as the ultimate model for moral action,' Hawthorne, *Philippians*, p. 79. See further Thurston, *Philippians*, pp. 89–90; Aletti, *Philippiens*, p. 147; O'Brien, *Philippians*, pp. 205, 262. O'Brien here closely follows Hawthorne – word for word on a few occasions – and often without referencing him.

38 For discussions of the hymn's structure, see O'Brien, *Philippians*, pp. 188–93; Hawthorne, *Philippians*, pp. 76–79; Thurston, *Philippians*, pp. 88–89; Martin, *Philippians*, pp. 112–13; Bockmuehl, *Philippians*, pp. 125–26.

39 See also Hawthorne, *Philippians*, p. 77; O'Brien, *Philippians*, pp. 192–93; Silva, *Philippians*, p. 93; Bockmuehl, *Philippians*, p. 125–26.

40 In *Greek Grammar Beyond the Basics: An Exegetical Syntax of the New Testament* (Grand Rapids: Zondervan, 1996), Daniel B. Wallace notes that a purpose-result ἵνα clause in the NT 'indicates *both the intention and its sure accomplishment*', p. 473. Italics original. Wallace lists Phil. 2.9-11 as an example of such a construction, *Greek Grammar*, p. 474.

41 We prefer the aorist subjunctive ἐξομολογήσηται over the future indicative ἐξομολογήσεται primarily because it continues the flow of thought from the ἵνα clause and because the verb which precedes it (κάμψῃ) is also aorist subjunctive, the two clauses being connected with καί. See also O'Brien, *Philippians*, pp. 249–50. Metzger defends the choice for the subjunctive as the reading supported by P[46] ℵ B *al*', *A Textual Commentary*, p. 546.

42 Much has been made over whether the confession made by πᾶν γόνυ and πᾶσα γλῶσσα is a glad confession proclaimed with thanksgiving. We agree with O'Brien who '(concludes) that on the last day every knee will bow and every tongue will "openly declare" that Jesus alone has the right to rule (cf. Rev. 5.13, etc.)', *Philippians*, p. 250. For those who now confess Jesus as Lord, their declaration will be glad, with thanksgiving, and in praise. Others, which includes both people who do not presently confess Christ as Lord and also the principalities and powers of Col. 2.15, will also openly declare but will do so as 'submitting against their wills to a power they cannot resist', O'Brien, *Philippians*, p. 250. Cf. Bockmuehl, *Philippians*, pp. 146–47.

43 These three adjectives in the genitive case refer back to πᾶν γόνυ and so depict the universality of the homage paid to Jesus when every knee of those in heaven, on the earth, and under the earth will bow to him.

issues – the gender of the adjectives, the references of the adjectives, and whether or not this expression represents a developed cosmology. Many earlier commentators and translations opted to understand the adjectives as neuter believing that they refer to all of creation including both animate and inanimate things.[44] However, we believe it is more plausible that the three adjectives are masculine and so refer to personal beings who are able to bend the knee and make confession.[45] While some commentators have argued that ἐπουρανίων καὶ ἐπιγείων καὶ καταχθονίων refer only to the spiritual powers believed to rule over the heavenly, earthly, and subterranean realms,[46] Paul's purpose here is to communicate the universality of the honour which will be given to Jesus. For this reason, we understand this adjectival expression to include both human beings and spiritual powers.[47] Gerald Hawthorne writes, 'In this series the writer describes angels, men and demons as ultimately joining together in an act of worship ... All – all principalities and powers ... as well as all people – [will] bow their knees before Jesus and do obeisance to him in adoration and awe.'[48] In agreement with the majority of commentators, we are hesitant to ascribe precise identities to the inhabitants of the three realms (ἐπουρανίων καὶ ἐπιγείων καὶ καταχθονίων)[49] or to

44 For brief discussions, see O'Brien, *Philippians*, pp. 243–44, and Hawthorne, *Philippians*, p. 93. As examples, O'Brien lists the Authorized Version; RV; ASV; J. B. Lightfoot, *Saint Paul's Epistle to the Philippians* (London: MacMillan, 1881), p. 115; H. C. G. Moule, *The Epistle to the Philippians* (Cambridge Bible for Schools and Colleges; Cambridge: Cambridge University Press, 1923), pp. 69–70; Carr, *Angels and Principalities*, pp. 86–89, esp. p. 87. As cited in O'Brien, *Philippians*, p. 244. See also Silva, who does not limit the reference to intelligent beings and who cites Ps. 19.1-6, Psalm 148, and Rom. 8.19-22 as examples of personification of creation in Scripture, *Philippians*, p. 116.

45 So Hawthorne, *Philippians*, p. 93; O'Brien, *Philippians*, pp. 244–45; Martin, *Philippians*, p. 110. Such an understanding would be in accord with a similar reference in Ignatius where the almost identical terms also appear to be masculine. In Ignatius, *Trall.* 9.1, Ignatius writes that Jesus 'was crucified and died while those in heaven and on earth and under the earth (τῶν ἐπουρανίων καὶ ἐπιγείων καὶ ὑποχθονίων) looked on'. For brief discussions of this passage from Ignatius, see Martin, *Philippians*, p. 110, and O'Brien, *Philippians*, p. 244. See also my brief analysis of Ignatius, *Trall.* 9.1 in chapter 3.

46 This seems to be the preference of Ralph P. Martin in *Carmen Christi*, pp. 262–64. For Martin's discussion of these three adjectives, their references, and the three-fold division of the universe, see *Carmen Christi*, pp. 257–65. For additional discussions of this view, see O'Brien, *Philippians*, pp. 244–45, and Hawthorne, *Philippians*, p. 93.

47 So also O'Brien, *Philippians*, pp. 244–45; Hawthorne, *Philippians*, p. 93; Fowl, *Philippians*, p. 103.

48 Hawthorne, *Philippians*, p. 93.

49 Silva, *Philippians*, p. 116; Fowl, *Philippians*, p. 103. Though Silva emphasizes that we cannot know with any certainty the precise identification of these three groups, he also writes that the least objectionable classification would be references to the spirits in heaven, people on earth, and the dead in Sheol, *Philippians*, p. 116, note 39. See also O'Brien who seems guarded in assigning identities to the terms but allows for the possibility that ἐπουρανίων could refer to angels in heaven and ἐπιγείων to earthly inhabitants.

insist that the three terms represent a developed cosmology.[50] Rather, Paul's intention here is to emphasize the universal lordship of Christ over all created beings.[51]

Just as every knee will bow (κάμψῃ), so also every tongue will confess (ἐξομολογήσηται). In these verses, we find an allusion to Isa. 45.18-25 where we also read that every knee will bow and every tongue confess. In the larger context of this passage, the God of Israel repeatedly proclaims his unique greatness.[52] He is the creator of the heavens (v. 18), he is the only God (vv. 18, 21, 22), and he is the hope of salvation for all the ends of the earth (v. 22). In v. 23 the Lord proclaims 'that to [him] every knee will bow (κάμψει), (and) every tongue will swear *allegiance* (ἐξομολογήσεται)'. Paul's allusion to Isa. 45.23 here is striking as he adopts the language attributed to the God of Israel and subsequently applies it to Jesus.[53] As Ralph Martin notes, 'No clearer proof could be forthcoming of our Lord's pre-eminent position at the Father's right hand than the use of this Old Testament quotation in reference to him.'[54] Of equal significance is the substance of the confession made by every tongue – that Jesus Christ is Lord. Not only is an Old Testament reference to God here applied to Jesus, but Jesus is also given the divine name. With such a declaration, this great hymn

O'Brien warns that one cannot be certain whether καταχθονίων refers to dead human beings, demons, or both, *Philippians*, p. 245.

50 Though it would be imprudent to investigate this issue in much detail, several arguments militate against the notion that Phil. 2.10 represents a developed Pauline cosmology. First, since Phil. 2.6–11 is a hymn, we cannot be certain whether Paul was even the original author. Regardless, Paul certainly appropriated and utilized the hymn for his own purposes here in Philippians, and the most likely purpose for this triadic phrase would have been to emphasize the universal homage attributed to Christ. Second, Hawthorne notes that belief in a three-storied universe was common in antiquity and consequently universality was often conveyed through corresponding triadic expressions, *Philippians*, p. 93. See also O'Brien, *Philippians*, p. 244, and Thurston, *Philippians*, p. 84. Third, O'Brien notes that Scripture often has varying categories for communicating universality. Revelation 5.13 has four groups and Exod. 20.4 has three groups but with a slight variation, O'Brien, *Philippians*, p. 245. In Col. 1.16 and Eph. 1.10, τὰ πάντα is clarified by ἐν τοῖς οὐρανοῖς καὶ ἐπὶ τῆς γῆς and τὰ ἐπὶ τοῖς οὐρανοῖς καὶ τὰ ἐπὶ τῆς γῆς respectively. See further Aletti, *Philippiens*, pp. 170–71.

51 O'Brien, *Philippians*, pp. 243–45; Hawthorne, *Philippians*, p. 93; Thurston, *Philippians*, p. 84; Silva, *Philippians*, p. 116; Fowl, *Philippians*, p. 103; Aletti, *Philippiens*, pp. 170–71; Bockmuehl, *Philippians*, pp. 144–48.

52 Martin, *Philippians*, p. 109; cf. Bockmuehl, *Philippians*, pp. 144–45.

53 For some concise discussions, see Hawthorne, *Philippians*, pp. 92–95; O'Brien, *Philippians*, pp. 240–42; Fowl, *Philippians*, p. 103; Martin, *Philippians*, pp. 109–10; Silva, *Philippians*, p. 112.

54 Martin, *Philippians*, p. 109. Also of importance is the fact that Paul cites Isa. 45.23 in Rom. 14.11 in order to demonstrate God's universal reign and his authority as supreme judge. Thus Paul grants to Jesus in Phil. 2.10–11 the same supremacy as God in Rom. 14.11 through his referencing of Isa. 45.23 in both instances, Fowl, *Philippians*, p. 103.

reaches its climax and clearly reveals the supreme name which God has granted to Jesus – κύριος.[55]

In this brief exegetical sketch, we can see that the meaning of ἐπουράνιος in Phil. 2.10 is consistent with our argument that the term always refers to that which is spatially distinct from the earth. Though there is no appearance of οὐρανός in this passage, we do once again find a contrast between the heavenly (ἐπουρανίων) and the earthly (ἐπιγείων). Also of significance is an appearance of οὐρανός in Phil. 3.18-21 where Paul writes that there are some who walk as enemies of the cross of Christ and who set their minds on earthly things (τὰ ἐπίγεια).[56] In contrast to these enemies of Christ, Paul writes, 'For our citizenship is in heaven (ἐν οὐρανοῖς), from which also we eagerly wait for a Savior, the Lord Jesus Christ.' It is of no minor significance that, in Philippians, there is a direct contrast not only between ἐπουράνιος and ἐπίγειος in 2.10, but also between οὐρανός and ἐπίγειος in 3.19-20. These examples serve as further proof that these two terms for heaven (ἐπουράνιος and οὐρανός), though one is a noun and one is an adjective, refer to the same location. Thus once again, we see that any argument to define ἐπουράνιος as some sort of spiritual atmosphere on the earth or as distinct in meaning from οὐρανός falls short.[57] Rather, the natural reading and understanding of ἐπουρανίων is as a reference to that part of the cosmos which is spatially distinct from the earth.

5. 2 Timothy 4.18

In 2 Timothy 4 Paul[58] writes of his impending death and the award that awaits him (vv. 6-8) and so urges Timothy to visit him soon (vv. 9-11). Paul then recounts various trials and persecutions he has

55 So Hawthorne, *Philippians*, p. 93, and O'Brien, *Philippians*, pp. 245–46. O'Brien also notes that the placement of κύριος at the beginning of the phrase is of significance, *Philippians*, pp. 245–46.

56 It is also of some significance to note the spatial terms once more employed by Paul to communicate an already/not yet eschatology. Here Paul writes that believers' citizenship (πολίτευμα) is in heaven (ἐν οὐρανοῖς) (already), from which they await a Saviour who will transform their bodies into conformity with the body of his glory (not yet).

57 In his assessment of Phil. 2.10, McGough provides no real contribution and does nothing to advance his argument. McGough merely writes that ἐπουρανίων might refer to spiritual powers, people, or both and that the point of the description is the universal exaltation of Christ, 'Investigation', p. 42. McGough also writes that the use of ἐπουράνιος in Phil. 2.10 is cosmological and Christological, 'Investigation', p. 42. The fact that McGough does not discuss the relationship between ἐπουρανίων and ἐπιγείων in Phil. 2.10 is unacceptable in light of his argument that the term ἐπουράνιος indicates either earthly and heavenly interaction or the spiritual atmosphere of the church on earth.

58 No discussion of the authorship of 2 Timothy will be attempted here and we use the title out of convenience.

undergone and writes of God’s strengthening, saving, and rescuing him (vv. 14-17). As a result of his impending death and the Lord’s faithfulness throughout his trials, Paul proclaims that ‘the Lord will rescue [him] from every evil deed, and will bring [him] safely to His heavenly (ἐπουράνιον) kingdom’ (v. 18). The ‘heavenly kingdom’ of which Paul here writes is a reference to the kingdom of Christ.[59] The kingdom’s description as ἐπουράνιος is not insignificant, in that Paul understood this ‘heavenly kingdom’ to be a present reality but yet also one which awaits its future consummation when Christ’s heavenly reign will be fully realized upon the earth.[60] The heavenly reign of Christ is an oft-appearing theme in the New Testament[61] and will be of significance in our discussion of Eph. 1.20.

The usage of the term ἐπουράνιος in 2 Tim. 4.18 is straightforward and is in accordance with the definition argued for throughout this chapter. The kingdom of which Paul writes is a heavenly (ἐπουράνιος) one and is therefore spatially distinct from the earth.[62] Though it is not explicit, there is an implied contrast with the earth in this passage. Since the trials which Paul experiences are on the earth, the implication is that when the Lord brings him into his heavenly kingdom, he will no longer experience those trials and persecutions. Donald Guthrie notes this contrast when he writes, ‘The use of the adjective “heavenly” (a characteristic Pauline word) draws attention to the emphatic contrast between God’s kingdom and the present earthly circumstances of sorrow and suffering.’[63] This analysis of 2 Tim. 4.18 continues to support our argument that though there is flexibility in the usage of ἐπουράνιος, its basic meaning remains the same – as a reference to that which is spatially distinct from the earth and as synonymous with other related terms for heaven, i.e. οὐρανός and οὐράνιος.[64]

59 I. Howard Marshall, *A Critical and Exegetical Commentary on the Pastoral Epistles* (International Critical Commentary on the Holy Scriptures of the Old and New Testaments; Edinburgh: T & T Clark, 1999), p. 826. Marshall correctly notes that Paul has already utilized βασιλεία to refer to Christ’s kingdom in 4.1. Cf. Philip H. Towner, *The Letters to Timothy and Titus* (NICNT; Grand Rapids: Eerdmans, 2006), p. 647; George Knight III, *The Pastoral Epistles: A Commentary on the Greek Text* (NIGTC; Grand Rapids: Eerdmans, 1992), p. 472; William D. Mounce, *Pastoral Epistles* (WBC 46; Nashville: Thomas Nelson, 2000), p. 598.

60 Towner, *Timothy and Titus*, p. 647.

61 See, e.g., Eph. 1.20, Phil. 3.20-21, 1 Thess. 1.10, 1 Thess. 4.16, 1 Pet. 3.21-22, Acts 2.30-36, Heb. 8.1, and Heb. 1.3-4.

62 See Knight III who correctly recognizes that ‘Paul uses both ἐπουράνιος, “heavenly”, and οὐρανός, “heaven”, of the realm that is distinguishable from the earth,’ *Pastoral Epistles*, p. 472.

63 Donald Guthrie, *The Pastoral Epistles: An Introduction and Commentary* (TNTC; Leicester: InterVarsity, 2nd edn, 1990), p. 189. Cf. Mounce who also finds an implicit contrast between an earthly kingdom and the true heavenly kingdom, and so also an earthly king and the heavenly king, *Pastoral Epistles*, p. 598.

64 See also Knight III, *Pastoral Epistles*, p. 472. We should note here, however, that

6. *Hebrews 3.1*

In Heb. 3.1 we read that the addressees (ἀδελφοὶ ἅγιοι) of the letter are partakers of a heavenly calling (κλήσεως ἐπουρανίου). Whether this κλῆσις ἐπουράνιος is a call from heaven or a call to heaven is open to interpretation.[65] It is not necessary, however, to posit a sharp distinction between these options since they are by no means mutually exclusive. Within the context of Hebrews, it is quite likely that this κλῆσις ἐπουράνιος is both Christ's call from heaven and Christ's call for believers to join him in heaven.[66] In light of this call to heaven, we find in Heb. 3.1 an additional New Testament passage in which believers on earth are granted a heavenly status of sorts. Though it would be misguided to conflate Paul's conception of union with Christ with the author of Hebrews' view, we nevertheless can observe that some sort of identification with Christ is also instrumental for the author of Hebrews in how he understands this 'heavenly call' of believers.

In our analysis of this κλῆσις ἐπουράνιος, it is significant to note how the author of Hebrews portrays both Christ's status and position in heaven and then believers' identity with Christ. Through a brief analysis of Christ's status and position in Hebrews, we observe that:

1 Christ is 'the radiance of [God's] glory and the exact representation of His nature' (1.3).
2 Christ is 'at the right hand of the Majesty on high' (1.3).
3 Christ's status is greater than that of the angels (1.4-14).
4 Christ 'has passed through the heavens (τοὺς οὐρανούς)' (4.14; cf. 7.26).
5 Christ 'has taken His seat at the right hand of the throne of the Majesty in the heavens (ἐν τοῖς οὐρανοῖς)' (8.1; cf. 9.24; 12.25).

these other related terms – οὐρανός and οὐράνιος – do not appear in 2 Timothy. In his assessment of 2 Tim. 4.18, McGough makes no attempt to advance his argument and simply writes that the use of ἐπουράνιος is as an adjective of the kingdom of the Lord, 'Investigation', p. 43.

65 Paul Ellingworth, *The Epistle to the Hebrews: A Commentary on the Greek Text* (NIGTC; Grand Rapids: Eerdmans, 1993), p. 198. Ellingworth provides a short discussion of this ambiguous phrase.

66 So Ellingworth who writes 'that the call is directly from, and indirectly to, heaven', *Hebrews*, p. 198. Similarly, Luke Timothy Johnson understands the reference as 'a call from God' and a call to 'the reality to which they have been summoned', *Hebrews: A Commentary* (NTL; Louisville: Westminster John Knox Press, 2006), p. 106. William L. Lane seems to understand the κλῆσις ἐπουράνιος as primarily a call to heaven when he writes that the reference is to 'those who are being led to enjoy the glory of God's presence', *Hebrews* (WBC 47a–b; 2 vols; Nashville: Thomas Nelson, 1991), p. a:74.

Through an examination of believers' identity with Christ, we observe that:

1 Christ partook (μετέσχεν) in humanity's flesh and blood (2.14).
2 Christ was made like his brothers so that he might become a merciful and faithful high priest (2.17-18).
3 Believers are referred to as brothers (ἀδελφούς) of Christ (2.11-13).
4 Believers have become partakers of Christ (μέτοχοι τοῦ Χριστοῦ) (3.14).

From this brief analysis, we see Christ's high and exalted status as the radiance of God's glory, as the exact representation of God's nature, as greater than the angels, and as seated at the right hand of God. In addition to Christ's exalted position, we also note that his location is supreme since he 'has taken His seat at the right hand of the throne of the Majesty in the heavens' (ἐν τοῖς οὐρανοῖς) (8.1). Furthermore, the author of Hebrews also emphasizes Christ's identity with believers in order to demonstrate his effectiveness as their high priest (2.14-3.1; 4.14-5.10). Christ partook (μετέσχεν) of flesh and blood (2.14) and was made like his brothers (ἀδελφοῖς) (2.17-18). As a result, the author of Hebrews can now depict believers as brothers of Christ (2.11-13) and as partakers of Christ (μέτοχοι τοῦ Χριστοῦ) (3.14).[67]

From our analysis, it seems the line of thought for the author of Hebrews is that since believers are both brothers and partakers of Christ and since Christ is in heaven (ἐν τοῖς οὐρανοῖς), believers are consequently partakers of a heavenly calling (κλήσεως ἐπουρανίου μέτοχοι). Thus believers' relationship and identity with Christ is determinative for their heavenly status and calling.[68] In this sense, the 'heavenly calling' in Heb. 3.1 is similar to those who are seated in the heavenlies in Christ in Eph. 2.6 since in both passages, believers can be depicted as 'heavenly' because of their relationship to and identity with Christ. In light of our purpose to determine the meaning and usage of ἐπουράνιος, it is significant that believers who are partakers of a heavenly calling (κλήσεως ἐπουρανίου μέτοχοι) are also partakers of Christ (μέτοχοι τοῦ Χριστοῦ) (3.14) who is located ἐν τοῖς οὐρανοῖς (8.1; cf. 7.26; 9.24; 12.25). The implication is that there is a connection between the

67 Thus the term 'partakers' (μέτοχοι) is significant for this conclusion. Within Hebrews, the author uses this term to demonstrate that Christ is above his μετόχους (1.9). The remaining references are to the addressees as μέτοχοι of a heavenly calling (3.1), μέτοχοι of Christ (3.14), μετόχους of the Holy Spirit (6.4), and μέτοχοι of discipline (12.8). Of equal significance is an appearance of the cognate verb in 2.14 where Christ partook (μετέσχεν) of flesh and blood. Cf. Ellingworth who also points out that μέτοχοι in 3.1 echoes μετέσχεν in 2.14, *Hebrews*, p. 198.

68 This appears close to the opinion of Lane who, when commenting on 3.1, notes that the addressees owe their privileged heavenly status to Jesus who, as their great high priest, has already entered heaven, *Hebrews*, p. a:74. See also Ellingworth, *Hebrews*, p. 198.

heavenly (ἐπουράνιος) calling of believers in Heb. 3.1 and the location of Christ ἐν τοῖς οὐρανοῖς in Heb 8.1.[69] As a result, the meaning and usage of ἐπουράνιος in Heb 3.1 are consistent with our argument that the term always refers to that which is spatially distinct from the earth and refers to the same location as οὐρανός.[70]

7. *Hebrews 6.4*

Though within this passage there are a number of significant theological and exegetical issues which we could explore, in light of our task, we will focus on the meaning and usage of ἐπουράνιος. The purpose of Heb. 6.4-6, and the larger passage of which it is a part,[71] is to encourage the community of believers to remain faithful to Christ in the midst of possible temptation to turn away from him. In vv. 4-5, the author of Hebrews describes the community as those who have been enlightened, tasted of the heavenly gift, partaken of the Holy Spirit, and tasted of the word of God and the coming age. These spiritual (i.e. Spiritual) blessings do not have either man or the earth as their origin but rather are from God who is in heaven (8.1) and are of the Holy Spirit (6.4). The precise identification of 'the heavenly gift' (τῆς δωρεᾶς τῆς ἐπουρανίου) is difficult to discern. Commentators have suggested such references as the Eucharist, an identification with God, a parallel with partaking of the Holy Spirit,[72] enlightenment, or baptism.[73] While these seem to be viable options, a more natural reading is to identify 'the heavenly gift' with salvation itself. Harold Attridge writes, 'The "heavenly gift" is best understood as a general image for the gracious bestowal of salvation, with all that entails – the spirit, forgiveness, and sanctification.'[74] Thus

69 Harold W. Attridge also notes this connection and writes, 'By describing the call, and later the "gift" (6.4), as heavenly, the text suggests something about the quality of the items mentioned. The quality ultimately depends on the source and goal of the call, the "true" realm of God's presence, which Christ by his sacrifice has entered,' *The Epistle to the Hebrews: A Commentary on the Epistle to the Hebrews* (Hermeneia; Philadelphia: Fortress Press, 1989), p. 106.

70 Cf. Ellingworth who also writes that ἐπουράνιος and οὐράνιος are synonymous, *Hebrews*, p. 198. Contra McGough who provides no real analysis of Heb. 3.1 or the use of ἐπουράνιος when he writes that 'believers participate in a spiritual realm in their bodily existence', 'Investigation', p. 43.

71 Ellingworth outlines the larger passage as 5.11–6.20, *Hebrews*, pp. 297–98; Lane's division is 5.11–6.12, *Hebrews*, pp. a:133–35.

72 Ellingworth, *Hebrews*, pp. 319–20.

73 Johnson doubts that the reference is to the Eucharist and concludes that it is either to enlightenment or baptism, *Hebrews*, p. 162.

74 Attridge, *Hebrews*, p. 170. Lane also seems to think along this line when he identifies τῆς δωρεᾶς τῆς ἐπουρανίου as a reference to 'redemption as the free gift of God', *Hebrews*, p. a:141.

we can refer to 'the heavenly gift' (τῆς δωρεᾶς τῆς ἐπουρανίου) as salvation but also as that which ultimately comes from God and has heaven as its origin and goal.[75] As a result, though the usage of ἐπουράνιος in Heb. 6.4 is qualitative, the term still carries its basic meaning as a reference to that which is spatially distinct from the earth since it represents that which comes from God in heaven.[76]

8. *Hebrews 8.5*

Harold Attridge writes that Heb. 8.1-6 reflects the entire letter of Hebrews' 'basic contention that Christ is an exalted High Priest'.[77] To emphasize Christ's unique position, the author of Hebrews contrasts the old and new covenants and, more specifically, the earthly, temporal high priests, and Jesus, the permanent, heavenly High Priest.[78] The author's depiction of Christ's priesthood and heavenly session[79] in 8.1-2 leads him to elaborate further on the contrast between the earthly priesthood in the earthly tabernacle and Christ's heavenly priesthood in the heavenly tabernacle (8.3-5). That Christ is a minister in the true sanctuary pitched by the Lord (8.2) reveals both the inherent weaknesses of the Levitical arrangement as well as the eschatological superiority of Christ's ministry.[80] Earthly priests offer gifts according to the Law and serve merely a copy and shadow of the heavenly things (τῶν ἐπουρανίων) (8.4-5).[81] This contrast between heaven and earth denotes heaven 'as the "place" of God's presence (which) transcends earth as the source of all reality and value'.[82] Thus the contrast between the perfection of heaven and the imperfection of earth can be viewed as a contrast between that

75 Cf. Attridge, *Hebrews*, p. 170.

76 Contra McGough who once again seems to spiritualize the meaning of ἐπουράνιος when he writes, 'Because the gift is heavenly, it is of a different order of reality,' 'Investigation', p. 44.

77 Attridge, *Hebrews*, p. 217.

78 This theme is really the subject of a much larger section beginning at 7.1 and ending at 10.39.

79 By uniting these two themes of priesthood and heavenly session, the author of Hebrews alludes to Ps. 110.1 (LXX Ps. 109.1) and probably to LXX Zech. 6.13 as well, where the priest is at the right hand of God. See Lane, *Hebrews*, p. a:205.

80 Lane, *Hebrews*, p. a:204. See in particular Lane's brief discussion of the weaknesses of the Levitical priesthood in comparison to Christ's ministry.

81 The clear implication here is that the copies of the heavenly things are the earthly things.

82 Lane, *Hebrews*, pp. a:210–11. Cf. Ellingworth who also notes that 'the contrast is mainly one of place (heaven/earth)', *Hebrews*, p. 399. We should also note that in this passage, we not only find a spatial contrast, but also a temporal contrast between the Levitical priesthood on earth in the old covenant and the present priesthood of Christ in heaven in the new covenant, Lane, *Hebrews*, p. a:207. Hebrews 8.6 serves to highlight this temporal contrast.

which is merely a 'shadow' to that which is reality.[83] The significance of Christ's heavenly priesthood lies in the fact that Jesus possesses complete access to the presence of God. An earthly priesthood which provided only limited and imperfect access to God no longer exists as a result of Christ's superior heavenly priesthood which provides complete access to the presence of God in the true tabernacle.[84]

For our purposes, it is significant that the author of Hebrews contrasts the priests on earth (ἐπὶ γῆς) who serve a copy and shadow of the heavenly things (τῶν ἐπουρανίων) with Jesus who is a minister in the true tabernacle. Within this contrast, the fact that ὑποδείγματι καὶ σκιᾷ τῶν ἐπουρανίων refers to earthly things is made explicit by the author's implication that the Levitical priests minister ἐπὶ γῆς.[85] Additionally, Jesus's location at the right hand of God ἐν τοῖς οὐρανοῖς[86] (8.1) also makes clear that Jesus is a minister of heavenly things (τῶν ἐπουρανίων) in the true sanctuary.[87] Thus we find in Heb. 8.1-6 both an implicit contrast between ἐπουράνιος and the earth and an identification between the location of Jesus's priestly ministry ἐν τοῖς οὐρανοῖς and the heavenly things (τῶν ἐπουρανίων) which are located there.[88] As a result, our analysis of Heb. 8.1-6 supports our argument that the term ἐπουράνιος refers to the same location as οὐρανός and always refers to that which is spatially distinct from the earth.[89]

83 Lane, *Hebrews*, pp. a:210–11.

84 Lane, *Hebrews*, pp. a:204–11.

85 See also Johnson, *Hebrews*, p. 200; Attridge, *Hebrews*, p. 219.

86 This statement in itself is striking when we realize the same thing is said of Christ in Eph. 1.20 with the exception that the expression ἐν τοῖς ἐπουρανίοις appears rather than ἐν τοῖς οὐρανοῖς. In our view, this is strong evidence indeed that these two expressions should be understood as synonymous and interchangeable. We will explore this idea through a comparison of ascension texts in our examination of Eph. 1.20.

87 Cf. Johnson who writes that 'the place where Jesus is now the eternal priest is in God's presence', *Hebrews*, p. 198.

88 See also Lane's discussion of Heb. 8.1-5 which supports our argument and conclusion, *Hebrews*, pp. a:198–211.

89 Contra McGough who provides almost no analysis of the passage when he writes, 'The significance of ἐπουράνιος in 8.5 appears to point to an order of existence brought about by Christ that is abiding and real,' 'Investigation', p. 45. With such an understanding, McGough continues to spiritualize the meaning and usage of ἐπουράνιος while neglecting the spatial component of the term. In his analysis of Heb. 8.5 McGough once again fails to interact with the appearance of οὐρανός in 8.1 and so he cannot comment on the relationship between these two 'heaven' terms. As we have previously stated, such an omission is unacceptable in light of his argument that there is a major distinction in meaning between ἐπουράνιος and οὐρανός.

9. Hebrews 9.23

Within the larger section of Heb. 9.11-28, the author of Hebrews depicts salvation as 'a forward movement into the presence of God'.[90] Through his discussion of various topics such as sacrifice, tabernacle, high priest, blood, and covenant, the writer contrasts the sacrificial system of the old covenant with the more efficacious sacrifice of Christ under the new covenant. On account of Christ's sacrifice and subsequent entrance into the heavenly sanctuary as a perfect high priest, 'every obstacle to union with God has been effectively removed'.[91] In Heb. 9.22-24 the author once again picks up the theme of Christ's heavenly priestly ministry.[92] In 9.22 the author summarizes his discussion of the importance of blood (9.11-22) when he writes that 'all things are cleansed with blood, and without shedding of blood there is no forgiveness'.[93] As a result, it was necessary for τὰ ὑποδείγματα τῶν ἐν τοῖς οὐρανοῖς (i.e. the earthly things)[94] to be cleansed with the Old Testament sacrifices and blood of animals (vv. 19-21), but for the heavenly things (τὰ ἐπουράνια) themselves to be cleansed with better sacrifices (9.23). Though the reference is quite elusive, it is best to understand the 'cleansing' of τὰ ἐπουράνια as a dedication of the sanctuary or a consecration rather than a cleansing from impurity.[95] In 9.24 the author gives the reason for the cleansing of τὰ ἐπουράνια – because Christ did not enter the earthly holy place, which is only a copy of the true one, but rather Christ entered into

90 Lane, *Hebrews*, p. b:251.

91 Lane, *Hebrews*, p. b:251.

92 As noted above, the author of Hebrews first introduces the theme of Christ's heavenly priestly ministry in 8.1-6 and now he continues to develop this theme in chapter 9. See Lane, *Hebrews*, p. b:234.

93 Lane correctly notes that cleansing by blood is highly significant to the author's argument since it provides the comparison for the limited effectiveness of the blood of animals under the old covenant with the fully effective blood of Christ in the new covenant. The blood of Christ is more powerful since it provides full access to God and complete cleansing from sin in Christ's one sacrifice, Lane, *Hebrews*, pp. b:246–47, 252. See also Johnson who lists Lev. 4.20, Lev. 19.22, and Num. 15.25–28 as additional passages which highlight the connection between the shedding of blood and forgiveness of sins, *Hebrews*, p. 242.

94 Τὰ ὑποδείγματα τῶν ἐν τοῖς οὐρανοῖς are undoubtedly a reference to the earthly things and, more specifically, most likely refer to the tabernacle and its cultus (v. 21). See Lane, *Hebrews*, pp. b:247–48. Ellingworth believes the reference here is to the essentials of the earthly sanctuary such as altars, priests, and sacrifices, *Hebrews*, p. 476.

95 So Ellingworth, *Hebrews*, p. 477. Contra Lane, *Hebrews*, pp. b:247–48. F. F. Bruce believes that it is the sinful conscience of people which needs to be cleansed so that God might dwell with his people, *The Epistle to the Hebrews* (NICNT; Grand Rapids: Eerdmans, rev. edn, 1990), pp. 228–29; cf. Attridge who also contends that the heavenly things cleansed by Christ are the consciences of believers in the new covenant, *Hebrews*, p. 262. For a brief discussion of the cleansing of τὰ ἐπουράνια and various interpretations, see Ellingworth, *Hebrews*, pp. 477–78.

the very presence of God, into heaven itself (εἰς αὐτὸν τὸν οὐρανόν).[96] For the author of Hebrews, Christ's access to God in the heavenly temple provides the basis for believers' free and complete access to God in the new covenant through Christ (cf. Heb. 10.19-22).

In light of our purpose in this chapter, Heb. 9.22-24 is another striking example which demonstrates that the terms ἐπουράνιος and οὐρανός are synonymous, and in the case of this passage, interchangeable. In 9.23 the author of Hebrews writes that cleansing was necessary both for the copies of the things in the heavens (τὰ ὑποδείγματα τῶν ἐν τοῖς οὐρανοῖς) and yet also for the heavenly things (τὰ ἐπουράνια) themselves. With these expressions, the author of Hebrews provides a clear contrast between 'the earthly things' and 'the heavenly things'.[97] The expression which he uses for the contrast with the earthly things, however, is not the typical τὰ ἐπὶ τῆς γῆς or τὰ ἐπίγεια. Rather, the writer employs τὰ ὑποδείγματα before the expression τῶν ἐν τοῖς οὐρανοῖς to denote 'the earthly things'. Of particular significance is the fact that the expressions τῶν ἐν τοῖς οὐρανοῖς and τὰ ἐπουράνια are complete equivalents and refer to the exact same thing.[98] In the great majority of the examples we have examined, there is a minor difference in usage between ἐπουράνιος and οὐρανός simply because one term is an adjective (ἐπουράνιος) and the other a noun (οὐρανός); however, in 9.23, since τὰ ἐπουράνια is a substantive, both phrases (τὰ ἐπουράνια and τῶν ἐν τοῖς οὐρανοῖς) are properly understood as 'noun' phrases and so are completely interchangeable. It is probable that the author of Hebrews here employs these two different terms and expressions simply for stylistic purposes.[99] Finally, Christ's entrance into heaven (οὐρανός) as

96 See Ellingworth, *Hebrews*, p. 479. From the appearance of the singular οὐρανόν, coupled with its description as the presence of God, Lane concludes that there is a distinction between the singular and plural forms of οὐρανός, οὐρανοί, respectively in Hebrews. Lane writes that the plural οὐρανοί is usually the description of choice for the writer, but in 9.24 he employs the singular οὐρανός to refer to the highest heaven as the abode of God, *Hebrews*, p. b:248. Lane's conclusion proves to be hasty and unfounded though, since the usage of οὐρανός, οὐρανοί in Hebrews does not warrant such a distinction. For example, the author uses the singular οὐρανοῦ in 11.12 to refer to the stars of heaven (τὰ ἄστρα τοῦ οὐρανοῦ) while he utilizes the plural οὐρανοῖς in 8.1 for the dwelling place of God (ὃς ἐκάθισεν ἐν δεξιᾷ τοῦ θρόνου τῆς μεγαλωσύνης ἐν τοῖς οὐρανοῖς). Ellingworth's conclusion that 'Hebrews' language about heaven is impossible to fit into a single consistent schema' and that 'there is almost certainly no distinction of meaning between the singular and the plural of οὐρανός' better accords with the citations in Hebrews, *Hebrews*, p. 476. Ellingworth also notes that the usage of ἐπουράνιος in Hebrews does not allow for a distinction in the heavens either, *Hebrews*, pp. 476–77.

97 As noted above, τὰ ὑποδείγματα τῶν ἐν τοῖς οὐρανοῖς is a clear reference to the earthly things. See also Johnson, *Hebrews*, p. 242.

98 Cf. Max Zerwick and Mary Grosvenor who also regard the expressions τὰ ἐν τοῖς οὐρανοῖς and τὰ ἐπουράνια as equivalent, *A Grammatical Analysis of the Greek New Testament* (vol. 2, Epistles – Apocalypse; Rome: Biblical Institute Press, 1979), p. 674.

99 We will explore this notion and its possible significance for a proper understanding of the heavenlies in Ephesians in more detail later in the book.

the presence of God (9.24) provides even further confirmation that the terms ἐπουράνιος and οὐρανός are synonymous and always refer to that which is spatially distinct from the earth.[100]

10. Hebrews 11.16

In Heb 11.4-12 the writer briefly recounts the stories of Abel, Enoch, Noah, and Abraham and commends them as examples of those who lived by faith. In 11.13-16 the author of Hebrews pauses in his description of Abraham's faith in order to '(give) his interpretation of the history of salvation'.[101] According to v. 13, all[102] of these Old Testament heroes died[103] in faith without receiving complete fulfilment of the promises made to them. Likewise they considered themselves to be strangers and exiles on the earth (ἐπὶ τῆς γῆς) (v. 13) who were seeking a homeland (v. 14). In v. 16 the author of Hebrews writes that these Old Testament heroes of faith were longing for a better homeland, a heavenly one (ἐπουρανίου). As a result, God has prepared a city for them.

For our purposes, we will focus our attention on two matters: (1) that these Old Testament heroes of faith were strangers and exiles[104] ἐπὶ τῆς γῆς and (2) that these Old Testament heroes of faith were seeking a heavenly (ἐπουρανίου) country. Within the context of Hebrews 11, the prepositional phrase ἐπὶ τῆς γῆς could be a reference either narrowly

100 Contra McGough who maintains that there is a distinction in meaning between the expressions τῶν ἐν τοῖς οὐρανοῖς and τὰ ἐπουράνια, 'Investigation', p. 45. McGough provides no real analysis when he writes that τὰ ἐπουράνια 'are spiritual realities made available for Christians through Christ', 'Investigation', p. 46. For his discussion, see McGough, 'Investigation', pp. 45–46.

101 Ellingworth, *Hebrews*, p. 592. Ellingworth notes that the author's placement of these verses in the centre of this passage underscores their prominence, *Hebrews*, p. 592.

102 Here we follow Ellingworth, who notes that the immediate reference of οὗτοι in v. 13 is to Abraham and Sarah (and also possibly Isaac and Jacob) who in Scripture were explicitly said to be temporary residents in Canaan. However, the author's use of πάντες suggests a broader reference which includes both the heroes previously mentioned (vv. 4–12) and the ones to be mentioned later (vv. 17–40), Ellingworth, *Hebrews*, p. 593. Cf. Heb. 11.39, where another appearance of οὗτοι πάντες clearly refers to all of the heroes of the faith in Hebrews 11. Contra Lane who limits the reference of οὗτοι πάντες primarily to Abraham and Sarah and secondarily to Isaac and Jacob, *Hebrews*, p. b:356. Bruce also limits the reference to Abraham, Isaac, Sarah, and Jacob, but notes that in a general sense it can be true of all of the OT men and women who died in faith, *Hebrews*, p. 298.

103 Though Enoch did not die, he is not an exception here since he also had not received the complete fulfilment of God's promises when he was taken up. It places too much emphasis on ἀπέθανον to make Enoch an exception. So Ellingworth, *Hebrews*, p. 593. Contra Lane, *Hebrews*, p. b:356; Attridge, *Hebrews*, p. 329.

104 Given the context, LXX Gen. 23.4 is probably the source of ξένοι καὶ παρεπίδημοί, though the precise expression which appears in Gen. 23.4 is πάροικος καὶ παρεπίδημος. Lane accounts for the different expression in Heb. 11.13 as stylistic variation, *Hebrews*, p. b:357.

to the land of Canaan[105] or broadly to the whole earth.[106] However, it seems best to understand this phrase, as well as the entire passage, as an immediate allusion to the Abraham story with a broader reference and application to all of the patriarchs that are mentioned in Hebrews 11. Thus the writer exploits Abraham's experience as a foreigner 'in the land' as a metaphor for the experiences of all of these heroes of faith who also were strangers 'on the earth' and longed for a better homeland, a heavenly one (ἐπουρανίου). Of significance in our examination is that in the description of these Old Testament heroes, there is a clear contrast between ἐπὶ τῆς γῆς[107] (11.13) and the heavenly (ἐπουράνιος) homeland (11.16).[108] The heavenly homeland which these Old Testament heroes desired is an obvious reference to the city which God has prepared for them (11.16), the heavenly Jerusalem (12.22). Luke Timothy Johnson appropriately describes this heavenly homeland when he writes:

> The city that God has prepared for the patriarchs is not an earthly one, but is located in the very homeland they seek; it is God's own city, toward which the author's hearers are themselves streaming in their faithful pilgrimage (Heb. 12.22). Again, the pilgrimage of the people of faith is continuous, having from beginning to end the same structure of obedience and loyalty, the same goal of the presence of the living God.[109]

Thus the description of the homeland as ἐπουράνιος not only signifies a clear distinction with that which is associated with the earth, but also signifies the ultimate goal of the Old Testament patriarchs and the Christian community – the presence of God. As a result, it is clear that the meaning and usage of ἐπουράνιος in Heb. 11.16 is consistent with our argument that the term always refers to that which is spatially distinct from the earth.[110]

105 So Lane who believes the reference to Abraham in vv. 8-10 signifies that the land of Canaan is in view, *Hebrews*, p. b:346, note w.

106 So Ellingworth who considers the contrast with ἐπουράνιος in v. 16 to reflect a broader view of the entire earth, *Hebrews*, p. 595. Similarly, Attridge does not limit the expression ἐπὶ τῆς γῆς to the land of Israel but rather understands it as a reference to the earth in general and also notes that it is typical in Hebrews for the author to reinterpret the biblical language for Canaan, *Hebrews*, pp. 330–31.

107 Regardless of whether one translates ἐπὶ τῆς γῆς (11.13) as 'in the land' or 'on the earth', the expression would still serve as a spatial contrast to ἐπουρανίου in 11.16.

108 See Ellingworth who also notes this contrast, *Hebrews*, pp. 593, 598.

109 Johnson, *Hebrews*, pp. 293–94.

110 Contra McGough who writes that 'ἐπουράνιος in Heb. 11.16 suggests a realm of reality, spiritual in nature, made explicit by the Christ event', 'Investigation', p. 47. With this analysis, McGough once again spiritualizes the meaning and usage of the term ἐπουράνιος.

11. Hebrews 12.22

Hebrews 12.14-29 serves as a final warning not to refuse God's gracious word and turn away from him.[111] In order to emphasize the severity of his warning, the author of Hebrews contrasts the old and new covenants through the metaphors of Mount Sinai and Mount Zion. He reminds his readers that they have not come (προσεληλύθατε) to a mountain that can be touched (i.e. Mount Sinai) (v. 18) or to the ominous, fearful dread evoked by the old covenant (vv. 18-21) which led Moses to say that he was full of fear (v. 21).[112] Rather, they have come (προσεληλύθατε)[113] to Mount Zion,[114] to the city of the living God,[115] to the heavenly Jerusalem (Ἰερουσαλὴμ ἐπουρανίῳ),[116] to myriads of angels in festal gathering,[117] to the assembly of the firstborn enrolled in heaven (ἐν οὐρανοῖς),[118] to God, to the spirits of the righteous,[119] and to Jesus who is the mediator of a

111 So Lane, *Hebrews*, pp. b:435–91, especially 488. See also Ellingworth, *Hebrews*, pp. 661–92.

112 Included within this notion of fear under the Sinai covenant is the great distance between God and those who worship. The description of Sinai in vv. 18–21 associates this covenant with fear and thus the unapproachability of God, Lane, *Hebrews*, p. b:464.

113 Note the contrast between the old Sinai covenant and the new Zion covenant through the repetition of the verb προσεληλύθατε with the conjunction ἀλλά; see also Lane, *Hebrews*, p. b:465. Whereas the old covenant represented by Sinai was characterized by fear, the writer characterizes the new Zion as a joyful atmosphere. Zion's description as 'city of the living God' and 'heavenly Jerusalem' along with the presence of angels in festal gathering and the church of the firstborn demonstrate the approachability of God under the new covenant in Christ, Lane, *Hebrews*, pp. b:464–65. See also Ellingworth who contends that the primary contrast is not between fear and joy but rather lesser and greater revelation, *Hebrews*, p. 682.

114 Johnson writes that the reference to 'Mount Zion' denotes 'God's eschatological rule through Christ', *Hebrews*, pp. 330–31.

115 Cf. Heb. 11.16.

116 All three phrases, 'Mount Zion', 'city of the living God', and 'heavenly Jerusalem', should be understood as references to the locus of God's presence. 'City of the living God' clarifies the meaning of 'Mount Zion' and 'heavenly Jerusalem' provides further identification for 'city of the living God'. So Lane, *Hebrews*, pp. b:441, note hh, 465–66, and Ellingworth, *Hebrews*, p. 677. For a brief analysis of the biblical and apocalyptic tradition behind these three designations, see Lane, *Hebrews*, p. b:466.

117 The position of the καί after πανηγύρει leads us to connect the term with the preceding μυριάσιν ἀγγέλων rather than the following ἐκκλησίᾳ πρωτοτόκων. So Lane, *Hebrews*, pp. b:441–42, note jj; cf. Johnson, *Hebrews*, pp. 331–32. This would be in contradistinction to the NASB translation.

118 The 'assembly of the firstborn enrolled in heaven' should be understood as a reference to the redeemed people of God rather than as a reference to angels, Lane, *Hebrews*, pp. b:467–69, 472. That this assembly of the whole people of God includes those presently on earth indicates that it is to be understood as an eschatological gathering in which those on earth take part through faith, Lane, *Hebrews*, pp. b:469, 472; cf. Bruce, *Hebrews*, p. 359; Attridge, *Hebrews*, p. 375.

119 Πνεύμασι δικαίων should be understood as 'an idiom for the godly dead' and 'refers to those who have died but now inhabit the heavenly city ... under both covenants', Lane, *Hebrews*, p. b:470.

new covenant (vv. 22-24).[120] Though the new covenant under Christ is characterized by a joyful atmosphere with full access to God, the writer reminds his readers that if there was no escape for those who refused God when he warned ἐπὶ γῆς, then there will surely be judgement for those who turn away from God when he warns ἀπ' οὐρανῶν (v. 25).[121] God will demonstrate this final, eschatological judgement through a shaking of not only the earth, but also of heaven (v. 26).[122]

Hebrews 12.22-26 also proves to be a significant passage for a proper understanding of ἐπουράνιος and its relationship to οὐρανός. The identification of the heavenly Jerusalem (Ἰερουσαλὴμ ἐπουρανίῳ) with the 'city of the living God' naturally leads to the conclusion that the location depicted by the 'heavenly Jerusalem' is the locus of God's presence.[123] This implication is made explicit when the author of Hebrews continues and writes that believers have also come to myriads of angels, to God, and to Jesus (9.22-24). For our purposes, it is of great significance that the description of Ἰερουσαλὴμ ἐπουρανίῳ is also identified as the location of the assembly of the firstborn enrolled ἐν οὐρανοῖς (9.23). Thus it is evident in this passage that the terms ἐπουράνιος and οὐρανός refer to the same location and are references to that which is spatially distinct from the earth.[124] An additional appearance of οὐρανός in 12.25 where God warns from heaven (ἀπ' οὐρανῶν) only serves to reinforce our argument.[125]

120 For brief discussions of the blood of Christ under the new covenant which speaks better than the blood of Abel, see Lane, *Hebrews*, pp. b:473–74, and Ellingworth, *Hebrews*, pp. 682–83. Lane notes that these two images of Jesus as the mediator of the new covenant and the superior, efficacious blood of Christ place this vision of the heavenly Jerusalem in a salvation-historical perspective, *Hebrews*, p. b:490.

121 Note in v. 25 the use of both temporal and spatial categories to represent the old and new covenants. Regarding the spatial contrast Lane writes, 'The expressions "on earth" and "from heaven" are used in a local sense to indicate the sphere of the old covenant and the new covenant respectively', *Hebrews*, p. b:476.

122 Lane writes that Heb. 12.26, and the surrounding context of 12.25-29, can be considered a 'parenetic midrash', *Hebrews*, p. b:447. Note the broadening of the earthly contrast from the earthly Mt Sinai in vv. 18-24 to the entire earth in 12.25-29. For brief discussions on 12.25-29 and the eschatological judgement through the shaking of both heaven and earth, see Lane, *Hebrews*, pp. b:474–88, 491, and Ellingworth, *Hebrews*, pp. 683–92.

123 Johnson compares the reference to Ἰερουσαλὴμ ἐπουρανίῳ with Rev. 3.12, Rev. 21.2, and Gal. 4.26, *Hebrews*, p. 331.

124 Contra McGough who writes that 'the heavenly Jerusalem seems to refer to an order of existence that is spiritual in nature', 'Investigation', p. 47. Similarly, McGough also writes that 'the significance of ἐπουράνιος in Heb. 12.22 concerns an order of existence, spiritual in nature, that is operative here and now', 'Investigation', p. 47. Here we do not dispute the fact that the experience of 'the heavenly Jerusalem' for believers has a spiritual component (i.e. of/from the Spirit). Rather, we dispute both McGough's argument that the term ἐπουράνιος lacks a spatial distinction with the earth and McGough's definition of the term ἐπουράνιος as 'spiritual'.

125 There is a final appearance of οὐρανός in 12.26 where God promises a final judgement which will consist of the shaking of both the earth (τὴν γῆν) and heaven (τὸν

Hebrews 12.22-24 proves to be of significance not only for a proper understanding of the term ἐπουράνιος, but also for its conceptual merit as an additional passage in which believers on earth are granted a heavenly status. As discussed briefly above, in 12.18-24 the author of Hebrews details some essential differences between the old Mosaic covenant represented by Sinai and the new covenant in Christ represented by Zion.[126] From these images, we contend that the fundamental difference between these respective covenants is the approachability of God in the new covenant in contrast to the severe restrictions for approaching God in the old covenant.[127] In 12.22-24 the author of Hebrews employs the metaphor of a pilgrimage to the heavenly Jerusalem to highlight believers' present access to and experience of God.[128] The fact that believers have already arrived (προσεληλύθατε) at the heavenly Jerusalem emphasizes the realized eschatological character of their experience. William Lane regards this arrival at the heavenly Jerusalem as proleptic and writes, 'Through new covenant faith, which grasps the future as though it were present reality (11.1), Christians have come to a reality that is not perceptible to the senses because it is essentially future, the city of the living God.'[129] Though the ultimate fulfilment of believers' life in the heavenly Jerusalem is still future, believers nevertheless already participate in the heavenly community through faith in Christ, the mediator of the new covenant.[130] Consequently, this proleptic experience of 'heaven' in Heb. 12.22-23 provides a possible parallel to Eph. 2.6 where believers are seated in the heavenlies because of their union with Christ.[131]

οὐρανόν). Whether, as Ellingworth maintains, οὐρανός here refers only to the visible heaven rather than the presence of God, is of no consequence for our argument. See Ellingworth, *Hebrews*, p. 687.

126 Lane, *Hebrews*, p. b:489.

127 Lane, *Hebrews*, p. b:490.

128 Lane, *Hebrews*, p. b:490; cf. Ellingworth who believes the theme of believers' pilgrimage to their heavenly goal is evident throughout the entire epistle, *Hebrews*, p. 678.

129 Lane, *Hebrews*, p. b:490; cf. Johnson who similarly describes this arrival at the heavenly Jerusalem as proleptic, *Hebrews*, p. 328.

130 See Lane, *Hebrews*, pp. b:465, 467–69, 472; Bruce, *Hebrews*, pp. 357–59.

131 Similar to studies in Ephesians, the heavenly status granted to believers in Heb. 12.22–23 has also led Hebrews' scholars to draw comparisons between this passage and the Qumran manuscripts. For brief discussions, see Ellingworth, *Hebrews*, pp. 676–78, and Lane, *Hebrews*, p. b:468.

12. Conclusions for New Testament Examination of Ἐπουράνιος

The results of our New Testament examination of the term ἐπουράνιος are conclusive. Of the ten passages examined,[132] the term ἐπουράνιος appears in five passages with the term οὐρανός with no distinction in the locations they represent (Jn 3.12-13; 1 Cor. 15.39-49; Heb. 8.1-6; Heb. 9.22-24; Heb. 12.22-26). Though the term οὐρανός does not appear in Heb. 3.1, there is nevertheless an implicit connection between the location of the κλήσεως ἐπουρανίου and the location of the risen Christ ἐν τοῖς οὐρανοῖς (8.1). Six of the ten passages associate the term ἐπουράνιος with the presence of God (Jn 3.12-13; 2 Tim. 4.18; Heb. 8.1-6; Heb. 9.22-24; Heb. 11.13-16; Heb. 12.22-26). Of particular interest and significance are the completely interchangeable and equivalent expressions τὰ ἐπουράνια and τῶν ἐν τοῖς οὐρανοῖς in Heb 9.23, where the author seemingly alternates between these various 'heaven' terms and expressions merely for stylistic purposes. In eight of the ten passages, there is either a direct contrast between ἐπουράνιος and the earth (Jn 3.12-13; 1 Cor. 15.39-49; Phil. 2.9-11; Heb. 8.1-6; Heb. 11.13-16) or an implicit contrast between ἐπουράνιος and the earth (2 Tim. 4.18; Heb. 9.22-24; Heb. 12.22-26). As we concluded in our examination of ἐπουράνιος outside the New Testament, what our findings demonstrate is that there is also no precedent for a major distinction in meaning between ἐπουράνιος and οὐρανός/οὐράνιος within the New Testament.[133] Additionally, our findings demonstrate that though the term ἐπουράνιος can have various meanings and nuances, it always refers to that which is spatially distinct from the earth. As a result, from our examination of ἐπουράνιος in the New Testament, we conclude that there is no precedent or basis for a spiritualization of the heavenlies in Ephesians or an interpretation such as Odeberg's wherein he defines the heavenlies as the spiritual environment of the church on earth.[134]

132 As previously stated, the term ἐπουράνιος appears fourteen times in the NT outside Ephesians; however; since five of these occurrences are in 1 Cor. 15.39-49, our examination consisted of ten NT passages.

133 Contra McGough, 'Investigation', pp. 45, 50.

134 See Odeberg, *View*, p. 12. See our history of interpretation for a list of NT scholars who have followed or been influenced by his interpretation. Additionally, our findings are also a direct refutation of McGough who similarly spiritualizes the heavenlies in 'Investigation', pp. 95–96, 102–103.

13. Conclusions for Lexical Examination of 'Ἐπουράνιος

Our purpose in chapters 3 and 4 was to examine the meaning and usage of the term ἐπουράνιος in both biblical and non-biblical texts. Consequently, our examination serves as a contribution to the field of New Testament studies as it represents the most comprehensive analysis of the term ἐπουράνιος. Within our examination, two primary arguments have informed our understanding of ἐπουράνιος. First, we have argued that though the term ἐπουράνιος can have different nuances in meaning, it always refers to that which is spatially distinct from the earth. Second, and of equal importance, we have argued that the term ἐπουράνιος is synonymous with other 'heaven' terms such as οὐράνιος and οὐρανός. Our development and demonstration of these two arguments also serve as another important contribution to the field of New Testament studies.[135] From our examination, we conclude that there is no justification within the New Testament, the Old Testament, the Apocrypha, the Old Testament Pseudepigrapha, Philo, the Apostolic Fathers, or other Greek literature either to understand the term ἐπουράνιος in the manner which Odeberg, McGough, and those who follow Odeberg have, or to posit a major distinction in meaning between ἐπουράνιος and οὐρανός/οὐράνιος. Additionally, it is not correct to reason, as Odeberg has, that since τὰ ἐπουράνια are not contrasted with the earth in Ephesians, they must consequently be distinguished from the οὐρανοί and understood as the spiritual atmosphere of the church on earth. As we have thoroughly demonstrated, the term ἐπουράνιος is regularly utilized in contrast with the earth, even within the New Testament and the larger Pauline corpus. Consequently, since there is no precedent or basis for the spiritualization of the heavenlies in Ephesians, we must conclude that commentators such as McGough and Odeberg are misguided in their interpretations.

In all probability, the primary concerns of Odeberg and McGough are to keep believers on the earth and the spiritual forces of evil out of heaven.[136] It does not seem plausible to them that the redeemed on earth should already be granted a heavenly status (Eph. 2.6) or that the forces of evil should be present in heaven (Eph. 6.12). As a result, these presuppositions drive their exegesis of these texts and in the case of McGough, also his exegesis of the texts in his word study. By spiritualizing the heavenlies in Ephesians and interpreting them as the spiritual life of the church on earth, they can make sense of their theological

135 As previously noted, there are others such as Caragounis (*Mysterion*, pp. 146–50) and Best (*Ephesians*, pp. 116–17) who have made similar arguments but they have also in turn done very little to develop and prove these arguments. As a result, our examination in chapters 3 and 4 serves to build upon, develop, and demonstrate the arguments of Caragounis and Best.

136 Similarly, Best also writes that Odeberg is concerned to keep believers on earth, *Ephesians*, p. 117.

presuppositions. The problem, as we have duly noted, is that there is no such precedent within the lexical usage of ἐπουράνιος for such an interpretation or for a distinction between the terms ἐπουράνιος and οὐρανός. On the contrary, the lexical usage of ἐπουράνιος is consistent with and synonymous with the meaning of οὐρανός/οὐράνιος.

14. Implications for 'the Heavenlies' in Ephesians

From our study of the term ἐπουράνιος, there are two primary implications for our examination of the heavenlies in Ephesians. The first implication is that in Ephesians the terms ἐπουράνιος and οὐρανός describe the same general location. The second implication is that the expressions ἐν τοῖς ἐπουρανίοις and ἐν (τοῖς) οὐρανοῖς in Ephesians are synonymous and interchangeable.[137] Since there is absolutely no basis for a major distinction in meaning between these terms or phrases in any Greek literature, it is necessary that we understand and interpret them within their lexical range and usage. As Ernest Best has argued, five appearances of ἐπουράνιος and four of οὐρανός in Ephesians are too few to sustain a major distinction between the terms when their normal meaning is the same.[138]

In the Old Testament, the שָׁמַיִם, or the LXX ὁ οὐρανός/οἱ οὐρανοί, generally could refer to any of the space above the earth such as either the sky/atmosphere where the birds fly or the firmament.[139] Within Old Testament and Jewish thought, however, the שָׁמַיִם, or the LXX ὁ οὐρανός/οἱ οὐρανοί, were also understood as the dwelling place of God.[140] Traub notes that 'in such cases שָׁמַיִם is the dimension above the firmament'.[141] The New Testament's usage of οὐρανός is consistent with the Old Testament's usage and we find references to the birds τοῦ οὐρανοῦ (Mt. 6.26), the stars τοῦ οὐρανοῦ (Heb. 11.12), and the dwelling place of God ἐν οὐρανοῖς (Eph. 6.9), ἐν τοῖς οὐρανοῖς (Heb. 8.1), and εἰς

137 For others who have argued that these expressions in Ephesians are more or less synonymous, see Traub, *TDNT*, p. 5:539; Percy, *Probleme*, pp. 181–82, note 7; Bietenhard, *Die himmlische Welt*, p. 211, note 1; Lincoln, 'Re-Examination', p. 479; Lincoln, *Paradise*, p. 140; Lincoln, *Ephesians*, p. 20; Best, *Ephesians*, pp. 116–18; Calvin R. Schoonhoven, *The Wrath of Heaven* (Grand Rapids: Eerdmans, 1966), p. 61.

138 Best, *Ephesians*, pp. 116–17.

139 See further the discussions of Traub, *TDNT*, pp. 5:497–543, especially 502–503, and H. Bietenhard, 'Heaven, Ascend, Above', *NIDNTT*, pp. 2:184–96 (188–96). See also Jonathan T. Pennington, *Heaven and Earth in the Gospel of Matthew* (NovTSup 126; Leiden: Brill, 2007), pp. 41–44. Additionally, see Pennington's detailed and thorough discussions of heaven in OT and Second Temple literature, οὐρανός in LXX and Second Temple literature, and οὐρανός in Matthew, Pennington, *Heaven and Earth*, pp. 39–161.

140 Traub, *TDNT*, pp. 5:497–543, especially 502–503; Bietenhard, *NIDNTT*, pp. 2:190–93; Pennington, *Heaven and Earth*, pp. 44–46.

141 Traub, *TDNT*, p. 5:503.

οὐρανόν (1 Pet. 3.22). Since the terms ἐπουράνιος and οὐρανός/οὐράνιος are properly understood as synonymous, the term ἐπουράνιος can likewise carry any of these basic meanings and so refer to the sky, the firmament, or the dwelling place of God. In the New Testament, we find references to the sun, moon, and stars as σώματα ἐπουράνια (1 Cor. 15.40-41) and a description of God's dwelling place ἐν τοῖς ἐπουρανίοις (Eph. 1.20). As a result, when we encounter the term ἐπουράνιος or the expression ἐν τοῖς ἐπουρανίοις in Ephesians, we should expect a reference either to the sky, the firmament, or the dwelling place of God.

In the introduction of this book, we argued that the session of earthly believers ἐν τοῖς ἐπουρανίοις and the presence of evil powers ἐν τοῖς ἐπουρανίοις are the two statements which have caused the most confusion for New Testament scholars. As we detailed in our history of interpretation, the result is that the majority of scholars have followed or been influenced by Odeberg's interpretation and spiritualized the heavenlies in Ephesians. Our examination of the term ἐπουράνιος has demonstrated, however, that there is no basis or justification for such an interpretation. As a result, we must turn elsewhere to make sense of the difficult statements about the heavenlies in Ephesians. In our examinations of Eph. 2.6 and Eph. 6.12, we will investigate similar concepts from Scripture, the Qumran manuscripts, and apocalyptic literature in order to shed light on these difficult statements. Within these investigations, we will also discuss the significance of Pauline eschatology, Pauline cosmology, and Paul's doctrine of union with Christ for a proper understanding of these statements. In our examinations of Eph. 1.3, Eph 1.20, and Eph. 3.10, we will investigate other significant concepts related to the heavenlies in Ephesians such as heavenly blessing, the heavenly reign of Christ, Paul's understanding of evil spiritual powers, and the revelation of God's mystery to the evil spiritual powers. It is to these tasks which we now turn.

Chapter 5

Exegetical and Conceptual Analysis of Ephesians 1.3-14

1. *Introduction*

Scholars of the New Testament have long noted the distinctive form and character of Eph. 1.3-14.[1] In the Greek text, the passage is one long sentence of 202 words and consists of a collection of participial phrases, genitive constructions, compound prepositional phrases, infinitive clauses, and relative clauses. The elevated language, liturgical style, and hymnic qualities of Eph. 1.3-14 have led some commentators to draw comparisons with the Qumran manuscripts and likewise have led others to explore the possibility that the passage was a hymn. Though there is divergence of opinion on the form, style, and structure of Eph. 1.3-14, we agree with O'Brien who contends that the passage 'is an *ad hoc* prosaic creation in which the author, by means of exalted liturgical language (some of which was possibly borrowed from early Christian worship), praises God for His glorious plan of salvation, and edifies the readers'.[2] In writing the eulogy, Paul's intent is likely to remind his readers of the greatness of their salvation so that they will also respond with praise to God.[3] Additionally, the eulogy serves to introduce many of the themes and important ideas in the letter.[4] Themes such as God's bringing all things together in Christ (vv. 9-10),[5] divine grace (vv. 4-8),

1 For discussions of the form, structure, and function of Eph. 1.3-14, see Peter T. O'Brien, 'Ephesians I: An Unusual Introduction to a New Testament Letter', *NTS* 25.4 (1979), pp. 504–16; Nils Alstrup Dahl, 'Das Proömium des Epheserbriefes', *Studies in Ephesians: Introductory Questions, Text- & Edition-Critical Issues, Interpretation of Texts and Themes* (ed. David Hellholm, Vemund Blomkvist, and Tord Fornberg; WUNT 131; Tübingen: Mohr Siebeck, 2000), pp. 315–34.

2 O'Brien, 'Unusual Introduction', p. 509.

3 See O'Brien, *Ephesians*, pp. 92–93, 123.

4 See O'Brien, 'Unusual Introduction', pp. 509–12; O'Brien, *Ephesians*, pp. 93, 117, 123; Turner, 'Ephesians', p. 1225; Aletti, *Éphésiens*, pp. 53–54.

5 From Eph. 1.9–10, O'Brien identifies 'cosmic reconciliation and unity in Christ (as) ... the central message of ... Ephesians', *Ephesians*, p. 58; cf. Max Turner, 'Mission and Meaning in Terms of "Unity" in Ephesians', *New Bible Commentary* (ed. D. A. Carson, R. T. France, J. A. Motyer, and G. J. Wenham; Leicester: InterVarsity, 4th edn, 1994), pp. 138–66. While scholars have often been hesitant to ascribe a central theme

mystery (vv. 8-10), the Spirit (vv. 3, 13-14), Jew–Gentile relations (vv. 11-14), the heavenlies (v. 3), and salvation through Christ are all significant ideas which will be expounded in Ephesians.[6]

Within our examination of Eph. 1.3-14, there are a host of scholarly, theological, and grammatical issues which we could explore.[7] It is not our purpose, however, merely to rehash academic and theological interests which have already been investigated in prior studies of Ephesians. As a result, we will focus our attention on issues which will advance a proper understanding of the heavenlies and the use of the expression ἐν τοῖς ἐπουρανίοις in Ephesians.[8] In our discussion of Eph. 1.3-14, we will examine three principal issues: (1) the 'berakah' form in the Old Testament, Septuagint, and the New Testament; (2) the notion of heavenly blessing in the Old Testament and Jewish literature; and (3) heavenly blessing in Eph. 1.3-14.

2. *The Berakah Form*

The first appearance of the expression ἐν τοῖς ἐπουρανίοις occurs near the very beginning of Ephesians when we read, 'Blessed *be* the God and Father of our Lord Jesus Christ, who has blessed us with every spiritual blessing in the heavenly *places* in Christ' (1.3). After his customary introductory greeting (vv. 1-2), Paul writes this statement as the beginning of an extended eulogy or 'berakah' which comprises one lengthy sentence of 202 words in the Greek text and spans 12 verses (vv. 3-14).[9] Paul begins his berakah with an outburst of praise and worship for the salvation accomplished by God through Christ in the lives of the readers.[10] From the very outset, the emphasis of this berakah can be seen

to Ephesians, we agree with O'Brien that this message provides the best summary and 'draws together ... many of its major themes ... to gain an integrated picture of the letter as a whole', O'Brien, *Ephesians*, p. 58. For a full discussion of this central message of Ephesians, see O'Brien, *Ephesians*, pp. 58–65, 88–123.

6 O'Brien, *Ephesians*, pp. 93, 117, 123; cf. Aletti, *Éphésiens*, pp. 53–54. O'Brien notes that Paul utilizes these themes both for didactic and exhortatory purposes, *Ephesians*, p. 93.

7 E.g., the structure of the passage, hymnic qualities, comparisons with Qumran, and possible themes and motifs in Ephesians.

8 Here we should state that this will also be the case for all of the passages we examine in Ephesians. Our purpose in the examinations of Eph. 1.3-14, 1.15-23, 2.1-10, 3.1-13, and 6.10-13 is to advance the discussion of and a proper understanding of the heavenlies in Ephesians. It is not our purpose merely to rehash the academic and theological interests covered in prior studies of Ephesians.

9 O'Brien writes that 'in the typical Old Testament *berakoth* the name of God is followed by a relative pronoun and a participial clause which gives the reasons for praising God', *Ephesians*, p. 94.

10 See O'Brien, *Ephesians*, p. 89; O'Brien, 'Unusual Introduction', pp. 504, 509.

through the play on words, '*Blessed* (Εὐλογητός) be the God and Father of our Lord Jesus Christ, who has *blessed* (εὐλογήσας) us with every spiritual *blessing* (εὐλογίᾳ) ...'[11]

This emphasis on praise coupled with its distinct stylistic features has led a number of commentators to conclude that this passage in Ephesians contains hymnic characteristics.[12] However, as previously noted, we believe it is better to understand the composition as the original work of Paul. That Eph. 1.3-14 is the work of Paul does not rule out the possibility that Paul adopted some of the language from the worship traditions of the church in his formulation of the passage.[13] The traditional material, however, is neither great enough nor distinct enough to warrant the conclusion that there is a pre-existent hymn or eulogy behind these verses.[14] Finally, in his assessment, Jack T. Sanders writes, 'Thus every attempt to provide a strophic structure for Eph. 1.3-14 fails, and places in very grave doubt the thesis that we have to do here with the quotation of a hymn.'[15]

Scholars have also observed that this berakah is characterized by an accumulation of participial phrases, genitive constructions, compound prepositional phrases, infinitive clauses, and relative clauses. Such a style is typical of liturgical language and is probably the result of Semitic influence.[16] In his article 'The Epistle to the Ephesians in the Light of the Qumran Texts', Karl Georg Kuhn draws attention to many of these characteristics and contends that they are reminiscent of the liturgical and hymnic language of the Qumran texts and their Hebraic style.[17] In

11 Emphasis mine.

12 See our brief discussion of the hymnic qualities in Eph. 1.3-14 in chapter 2, 'The History of Interpretation'; see also Sanders, 'Hymnic Elements'.

13 Lincoln, *Ephesians*, pp. 14, 20; cf. O'Brien, *Ephesians*, pp. 90–91.

14 So Lincoln, *Ephesians*, p. 14. In arriving at this conclusion, Lincoln rightly observes the similarity in language and style with the rest of chapters 1–3 in Ephesians and also the close connections between Ephesians and Colossians, *Ephesians*, p. 14. See further Aletti's discussion of the structure, composition, and character of Eph. 1.3–14, *Éphésiens*, pp. 44–54.

15 Sanders, 'Hymnic Elements', p. 227. O'Brien notes that Sanders's conclusion still remains true even though there have been subsequent attempts to discern the structure of a hymn since Sanders wrote his article, O'Brien, *Ephesians*, p. 90.

16 O'Brien, *Ephesians*, p. 90. Additionally, in his rhetorical analysis of Ephesians, Ben Witherington III has demonstrated that the language and style of Ephesians, and in particular Eph. 1.3-14, are consistent with Asiatic epideictic rhetoric which was also characterized by rhythm, ornate language, elegant diction, ornamentation, repetition, praise, and long sentences, *Letters*, pp. 1–10, 219–23, 227–37. Witherington III writes that it is not surprising to find such Asiatic rhetoric in a document which was addressed to Asia Minor, *Letters*, pp. 2, 9, 222–23.

17 See, e.g., Karl Georg Kuhn, 'The Epistle to the Ephesians in the Light of the Qumran Texts', in *Paul and Qumran: Studies in New Testament Exegesis* (ed. Jerome Murphy-O'Connor; London: Geoffrey Chapman, 1968), pp. 115–31, especially 116–17. In addition to these stylistic similarities, Kuhn maintains that there are parallels in the

his summary, Kuhn argues that 'it is difficult to avoid the conclusion that the relationship of the language and style of the Epistle to the Ephesians to that of the Qumran texts can hardly be explained except on the basis of a continuity of a tradition'.[18] While such parallels have proved convincing to some, it would be misguided to conclude that the author of Ephesians, whether Paul or one who wrote in the Pauline tradition, was a member of the Qumran or Essene community.[19] The similarities can be accounted for from the more general influence of the liturgical language common to a variety of Jewish writings and traditions.[20]

The use of the berakah form is found in all types of Jewish literature from the Pentateuch and the Psalter in the Old Testament[21] to Second Temple Jewish writings including Qumran and rabbinic literature.[22] In the Old Testament, we find a few examples which exhibit some loose similarities with some of the themes in Ephesians. In 1 Chron. 29.10-13 the God of Israel is to be praised (εὐλογητός) for his power, glory, victory, and majesty (vv. 10-11). The Lord has dominion over all, including everything ἐν τῷ οὐρανῷ καὶ ἐπὶ τῆς γῆς (v. 11), and he is also the source of all blessing as riches and honour come from him (v. 12). In LXX Ps. 67.19-22 the Lord is to be praised (εὐλογητός) because he is the one who bears burdens and because he is the source of salvation (ὁ θεὸς τῶν σωτηρίων) (v. 20). He is the God of deliverance (ὁ θεὸς ἡμῶν θεὸς τοῦ σῴζειν) (v. 21), the source of escape from death (v. 21), and the ruler over his enemies (v. 22). In Prayer of Azariah 1.29-68 (LXX Dan. 3.52-90), the Lord is to be praised (εὐλογητός) and highly exalted forever. All that is on the earth and all that is in the heavens are to praise

Qumran manuscripts with a number of expressions found in Ephesians, one of which is 'the purpose of his will' (1.9; 3.3; 6.19) which appears in Eph. 1.3-14, pp. 117–19. See also O'Brien's discussion in 'Unusual Introduction', pp. 507–509.

18 Kuhn, 'Epistle', p. 120.

19 See Best, *Ephesians*, pp. 8, 91–92.

20 See also O'Brien, 'Unusual Introduction', pp. 507–509; Aletti, *Éphésiens*, pp. 34–36.

21 The OT and LXX are filled with appearances of the berakah in various forms. Examples include Gen. 9.26; Gen. 14.19-20; Gen. 24.27; Exod. 18.10; Ruth 4.14; 1 Sam. 25.32-33; 1 Sam. 25.39; 2 Sam. 18.28; 1 Kgs 1.48; 1 Kgs 5.7; 1 Kgs 8.15; 1 Kgs 8.56; 1 Kgs 10.9; 1 Chron. 16.36; 1 Chron. 29.10-13; 2 Chron. 2.11; 2 Chron 6.4; Ezra 7.27-28; Ps. 27.6; Ps. 30.22; Ps. 40.14; Ps. 65.20; Ps. 67.19; Ps. 67.36; Ps. 71.18-19; Ps. 88.53; Ps. 105.48; Ps. 118.12; Ps. 123.6; Ps. 134.21; Ps. 143.1; Zech. 11.5; Prayer of Azariah 1.3; Prayer of Azariah 1.29; Dan. 3.95; 1 Esd. 4.40; 1 Esd. 4.60; 1 Esd. 8.25; Jdt. 13.17-18; Tob. 3.11; Tob. 8.5; Tob. 8.15-17; Tob. 11.14; Tob. 13.2; 1 Macc. 4.30. All references cited are from the LXX.

22 See further Nils Alstrup Dahl, 'Benediction and Congratulation', *Studies in Ephesians: Introductory Questions, Text- & Edition-Critical Issues, Interpretation of Texts and Themes* (ed. David Hellholm, Vemund Blomkvist, and Tord Fornberg; WUNT 131; Tübingen: Mohr Siebeck, 2000), pp. 279–314. Dahl conducts an extensive study of the berakah form in both Jewish and Christian literature with numerous examples. Cf. O'Brien, *Ephesians*, pp. 89–90.

the Lord who saves from death (1.66) and whose mercy endures forever (1.67-68).

From its Old Testament and Jewish roots, we find that a Christian form of the berakah also develops.[23] Outside Ephesians 1, we find other examples of the New Testament berakah in Lk. 1.68-75, 2 Cor. 1.3-4, and 1 Pet. 1.3-5. Luke 1.68-75 follows closely the Old Testament pattern in which the name of God is followed by a relative pronoun and a participial clause[24] and reads, 'Blessed *be* the Lord God of Israel, For He has visited us and accomplished redemption for His people ...' In the other New Testament examples (2 Cor. 1.3-4; Eph. 1.3-14; 1 Pet. 1.3-5) we find a distinctively Christian emphasis with the inclusion of Christ in the introductory phrase 'Blessed be the God *and Father of our Lord Jesus Christ*'[25] (Εὐλογητὸς ὁ θεὸς καὶ πατὴρ τοῦ κυρίου ἡμῶν Ἰησοῦ Χριστοῦ). In 2 Cor. 1.3-4 we find another example of a letter in the Pauline corpus which begins with the distinctive New Testament berakah, though the themes and length of the berakah in 2 Cor. 1.3-4 are quite different than in Eph. 1.3-14. In 1 Pet. 1.3-5, which also appears at the beginning of the letter, we find some similar themes to those found in Ephesians 1. God is praised for the salvation accomplished through Christ (cf. Eph. 1.13) which is revealed in the last time (cf. Eph. 1.10). Furthermore, this salvation is a result of the great mercy of God (cf. Eph. 1.5, 7) and is described as an inheritance (cf. Eph. 1.13-14) which is reserved ἐν οὐρανοῖς[26] and protected by the power of God.

3. *Implications from Berakah Study*

From this brief analysis, we see that the berakah form was widespread in Old Testament and Jewish literature. From these roots, early Christian writers also adopted the form and imbued it with a distinctively Christian flavour by inserting καὶ πατὴρ τοῦ κυρίου ἡμῶν Ἰησοῦ Χριστοῦ to the standard Εὐλογητὸς ὁ θεός formula. In addition, New Testament writers often employed this Christian form of the berakah to begin their letters.[27] Some of the distinctive themes which appear in Ephesians'

23 O'Brien, *Ephesians*, p. 89; cf. Dahl, 'Benediction', pp. 280–81, 301; Dahl, 'Proömium', p. 315.

24 O'Brien, *Ephesians*, p. 94.

25 Emphasis mine.

26 First Peter 1.3-4's description of salvation as being born again through the resurrection of Jesus Christ from the dead and an inheritance which is reserved in heaven (τετηρημένην ἐν οὐρανοῖς) also bears some similarities with Paul's description of salvation in Eph. 2.5-6 where believers are made alive and seated with Christ in the heavenlies.

27 See also the discussions of Dahl in 'Benediction', pp. 296–308, and 'Proömium', pp. 315–19. Dahl notes that there is precedent for an opening benediction in Jewish letters, 'Benediction', pp. 296–300, 307–308.

berakah are also found in other Old Testament and New Testament eulogies. While the evidence does not warrant any sort of allusion or direct dependence, it does allow for the possibility that Paul here drew upon traditional Old Testament, Jewish, and Christian material in formulating the opening eulogy of Eph. 1.3-14.[28] Thus it is quite possible that Jewish or Christian traditional liturgical language served as the origin of the expression ἐν τοῖς ἐπουρανίοις in Ephesians.[29]

4. *Heavenly Blessing in the Old Testament and Jewish Literature*

The notion of 'blessing' which is associated with heaven has some minor attestation both in the Old Testament and in Jewish literature. Often, heavenly blessing is associated with the cosmological and meteorological function of rain on the land. This seems to be the case in Deut. 28.12 when the Lord proclaims to his people, 'The LORD will open for you His good storehouse, the heavens (אֶת־הַשָּׁמַיִם) (τὸν οὐρανόν), to give rain to your land in its season and to bless all the work of your hand; and you shall lend to many nations, but you shall not borrow.'[30] In *1 En.* 11.1-2, in an eschatological context, God promises that he 'shall open the storerooms of blessing which are in the heavens, so that (he) shall send them down upon the earth, over the work and the toil of the children of man' (Isaac). Similarly, in 11Q14, the writer proclaims:

> May the Most High God bless you. May he shine His face towards you and open to you His good treasure which is in heaven to bring down on your land showers of blessing, dew, rain, early rain, and late rain in His/its time to give you the fruit of the produce of corn, wine and oil plentiful. May the land produce for you fruits of delight ...[31]

Obviously this sort of heavenly blessing should be understood as God's provision of rain from the heavens (skies) for God's people.

At other places, it is difficult to identify precisely the nature of the heavenly blessing. In Gen. 49.25-26, the Almighty blesses Joseph with the blessings of heaven above (וִיבָרְכֶךָּ בִּרְכֹת שָׁמַיִם) (εὐλόγησέν σε εὐλογίαν οὐρανοῦ ἄνωθεν). In Tob. 9.6 Gabael blesses Tobias when he proclaims,

28 Lincoln, *Ephesians*, p. 14; cf. O'Brien, *Ephesians*, p. 91; Dahl, 'Benediction'. In his comparison of 2 Cor. 1.3-7, Eph. 1.3-14, and 1 Pet. 1.3-7, Dahl writes that 'it (is) likely that these eulogies reflect a form that was used also by Paul and other preachers', 'Benediction', p. 301.

29 We have already seen the expression in *Testament of Job*. As previously mentioned, Lincoln also allows for this possibility as an analogy with expressions such as ἐν ὑψίστοις in Mk 11.10 or ἐν ὑψηλοῖς in Heb. 1.3, *Ephesians*, p. 20.

30 Cf. Mal. 3.10-12.

31 See also 4Q285, fragment 1.

'May the Lord grant the blessing of heaven to you and your wife, and to your wife's father and mother' (NRSV). At still other times, the notion of heavenly blessing seems to imply a primarily future fulfilment such as in *Gk. Apoc. Ezra* 1.14 when the righteous man receives his reward in the heavens. Perhaps the closest parallel to the heavenly blessing depicted in Eph. 1.3-14 is found in Qumran's 1QSb 1.4-6 which reads:

> May the [Lord bless you from the Abode of His holiness]; may He open for you from heaven an eternal fountain which [shall not fail]! May He [favour] you with every [heavenly] blessing; [may He teach you] the knowledge of the Holy Ones! [May He unlock for you the] everlasting [fountain; may He not withhold the waters of life from] them that thirst![32] (Vermes)

In this passage, the writer beseeches the Lord to bless the faithful from his abode (i.e. heaven), to open for them from heaven an eternal fountain, to grant them every heavenly blessing, and to teach them the knowledge of the Holy Ones. From the context, the identification of this heavenly blessing should probably be understood as the knowledge of the Holy Ones. In 1QSb 1.4-6 we find, therefore, a subtle distinction between its more spiritual blessing and the physical heavenly blessing of most Old Testament and Jewish passages.[33]

5. *Heavenly Blessing in Ephesians 1.3-14*

When we read Eph. 1.3-14, what is immediately striking is the explicit nature and character of the heavenly blessing conferred on believers by God himself. In an astounding statement, Paul writes in Eph. 1.3 that God has blessed believers with every spiritual blessing in the heavenlies in Christ. The interpretive grid for understanding these blessings no doubt lies in the significance of the three prepositional phrases found in this verse: (1) ἐν πάσῃ εὐλογίᾳ πνευματικῇ; (2) ἐν τοῖς ἐπουρανίοις; (3) ἐν Χριστῷ.[34] In our examination of the heavenly blessing of Eph. 1.3-14, we will focus our attention on these three significant phrases.

32 Unless otherwise noted, all citations from Qumran are from Vermes. Hypothetical but likely reconstructions are enclosed in [ ].

33 See also 1QS 11.3-10 and 1QH 11, Hymn 10 for additional examples from Qumran of blessings of a spiritual and heavenly nature, though the gifts listed are neither explicitly described as 'blessings' or 'from (or of) heaven'. On the other hand, the present blessings of 1QS 4.8-9 – healing, peace, long life, and fruitfulness – appear to be of a more earthly and physical nature.

34 So Lincoln who writes that 'the three ἐν phrases in v. 3 combine to sum up in a general way the content of God's blessing of believers for which he is to be blessed and which will be elaborated in the rest of the eulogy', *Ephesians*, p. 19.

In the Old Testament, blessing from God is almost uniformly of an earthly and physical nature. The typical Old Testament blessings from God include descendants, (good) land, rain, produce, victory over enemies in battle, wealth, honour, and prosperity. Perhaps the general nature of blessing in the Old Testament is best characterized in Deut. 28.1-14 where the Lord promises Israel prosperity, land, offspring, produce, protection, and military success for obedience. In stark contrast to these Old Testament blessings, we read in Eph. 1.3 that God has blessed believers with *every spiritual blessing* in the heavenlies in Christ.[35] At first glance, such a statement may appear enigmatic to the reader of Ephesians; however, the identification of these blessings should be understood and identified within the context of the passage. The spiritual blessings which Paul has in mind then are election (vv. 3-4, 11), sonship (v. 4), lavished grace (vv. 6-8), redemption (vv. 7, 14), forgiveness of sins (v. 7), revelation of the mystery of his will (v. 9), salvation (v. 13), and sealing with the Holy Spirit (vv. 13-14).[36] In addition to the context, the adverb καθώς also links the phrases ἐν πάσῃ εὐλογίᾳ πνευματικῇ ἐν τοῖς ἐπουρανίοις ἐν Χριστῷ of v. 3 with the blessings that follow in vv. 4-14. With his use of the aorist εὐλογήσας,[37] Paul clearly intends to communicate both a present receiving and a present experience of these spiritual blessings in the lives of believers, though their final fulfilment and realization still lie in the future.[38]

Paul's description of these blessings as πνευματικός should evoke conceptions neither of a general mystical nature nor of a personal, private character.[39] Rather, their description as πνευματικός signifies that the blessings are 'bound up with the Holy Spirit'.[40] Further con-

35 Emphasis mine. O'Brien argues that these spiritual blessings are not primarily a contrast to the material blessings of Deut. 28.1-14, *Ephesians*, p. 95. While it is in all probability true that Paul did not have in mind the material blessings of Deut. 28.1-14 when he wrote of God's spiritual blessings in 1.3-14, there is nevertheless a distinction between the material blessing in Deuteronomy and the spiritual blessing in Ephesians. Thus there is a clear contrast in the nature of these respective blessings even if the explicit contrast was not the primary intent of Paul.

36 See also O'Brien, *Ephesians*, p. 89; O'Brien, 'Unusual Introduction', p. 504; cf. Dahl, 'Proömium', pp. 319–24.

37 The aorist εὐλογήσας is indicative of the completed and past action of God. See Best, *Ephesians*, p. 114; Lincoln, 'Re-Examination', p. 470.

38 Cf. Lincoln, *Paradise*, pp. 141–42; O'Brien, *Ephesians*, p. 97. Turner tends to regard God's blessing of believers ἐν πάσῃ εὐλογίᾳ πνευματικῇ in Eph. 1.3 primarily as future when he writes, 'Paul is, of course, aware that he and his readers have not yet themselves experienced *every spiritual blessing*, hence his qualifications. We have received this blessing only *in the heavenly realms* and *in Christ* ... The essentially future blessing, which we have begun to experience in Christ, is further assured on the grounds of God's election ...,' Turner, 'Ephesians', p. 1225. There is no reason, however, to understand the receipt and experience of these spiritual blessings as primarily future if we identify the spiritual blessings as what follows in vv. 4-14.

39 See also Lincoln, *Ephesians*, p. 19.

40 Lincoln, *Ephesians*, p. 19; cf. O'Brien, *Ephesians*, p. 95.

firmation of this can be found with the description of these blessings as ἐν Χριστῷ (1.3) and with Paul's declaration that believers have been sealed τῷ πνεύματι τῆς ἐπαγγελίας τῷ ἁγίῳ (1.13). M.-É. Boismard notes well this connection between the Holy Spirit, being 'in Christ', and the spiritual blessing when he writes, 'C'est une bénédiction "spirituelle" car Dieu la réalise par le don de son Esprit Saint (v. 13b; cf. *infra*) "dans les cieux et dans le Christ."'[41] Paul's depiction of this divine blessing as ἐν Χριστῷ means that it is both the result of Christ's agency and also the result of believers' incorporation into Christ.[42] The sealing of the Spirit and the Spirit's description as an ἀρραβών of believers' inheritance also serve to highlight the present experience of these spiritual blessings 'in Christ' as well as their complete realization in the future.[43] What we find in Eph. 1.3-14, therefore, is an intimate connection between believers' union with Christ, sealing with the Holy Spirit, and sharing in the blessings of the Holy Spirit.[44] Thus the blessings of the Holy Spirit are bestowed on those who are 'in Christ' and who have been sealed with the Holy Spirit.[45]

In Eph. 1.3-14, not only do we find an intimate connection between believers' union with Christ and sharing in the blessings of the Holy Spirit, but we also find a connection between believers' union with Christ, the blessings of the Spirit, and believers sharing in heavenly reality.[46] It is interesting to note here that no other New Testament passage speaks explicitly of heavenly blessing. There are, however, a few additional places in the New Testament in which spiritual benefits are associated with heaven.[47] In 2 Cor. 5.1-2 Paul writes that believers possess a building from God, a house αἰώνιον ἐν τοῖς οὐρανοῖς and that they long to be clothed with this dwelling ἐξ οὐρανοῦ. In Col. 1.5 Paul

41 Boismard, *Éphésiens*, p. 20. See further Boismard's full discussion where he identifies the three primary themes and structural parts of the benediction as God, Christ, and the Spirit, *Éphésiens*, pp. 18–23.

42 Lincoln, *Ephesians*, pp. 21–22; O'Brien, *Ephesians*, pp. 97–98.

43 H. R. Lemmer, 'Reciprocity between Eschatology and Pneuma in Ephesians 1:3-14', *Neot* 21 (1987), pp. 159–82 (174). See also Neill Q. Hamilton's excellent discussion on the Spirit and eschatological tension in *The Holy Spirit and Eschatology in Paul* (Scottish Journal of Theology Occasional Papers 6; Edinburgh: Oliver and Boyd, 1957), pp. 26–40.

44 For an excellent discussion, see Lemmer, 'Reciprocity', pp. 159–82, especially 169; cf. Hamilton, *Holy Spirit*, pp. 20, 83.

45 See Hamilton, *Holy Spirit*, p. 83. Hamilton writes, 'By virtue of the fact that the benefits are inseparable from Christ's person, the Spirit, in communicating the benefits of redemption, in effect communicates Christ. Thus from the standpoint of the believer receiving these benefits the Spirit and the Lord are one,' Hamilton, *Holy Spirit*, p. 83.

46 Lemmer, 'Reciprocity', p. 176. Lincoln also closely associates the heavenly world with the spiritual world (i.e. of the Spirit) in 'Re-Examination', pp. 469–71; cf. Lincoln, *Ephesians*, pp. 19–21.

47 Lincoln references Col. 1.5 and 2 Cor. 5.1-2 in 'Re-Examination', p. 471.

insists that believers' hope is laid up ἐν τοῖς οὐρανοῖς. As we noted above, the closest New Testament parallel is 1 Pet. 1.3-5 which describes salvation as an inheritance reserved ἐν οὐρανοῖς to be revealed in the last time.

Of these New Testament references, what is immediately striking is the realized eschatological emphasis of Eph. 1.3 in comparison with the more future eschatological tone of the other passages. Though in Eph. 1.3-14 the blessings are from heaven, they are nonetheless present benefits for believers since these spiritual blessings are the result of God's salvation which he has accomplished in Christ.[48] It is probable that Paul's emphasis on the ἀνακεφαλαιώσασθαι of all things in Christ, the things ἐπὶ τοῖς οὐρανοῖς and ἐπὶ τῆς γῆς (Eph. 1.10), accounts for some of this realized eschatological emphasis. The fact that Paul stresses that God has granted every spiritual blessing ἐν τοῖς ἐπουρανίοις to those in Christ also implies that believers need not look elsewhere or outside Christ for God's rich spiritual blessing. This realized eschatological emphasis of Ephesians reaches its culmination when we read in 2.6 that God has raised believers with Christ and seated them with him ἐν τοῖς ἐπουρανίοις in Christ Jesus. In Eph. 1.3, therefore, Paul introduces a theme of Ephesians in which believers in Christ are closely associated with the blessings of heaven.

The fact that the blessings which God grants to believers are described as ἐν τοῖς ἐπουρανίοις carries a local connotation. Since, as we previously noted, the expression ἐν τοῖς ἐπουρανίοις is utilized as a fixed formula throughout Ephesians, the force of the preposition ἐν is clearly local.[49] In Eph. 1.3 the phrase indicates that the source and origin of the spiritual blessing is heaven or as Paul writes in Ephesians ἐν τοῖς ἐπουρανίοις.[50] The reference to the heavenlies as the origin and location of God's rich blessing indicates its 'other-worldly' character. In this sense, there is an implicit contrast between the source of God's blessing ἐν τοῖς ἐπουρανίοις and the earth. Moreover, since God, as the giver, is also the source of the spiritual blessing, the expression ἐν τοῖς ἐπουρανίοις is almost certainly a reference to the abode of God. Thus the meaning of ἐν τοῖς ἐπουρανίοις in Eph. 1.3 is consistent with our argument that the expression is synonymous with ἐν (τοῖς) οὐρανοῖς and is a reference to that which is spatially distinct from the earth.[51]

48 See also Lincoln, *Ephesians*, pp. 19–22.

49 For our discussion, see history of interpretation.

50 Cf. Best, *Ephesians*, p. 114; Hoehner, *Ephesians*, p. 168.

51 Contra McGough who argues that in Eph. 1.3 the heavenlies refer to 'a realm of existence that embraces both temporal and eternal realities' which 'is not to be defined or located as a region or locality above the earth', 'Investigation', p. 58.

6. *Conclusions*

In our examination of Eph. 1.3-14, we noted that the berakah form was quite common and was utilized in various types of Jewish literature. Some New Testament writers also made use of the berakah form but yet also imbued it with a distinctly Christian character. Additionally, we discovered that themes such as God's deliverance, God's reign over his enemies, God's salvation for his people, and God's bestowal of blessing on his people are all common in Jewish and Christian eulogies and so allow for the possibility that Paul drew upon traditional material in his formulation of Eph. 1.3-14. As a result, we concluded that such traditional material might have indeed served as the origin for the initial appearance of the expression ἐν τοῖς ἐπουρανίοις in Ephesians.[52] In our examination of Eph. 1.3-14, we also provided an original contribution to the field of the New Testament with our study of heavenly blessing. In this study, we observed that it was somewhat common to associate God's blessing with the spatial 'heaven' designation. The most common example of heavenly blessing in Jewish literature was God's physical provision of rain for the land, though we also noted more ambiguous examples of heavenly blessing. The Qumran text 1QSB 1.4-6 proved to be the closest parallel to Eph. 1.3-14 as it linked heavenly blessing with knowledge and salvation. Finally, in our examination of Eph. 1.3-14, we noted that there is an intimate connection between the Holy Spirit, the eschatological heavenly blessing which is bestowed on those 'in Christ', and believers' participation in heavenly realities. As a result, in Eph. 1.3, Paul introduces a theme for Ephesians in which believers are closely associated with the blessings of heaven.

52 We have already noted an appearance of the expression in *T. Job* 36.3.

Chapter 6

Exegetical, Conceptual, and Lexical Analysis of Ephesians 1.15-23

1. *Introduction*

Like the eulogy which precedes it, Eph. 1.15-23 is similarly characterized by liturgical language. These verses also comprise one lengthy sentence in Greek with multiple participial phrases, genitive constructions, compound prepositional phrases, and various subordinate clauses.[1] In regard to its structure, most commentators agree that the passage includes a thanksgiving (vv. 15-16a), an intercessory prayer (vv. 16b-19), and confessional material about Christ's resurrection and exaltation (vv. 20-23), though these categories and sections blend together and are at times difficult to distinguish.[2] Ephesians 1.15-23 is logically and clearly connected with 1.3-14 with the opening words Διὰ τοῦτο.[3] Thus for Paul, the natural result of the Lord's abundant blessing of believers is to give thanks for his addressees' faith in Christ and love for the saints. As he gives thanks, Paul moves seamlessly into intercession for his readers when he prays that God would grant them the Spirit[4] of wisdom and revelation in the knowledge of Christ, that the eyes of their heart would be enlightened, and that they would know the hope of God's calling, the riches of God's inheritance in the saints,[5] and God's great power for believers. As many of the themes in his prayer are reminiscent of those in the eulogy, Paul in effect prays here for the full

1 On account of the elevated language and stylistic features, some scholars have argued that 1.20-23 should also be regarded as an early Christian hymn. For brief discussions, see Sanders, 'Hymnic Elements', pp. 220–23; Lincoln, *Ephesians*, pp. 50–52; Best, *Ephesians*, p. 157.

2 So Lincoln, *Ephesians*, pp. 47–54; O'Brien, *Ephesians*, pp. 124–26.

3 See O'Brien, *Ephesians*, pp. 124–27.

4 We take πνεῦμα here as a reference to the Holy Spirit. For brief discussions, see O'Brien, *Ephesians*, pp. 131–33; Lincoln, *Ephesians*, pp. 56–58; Best, *Ephesians*, pp. 162–64.

5 Here we take ἁγίοις in 1.18 and ἁγίους in 1.15 as references to believers, or more specifically, all of God's people which include both Jews and Gentiles; see also O'Brien, *Ephesians*, pp. 128, 136, note 177; Lincoln, *Ephesians*, pp. 55, 59–60; Best, *Ephesians*, pp. 160, 167–68; Hoehner, *Ephesians*, pp. 250, 267.

realization of the blessings (vv. 3-14) which God has so richly bestowed on those who are in Christ.[6]

Paul's prayer for his readers to know the greatness of God's power then leads him to write what commentators have termed 'confessional material' concerning Christ's resurrection, enthronement, and reign (1.20-23). In order to convince his readers, Paul writes that the power that is at work in believers (v. 19) is the same power which God used to raise (ἐγείρας) Christ from the dead and seat (καθίσας) him at God's right hand ἐν τοῖς ἐπουρανίοις (v. 20).[7] Paul also emphasizes Christ's exalted status at God's right hand through his declaration that Christ rules over his enemies (v. 21), has authority over all things (v. 22), and is the head over the church (v. 22).[8] Finally, Paul concludes this section with his statement that the church is Christ's body,[9] the fullness of him who fills all in all.[10] For our purposes, we will focus our attention on the confessional material which describes Christ's resurrection, enthronement, and exaltation. Our

6 So O'Brien, *Ephesians*, pp. 125, 129; O'Brien, 'Unusual Introduction', p. 514; cf. Lincoln, *Ephesians*, p. 50.

7 See O'Brien who writes that 'the decisive demonstration of God's power available to believers occurred in the resurrection and exaltation of Christ, as well as in the subjection of the powers to him and his being given as head over everything to the church', *Ephesians*, p. 139. God's life-giving power which is also at work in believers who are united with Christ is what can lead Paul later to write in Eph. 2.5-6 that believers are raised and seated with Christ in the heavenlies. Cf. Col. 2.12. See O'Brien's discussion in *Ephesians*, pp. 139–41.

8 Here we take τῇ ἐκκλησίᾳ as a reference to the universal church. See also Lincoln, *Ephesians*, p. 67; Andrew T. Lincoln and A. J. M. Wedderburn, *The Theology of the Later Pauline Letters* (New Testament Theology; Cambridge: Cambridge University Press, 1993), pp. 92–93; Best, *Ephesians*, pp. 625–26, 639; Hoehner, *Ephesians*, p. 287. Contra O'Brien who insists that the term ἐκκλησία must always refer to a local congregation and so concludes that it refers to a heavenly gathering of believers around Christ, O'Brien, *Ephesians*, pp. 146–47; see also O'Brien's more thorough discussion in Peter T. O'Brien, 'The Church as a Heavenly and Eschatological Entity', *The Church in the Bible and the World: An International Study* (ed. D. A. Carson; Exeter: Paternoster, 1987), pp. 88–119, 307–11. For a brief critique of this particular view, see Lincoln, *Ephesians*, pp. 66–67. Lincoln correctly recognizes that in numerous places, Paul utilizes the term ἐκκλησία to refer to 'an entity which is broader than the merely local congregation (cf. Gal. 1.13; 1 Cor. 10.32; 12.28; 15.9; Phil. 3.6)', *Ephesians*, p. 67. Similarly, Col. 1.18, 24 and all nine of the references in Ephesians describe the universal church as the entire Christian community, Lincoln, *Ephesians*, p. 67; cf. Lincoln and Wedderburn, *Theology*, pp. 92–93.

9 This mysterious identification of the church as Christ's body is possibly another outworking of Paul's doctrine of believers' union with Christ (cf. Eph. 2.5-6). On Christ as the head of the church and the head's relation to the body in 1.22-23, see O'Brien, *Ephesians*, pp. 144–48 and Best, *Ephesians*, pp. 189–96.

10 We take the phrase τὸ πλήρωμα τοῦ τὰ πάντα ἐν πᾶσιν πληρουμένου as a metaphor in which the church is the fullness of Christ which Christ fills. See Turner, 'Ephesians', p. 1228. Turner writes, 'To "fill" is a metaphor for "become present to, and active in respect of" or "extend influence, or rule, over",' Turner, 'Ephesians', p. 1228. Though Christ fills all things, it is the church which Paul specifically calls his πλήρωμα, Turner, 'Ephesians', p. 1228; cf. Lincoln, *Paradise*, p. 147.

analysis will include discussions of three significant themes: (1) Christ's heavenly reign in Eph. 1.20-23; (2) the relationship between the resurrection of Christ and his enthronement; (3) the use of the expression ἐν τοῖς ἐπουρανίοις in Eph. 1.20 and a comparison with other ascension and exaltation texts.

2. *Christ's Heavenly Reign in Ephesians 1.20-23*

In Eph. 1.20 Paul proclaims that God has raised Christ from the dead and seated Christ at God's right hand in the heavenlies. These two events have traditionally been referred to as the resurrection and enthronement (or exaltation) of Christ. In order to emphasize the unique rule and authority granted to Christ, Paul draws upon and alludes to two psalms – Ps. 110 and Ps. 8.[11] Early Christian writers frequently exploited Ps. 110 to communicate the exalted status and power of Christ.[12] In Ps. 110.1-2 (LXX Ps. 109.1-2) we read, 'The LORD says to my Lord: "Sit at My right hand (ἐκ δεξιῶν μου) Until I make Your enemies a footstool for Your feet." [2] The LORD will stretch forth Your strong scepter from Zion, *saying*, "Rule (κατακυρίευε) in the midst of Your enemies."' The king's position at the right hand of God and his rule over his enemies are themes which Paul draws upon and applies directly to Christ in Eph. 1.20-22.[13] Additionally, Paul also draws upon Ps. 8.6 (LXX Ps. 8.7) where God has granted man dominion over all things (καὶ κατέστησας αὐτὸν ἐπὶ τὰ ἔργα τῶν χειρῶν σου πάντα ὑπέταξας ὑποκάτω τῶν ποδῶν αὐτοῦ) when Paul writes in Eph. 1.22 that God has subjected all things under Christ's feet (πάντα ὑπέταξεν ὑπὸ τοὺς πόδας αὐτοῦ).[14]

In his monograph *Messiah and the Throne*, Timo Eskola sets out 'to investigate the relationship between Jewish merkabah mysticism and New Testament exaltation Christology by focusing on the central metaphor of

11 For discussions of Paul's use of Ps. 8 and Ps. 110 in Eph. 1.20-22, see Andrew T. Lincoln, 'The Use of the OT in Ephesians', *JSNT* 14 (1982), pp. 16–57 (40–42), and Frank S. Thielman, 'Ephesians', *Commentary on the New Testament Use of the Old Testament* (ed. G. K. Beale and D. A. Carson; Grand Rapids: Baker Academic, 2007), pp. 813–33 (814–17).

12 For a thorough discussion on the use of Ps. 110 in the formation of early exaltation Christology, see Martin Hengel, '"Sit at My Right Hand!" The Enthronement of Christ at the Right Hand of God and Psalm 110:1', *Studies in Early Christology* (Edinburgh: T & T Clark, 1995), pp. 119–225. For an examination of the development of early Christology and Christ's exalted position next to God in heaven, see Larry W. Hurtado, *One God, One Lord: Early Christian Devotion and Ancient Jewish Monotheism* (Edinburgh: T & T Clark, 2nd edn, 1998).

13 Cf. Erwin Penner who notes that the most important Christological theme in Ephesians is Christ's enthronement, 'Enthronement', p. 12.

14 Cf. 1 Cor. 15.23-28.

the throne'.[15] As Eskola traces the metaphor of the throne through both Old Testament and Jewish literature, he contends that 'the depiction of God as a heavenly King, or the symbol of the throne, belonged to the very core of Jewish Temple liturgy'.[16] Concerning Ps. 110.1, Eskola argues that sitting at God's right hand is a 'submetaphor for the enthronement theme (which) expresses both the great significance of the throne of God and the special status of the enthroned one'.[17] This particular statement in turn began to be utilized and appropriated in Second Temple Jewish theology and New Testament Christology.[18] Eskola subsequently argues that the themes of heavenly court, Temple, and God's throne are metaphors which are common to both Jewish apocalyptic and the New Testament. Whereas Jewish apocalyptic contains ascensions and throne visions, the New Testament writers place Christ at the centre of all these themes and adopt them for Christological purposes in order to demonstrate that Christ has ascended into heaven and now sits on the throne of glory.[19] In Eph. 1.20 Paul clearly draws upon and unites these themes of heavenly ascension and heavenly kingship in his statement that God raised Christ from the dead and seated him at God's right hand in the heavenlies.[20]

In his appropriation of Psalm 110, it is probable that Paul also draws upon the theme of the king's reign over his enemies in Ps. 110.2 (LXX Ps. 109.2) when he writes in Eph. 1.21 that Christ's position at God's right hand is ὑπεράνω πάσης ἀρχῆς καὶ ἐξουσίας καὶ δυνάμεως καὶ κυριότητος καὶ παντὸς ὀνόματος ὀνομαζομένου.[21] A number of scholars have dedicated a

15 Timo Eskola, *Messiah and the Throne: Jewish Merkabah Mysticism and Early Christian Exaltation Discourse* (WUNT 2:142; Tübingen: Mohr Siebeck, 2001), pp. 16–17.

16 Eskola, *Messiah*, p. 63. See chapter 2 of Eskola's monograph for his analysis.

17 Eskola, *Messiah*, p. 61.

18 Eskola, *Messiah*, p. 61.

19 Eskola, *Messiah*, p. 159. Eskola has been especially helpful in elucidating some of the common themes which run throughout Jewish merkabah mysticism and NT Christology. However, we are sceptical of Eskola's supposition that Jewish merkabah mysticism provided the exaltation discourse for the formation of NT exaltation Christology, *Messiah*, pp. 154, 196, 389–90. This notion is true insofar as we also recognize the deep indebtedness of Jewish apocalyptic to the OT and its themes of heavenly kingship, the heavenly throne, and the heavenly Temple found among other places in Psalms, Isaiah, Ezekiel, and Daniel. Eskola also clearly recognizes this great indebtedness (see *Messiah and the Throne*, pp. 52–55, 63, 125, 154), but nonetheless, in our estimation, grants too much prominence to the role of Jewish merkabah mysticism in the formation of NT Christology.

20 Christ's exalted position at the right hand of God demonstrates his authority, sovereignty, and primacy over all of creation, Lincoln, 'Re-Examination', pp. 471–72. In accordance with the usual early Christian tradition, Paul writes ἐν δεξιᾷ in Eph. 1.20 rather than ἐκ δεξιῶν from LXX Ps. 109.1, Best, *Ephesians*, p. 172. Lincoln notes that this change was common in NT passages where the full verse of LXX Ps. 109.1 was not cited, 'Use of the OT', p. 40. For a brief discussion of ἐν δεξιᾷ αὐτοῦ and its relationship to ἐν τοῖς ἐπουρανίοις in 1.20, see Lincoln, 'Re-Examination', pp. 471–72.

21 Alan F. Segal regards Christ's exalted position above παντὸς ὀνόματος ὀνομαζομένου as an implication that Christ 'has been awarded the secret name of God', *Two Powers in*

vast amount of work to the task of identifying the precise meaning of these terms for spiritual powers in the Pauline corpus.[22] It is beyond the scope of this study to engage this conversation in great detail and it would not be beneficial simply to rehash the positions of significant works or major commentaries.[23] For our purposes, it is significant to note that in Ephesians (and the rest of the Pauline corpus), the ἀρχαί, ἐξουσίαι and other related terms[24] are personal,[25] spiritual (or supernatural), and evil[26]

Heaven: Early Rabbinic Reports about Christianity and Gnosticism (SJLA 25; Leiden: Brill, 1977), p. 212; cf. Hoehner who compares this expression with Phil. 2.9 where God has conferred upon Christ τὸ ὄνομα τὸ ὑπὲρ πᾶν ὄνομα and concludes that Christ's status and title as Lord is greater than any other name in heaven or on the earth, Hoehner, *Ephesians*, pp. 280–81. Additionally, Segal writes that rabbinic tradition reserved exclusively for God Paul's description of Christ as sovereign both in this age and in the age to come, *Two Powers*, p. 212.

22 In addition to the normal treatments in commentaries, see, e.g., Sydney H. T. Page, *Powers of Evil: A Biblical Study of Satan and Demons* (Grand Rapids: Baker Books, 1995), especially pp. 184–203, 223–55; Peter T. O'Brien, 'Principalities and Powers: Opponents of the Church', *Biblical Interpretation and the Church: Text and Context* (ed. D. A. Carson; Exeter: Paternoster, 1984), pp. 110–150; Clinton E. Arnold, *Powers of Darkness: Principalities and Powers in Paul's Letters* (Downers Grove, IL: InterVarsity, 1992); Pierre Benoit, 'Pauline Angelology and Demonology: Reflexions on the Designations of the Heavenly Powers and on the Origin of Angelic Evil According to Paul', *Religious Studies Bulletin* 3.1 (1983), pp. 1–18; Carr, *Angels*; Walter Wink, *Naming the Powers: The Language of Power in the New Testament* (Philadelphia: Fortress Press, 1984); Heinrich Schlier, *Principalities and Powers in the New Testament* (Quaestiones Disputatae 3; New York: Herder and Herder, 1961); Timothy G. Gombis, 'Ephesians 2 as a Narrative of Divine Warfare', *JSNT* 26.4 (2004), pp. 403–18; Hoehner, *Ephesians*, pp. 276–80; Best, *Ephesians*, pp. 174–80.

23 Since the powers are a somewhat prominent theme of the heavenlies and appear in three of the five passages which contain the expression ἐν τοῖς ἐπουρανίοις (1.15-23, 3.1-13, and 6.10-20), we will, however, briefly detail our view of the spiritual powers in an excursus which will take into account the passages in Ephesians as well as additional passages from the Pauline corpus.

24 E.g. δυνάμεως and κυριότητος in Eph. 1.21, κοσμοκράτορας τοῦ σκότους τούτου and τὰ πνευματικὰ τῆς πονηρίας in Eph. 6.12 (though τὰ πνευματικὰ τῆς πονηρίας depicts the entire group of evil forces as opposed to a specific class of spiritual powers), θρόνοι in the list of Col. 1.16, and ἄγγελοι in Rom. 8.38, though it is not clear whether the angels in Rom. 8.38 are good or evil. We should clarify here that Paul does not always utilize these terms in the same context or with the same meanings. For example, Paul writes in Phil. 4.15 that at the first preaching of the gospel (ἐν ἀρχῇ τοῦ εὐαγγελίου), only the Philippian church shared in giving and receiving with Paul. Here Paul utilizes the term ἀρχή in its more basic sense of 'beginning'. Additionally, in Rom. 13.1, when Paul writes that every person should be subject to the governing authorities (ἐξουσίαις), he utilizes the term in the more general sense of 'authority'. The passages in the Pauline corpus with references to these terms (in varying lists) as evil, spiritual, and personal powers are Rom. 8.38, 1 Cor. 15.24, Eph. 1.21, Eph. 3.10, Eph. 6.12, Col. 1.16, Col. 2.10, and Col. 2.15. See also the ἀρχόντων of 1 Cor. 2.6-8 as an ambiguous example.

25 Contra Wink who too readily identifies the powers with institutions and political structures, *Naming the Powers*.

26 Contra Carr who argues that in Paul the ἀρχαί, ἐξουσίαι, and other related terms

powers.[27] Additionally, whatever the terms' background, Paul's main point in Eph. 1.20-22 is to emphasize the universality of Christ's rule. Though a number of the terms in Eph. 1.21 also appear in apocalyptic and other Jewish literature to refer to specific ranks of angels, it is not Paul's intent in 1.21 to describe a specific angelology or hierarchy of angels.[28] Rather, Paul's point is that whatever evil spiritual powers there are, Christ is seated at God's right hand, above all of them, and they are all subject to him.[29]

3. The Relationship between the Resurrection of Christ and his Enthronement

As referenced above, scholars have traditionally referred to the two events in Eph. 1.20 as the resurrection and enthronement of Christ. The close association of these events in several biblical texts has sparked some debate among scholars as to their precise relationship. In addition to his central argument that 'the depiction of God as a heavenly King ... belonged to the very core of Jewish Temple theology',[30] Timo Eskola also contends that the resurrection of Christ from the dead serves as his enthronement or installation as king.[31] With this claim, Eskola effectively identifies Christ's resurrection and enthronement as the same event. Though his discussion of this relationship between resurrection and enthronement includes a number of passages, Eskola argues that this connection is explicit in Eph. 1.20.[32]

are references to the good angelic multitude around God's throne, *Angels*. For critiques of Carr's argument, see Clinton E. Arnold, 'The "Exorcism" of Ephesians 6.12 in Recent Research: A Critique of Wesley Carr's View of the Role of Evil Powers in First-Century AD Belief', *JSNT* 30 (1987), pp. 71–87; O'Brien, 'Principalities', pp. 125–28.

27 For additional support of our view, see Page, *Powers*, pp. 244–45; O'Brien, 'Principalities', pp. 133–41; O'Brien, *Ephesians*, p. 144; Lincoln, *Ephesians*, pp. 62–65; Hoehner, *Ephesians*, pp. 279–80; Best, *Ephesians*, p. 176; Arnold, *Power and Magic*, pp. 41–56; Arnold, 'Ephesians', p. 247; Arnold, *Powers of Darkness*, pp. 89–91.

28 So Page, *Powers*, p. 245. Page correctly notes that the various lists in the NT with different terms and the addition of the phrase παντὸς ὀνόματος ὀνομαζομένου to the list in Eph. 1.21 make clear that Paul did not intend here a comprehensive list or an angelic hierarchy; cf. O'Brien, *Ephesians*, pp. 142–43.

29 So also Page, *Powers*, p. 245, and Lincoln, *Paradise*, pp. 145–46. Cf. Col. 2.10 where Christ is κεφαλὴ πάσης ἀρχῆς καὶ ἐξουσίας and 1 Cor. 15.24 where Christ abolishes πᾶσαν ἀρχὴν καὶ πᾶσαν ἐξουσίαν καὶ δύναμιν.

30 Eskola, *Messiah*, p. 63.

31 See Eskola's discussions of Acts 2.22-26, Acts 5.30-31, 1 Cor. 15.4-5, 23-28, and Rom. 8.34 in *Messiah*, pp. 163–64, 183–86, and his detailed analysis of Rom. 1.3-4, *Messiah*, pp. 217–50. See also Eskola's discussion of the relationship between enthronement and resurrection language, namely wordplays with the Hebrew קום and the Greek ἀναστήσω, *Messiah*, pp. 166–67.

32 Eskola, *Messiah*, p. 183.

Eskola's discussions of resurrection and enthronement prove to be valuable for our understanding of the close relationship between resurrection and enthronement. Several passages in Scripture demonstrate this close association and could perhaps lead to the conclusion that resurrection and enthronement refer to the same event; however, we should also note the way in which Christ's resurrection and ascension/enthronement, though closely related, are still separate events and distinct phenomena.[33] Within Jewish literature and tradition, there was often an expectation of resurrection but not necessarily enthronement. The idea of resurrection from the dead was therefore not equated with enthronement or exaltation.[34] In the case of Christ then, his resurrection from the dead by itself does not prove his Messiahship or his status as the exalted Lord. Rather, Christ's resurrection proclaims that he lives forever and his exaltation or enthronement proclaims that he reigns forever.[35] In this sense, the resurrection and ascension/exaltation should be understood as two distinct events; however, many New Testament writers do indeed at times seem to associate closely and even unite these two events (e.g. Eph. 1.20). Their justification for this is likely from their view of Christ who, as the Messiah who is raised from the dead, surely must also be exalted and reign in heaven. Alan Segal writes, 'In most other places in the New Testament, the ascension is closely associated with resurrection ... In the Pauline corpus most of the evidence implies that ascension was implicit in resurrection.'[36] As a result, while on the one hand we can clearly distinguish between the events of resurrection and ascension/enthronement, we can also on the other hand closely associate the two events as they apply to Christ as Messiah.[37] This close relationship between Christ's resurrection and ascension/enthronement

33 See O'Brien for a brief discussion of the distinction between Christ's resurrection and exaltation, *Ephesians*, pp. 140–41. Interestingly, O'Brien cites many of the same texts (Rom. 8.34; Eph. 1.20; Eph. 2.6; Acts 2.32-33) for proof of a distinction between resurrection and enthronement as Eskola does for an identification of the two events. In addition to the references above, O'Brien lists Col. 3.1 and 1 Pet. 3.21-22 in his argument, *Ephesians*, p. 141, note 197. It seems then that an appeal to these NT texts does not provide evidence either for an identification of or a distinction between resurrection and enthronement. Thus any basis for a distinction between or an identification of these two events must come from elsewhere.

34 This idea was first brought to my attention through a conversation with Professor Larry Hurtado, the supervisor of my NT PhD studies.

35 O'Brien, *Ephesians*, p. 141. O'Brien cites and follows Murray J. Harris, *Raised Immortal: Resurrection and Immortality in the New Testament* (London: Marshall, Morgan & Scott, 1983), p. 85. As cited in O'Brien, *Ephesians*, p. 141.

36 Alan F. Segal, 'Heavenly Ascent in Hellenistic Judaism, Early Christianity and their Environment', *ANRW* 23.2, pp. 1333–94 (1373). See further Segal, 'Heavenly Ascent', *ANRW* 23.2, pp. 1371–74.

37 So Segal who writes, 'Thus while resurrection and ascension must be viewed as different phenomena in the strict sense, they are so closely associated by Paul that one virtually implies the other', *ANRW* 23.2, p. 1374.

will also be significant for our understanding of Eph. 2.6 where believers who are united to Christ are also raised up with him and seated with him in the heavenlies.

4. The Use of the Expression ἐν τοῖς ἐπουρανίοις in Ephesians 1.20 and a Comparison with other Ascension and Exaltation Texts

In our examination of the term ἐπουράνιος, we concluded that there was no basis for a major distinction in meaning between the terms ἐπουράνιος and οὐρανός/οὐράνιος or between the phrases ἐν τοῖς ἐπουρανίοις and ἐν (τοῖς) οὐρανοῖς. The implication of our conclusions was that we would proceed on the basis that the expressions ἐν τοῖς ἐπουρανίοις and ἐν (τοῖς) οὐρανοῖς in Ephesians are synonymous and interchangeable. Indeed, the evidence from a wide range of Greek literature including the Old Testament, the New Testament, the Apocrypha, the Old Testament Pseudepigrapha, and the Apostolic Fathers demanded such a course of action. We would be remiss, however, to ignore the equally clear evidence from Ephesians that these 'heaven' expressions are synonymous and interchangeable. As a result, the purpose of this section is to compare the ascension text of Eph. 1.20-23 with other New Testament ascension texts in order further to substantiate our argument that the expressions ἐν τοῖς ἐπουρανίοις and ἐν (τοῖς) οὐρανοῖς are synonymous and interchangeable.

Of critical importance in our analysis of Eph. 1.20 is to establish the original reading of the text. The textual variant ἐν τοῖς οὐρανοῖς rather than the reading ἐν τοῖς ἐπουρανίοις appears in B, 365, 629, a few other manuscripts (designated by *pc*), Syriac Vulgate (Peshitta), and Marius Victorinus. The overwhelming textual evidence, however, confirms that ἐν τοῖς ἐπουρανίοις is the original reading.[38] The textual evidence also coheres with the internal evidence of Christ's resurrection (ἐγείρας) from the dead and subsequent session (καθίσας) ἐν τοῖς ἐπουρανίοις in 1.20 and believers' resurrection (συνήγειρεν) and session (συνεκάθισεν) ἐν τοῖς ἐπουρανίοις in Christ in 2.6. A secondary question is whether or not we should attach any significance to the fact that this textual variant even exists. This is in fact what Lincoln does when he argues that the appearance of the textual variant is evidence for the synonymity of these two expressions.[39] The most likely explanation for the variance in the textual tradition is that copyists, whether knowingly or unknowingly, desired to bring Eph. 1.20 in closer conformity with other ascension and exaltation texts. Whether such an alteration represents the copyists'

38 See also Hoehner, *Ephesians*, p. 275, note 2, though Hoehner incorrectly identifies the variant as οὐρανιοῖς.

39 Lincoln, 'Re-Examination', p. 471.

understanding of the expressions as synonymous is impossible to discern.[40] As a result, we believe it is misguided to argue for a particular interpretation or understanding of ἐν τοῖς ἐπουρανίοις based upon the existence of the textual variant ἐν τοῖς οὐρανοῖς.[41]

In Eph 1.15-23 the term οὐρανός does not appear and the expression ἐν τοῖς ἐπουρανίοις is not directly contrasted with the earth.[42] However, throughout the New Testament, there are numerous examples of other ascension and enthronement texts which should inform our understanding of ἐν τοῖς ἐπουρανίοις in Eph. 1.20. Below are the New Testament ascension and exaltation texts with an appearance of οὐρανός or another related term:

> **Acts 2.32-35** This Jesus God raised up again, to which we are all witnesses. [33] Therefore having been exalted to the right hand of God, and having received from the Father the promise of the Holy Spirit, He has poured forth this which you both see and hear. [34] For it was not David who ascended into heaven (εἰς τοὺς οὐρανούς), but he himself says: 'THE LORD SAID TO MY LORD, "SIT AT MY RIGHT HAND, [35] UNTIL I MAKE YOUR ENEMIES A FOOTSTOOL FOR YOUR FEET."'

> **Acts 7.55-56** But being full of the Holy Spirit, he gazed intently into heaven (εἰς τὸν οὐρανόν) and saw the glory of God, and Jesus standing at the right hand of God; [56] and he said, 'Behold, I see the heavens (τοὺς οὐρανούς) opened up and the Son of Man standing at the right hand of God.'

> **Col. 3.1** Therefore if you have been raised up with Christ, keep seeking the things above (ἄνω), where Christ is, seated at the right hand of God.

> **Heb. 1.3** And He is the radiance of His glory and the exact representation of His nature, and upholds all things by the word of His power. When He

40 Though they do not, it seems quite reasonable that commentators such as Odeberg and McGough could actually argue for a distinction in meaning between ἐν τοῖς ἐπουρανίοις and ἐν τοῖς οὐρανοῖς based upon the appearance of the textual variant. One could contend that a copyist or editor made such a change to distinguish between the location of the risen Christ in Eph. 1.20 and believers in Eph. 2.6.

41 We should clarify here that we obviously agree with Lincoln's argument that the two expressions are synonymous, Lincoln, 'Re-Examination', p. 479. In addition, we also agree with his contention that 'ἐν τοῖς ἐπουρανίοις has similar force in Eph i. 20 as ἐν τοῖς οὐρανοῖς has in...other references to the ascension', 'Re-Examination', p. 471. Our disagreement is with Lincoln's assertion that the appearance of the textual variant in 1.20 confirms that the expressions are synonymous.

42 Ephesians 6.9 does state, however, that the Lord is ἐν οὐρανοῖς. The location of the Lord ἐν οὐρανοῖς (6.9) should be understood as the same location of the risen Christ at the right hand of God ἐν τοῖς ἐπουρανίοις (Eph. 1.20). See also Bietenhard, *Die himmlische Welt*, p. 211, note 1, and Lincoln, who follows Bietenhard, in 'Re-Examination', p. 471. Contra Odeberg, *View*, p. 9, and McGough, 'Investigation', pp. 158–60, who argue for a distinction in meaning between the expressions ἐν τοῖς ἐπουρανίοις in 1.20 and 2.6 and ἐν οὐρανοῖς in 6.9.

had made purification of sins, He sat down at the right hand of the Majesty on high (ἐν ὑψηλοῖς) ...

Heb 8.1 Now the main point in what has been said *is this*: we have such a high priest, who has taken His seat at the right hand of the throne of the Majesty in the heavens (ἐν τοῖς οὐρανοῖς).

1 Pet. 3.21-22 Corresponding to that, baptism now saves you – not the removal of dirt from the flesh, but an appeal to God for a good conscience – through the resurrection of Jesus Christ,[22] who is at the right hand of God, having gone into heaven (εἰς οὐρανόν), after angels and authorities and powers had been subjected to Him.

In Acts 2.32-35 Peter declares that God has raised Jesus and exalted him to the right hand of God. The implication of v. 34 is that, in contrast to David, Jesus has ascended εἰς τοὺς οὐρανούς, the very place of Christ's exaltation and authority at the right hand of God. Similarly, in Acts 7.55-56 Stephen gazes εἰς τὸν οὐρανόν and sees the glory of God and Jesus at the right hand of God.[43] Neither Col. 3.1 nor Heb 1.3 employ a 'heaven' term but they both utilize spatial terms to describe the location of the risen Christ at the right hand of God, ἄνω meaning 'above' and ἐν ὑψηλοῖς meaning 'on high' or 'in the high places' respectively.[44] In Heb. 8.1 Christ is at the right hand of God ἐν τοῖς οὐρανοῖς. This particular description of the location of the risen Christ is almost identical with Eph. 1.20, the obvious difference being that Ephesians employs the adjectival substantive ἐπουρανίοις. The exaltation discourse of 1 Pet. 3.21-22 has many similarities with Eph. 1.20-21 as the location of the risen Christ is at the right hand of God in heaven (εἰς οὐρανόν) with angels, authorities, and powers subjected to Christ.

The significance of these six passages is that they, like Eph. 1.20, describe the location of the risen Christ at the right hand of God but with the term οὐρανός (or in some cases another spatial term) rather than ἐπουράνιος. A comparison of these ascension texts with Eph. 1.20 once more confirms our argument that the expressions ἐν τοῖς ἐπουρανίοις and ἐν (τοῖς) οὐρανοῖς, both within and outside Ephesians, are synonymous and indeed even interchangeable.[45] It would be severely misguided and indeed even absurd to conclude that the location of the

43 Whether εἰς τὸν οὐρανόν should be understood here as the abode of God or simply the sky is not certain. It is certain, however, that Stephen beholds a vision of Jesus at the right hand of God and that whatever location is intended by τὸν οὐρανόν, it is spatially distinct from the earth.

44 In these verses, these spatial terms should also be understood as spatially distinct from the earth and as periphrases for heaven.

45 Cf. Traub, *TDNT* 5, p. 539; Percy, *Probleme*, pp. 181–82, note 7; Bietenhard, *Die himmlische Welt*, p. 211, note 1; Lincoln, 'Re-Examination', p. 479; Lincoln, *Paradise*, p. 140; Lincoln, *Ephesians*, p. 20; Best, *Ephesians*, pp. 116–18.

risen Christ at the right hand of God ἐν τοῖς ἐπουρανίοις in Eph. 1.20 is different from the location of Christ at the right hand of God ἐν τοῖς οὐρανοῖς in Heb. 8.1. As a result, we must once more conclude that commentators such as Odeberg, McGough, and others who spiritualize the heavenlies are flawed in their interpretation. Finally, our examinations of the term ἐπουράνιος in Greek literature and the expression ἐν τοῖς ἐπουρανίοις in Eph. 1.20 must inform our understanding of the expression ἐν τοῖς ἐπουρανίοις throughout the whole of Ephesians, even in difficult passages where believers are seated ἐν τοῖς ἐπουρανίοις (2.6) and the spiritual forces of evil reside ἐν τοῖς ἐπουρανίοις (6.12).

5. Conclusions

In Eph. 1.15-23 Paul draws upon and alludes to Psalm 110 and Psalm 8 in order to depict the exalted status and power of Christ in his heavenly reign. Though the resurrection and enthronement of Christ are in the strict sense distinct phenomena, the two events are often intimately associated in the Pauline corpus and this close relationship is explicit in Eph. 1.20. This intimate relationship is significant for our understanding of Eph. 2.6, where believers who are united to Christ are not only raised up with him, but are also seated with him in the heavenlies. Though our discussion of Eph. 1.15-23 has not proved to be groundbreaking within the field of New Testament studies, we have nonetheless highlighted some central Christological themes and demonstrated their significance within the exaltation discourse of Eph. 1.20-23. However, our comparison of Eph. 1.20 with other New Testament ascension and enthronement texts has provided further confirmation for one of our central arguments in this book, namely that the expressions ἐν τοῖς ἐπουρανίοις and ἐν (τοῖς) οὐρανοῖς, both within and outside Ephesians, are synonymous and interchangeable.

Chapter 7

Exegetical and Conceptual Analysis of Ephesians 2.6

1. Introduction

Students of the New Testament encounter various interpretive difficulties when attempting to understand the tension between realized and future eschatology. From the very beginning of the New Testament, this tension finds expression in the descriptions of the Kingdom of God in the gospels. In recent years, interpreters of Paul have paid more attention to the tension of realized and future eschatology within the Pauline corpus. In his commentary on Ephesians, Andrew Lincoln writes 'that the coherent core of Paul's thought, which comes to different expression in a variety of settings, is his eschatology which centers in Christ, and that this is fundamental for the rest of his thinking'.[1] Similarly, Hermann Ridderbos writes:

> one can speak of a growing consensus insofar that scholars are more and more finding the point of departure for an adequate approach to the whole in the *redemptive-historical, eschatological character of Paul's proclamation* ... It is this great redemptive-historical framework within which the whole of Paul's preaching must be understood and all of its subordinate parts receive their place and organically cohere.[2]

While there are references in Ephesians to a future eschatological fulfilment (cf. 1.14; 2.7; 4.30; 5.5; 6.8, 13), the distinctive emphasis remains that of present or realized eschatology.[3] As previously examined, this emphasis is evident from the very beginning of the epistle when we read in Eph. 1.3 that God has blessed believers with every spiritual blessing in the heavenlies in Christ. Indeed, this emphasis on realized eschatology reaches its culmination when we read in Eph. 2.6 that God

1 Lincoln, *Ephesians*, p. lxxxix; cf. also Lincoln's monograph *Paradise Now and Not Yet*.

2 Hermann Ridderbos, *Paul: An Outline of His Theology* (trans. J. R. de Witt; Grand Rapids: Eerdmans, 1975), p. 39. Italics original. See also Geerhardus Vos, *The Pauline Eschatology* (Princeton: Princeton University Press, 1930), p. 11.

3 Lincoln, *Ephesians*, pp. lxxxix–xc.

has raised believers with Christ (συνήγειρεν) and seated them with him (συνεκάθισεν) in the heavenlies in Christ Jesus.[4] Whereas elsewhere in the New Testament believers' reign and session in heaven with Christ is reserved as a future promise, in Eph. 2.6 the redeemed already participate in Christ's rule and exaltation.[5]

Within the larger pericope of Eph. 2.1-10, we find perhaps Paul's clearest picture and presentation of the salvation accomplished by God through Christ.[6] In vv. 1-3 Paul depicts in graphic terms the past sinful and hopeless condition of his readers. In vv. 4-7 Paul writes of the great mercy, love, and grace of God which has been lavished upon believers through Christ. Finally, in vv. 8-10 Paul summarizes the nature of God's salvation accomplished in Christ.[7] We have already observed that in Ephesians certain themes recapitulate and appear in a number of places within the letter. In Eph. 1.15-23 Paul writes of the death, resurrection, and present reign of Christ over his enemies and the church. In 2.1-10, through some remarkable statements, Paul applies these very themes to those who are 'in Christ'. Indeed, the most astonishing statement and the one that has been the most troublesome for New Testament scholars is Paul's declaration that believers have been raised up and seated with Christ ἐν τοῖς ἐπουρανίοις.

For the purposes of this book, we will focus our attention on this perplexing issue – the heavenly status granted to believers in Eph. 2.6. Since we have already established that any interpretation which spiritualizes the heavenlies is not a viable option, we must investigate other alternatives which will assist in making sense of this enigmatic statement. It is our contention that a study of Jewish mysticism sheds light on the heavenly status granted to believers in Eph. 2.6. In our examination, however, we will cast our net more broadly and investigate a host of issues which we believe will illumine Paul's enigmatic statement that believers are seated with Christ ἐν τοῖς ἐπουρανίοις. First, we will provide an abbreviated introduction to the tradition of Jewish (merkabah) mysticism with a brief survey of relevant texts from this

4 On the realized eschatological emphasis of Eph. 2.4-10, Arnold writes, 'There is surely no doubt that the author has emphasized the present aspect of salvation to a degree unparalleled in Paul', *Power and Magic*, p. 147.

5 Lincoln, *Ephesians*, pp. lxxxix–xc. Cf. Rom. 6.5-8 where the resurrection and life of believers with Christ is future. Lincoln compares the present rule depicted in Eph. 2.6 with the future eschatological emphasis of Rev. 3.21 ('He who overcomes, I will grant to him to sit down with Me on My throne, as I also overcame and sat down with My Father on his throne'), *Ephesians*, pp. lxxxix–xc. Believers' resurrection, reign, and session with Christ ἐν τοῖς ἐπουρανίοις in Eph. 2.6 is also somewhat different from Col. 3.1-4, where the heavenly status granted to believers is only implicit, Lincoln, *Paradise*, p. 148.

6 Cf. Arnold who regards Eph. 2.4-10 as 'the crux for discerning the author's understanding of eschatology and salvation', *Power and Magic*, p. 147.

7 These structural divisions correspond to those of Lincoln's in *Ephesians*, p. 84; cf. O'Brien, *Ephesians*, p. 154.

tradition. Second, we will explore the notion of apocalyptic and mystical thought within Paul's writings. Third, we will examine Col. 2.16-3.4 for insights which might shed light on our study of Eph. 2.6. Fourth, we will examine Eph. 2.6 and its surrounding context in the light of Jewish mysticism. Fifth and finally, we will conduct a brief exegetical sketch of Eph. 2.1-10 and attempt to make sense of the heavenly status granted to believers in Eph. 2.6. Within our examination, we will also address Paul's possible motivation for utilizing this realized eschatological language in Eph. 2.6, a subject by and large overlooked in studies of Ephesians.[8] It is to these tasks which we now turn.

2. *Introduction to Jewish (Merkabah) Mysticism*

The concept of apocalyptic Jewish mysticism is rooted in themes such as heavenly journeys, ascensions, throne visions, and enthronements.[9] The term 'merkabah mysticism', or 'throne-chariot mysticism', finds its inception in the mishnaic period (c. 220 CE) and is the usual designation for these Jewish mystical traditions.[10] Merkabah mysticism can thus be defined as a Jewish tradition which is centred around heavenly journeys and throne visions of the heavenly merkabah, or the throne chariot of God.[11] Frequently included within these visions is an ascent structure whereby certain persons of honour, often Old Testament heroes, ascend to the throne of God in heaven.[12] In addition, the setting of many of these ascents is the heavenly Temple where heavenly worship is detailed.[13] Though the term 'merkabah mysticism' is most often applied to the Hekhalot literature beginning in the third century AD, many scholars believe the tradition to be the result of a long process of development.[14] Indeed, the earlier forms of Jewish mysticism identified in a

8 So Arnold who writes that apart from the work of Lona (and now Arnold), there has not been a significant effort to discern Paul's motivation for the realized eschatological emphasis in Eph. 2.4-10, *Power and Magic*, p. 147.

9 Eskola, *Messiah*, p. 1.

10 Segal, *Paul*, p. 39. The term 'merkabah' appears throughout the Old Testament as a common designation for 'chariot'. In rabbinic writings, it is later applied to the heavenly conveyance depicted in Ezekiel 1, Segal, *Paul*, p. 39.

11 Eskola, *Messiah*, pp. 1–2; Gershom G. Scholem, *Major Trends in Jewish Mysticism* (New York: Schocken Books, 3rd edn, 1954), p. 44.

12 Eskola, *Messiah*, p. 6.

13 Eskola, *Messiah*, pp. 6, 15.

14 Eskola, *Messiah*, pp. 2, 6, 15; cf. Christopher Rowland, *The Open Heaven: A Study of Apocalyptic in Judaism and Early Christianity* (London: SPCK, 1982); Ithamar Gruenwald, *From Apocalypticism to Gnosticism: Studies in Apocalypticism, Merkavah Mysticism and Gnosticism* (Beiträge zur Erforschung des Alten Testaments und des Antiken Judentums 14; Frankfurt am Main: Peter Lang, 1988); Ithamar Gruenwald, *Apocalyptic and Merkavah Mystcism* (AGJU 14; Leiden: Brill, 1980); Segal, *Paul*, pp. 34–71.

number of Qumran manuscripts, portions of *1 Enoch*, and *Testament of Levi* are pre-Christian.[15]

a. Heavenly kingship in the Old Testament

As a precursor to Jewish merkabah mysticism, Timo Eskola begins his examination with an investigation of heavenly kingship in the Old Testament. Since, as discussed briefly, merkabah mysticism can be summarized as throne mysticism and since this tradition has undergone a centuries-long development,[16] we should expect to encounter the concept of heavenly kingship in the Old Testament. Eskola devotes a chapter of his monograph to this analysis, and, while it is impractical for us to review his entire examination, it is beneficial to highlight some of his findings which are relevant for our analysis.

Of particular interest is the fact that in the Old Testament the throne of God is located on the earth with the dwelling place of God in the Holy of Holies inside the Tabernacle and subsequently in the Temple. The Holy of Holies is not only the place of God's presence but it is also the location of God's throne. In several passages, God is enthroned on the cherubim above the ark.[17] In Exod. 25.20-22 the place where God is to be met is the mercy seat on top of the ark and between the two cherubim. In 1 Sam. 4.4, 2 Kgs 19.15, Ps. 80.1, and Ps. 99.1 the Lord is enthroned above the cherubim. Not only does the Old Testament speak of God's throne in the earthly Temple, but it also speaks of God's throne in heaven and often even in the heavenly Temple. According to Eskola, these references evince characteristics of merkabah speculation:[18]

> **Ps. 11.4** The LORD is in His holy temple; the LORD'S throne is in heaven ...
>
> **Ps. 103.19** The LORD has established His throne in the heavens, And His sovereignty rules over all.
>
> **Ps. 33.13-14** The LORD looks from heaven; He sees all the sons of men; From His dwelling place He looks out On all the inhabitants of the earth ...

The significance of these passages is that they reveal a special relationship between the earthly and heavenly realms. In some respects, we might regard the Temple as a uniting of the heavenly and earthly realms.[19] The earthly Temple can be regarded as an imitation of the heavenly one but

15 Eskola, *Messiah*, pp. 2–3, 6.

16 Eskola, *Messiah*, pp. 2–3, 43.

17 Eskola, *Messiah*, pp. 50–51. Eskola lists and discusses briefly the Scriptures which follow above.

18 Eskola, *Messiah*, p. 52. Eskola lists and briefly discusses the references which follow above.

19 Eskola, *Messiah*, p. 53.

yet also as a place where God can be met.[20] This unique relationship between the heavenly and earthly Temple is of great significance when we consider the context of Second Temple Jewish mystical writings. From this survey of appropriate Old Testament texts, we can agree with Eskola that 'the depiction of God as a heavenly King, or the symbol of the throne, belonged to the very core of Jewish Temple liturgy'.[21]

b. The biblical roots of the merkabah mysticism tradition

The central image of Jewish merkabah mysticism is the vision of the throne chariot of God depicted in Ezekiel 1.[22] In Ezekiel's vision, he sees something resembling a throne and a figure with the appearance of a man on the throne (1.26). In 1.28 Ezekiel describes this appearance as the likeness of the glory of the Lord which causes him to fall on his face upon seeing it. There are additional visions of God in human form in the Old Testament.[23] Exodus 23.20-21 depicts an angel who carries the name of the Lord within him. Daniel 7 also details a human figure on the throne of God. In Exod. 24.9-11 Moses, along with Aaron, Nadab, Abihu, and seventy elders of Israel, sees the God of Israel seemingly depicted in human form. In Exod. 33.18-23, when Moses asks to see the glory of the Lord, the Lord responds that no man can see the face of the Lord and live. As a result, Moses is allowed to see the back of the Lord after his glory has passed by. Finally, in Isa. 6.1-2 Isaiah has a vision of the Lord 'sitting on a throne, lofty and exalted, with the train of his robe filling the temple'. The setting here appears to be the heavenly Temple.

Along with others, these Old Testament references to the enthroned Lord provided the necessary backdrop for the continuation of a Jewish apocalyptic and mystical tradition.[24] In addition, the departing of God's glory from the Temple as detailed in Ezekiel 10, the subsequent destruction of the Temple, and Israel's exile provided the impetus for new ways to approach God. In her monograph *Ascent to Heaven in Jewish and Christian Apocalypses*, Martha Himmelfarb writes that the Second Temple 'is never able to emerge from the shadow of the dis-

20 Eskola, *Messiah*, p. 55.

21 Eskola, *Messiah*, p. 63.

22 Segal, *Paul*, p. 39.

23 Segal, *Paul*, pp. 40–41. In his discussion of the predecessors to merkabah mysticism, Segal discusses briefly Exod. 23.21, Ezekiel 1, Daniel 7, Exodus 24, and Exod. 33.18-23. In addition to these references, Eskola also lists and briefly discusses Gen. 21.18; 22.11; 18.1-2; 31.11-13; 28.11-17; Exodus 19; Deut. 4.11-15; 1 Kgs 22.19; Isa. 6.1-2, Eskola, *Messiah*, pp. 66–70.

24 On the Scriptural and exegetical nature of apocalyptic esotericism, see Gruenwald, *From Apocalypticism to Gnosticism*, pp. iv–v, 55–59; cf. Mary Dean-Otting, *Heavenly Journeys: A Study of the Motif in Hellenistic Jewish Literature* (Judentum und Umwelt 8; Bern: Peter Lang, 1984), p. 58.

engagement of the glory of God'.[25] Consequently, faithful Jews began to locate the true Temple in heaven and the only way to access the true Temple was by way of a heavenly ascent.[26] In *The Open Heaven*, Christopher Rowland notes well this theological shift in Judaism and writes:

> By the time we reach the apocalyptic writings of the third and second centuries BC and later, we find that a cosmology has developed in which God is enthroned in glory in heaven, and his activities are carried out among men either by angelic intermediaries or other modes of divine operation like the spirit or *shekinah*. The cosmological beliefs were such that it often became necessary for anyone who would enter the immediate presence of God to embark on a journey through the heavenly world, in order to reach God himself.[27]

This heavenly journey to the very presence of God will be the primary focus of our examination of Jewish mystical texts.

c. Examination of Jewish mystical and apocalyptic texts[28]

In this study, we will examine six books which are relevant for our discussion of Eph. 2.6. For the most part, these six works are dated early in comparison with others and have often been considered by scholars to be significant for New Testament studies. It is beyond the scope of this chapter to undertake a more comprehensive examination in the

25 Martha Himmelfarb, *Ascent to Heaven in Jewish and Christian Apocalypses* (Oxford: Oxford University Press, 1993), p. 13.

26 Himmelfarb, *Ascent to Heaven*, p. 13; cf. Martha Himmelfarb, 'Apocalyptic Ascent and the Heavenly Temple' *SBLSP 1987* (ed. Kent Harold Richards; Atlanta: Scholars Press, 1987), pp. 210–17.

27 Rowland, *Open Heaven*, p. 80. Similarly, James H. Charlesworth writes, 'After the exile God is usually perceived as one who is above ... Knowledge of him is obtained almost always only through the sacred books, the descent of angels (Tab 2.15), the gift of vision (1En 1.2), or the journey of a seer through the various heavens (2En, AscenIs),' 'Introduction for the General Reader' *OTP* 1, pp. xxi–xxxiv (xxxi). See also Gruenwald, *From Apocalypticism to Gnosticism*, pp. 7, 23, 52, 129–30.

28 The focus of our investigation is the notion of a heavenly journey or ascent to the throne of God in Jewish mystical and apocalyptic texts. Here we should state that Judaism was not the only religion with a heavenly journey. For an excellent discussion of heavenly ascent in other cultures and religions, see Segal, 'Heavenly Ascent', *ANRW* 23.2, pp. 1334–51. Segal examines the notion of heavenly ascent in Persian, Greek (including Roman), Egyptian, Babylonian, and Eastern European thought. While there are certain similarities between the ascent structures of Judaism and other religions, there are also at times differences such as a descent (rather than an ascent) to the perfect realm or the occasion for the journey after death. Additionally, Dean-Otting has successfully argued 'that the heavenly journey motif is firmly rooted in Biblical Judaism and not to be explained as a development resulting from foreign influence', *Heavenly Journeys*, p. 58. For reasons detailed below, the focus of our examination is the notion of a heavenly journey to the throne of God in Jewish mystical and apocalyptic texts.

manner of a number of scholars.[29] Rather, our intention is to provide an abbreviated study which serves to highlight those passages and themes which are relevant for our study of Ephesians.[30] At the end of the analysis, we will provide a summary of our findings which will highlight those issues which are most significant for our study of Ephesians. In the summary, we will also provide references from a larger sample of Jewish texts. Finally, we will reserve any discussion of Qumran texts, many of which also exhibit similarities with Jewish apocalyptic and merkabah mysticism,[31] for our examinations of Colossians 2 and Ephesians 2.

1 Enoch 1-36 (Book of the Watchers)

The Book of the Watchers is of central importance because it represents one of the earliest records of a heavenly ascent.[32] Portions of the text have been recovered at Qumran and the dating of the manuscripts is consigned to the early second century BC.[33] Concerning the Book of the Watchers, Himmelfarb writes that it 'was among the most influential works outside the canon for both Jews and Christians'.[34] She reiterates that the book's central theme, 'the depiction of the visionary's ascent to

29 For more comprehensive examinations of apocalyptic and/or Jewish mystical thought with heavenly ascent as a primary consideration, see Eskola, *Messiah*; Rowland, *Open Heaven*; Thomas J. Sappington, *Revelation and Redemption at Colossae* (JSNTSup 53; Sheffield: Sheffield Academic Press, 1991), pp. 26–54; Ian K. Smith, *Heavenly Perspective: A Study of the Apostle Paul's Response to a Jewish Mystical Movement at Colossae* (Library of New Testament Studies 326; London: T & T Clark, 2006); Segal, 'Heavenly Ascent', *ANRW* 23.2, pp. 1352–94.

30 In our examination, we will not interact with Philo primarily because in Philo there is not a heavenly journey such as in apocalyptic but rather a metaphor for the journey of the soul; cf. Dean-Otting, *Heavenly Journeys*, pp. 31–33.

31 Cf. Rowland, *Open Heaven*, p. 16; James M. Scott, 'Throne-Chariot Mysticism in Qumran and in Paul', *Eschatology, Messianism, and the Dead Sea Scrolls* (ed. Craig A. Evans and Peter W. Flint; Studies in the Dead Sea Scrolls and Related Literature 1; Grand Rapids: Eerdmans, 1997), pp. 101–19. On the relation between apocalyptic and Qumran, see John J. Collins, 'Was the Dead Sea Sect an Apocalyptic Movement?', *Archaeology and History in the Dead Sea Scrolls: The New York University Conference in Memory of Yigael Yadin* (ed. Lawrence H. Schiffman; JSPSup 8/American Schools of Oriental Research/Journal for the Study of the Old Testament Monograph Series 2; Sheffield: Sheffield Academic Press, 1990), pp. 25–51.

32 See John J. Collins, 'A Throne in the Heavens: Apotheosis in Pre-Christian Judaism', *Death, Ecstasy, and Other Worldly Journeys* (ed. John J. Collins and Michael Fishbane; Albany: State University of New York Press, 1995), pp. 43–58. Collins notes that the Book of the Watchers is one of the only references for the notion of ascent in pre-Christian Judaism.

33 For discussions of *1 Enoch* and its date, see George W. E. Nickelsburg, *Jewish Literature between the Bible and the Mishnah: A Historical and Literary Introduction* (Philadelphia: Fortress Press, 1981), pp. 48–55; John J. Collins, *The Apocalyptic Imagination: An Introduction to the Jewish Matrix of Christianity* (New York: Crossroad, 1984), pp. 36–46.

34 Himmelfarb, *Ascent to Heaven*, p. 29.

heaven in terms drawn from the understanding of heaven as a temple', is exploited by many later apocalypses and indeed 'sets the tone for the entire body of later apocalyptic literature'.[35] In *1 Enoch* 14 Enoch recalls his heavenly journey when he says, 'And behold I saw the clouds: And they were calling me in a vision ... and in the vision, the winds were causing me to fly and rushing me high into heaven' (14.8). In his vision, Enoch enters two houses which correspond to the heavenly Temple. In the second house, which should most likely be identified as the Holy of Holies,[36] Enoch sees a vision of the enthroned Lord. He recalls,

> And I observed and saw inside it a lofty throne – its appearance was like crystal and its wheels like the shining sun; and (I heard?) the voice of the cherubim; and from beneath the throne were issuing streams of flaming fire. It was difficult to look at it. And the Great Glory was sitting upon it ... (*1 En.* 14.18-20a, Isaac)

Enoch's heavenly journey to the throne of God in the heavenly Temple is significant for its influence on the themes and trends exhibited in Jewish merkabah mysticism.[37]

Jubilees

Though *Jubilees* should not be classified strictly as an apocalypse, its early date (c. 160 BC)[38] and the fact that many apocalyptic themes are present in the work emphasize its significance for our examination.[39] In the book of Jubilees, though there is no explicit reference to a heavenly ascent, we do read of Enoch's role as a visionary when Enoch is described as 'with the angels of God six jubilees of years (when) they showed him everything which is on earth and in the heavens ...' (*Jub.* 4.21, Wintermute). This theme of the revelation of heavenly mysteries is of primary significance in our study of Jewish mysticism and also for our examination of Ephesians. In 4.23 there is an allusion to Enoch's ascent to heaven when Enoch is taken from the children of men and led into the Garden of Eden. In addition, Eskola regards the incense which

35 Himmelfarb, *Ascent to Heaven*, p. 29. Himmelfarb notes that whether the dependence was direct or indirect, many of the later apocalypses are indebted to the Book of the Watchers; cf. Himmelfarb, 'Apocalyptic Ascent', and Dean-Otting, *Heavenly Journeys*, pp. 46–58, 70.

36 For a brief discussion, see Himmelfarb, *Ascent to Heaven*, pp. 25–28.

37 Collins writes that the throne vision in the Book of the Watchers reveals the mystical component in apocalyptic and he regards the work as the oldest merkabah vision outside Scripture, *Apocalyptic Imagination*, p. 42.

38 For discussions of date, see Nickelsburg, *Jewish Literature*, p. 77; Collins, *Apocalyptic Imagination*, p. 67; O. S. Wintermute, 'Introduction to Jubilees', *OTP* 2, pp. 35–51 (43–44).

39 Collins does note, however, that *Jubilees* has an apocalyptic dimension and regards it as a borderline apocalypse, *Apocalyptic Imagination*, pp. 65–66.

Enoch offered in 4.25 as a participation in heavenly worship.[40] Finally, the strict adherence to a particular calendar in the book of Jubilees will be significant in our examination of Colossians.

Testament of Levi

The manuscript history of *Testaments of the Twelve Patriarchs* is most complex and, consequently, the dating of the texts is difficult. Some scholars argue for an original Jewish composition with later Christian redactions and therefore an early pre-Christian date.[41] Others contend that *Testaments of the Twelve Patriarchs* is a Christian work which is dependent on Jewish sources.[42] The manuscript history of *Testament of Levi* is further complicated with the discoveries of an Aramaic Levi document from Qumran and the Cairo Genizah fragment.[43] The discoveries of the Aramaic Levi document lend weight to the conclusion that there is a long tradition of literature associated with the document and possibly all of *Testaments of the 12 Patriarchs.*[44] As a result, we regard *Testament of Levi* as a pre-Christian Jewish document with Christian interpolations.[45]

Similarly to *1 Enoch*, we also find in *Testament of Levi* a significant and influential account of a heavenly ascent to the throne of God.[46] We read of Levi's heavenly journey in *T. Levi* 2.5-8:

> Then sleep fell upon me, and I beheld a high mountain, and I was on it. And behold, the heavens were opened, and an angel of the Lord spoke to me: 'Levi, Levi, enter!' And I entered the first heaven, and saw there much

40 Eskola, *Messiah*, p. 76.

41 For a brief discussion, see H. C. Kee, 'Introduction to Testaments of the Twelve Patriarchs', *OTP* 1, pp. 775–81, (777–78). Kee argues for a second-century-BC composition. See also Eskola's brief discussion in *Messiah*, p. 77.

42 See Himmelfarb, *Ascent to Heaven*, pp. 30–33 and the relevant footnotes. For a discussion of the controversial history of composition for *Testament of Levi*, see Collins, *Apocalyptic Imagination*, pp. 106–107.

43 See further Kee, 'Introduction', pp. 775–78; Himmelfarb, *Ascent to Heaven*, pp. 30–31; Eskola, *Messiah*, p. 77.

44 See Kee, 'Introduction', pp. 777–78. James H. Charlesworth finds the similarities between the Aramaic fragment and the Greek Testament to be strong and concludes that there is a strong relation between the two works, *The Old Testament Pseudepigrapha and the New Testament: Prolegomena for the Study of Christian Origins* (SNTSMS 54; Cambridge: Cambridge University Press, 1985), pp. 38–40. On the other hand, Collins writes that the correspondences between the two documents are not exact and is hesitant to argue for a close relationship, *Apocalyptic Imagination*, pp. 107–10.

45 See the discussion of Charlesworth, *The Old Testament Pseudepigrapha and the New Testament*, pp. 38–40. Charlesworth concludes that *Testament of Levi* should be examined as evidence for early Judaism and for its influence on early Christianity, *The Old Testament Pseudepigrapha and the New Testament*, p. 40.

46 See Collins, *Apocalyptic Imagination*, pp. 109–10; Dean-Otting, *Heavenly Journeys*, pp. 76–94.

water suspended. And again I saw a second heaven much brighter and more lustrous... (Kee)

In the second heaven, the angel promises Levi that he '(will) see another heaven more lustrous and beyond compare' (2.9b) where he '(will) stand near the Lord' (2.10a). The angel describes this highest heaven with Temple terminology and as the location of God:

> In the uppermost heaven of all dwells the Great Glory in the Holy of Holies superior to all holiness. There with him are the archangels, who serve and offer propitiatory sacrifices to the Lord in behalf of all the sins of ignorance of the righteous ones. They present to the Lord a pleasing odor, a rational and bloodless oblation ... There with him are thrones and authorities; there praises to God are offered eternally.[47] (*T. Levi* 3.4-6, 8, Kee)

Later in the narrative, the angel opens the gates of heaven and Levi sees the 'Holy Most High' sitting on his throne (5.1).

In his notes on *Testament of Levi*, H. C. Kee writes that 'the sleep, the vision, the mountain, the ascent to the heavens and on to the throne of God are standard elements in Merkabah (throne) mysticism'.[48] For our purposes, it is significant to note that the throne of God is the place where God is to be met.[49] In addition, the apocalyptic theme of the heavenly Temple is significant for our discussion of Eph. 2.6 and its surrounding context. Finally, the identification of three heavens in *Testament of Levi* is of possible significance for our understanding of 2 Corinthians 12 and Pauline cosmology.

1 Enoch 37-71 (The Book of the Similitudes)

Like the majority of the apocalypses, the date and origin of the Similitudes of Enoch are complex with the result that there is often little agreement among scholars over these issues. The majority of scholars contend that the Similitudes are Jewish and should be dated within the first century

47 There is disagreement over the original number of heavens in *Testament of Levi*. We follow Kee who argues for three heavens – the heavens of water (2.7; 3.2), light (2.8; 3.3), and God's dwelling place (2.9–10; 3.4), 'Introduction', pp. 779, 789, note 3a. In this matter, Kee follows the α text which 'contains fewer evidences of expansion of the (original) account of the three heavens', 'Introduction', p. 789, note 3a. R. H. Charles also gives preference to the α text in *T. Levi* 2.7-10, *The Greek Versions of the Testaments of the Twelve Patriarchs* (Oxford: Clarendon Press, 1908), p. xv. In 3.1–5 Charles believes A^{α} to be less corrupt and a better representation of the original, *Greek Versions*, p. xv. Neither the α text nor the A^{α} text includes the later expansion in the number of heavens to seven which is found in the β text. Eskola also follows Kee in *Messiah*, p. 77. For a differing viewpoint, see Himmelfarb who argues for only a single heaven in the original composition, *Ascent to Heaven*, p. 127.

48 Kee, 'Introduction', p. 788, note c.

49 Eskola, *Messiah*, p. 79.

AD.[50] Martha Himmelfarb argues that the Book of the Watchers is the most important influence on the Similitudes and that it is best to understand the Similitudes 'as a retelling of the Book of the Watchers that integrates elements of the story of the fallen angels, the ascent to the heavenly temple, and the journey to the ends of the earth ...'[51] The purpose of the book is to demonstrate 'the ultimate vindication of the righteous and punishment of the wicked'.[52]

In *1 Enoch* 39 whirlwinds lift Enoch from the earth and set him down at the ends of the heavens (39.3) where he sees the dwelling place of the righteous with the angels (39.4-8). In *1 En.* 39.6-8 we read,

> And in those days my eyes saw the Elect One of righteousness and of faith, and righteousness shall prevail in his days, and the righteous and elect ones shall be without number before him forever and ever. And I saw a dwelling place underneath the wings of the Lord of the Spirits; and all the righteous and the elect before him shall be as intense as the light of fire ... There (underneath his wings) I wanted to dwell; and my soul desired that dwelling place. Already my portion is there; for this it has been reserved for me before the Lord of the Spirits. (Isaac)

These verses record Enoch's vision and also serve to demonstrate the central concern of the Similitudes as the righteous have their eternal dwelling with the Lord.[53] Not only do we observe here the heavenly dwelling place of the righteous dead, but we also note a realized eschatology of sorts. In 39.8 Enoch desires the dwelling place underneath the wings of the Lord and subsequently declares that his portion was already[54] there because the Lord had reserved it for him. Such a declaration is reminiscent of Paul's statement in Phil. 3.20 when he writes that 'our citizenship is in heaven, from which also we eagerly wait for a Savior, the Lord Jesus Christ'. Both of these statements speak of a heavenly status which is guaranteed or reserved for those on earth. Additionally, the fact that Enoch's portion is already in the heavens suggests a heavenly status which might be described as proleptic. We

50 E. Isaac, 'Introduction to 1 (Ethiopic Apocalypse of) Enoch', *OTP* 1, pp. 5–12, (6–7); Nickelsburg, *Jewish Literature*, pp. 221–23; Collins, *Apocalyptic Imagination*, pp. 142–54; Ėskola, *Messiah*, p. 91; Himmelfarb, *Ascent to Heaven*, p. 59; Charlesworth, *The Old Testament Pseudepigrapha and the New Testament*, p. 89. Segal, on the other hand, considers the Similitudes a Christian work which should reflect a post-Christian date, 'Heavenly Ascent', *ANRW* 23.2, pp. 1377–78.

51 Himmelfarb, *Ascent to Heaven*, p. 59.

52 Himmelfarb, *Ascent to Heaven*, p. 59.

53 See also *1 En.* 62.13-14 where the righteous and elect ones will 'eat and rest and rise with that Son of Man forever and ever'.

54 Isaac writes that the word 'already' clarifies Enoch's prior possession of this heavenly status of sorts. The word is literally translated as 'before', 'previously', or 'of old', Isaac, *OTP* 1, p. 31, note k.

will later argue that prolepsis is one of the keys to understanding the heavenly status granted to believers in Eph. 2.6.

At the conclusion of the Similitudes (after the third parable), Enoch is taken up from the earth by a wind chariot to the dwelling place of the elect and righteous ones (chapter 70). This ascent is expanded upon in *1 Enoch* 71[55] which Timo Eskola describes as 'a perfect description of a heavenly journey and a *merkabah* vision'.[56] At the beginning of the chapter, Enoch's spirit ascends into the heavens (71.1), Enoch sees angels clothed in white garments (71.1),[57] and Enoch falls on his face before the Lord (71.2). The archangel Michael then seizes Enoch's hand and lifts him up in order to reveal the secrets of righteousness and heaven (71.3-4). Next, Michael carries Enoch's spirit and Enoch finds himself in the heaven of heavens (71.5) where he sees the throne of glory with countless angels around it (71.7-8). Finally, Enoch sees a vision of the Antecedent of Time whose head is white and pure and whose garment is of indescribable glory (71.10). In his recollection of this vision, Enoch says, 'I fell on my face, my whole body mollified and my spirit transformed' (71.11).[58] After his transformation, Enoch begins to praise the Antecedent of Time (71.11-12).[59] The final result of his transformation is the angel's proclamation that Enoch is the Son of Man (71.14).[60]

Several features of this apocalypse are important for our discussion of Eph. 2.6 and its surrounding context. First, we witness a heavenly journey with an ascent to God's throne in the highest heaven. Second, some New Testament scholars compare the mystical transformation of Enoch's body and spirit when he sees the Antecedent of Time with the Pauline descriptions of the transformation of believers who are united to Christ. Third, Enoch's worship of the Lord at the conclusion of his heavenly ascent should probably be understood as his joining in the angelic praise. Fourth, though it is less explicit than in other apocalypses, Enoch's participation in the heavenly liturgy and his vision of a structure similar to the heavenly Temple of *1 Enoch* lead to the conclusion that the apocalyptic notion of the heavenly Temple is also significant in the Similitudes.[61]

55 Himmelfarb (*Ascent to Heaven*, p. 60, note 45) and Collins (*Apocalyptic Imagination*, pp. 152–53) regard ch. 71 of the Similitudes as a later addition to the text.

56 Eskola, *Messiah*, p. 95.

57 Presumably, these are the same garments of glory which are promised both to Enoch and to the righteous dead in *1 En*. 62.15–16.

58 Cf. *1 En*. 39.14b.

59 Cf. *1 En*. 39.9-14.

60 Whether or not Enoch here is transformed into the eschatological and enthroned Son of Man in *1 En*. 37-71 is insignificant for our examination. What is significant is Enoch's transformation upon his encounter with the enthroned Lord in heaven.

61 Himmelfarb, *Ascent to Heaven*, pp. 59–61.

2 Enoch

Second Enoch continues the apocalyptic tradition of heavenly ascension which we have traced in our study. Although the dating of *2 Enoch* is complex and controversial,[62] its contents are relevant for both our study of Paul's mystical thought and our discussion of Eph. 2.6. Of primary significance is the recasting from earlier apocalypses of Enoch's heavenly ascent. In his assessment, Timo Eskola contends that *2 Enoch* is a good example of the mystical contemplation found in many apocalypses and writes that it 'passes on the tradition in which God's heavenly throne is the centre of Jewish mysticism'.[63]

Second Enoch opens with the appearance of two angels who tell Enoch, 'Do not fear! The eternal God has sent us to you. And behold, you will ascend with us to heaven today' (*2 En.* 1.8, Andersen). In his journey, Enoch ascends through six heavens before his vision of the Lord in the seventh heaven.[64] In these six heavens, Enoch observes: (1) the clouds, the air higher up, the ether, the heavenly ocean, and the angels who govern the heavenly elements in the first heaven (chapters 3–6); (2) darkness and the angels of darkness who turned away from the Lord in the second heaven (chapter 7); (3) Paradise (chapters 8–9) and possibly the place of punishment in the third heaven[65] (chapter 10); (4) the secrets of the solar and lunar elements in the fourth

62 For a discussion of the textual history, date, provenance, and possible origins, see F. I. Andersen, 'Introduction to 2 (Slavonic Apocalypse of) Enoch', *OTP* 1, pp. 91–100, (92–97). Scholars are in disagreement over whether the work originated in Jewish or Christian circles and are equally divided on the question of date, as some contend for a pre-Christian original and others for a composition in the Middle Ages, Andersen, 'Introduction', pp. 94–95. Andersen 'is inclined to place the book – or at least its original nucleus – early rather than late; and in a Jewish rather than a Christian community', 'Introduction', p. 97. We find Andersen's date in the late first century the least objectionable of the options; cf. Nickelsburg, *Jewish Literature*, pp. 185–88, and Collins, *Apocalyptic Imagination*, pp. 195–98.

63 Eskola, *Messiah*, p. 105.

64 For several reasons, we follow here the shorter recension (A text) which contains seven heavens in contrast to the longer recension (J text) which contains ten heavens. First, a possible reason for the expansion from seven to ten heavens in the J text is a redactor's attempt to harmonize the number of heavens with the ranks of the heavenly armies and their corresponding ten steps (see *2 Enoch* 20). Andersen agrees and writes, 'The tradition of ten ranks of angels in the seventh heaven with corresponding lists has a better claim to be authentic than the scheme of ten heavens', *OTP* 1, p. 134, note a. Second, in 27.3, there is a reference to the seven stars, each one assigned to its own heaven. Third, Enoch's proclamation that he 'wrote down the height from the earth to the seventh heaven, and the depth to the lowermost hell, and the place of condemnation, and the supremely large hell, open and weeping' in *2 En.* 40.12 (J text) provides further confirmation for an original schema of seven heavens. Finally, the comparatively much shorter descriptions of the eighth and ninth heavens confined to 21.6, also lend support for an original cosmology of seven heavens.

65 See Andersen's comment on 40.12 where he notes that the longer manuscripts are open to the possibility that 'hell' is located in one of the heavens, *OTP* 1, p. 166, note j.

heaven (chapters 11–17); (5) the Grigori[66] who turned aside from the Lord in the fifth heaven (chapter 18); (6) seven groups of angels in the sixth heaven (chapter 19) before his vision of the Lord in the seventh heaven.

In the seventh heaven, Enoch sees the fiery armies of heaven – the archangels, incorporeal forces, dominions, origins authorities, cherubim, seraphim, thrones, regiments, and shining *otanim* stations – and subsequently, from a distance, sees the Lord on his high throne (20.1-3). The angel Gabriel then brings Enoch before the face of the Lord (21.3-6) whereupon Enoch falls down and worships (22.4). The Lord responds by encouraging Enoch to be brave and declaring, 'Let Enoch join in and stand in front of my face forever!' (*2 En.* 22.5-6, Andersen). The Lord then commands Michael:

> Go, and extract Enoch from |his| earthly clothing. And anoint him with my delightful oil, and put him into the clothes of my glory.' And so Michael did, just as the Lord had said to him. He anointed me and he clothed me ... And I looked at myself, and I had become like one of his glorious ones, and there was no observable difference. (*2 En.* 22.8-10, Andersen)

As in *1 En.* 71.11, when Enoch comes into contact with the Lord, he experiences some sort of transformation. Martha Himmelfarb believes that Enoch here becomes an angel through 'a heavenly version of priestly investiture'[67] and also compares the heavenly clothing which Enoch receives with the spiritual, heavenly body which Paul describes in 1 Cor. 15.42-50.[68] After Enoch's transformation, the Lord summons one of his archangels to bring Enoch the books of the Lord's deeds and a pen for 'speed-writing' (22.10-11). Chapters 23–33 then are the archangel Vrevoil's and the Lord's revealing of the secrets of God, evil, heaven, and earth to Enoch.

Several apocalyptic themes from *2 Enoch* are significant for our discussion of Ephesians 2. First, Enoch's heavenly ascent to the throne of God in the highest heaven continues this apocalyptic theme and tradition.[69] Second, the Lord and his angels reveal the secrets of God, along with various heavenly and earthly mysteries, to Enoch after his ascent to heaven and appearance before the throne of God. Third, the transformation of Enoch into a heavenly being, possibly an angel, continues the apocalyptic motif of transformation when the visionary encounters the throne and presence of God. Fourth, the location of

66 The Grigori who turned aside from the Lord most likely refer to the Watchers from *1 Enoch*. See Andersen, *OTP* 1, p. 130, note 18a.

67 Himmelfarb, *Ascent to Heaven*, p. 40.

68 Himmelfarb, *Ascent to Heaven*, p. 40.

69 Eskola writes that in this respect, '2 Enoch passes on the tradition in which God's heavenly throne is the centre of Jewish mysticism', *Messiah*, p. 105.

Paradise in the third heaven (chapter 8) is of possible significance for our understanding of 2 Cor. 12.1-4.[70] Finally, many of the ranks and classes of angels which stand before the Lord in the seventh heaven also appear both in Ephesians and in the larger Pauline corpus.

Testament of Job

Testament of Job differs somewhat from the works we have analysed thus far in that, though it exhibits some apocalyptic characteristics, it should not be characterized as a traditional apocalypse or included in the apocalyptic genre. Many of the concerns of apocalyptic such as an ascent to the highest heaven, a journey through the heavenly realms, the naming of various angels, an emphasis on eschatology, and some concept of messianism, are noticeably absent.[71] However, its notable characteristics such as concern with the upper world[72] and charismatic communion with the angels demonstrate some similarities with the Qumran texts and an even greater resemblance to Jewish merkabah mysticism.[73] These themes are also present in a number of apocalypses and are significant for our examination of Colossians 2 and Ephesians 2. Additionally, since *Testament of Job* is a first-century-BC or AD. Jewish composition,[74] its proximity to the dating of the New Testament and its Jewish theology demonstrate its significance for our examination of Colossians 2 and Ephesians 2.

Common themes in Jewish merkabah mysticism

From our brief analysis of the passages above, we can identify a number of themes which are common to Jewish apocalyptic and mystical texts. In his examination of Jewish mystical and apocalyptic texts, Timo Eskola identifies several common features which appear frequently throughout these writings: [75]

70 Cf. *Apoc. Mos.* 37.5; 40.1.

71 Spittler, 'Introduction', p. 832.

72 Spittler, 'Introduction', p. 833.

73 Spittler, 'Introduction', p. 833. Spittler clarifies the term 'merkabah mysticism' and defines it as 'Jewish mystical speculation focusing on God's chariot, *mrkbh*'. See also Spittler's comparison of these themes with merkabah mysticism in his notes on *Testament of Job*, p. 857, note 36a, and p. 864, note 46a.

74 Spittler, 'Introduction', pp. 830–33.

75 The first four characteristics listed are from Eskola, *Messiah*, p. 123. The second and third characteristics include themes which are listed separately by Eskola but we have combined them because of their evident similarity. The references in parentheses are the product of our research.

1 Heavenly journey (*1 En.* 14.8; *T. Levi* 2.5-8; *1 Enoch* 39; *1 Enoch* 70–71; *2 Enoch* 1–22; *3 Enoch* 1–2; *4 Ezra* 8.19-21; *Gk. Apoc. Ezra* 1, 5; *Apocalypse of Sedrach* 2; *3 Baruch* 2–11; *Apocalypse of Abraham* 15–18; *Testament of Abraham* A, 9–10; *Ascension of Isaiah* 6–9)
2 Ascent to God's throne in the highest heaven/early Jewish mysticism as throne mysticism (*1 En.* 14.18-22a; *T. Levi* 5.1; *2 Enoch* 21-22; *3 Enoch* 2; *Apocalypse of Abraham* 18; *Asc. Isa.* 9.37)
3 Apocalyptic idea of a heavenly Temple/Temple terminology transferred to the heavenly realm (*1 Enoch* 14; *T. Levi.* 3.4-6)
4 Differing descriptions of heavenly enthronements
   (a) A special relationship between God's throne of glory and other heavenly thrones (*1 En.* 45.3; 51.3; 62.5; *3 Enoch* 10)
   (b) The throne as a place of honour that is promised for the righteous (*1 En.* 45.3; *T. Benj.* 10.5-7; *1 En.* 51.3; 62.5; *1 En.* 108.11-15; T. *Dan* 5.13; *T. Moses* 10; *Asc. Isa.* 9.24-26; 11.40; 4Q 491, fragment 11).

To this list, we will add two additional characteristics:

5 On most occasions, when there is an ascent to the throne of God, the visionary either witnesses or takes part in the heavenly worship before the throne (*Jub.* 4.25; *1 Enoch* 71; *Testament of Job* 46–53; *3 Enoch* 2; *Apocalypse of Abraham* 17; 4Q 491, fragment 11)
6 The purpose/result of the ascent to the presence of God in heaven is usually the revelation of divine knowledge and mysteries (*Jub.* 4.21; *1 En.* 71.3-4; *1 Enoch* 72–82; *2 Enoch* 22–33; *Apocalypse of Abraham* 18–32; *Greek Apocalypse of Ezra* 1; *3 Baruch* 1–17).[76]

These characteristics, themes, and features of apocalyptic literature and Jewish merkabah mysticism will be significant for our discussion of both Colossians 2 and Ephesians 2.

3. *Paul as Mystic*

Following our brief examination of Jewish merkabah mysticism, it is appropriate now to consider the extent to which the life and writings of Paul bear similarities to Jewish mystical thought. As we read through the pages of the New Testament, it is evident that Paul was a visionary as both his earliest biographer and also his own writings testify to his mysticism.[77] Our claim here that Paul is a 'visionary' or a 'mystic' refers

76 On the notion of heavenly ascent and the revelation of divine mysteries, see especially Gruenwald, *Apocalyptic and Merkavah Mysticism*; Gruenwald, *From Apocalypticism to Gnosticism*; Rowland, *Open Heaven*.

77 In this section, I am particularly indebted to Segal's *Paul the Convert*, pp. 34–71. See further Lincoln, *Paradise*, pp. 71–73; Andrew T. Lincoln, '"Paul the Visionary": The Setting and Significance of the Rapture to Paradise in 2 Corinthians 12.1-10', *NTS* 25

to his supernatural visions and revelations (cf. 2 Cor. 12.1) of God or from God and has no direct bearing on whether Paul should be situated in or interpreted within the thought of Jewish merkabah mysticism. In the three accounts of Paul's conversion, Luke depicts ecstatic experiences.[78] In Acts 9.3-9 'a light from heaven (φῶς ἐκ τοῦ οὐρανοῦ) [flashes] around (Paul)', he falls to the ground, and he hears the voice of Jesus speaking to him. Similarly in Acts 22.6-11 'a very bright light suddenly [flashes] from heaven (ἐκ τοῦ οὐρανοῦ) all around [Paul]', he falls to the ground, and he hears the voice of Jesus. Later in this account of Paul's conversion, Luke records another vision in which the Lord reveals to Paul that Ananias will lay his hands on him to restore his sight (Acts 9.12). In Acts 26.12-18 Paul sees a light from heaven (οὐρανόθεν), falls to the ground along with his companions, and hears the voice of Jesus speaking to him. In 26.19 Paul tells King Agrippa that '[he] did not prove disobedient to [this] heavenly vision (οὐρανίῳ ὀπτασίᾳ)'.

In addition to the conversion experiences, Luke also recounts other ecstatic visions in the life of Paul.[79] In Acts 16.9-10 Paul sees a vision (ὅραμα) of a man from Macedonia urging him to come and help those in Macedonia. In 18.9-10 the Lord speaks to Paul in a vision (δι' ὁράματος) in which he exhorts Paul not to be afraid but to continue to speak. In 22.17-21, while praying in the temple, Paul falls into a trance (ἐν ἐκστάσει) and sees the Lord who tells Paul to leave Jerusalem. Finally, the Lord's direct instructions for Paul to 'witness at Rome' in Acts 23.11 should probably also be regarded as some sort visionary experience.[80]

Within Paul's own writings, he emphasizes that he is an apostle 'not *sent* from men nor through the agency of man, but through Jesus Christ and God the Father' (Gal. 1.1). Indeed, in his apostleship, Paul also underscores that the gospel which he preaches is 'not according to man, for [he] neither received it from man, nor was [he] taught it, but *[he] received it* δι' ἀποκαλύψεως Ἰησοῦ Χριστοῦ' (Gal. 1.11-12).[81] Paul also writes that it was in response to a revelation (κατὰ ἀποκάλυψιν)

(1979), pp. 204–20; C. R. A. Morray-Jones, 'Paradise Revisited (2 Cor. 12.1-12): The Jewish Mystical Background of Paul's Apostolate: Part 1: The Jewish Sources', *HTR* 86.2 (1993), pp. 177–217; C. R. A. Morray-Jones, 'Paradise Revisited (2 Cor. 12.1-12): The Jewish Mystical Background of Paul's Apostolate: Part 2: Paul's Heavenly Ascent and Its Significance', *HTR* 86.3 (1993), pp. 265–92; Seyoon Kim, *The Origin of Paul's Gospel* (WUNT 2:4; Tübingen: J. C. B. Mohr, 1981); Rowland, *Open Heaven*, pp. 374–86; Scott, 'Throne-Chariot Mysticism'. Contra Michael D. Goulder who contends that Paul was not a visionary, distinguished sharply between ἀποκάλυψις and ὀπτασία, and opposed all visionary and mystical claims, 'Vision and Knowledge', *JSNT* 56 (1994), pp. 53–71.

78 Segal, *Paul*, p. 37.

79 Segal lists the following three passages above as further ecstatic experiences in Acts' account of Paul's life, *Paul*, p. 37.

80 Cf. Lincoln, *Paradise*, p. 72.

81 Segal, *Paul*, p. 35.

that he went to Jerusalem (Gal. 2.2).[82] Without doubt, however, the greatest of Paul's mystical experiences is his ascent to the third heaven in 2 Cor. 12.1-10.[83] In 12.1, though he believes it is not profitable, Paul boasts of visions and revelations of the Lord (ὀπτασίας καὶ ἀποκαλύψεις κυρίου). Whether κυρίου is to be understood here as a subjective[84] or objective[85] genitive has been greatly debated. In our view, it seems best to understand κυρίου primarily as a subjective genitive in which the Lord is the giver of the visions and revelations, but also secondarily in an objective sense in which Christ is also the content of the visions and revelations.[86] Paul then speaks of being caught up (ἁρπαγέντα) ἕως τρίτου οὐρανοῦ where he hears ἄρρητα ῥήματα which are not proper for a man to speak. As a result of his great revelations, Paul reports that he is given 'a thorn in the flesh, a messenger of Satan (σκόλοψ τῇ σαρκί, ἄγγελος σατανᾶ) to torment [him]' (12.7). He implores the Lord three times that it might be taken away (12.8). In response to Paul's request, Jesus says, 'My grace is sufficient for you, for power is perfected in weakness' (12.9). This correspondence between Jesus and Paul also implies interaction of a visionary or apocalyptic nature.[87]

In his assessment of 2 Corinthians 12, Alan Segal calls Paul's vision 'both mystical and apocalyptic'[88] and believes that it is best understood within the context of first-century Jewish apocalyptic thought.[89] Segal writes, 'Paul's claim is not strange or ridiculous for a first-century Jew, since this experience parallels ecstatic ascents to the divine throne in other apocalyptic and merkabah mystical traditions in Jewish Hellenism.'[90] Furthermore, Paul's identification of the third heaven as Paradise (12.2, 4) is similar to *2 Enoch* 8 and *Apoc. Mos.* 37.5, 40.1, and so might also be indicative of a Jewish apocalyptic context.[91]

82 Segal, *Paul*, p. 36.

83 In 2 Cor. 12.2 Paul describes the person who ascends to heaven as ἄνθρωπον ἐν Χριστῷ; however, as 12.7 makes clear, the 'man in Christ' Paul referred to in 12.2 was indeed Paul himself. Paul's hesitancy to identify himself was most likely related to his hesitancy to boast of his ὀπτασίας καὶ ἀποκαλύψεις κυρίου (12.1), Lincoln, 'Paul the Visionary', pp. 208–209. Other possible motivations are Paul's adhering to pseudepigraphal apocalyptic conventions, Rowland, *Open Heaven*, pp. 384–86, or Paul's distinguishing between his 'weak, human self' and his 'visionary, heavenly self', Morray-Jones, 'Paradise Revisited: Part 2', pp. 273–74; Rowland, *Open Heaven*, pp. 384–86. Contra Goulder who argues that Paul was not speaking of himself in 2 Cor. 12.1-4, 'Vision and Knowledge', pp. 53–58.

84 Peter Schäfer, 'New Testament and Hekhalot Literature: The Journey into Heaven in Paul and in Merkavah Mysticism', *JJS* 35.1 (1984), pp. 19–35 (21).

85 Morray-Jones, 'Paradise Revisited: Part 2', p. 268, note 12.

86 So Lincoln, 'Paul the Visionary', pp. 205–206.

87 Segal, *Paul*, p. 36; cf. Lincoln, *Paradise*, p. 72.

88 Segal, *Paul*, p. 35.

89 Segal, *Paul*, p. 36.

90 Segal, *Paul*, p. 36.

91 Segal, *Paul*, pp. 313, note 5, 35–36; cf. Lincoln, *Paradise*, pp. 77–84.

Regardless of whether or not Paul's account of his heavenly ascent should be understood within the context of apocalyptic[92] and/or Jewish merkabah mystical thought,[93] his heavenly ascent in 2 Cor. 12.1-10 is nevertheless reminiscent of one of the primary characteristics of Jewish apocalyptic – the ascent to the throne of God in the highest heaven.[94]

The records of Paul's visions and ecstatic experiences found in Acts and within Paul's writings are not the only evidence of his interaction with a Jewish mystical tradition. His writings themselves on the doctrine of Christ and the transformation of believers also reveal and reflect the mystical tradition of the first century.[95] Paul's references to Christ as the image of God (2 Cor. 4.4-6), the image of the invisible God (Col. 1.15), in the form of God (Phil. 2.6), and as having been granted the name which is above every name (Phil. 2.9-11) all reveal similarities with the tradition of merkabah mysticism.[96] In addition to these references to Christ, Paul also exhibits mystical language when he writes of believers and their transformation into the image of Christ (Rom. 8.29; Rom. 12.2; 2 Cor. 3.18; Gal. 4.19; Phil. 3.10; Phil. 3.20-21; 1 Cor. 15.49; Col. 3.9-10; Eph. 4.22-24).[97] As noted above, this motif of transformation when a visionary stands before the throne of God occurs frequently in apocalyptic literature (*1 En.* 62.15-16; 71.11; 90.37-39; *2 En.* 22.8-10) and in Jewish merkabah mysticism.[98] Of particular interest is that these apocalyptic examples of transformation occur relatively late. Since the

92 On the differences between Paul's heavenly ascent and heavenly ascents in apocalyptic and other related literature, see Paula R. Gooder, *Only the Third Heaven?: 2 Corinthians 12:1-10 and Heavenly Ascent* (Library of New Testament Studies 313; London: T & T Clark, 2006), especially pp. 165–89.

93 Those who contend that Paul's heavenly ascent in 2 Corinthians 12 should be understood within the context of Jewish merkabah mysticism include: Segal, *Paul*, pp. 35–36; Gershom G. Scholem, *Jewish Gnosticism, Merkabah Mysticism, and Talmudic Tradition* (New York: The Jewish Theological Seminary of America, 1960), pp. 14–19; Morray-Jones, 'Paradise Revisited: Part 1'; Morray-Jones, 'Paradise Revisited: Part 2'; Scott, 'Throne-Chariot Mysticism'; Rowland, *Open Heaven*, pp. 379–86. Scholem argues that there is a continuity of tradition between apocalyptic, Paul, the Talmudic writings, and the Hekhalot texts, *Jewish Gnosticism*, pp. 14–19. Peter Schäfer, on the other hand, contends that there is no direct connection either between apocalyptic and merkabah mysticism or between 2 Cor. 12.1-4 and merkabah mysticism, Schäfer, 'New Testament and Hekhalot Literature'.

94 For a discussion of and justification for our argument that Paul ascended to the presence of God in 2 Corinthians 12, see our excursus of cosmology in Paul and Ephesians. Contra Gooder who contends that Paul's account in 2 Corinthians 12 should be understood as a failed ascent in which Paul only ascends to the third of seven heavens and which provided the occasion for Paul to boast in his weaknesses, *Only the Third Heaven?*, especially pp. 190–211.

95 Segal, *Paul*, p. 59.

96 Segal, *Paul*, pp. 59–63.

97 Segal, *Paul*, pp. 58–71.

98 See Segal, *Paul*, pp. 38–56.

date for the Similitudes of Enoch is not certain, it is quite possible that Paul is the first author to communicate explicitly this sort of transformation within Judaism.[99] On account of the uncertain date of the Similitudes, it is fruitless to speculate on any sort of dependence.

From our examination of Paul's life as recorded in Acts and Paul's writings, it is evident that Paul was a mystic and a visionary. Alan Segal summarizes Paul's mysticism well when he writes:

> Paul describes his own spiritual experiences in terms appropriate to a Jewish apocalyptic-mystagogue of the first century. He, like Enoch, relates his experiences of heavenly travel, in which he sees the secrets of the universe revealed. He believes his salvation to lie in a body-to-body identification with his heavenly savior, who sits on the divine throne and functions as God's glorious manifestation.[100]

In this sense, we can see that Paul's visionary experiences were a fundamental part of his life and his ministry. What is of particular interest and significance, though, is that we also find clear instances of Paul's condemnation of certain mystical and visionary practices. There is perhaps no clearer example of this than Paul's condemnation of the Colossian error.

4. *The Colossian Heresy and Jewish Mysticism*

We now turn our attention to the most complex and elusive 'Colossian heresy' or 'Colossian philosophy'. There is no shortage of opinions in regard to the identity of this 'philosophy' which posed a threat to the believers in Colossae and quite possibly also their near neighbours.[101] In fact, John J. Gunther identifies forty-four different proposals from nineteenth and twentieth-century scholarship.[102] For our purposes, there has been a growing contingent among those who identify the

99 Segal, *Paul*, p. 48.

100 Segal, *Paul*, p. 35.

101 Peter T. O'Brien notes that the Colossian heresy might also have been a threat to the near neighbours of Colossae, *Colossians, Philemon* (WBC 44; Nashville: Thomas Nelson, 1982), p. xxx; cf. Ernest W. Saunders, 'The Colossian Heresy and Qumran Theology', *Studies in the History and Text of the New Testament* (ed. Boyd L. Daniels and M. Jack Suggs; Studies and Documents 29; Salt Lake City: University of Utah Press, 1967), pp. 133–45 (133).

102 John J. Gunther, *St. Paul's Opponents and Their Background: A Study of Apocalyptic and Jewish Sectarian Teachings* (NovTSup 35; Leiden: Brill, 1973), pp. 3–4. To be accurate, however, the great majority of the proposals for the Colossian error which Gunther lists are quite similar to some of the others listed. For the full list, see Gunther, *St. Paul's Opponents*, pp. 3–4.

Colossian philosophy with Jewish mysticism.[103] It is our contention that this background of Jewish mysticism does indeed most accurately characterize the Colossian philosophy. We now turn our attention to a concise survey of some of the significant issues in Col. 2.16-23.[104]

When we read Paul's direct address of the Colossian heresy in Col. 2.16-23, what becomes immediately apparent is the Jewish nature of the false teaching. In 2.16 Paul exhorts the Colossians not to let anyone judge them in regard to food, drink, a festival, a new moon, or a Sabbath. He then points out that these things are a shadow (σκιά) of the things to come, but the substance (σῶμα) belongs to Christ (2.17).[105] One of the significant advantages of understanding the 'Colossian philosophy' against the backdrop of a Jewish mystical tradition is that the legalistic requirements of its adherents are intelligible in this framework.[106]

103 Eskola, *Messiah*, pp. 187–98; Von N. Kehl, 'Erniedrigung und Erhöhung in Qumran und Kolossä', *ZKT* 91 (1969), pp. 364–94; O'Brien, *Colossians*; Fred O. Francis, 'The Background of Embateuein (Col. 2.18) in Legal Papyri and Oracle Inscriptions', *Conflict at Colossae: A Problem in the Interpretation of Early Christianity Illustrated by Modern Studies* (ed. and trans. Fred O. Francis and Wayne A. Meeks; Missoula, MT: Society of Biblical Literature and Scholars Press, 1975), pp. 197–207; Fred O. Francis, 'Humility and Angelic Worship in Col. 2.18', *Conflict at Colossae: A Problem in the Interpretation of Early Christianity Illustrated by Modern Studies* (ed. and trans. Fred O. Francis and Wayne A. Meeks; Missoula, MT: Society of Biblical Literature and Scholars Press, 1975), pp. 163–95; Stanislas Lyonnet, 'Paul's Adversaries in Colossae', *Conflict at Colossae: A Problem in the Interpretation of Early Christianity Illustrated by Modern Studies* (ed. and trans. Fred O. Francis and Wayne A. Meeks; Missoula, MT: Society of Biblical Literature and Scholars Press, 1975), pp. 147–61; Christopher Rowland, 'Apocalyptic Visions and the Exaltation of Christ in the Letter to the Colossians', *JSNT* 19 (1983), pp. 73–83; Craig A. Evans, 'The Colossian Mystics', *Bib* 63 (1982), pp. 188–205; Andrew J. Bandstra, 'Did the Colossian Errorists Need a Mediator?', *New Dimensions in New Testament Study* (ed. Richard N. Longenecker and Merrill C. Tenney; Grand Rapids: Zondervan, 1974), pp. 329–43; J. H. Roberts, 'Jewish Mystical Experience in the Early Christian Era as Background to Understanding Colossians', *Neot* 32.1 (1998), pp. 161–89; Smith, *Heavenly Perspective*; Sappington, *Revelation and Redemption*; Saunders, 'The Colossian Heresy'; Edwin Yamauchi, 'Qumran and Colosse', *BSac* 121 (1964), pp. 141–52; E. Earle Ellis, 'Paul and His Opponents: Trends in the Research', *Christianity, Judaism and Other Greco-Roman Cults: Studies for Morton Smith at 60* (ed. Jacob Neusner; vol. 1, New Testament; SJLA 12; Leiden: Brill, 1975), pp. 295–96; Markus N. A. Bockmuehl, *Revelation and Mystery in Ancient Judaism and Pauline Christianity* (WUNT 2:36; Tübingen: J. C. B. Mohr, 1990), pp. 178–91; Jean-Noël Aletti, *Saint Paul Épitre aux Colossiens: Introduction, traduction et commentaire* (*EBib* new series 20; Paris: J. Gabalda, 1993), pp. 190–213.

104 Our discussion of the Colossian error will highlight some of the principal exegetical issues and communicate our view of the interpretive difficulties. It is beyond the scope of this book to investigate these matters at any length and such an effort would be of little value since a number of scholars have already argued at greater length and depth for our general interpretation. See the references cited above for more detailed examinations.

105 We detect a similar idea in Heb. 10.1 when the Law (ὁ νόμος) is a shadow (σκιά) of the good things to come (τῶν μελλόντων ἀγαθῶν), O'Brien, *Colossians*, p. 140.

106 So Eskola, *Messiah*, p. 193. Eskola correctly notes that the legalistic requirements of Col. 2.16 are troublesome for advocates of a syncretistic background.

Additionally, the terms ἑορτή, νεομηνία, and σάββατα are often utilized in the Old Testament to refer to special days dedicated to God.[107] Perhaps even more convincing is that the notion of 'new moons', 'festivals', and 'Sabbaths' all figure prominently in *Jubilees*, a Jewish document which has many similarities with apocalyptic and which was revered in sectarian Jewish groups (*Jub.* 1.14; 2.8-9; 6.17-38), and in the Qumran manuscripts (4Q320-330; 4Q319; 4Q317).[108] The references to food and drink in 2.16 perhaps point to purity laws but it is also likely that, in the context of this passage, they are part of the ascetic practices for obtaining visions.[109] Similarly, the legalistic requirements of 2.20-22 are also characteristic of the Jewish nature of the error.[110]

Colossians 2.18 proves to be the central verse for interpreting the Colossian philosophy. Our translation of Col. 2.18 will generally follow Francis's translation in his article the 'Humility and Angelic Worship in Col. 2.18':[111] Let no one disqualify you, delighting in (false) humility (ταπεινοφροσύνῃ) and the worship of the angels (θρησκείᾳ τῶν ἀγγέλων) – which he has seen upon entering (ἃ ἑόρακεν ἐμβατεύων) – being vainly puffed up by his mind of flesh.[112] In our analysis, we will briefly discuss three significant terms/phrases from 2.18 which support the notion that Paul here opposed a form of Jewish mysticism: (1) ταπεινοφροσύνη; (2) θρησκεία τῶν ἀγγέλων; (3) ἃ ἑόρακεν ἐμβατεύων.

The reference to ταπεινοφροσύνη in Col. 2.18 should not be understood as a virtue such as in Col 3.12 where Paul exhorts the elect of God to put on hearts of compassion, kindness, humility (ταπεινοφροσύνη), gentleness, and patience. In the context of Colossians 2, it refers to a sort of asceticism which involves fasting or self-abasement for the purpose of obtaining visions.[113] The references to food and drink in v. 16, the

107 O'Brien, *Colossians*, p. 139. O'Brien lists LXX Hos. 2.13, Ezek. 45.17, 1 Chron. 23.31, 2 Chron. 2.3, and 2 Chron. 31.3 as references.

108 Cf. also the strict adherence to a sectarian Jewish calendar in the Qumran MMT document.

109 So Eskola, *Messiah*, pp. 189–90; cf. O'Brien, *Colossians*, pp. 138–39; Lincoln, *Paradise*, pp. 111–12; Aletti, *Colossiens*, pp. 192–99.

110 Eskola, *Messiah*, pp. 189–90; Bockmuehl, *Revelation and Mystery*, p. 179; Smith, *Heavenly Perspective*, p. 2; O'Brien, *Colossians*, pp. 152–53; cf. Benoit who connects τὰ στοιχεῖα τοῦ κόσμου (2:20) with the Jewish law, 'Pauline Angelology', pp. 14–15.

111 Francis, 'Humility', pp. 166–67; cf. Eskola, *Messiah*, p. 193.

112 My translation but with Francis's translation as a model and guide.

113 So also Francis, 'Humility', pp. 166–69; Rowland, 'Apocalyptic Visions', pp. 75–78; O'Brien, *Colossians*, p. 142; Eskola, *Messiah*, p. 190; Lincoln, *Paradise*, pp. 111–13; Aletti, *Colossiens*, pp. 192–99. Martha Himmelfarb regards such ascetic practices and techniques in apocalyptic literature as preparatory rituals for purification to make the person worthy of revelation rather than directly for heavenly ascent or visions, Martha Himmelfarb, 'The Practice of Ascent in the Ancient Mediterranean World', *Death, Ecstasy, and Other Worldly Journeys* (ed. John J. Collins and Michael Fishbane; Albany: State University of New York Press, 1995), pp. 123–37, especially 130. Even if this is the case, Himmelfarb's argument is still unconvincing since the would-be-visionaries still

use of ταπεινοφροσύνη in v. 18, the legalistic requirements of v. 21, and another appearance of ταπεινοφροσύνη in v. 23, this time in connection with 'severe treatment of the body', all make this interpretation evident. Furthermore, Jewish and Christian writings are replete with examples of such ascetic practices for the purposes of obtaining visions (Daniel 9; *Gk. Apoc. Ezra* 1.1-5; *4 Ezra* 5.20; 6.35-37; 9.23-25; 12.50-51; *Apocalypse of Abraham* 9; *Asc. Isa.* 2.7-11).[114]

The meaning of the phrase θρησκεία τῶν ἀγγέλων is one of the most complex and controversial issues in studies of the Colossian error. At the heart of the controversy is the question of whether τῶν ἀγγέλων should be understood as an objective or subjective genitive. Traditionally, scholars have interpreted the phrase as an objective genitive and so understood the angels as the recipients of the worship. However, perhaps in light of the discovery and publication of the Qumran manuscripts, a number of recent commentators have elected to interpret θρησκεία τῶν ἀγγέλων as a subjective genitive.[115] In light of the context of Colossians 2 and comparisons with the Dead Sea Scrolls, we regard the subjective genitive as the proper meaning and interpretation. As a result, the proponents of the Colossian philosophy are not involved in directing worship towards angels; rather, they claim either to witness or take part in the worship which the angels direct to God.

Like θρησκεία τῶν ἀγγέλων, the meaning of the phrase ἃ ἑόρακεν ἐμβατεύων is also a source of controversy among commentators who attempt to identify the Colossian philosophy. At the source of the controversy is the meaning and usage of the term ἐμβατεύων. Until recently, the majority of scholars have understood ἃ ἑόρακεν ἐμβατεύων as a technical expression describing entry and initiation into mystery religions.[116] However, in his articles 'Humility and Angelic Worship in Col. 2.18' and 'The Background of ἐμβατεύων (Col. 2.18) in Legal Papyri and Oracle Inscriptions', F. O. Francis has argued successfully against the notion that ἐμβατεύων always carries the technical meaning of entrance into the mystery cults.[117] In the Septuagint, the term's basic meaning is 'to enter' or 'to enter into possession of' and the result of Israel's entrance into the promised land was to have a portion in the Lord.[118] As a result,

take part in various ascetic practices to make themselves worthy for the ultimate goal of heavenly ascent or visions.

114 See Francis, 'Humility', pp. 167–71.

115 See further Francis, 'Humility', pp. 176–81; Rowland, 'Apocalyptic Visions', p. 75; Evans, 'Colossian Mystics', pp. 196–97; O'Brien, *Colossians*, pp. xxxvii, 142–43; Eskola, *Messiah*, pp. 190–92; Lincoln, *Paradise*, pp. 111–12; Aletti, *Colossiens*, pp. 196–97.

116 Cf. Francis, 'Humility', pp. 166, 171–73; Francis, 'Background'; O'Brien, *Colossians*, p. 144.

117 Francis, 'Humility', pp. 171–76; Francis, 'Background'.

118 So Francis, 'Background', pp. 198–99; Francis, 'Humility', pp. 165, 171–72.

the ‘entrance’ in Col. 2.18 should be understood as an entrance to the heavenly realm wherein the worshippers enter into the presence of the Lord and so experience the heavenly worship.[119]

In our survey above, we noted that apocalyptic literature is full of examples of heavenly ascents in which the visionaries or Old Testament heroes often witness or participate in heavenly worship. In addition, a number of scholars have compared the pre-Christian (c. 100 BC)[120] Qumran text *Songs of the Sabbath Sacrifice* (or the Angelic Liturgy) to the error which Paul addresses in Colossians 2.[121] Whereas the majority of the texts from Qumran have either few or brief references to heaven, in the Songs of the Sabbath Sacrifice there is a substantial amount of attention given to the heavenly Temple and the angelic praise in the heavenly Temple.[122] The Angelic Liturgy draws heavily from the Book of Ezekiel with its emphasis on the throne chariot and the heavenly Temple. In 4Q405 20 ii, 21-2 we read,

> [Praise the God of ... w]onder, and exalt Him ... of glory in the te[nt of the God of] knowledge. The [cheru]bim prostrate themselves before Him and bless. As they rise, a whispered divine voice [is heard], and there is a roar of praise. When they drop their wings, there is a [whispere]d divine voice. The cherubim bless the image of the throne-chariot above the firmament, [and] they praise [the majes]ty of the luminous firmament beneath His seat of glory. When the wheels advance, angels of holiness come and go. From between His glorious wheels, there is as it were a fiery vision of most holy spirits. About them, the appearance of rivulets of fire in the likeness of gleaming brass, and a work of ... radiance in many-coloured glory, marvellous pigments, clearly mingled. The spirits of the living ‘gods’ move perpetually with the glory of the marvellous chariot(s). The whispered voice of blessing accompanies the roar of their advance, and they praise the Holy One on their way of return. When they ascend, they ascend marvellously and when they settle, they stand still. The sound of joyful praise is silenced and there is a whispered blessing of the ‘gods’ in all the camps of God. And the

119 Francis, ‘Humility’, pp. 171–76; Francis, ‘Background’; cf. Rowland, ‘Apocalyptic Visions’, p. 76; Evans, ‘Colossian Mystics’, p. 198; O’Brien, *Colossians*, pp. 144–45; Eskola, *Messiah*, pp. 192–93; Roberts, ‘Jewish Mystical Experience’, pp. 166, 171.

120 Carol A. Newsom assigns a general date of 100 BC for the composition of *Songs of the Sabbath Sacrifice*, ‘Songs of the Sabbath Sacrifice’, *Encyclopedia of the Dead Sea Scrolls* 2, pp. 887–89 (887); cf. Geza Vermes who also argues for a first-century-BC composition, *An Introduction to the Complete Dead Sea Scrolls* (London: SCM Press, 1999), p. 54.

121 Rowland notes that the Songs of the Sabbath Sacrifice with its details of heavenly mysteries and secrets has a ‘similar ethos’ to apocalyptic literature, Rowland, *Open Heaven*, p. 16.

122 Carol A. Newsom, ‘Heaven’, *Encyclopedia of the Dead Sea Scrolls* 1, pp. 338–40. Newsom notes that the Songs of the Sabbath Sacrifice contain ‘the most extensive description of the heavenly realm in Qumran literature’, ‘Heaven’, p. 339.

> sound of praise ... from among their divisions ... and all their numbered ones praise, each in his turn. (4Q405 20 ii, 21-2) (Vermes)

In her examination, Carol Newsom describes the function of the Songs of the Sabbath Sacrifice 'as the means for a communion with angels in the act of praise, in short, as a form of communal mysticism'.[123] Furthermore, it is possible that the thirteen Songs were utilized as liturgy during a time of festival whereby the members join in the angelic heavenly worship.[124] Within the course of the thirteen-week cycle, the members of the worshipping community undergo a lengthy preparation, recount the mysteries of the angelic priesthood, celebrate the sabbatical number seven, and finally are led through the heavenly Temple until they experience the merkabah and the worship of the angels.[125]

The Angelic Liturgy's mystical communion with the angels, experience of the merkabah, and joining in the worship of the angels are all reminiscent of the Colossian heresy.[126] Timo Eskola writes, 'In this respect the Colossian "heretics", i.e. Jewish teachers, may have been kindred souls of Qumran or Essene ascetics who possessed a rich angelology and based their faith in angelic liturgy. Their description of the heavenly world was fascinating and offered great mystical experience.'[127] Such an interpretation indeed fits well with the description of the Colossian error (2.16-23), Paul's response to the error (1.15-20; 2.8-15; 3.1-4), the notion of heavenly ascent in Jewish apocalyptic, and descriptions of heavenly participation in the Qumran manuscripts.

For Paul, the most significant problem with the Colossian philosophy was either that Christ was completely absent or, in the least, that their Christology was severely deficient.[128] Their religious rituals were but shadows and their teaching only the traditions of men, while Paul clearly insisted that Christ was the substance (2.17). Their asceticism and self-abasement had no value against fleshly indulgence. As a result, Paul refutes this Colossian error with a cosmic Christology. In Col.

123 Newsom, 'Songs', p. 888. See further Carol A. Newsom, *Songs of the Sabbath Sacrifice: A Critical Edition* (Harvard Semitic Studies 27; Atlanta: Scholars Press, 1985), pp. 5–21, especially 17–19.

124 Newsom, 'Songs', p. 888.

125 Newsom, *Songs*, p. 19.

126 Cf. Newsom, 'Songs', p. 889; Eskola, *Messiah*, pp. 190–92; Bandstra, 'Colossian Errorists', p. 333.

127 Eskola, *Messiah*, p. 192.

128 Cf. Eskola, *Messiah*, pp. 194–96; Bandstra, 'Colossian Errorists'; Roberts, 'Jewish Mystical Experience', pp. 169–75. In this sense, we disagree with Francis's more positive view of the errorists when he writes that the errorists also believed in the pre-eminence of Christ and would have sung praises both to God and to Christ at God's right hand, 'Humility', pp. 183–84. Others who more or less adhere to Francis's view include: Rowland, 'Apocalyptic Visions', pp. 77–78; Evans, 'Colossian Mystics', pp. 195–204.

1.15-20 Paul most likely addresses, albeit implicitly, the Colossian heresy and demonstrates that Christ is the fullness of God and that he is the one who has reconciled both things on earth and things in heaven. Furthermore, rather than any revelations which the Colossian errorists might have received through heavenly visions, Paul communicates in Col 2.3 that all the treasures of wisdom and knowledge are hidden in Christ.[129] In Col 2.8-15 we read that the πλήρωμα of the Deity dwells in Christ (2.9) and that believers have been given fullness (πεπληρωμένοι) in Christ (2.10).[130] Furthermore, Christ is the head of the rulers and authorities (2.10) and has also triumphed over them (2.15).

After Paul's direct address of the Colossian error in Col. 2.16-23, he writes:

> Therefore if you have been raised up with Christ, keep seeking the things above, where Christ is, seated at the right hand of God. [2] Set your mind on the things above, not on the things that are on earth. [3] For you have died and your life is hidden with Christ in God. [4] When Christ, who is our life, is revealed, then you also will be revealed with Him in glory. (Col. 3.1-4)

These verses represent the climax of Paul's thoughts on the Colossian philosophy. It is interesting and significant to note that Paul here combats the realized eschatology of the mystical visionaries with a realized eschatology which is found in Christ when he writes that believers have been raised up with Christ (3.1) and that believers' lives are hidden with Christ in God (3.3).[131] Indeed, Paul's instruction makes it clear that believers already participate in the heavenly reign of God since their lives are incorporated into Christ who is seated at the right hand of God. Timo Eskola appropriately summarizes Paul's response to the Colossian error when he writes:

> The Colossean Jewish mystics had relied on visions. They had sought the things that are above by conducting ascetic humility and joining angelic worship. For Paul, there was but one center in the heavenly Temple. It was the throne of Glory, and Christ, the Lord of the Church, was sitting on that throne.[132]

Since Christ is on the throne and in heaven, the Colossian believers are

129 Cf. Evans, 'Colossian Mystics', pp. 200–201, and Bandstra, 'Colossian Errorists', pp. 340–43, who also contend that Col. 2.3 served as part of Paul's polemical teaching against the Colossian error.

130 Others who also understand Col. 2.9-10 in the light of Paul's polemical teaching against the Colossian error include: Rowland, 'Apocalyptic Visions', pp. 82–83, note 35; Evans, 'Colossian Mystics', p. 202; Eskola, *Messiah*, p. 195.

131 Cf. Lincoln, *Paradise*, pp. 126–27.

132 Eskola, *Messiah*, p. 195.

to seek God in the proper manner – through Christ. It is not that the Colossian believers should not seek God or the heavenly things, but that they should seek them through Christ. Indeed they should seek these heavenly things since their lives are already raised up with Christ and hidden with Christ in God (Col. 3.1-4).

5. *Summary of the Colossian Heresy*

Our analysis thus far has led to the conclusion that in Colossians, Paul addresses a Jewish mystical ascetic heresy. It seems probable that there was a Jewish group in Colossae who adhered to a form of asceticism and various Jewish practices in order to experience visions and gain entry into the heavenly realm whereby they participated in the angelic worship before the throne of God. It is Paul's desire that the Colossian church not be deceived by this false teaching (2.4, 8) and so Paul communicates clearly that believers should not let themselves be condemned (2.16) or disqualified (2.18) on account of these Jewish demands and ascetic practices which are a mere shadow while Christ is the substance (2.17). Additionally, these commands are but the teachings of men (2.22) and have no value against fleshly indulgence (2.23). As detailed above, Paul's primary polemics against this false teaching are his presentation of a cosmic Christology, his teaching on the great salvation accomplished in Christ, and the implications of this great salvation for believers.

Whether this false teaching should be understood as inside[133] or outside[134] the church we cannot be completely certain, but based on Paul's positive description of the Colossian believers and his relatively subdued response to the Colossian heresy, it is our view that the latter is more likely.[135] A number of scholars have noted Paul's much more gentle response to the Colossian heresy than, for example, Paul's response to the issues of faith in Galatians (Gal. 1.6-9; 3.1-3; 4.9-21; 5.1-12). In light of this, it seems either that the heresy was not as egregious or that the heresy was primarily outside the church. In regard to the first consideration, as noted above, we cannot agree with Francis and others

133 Francis, 'Humility', pp. 183–84; Rowland, 'Apocalyptic Visions', pp. 77–78; Evans, 'Colossian Mystics', pp. 199–204.

134 Eskola, *Messiah*, pp. 195–96; Bandstra, 'Colossian Errorists', p. 343, note 81; Roberts, 'Jewish Mystical Experience', pp. 164, 169–75; Ellis, 'Paul and His Opponents', p. 295.

135 We also cannot accept Morna D. Hooker's proposal that in Colossians, Paul does not address a specific error or false teaching either inside or outside the church. Hooker contends that the Colossian believers were merely under the more general daily pressure from Judaism and paganism rather than a specific false teaching, Morna D. Hooker, 'Were there False Teachers in Colossae?', *Christ and Spirit in the New Testament: In Honor of Charles Francis Digby Moule* (ed. Barnabas Lindars and Stephen S. Smalley; Cambridge: Cambridge University Press, 1973), pp. 315–31.

who maintain that the errorists would have worshipped Christ at the right hand of God and so make the Colossian error only a matter of praxis rather than doctrine.[136] In support of the second consideration – that the heresy was primarily outside the church – we note Paul's relatively positive description of the Colossians as growing in the gospel (1.5-6) and as steadfast in their faith in Christ (2.5). The submission to the ascetic decrees of the false teaching in 2.20-21 indicates that the error had probably made some inroads into the church[137] but it seems unlikely that the heresy was widespread or that it had led to the defunct Christology or the heavenly visions of the errorists. Thus Paul's teaching in Colossians serves as a safeguard and a warning so that the community of believers would not be deceived by this Jewish ascetic mysticism. For those in the community of believers (perhaps Jewish Christians) who might have been attracted to the ascetic practices of this Jewish group, Paul's instruction makes it clear that this false teaching is only the teaching of man and has no value against fleshly indulgence (2.20-23). Additional questions such as the precise role of the powers[138] and whether there was a need for a mediator[139] in the Colossian heresy are interesting but also subsidiary.

As noted in the introduction to this book, there is a close relationship between the New Testament letters Colossians and Ephesians. If, as we have maintained, Paul wrote Colossians in order to address the specific needs of that church and then wrote Ephesians to address some similar concerns but in a more general nature and for a wider readership, then

136 Francis, 'Humility', pp. 183–84. Others who more or less adhere to Francis's view include: Rowland, 'Apocalyptic Visions', pp. 77–78; Evans, 'Colossian Mystics', pp. 195–204.

137 Cf. Peter T. O'Brien, 'Colossians', *New Bible Commentary* (ed. D. A. Carson, R. T. France, J. A. Motyer, and G. J. Wenham; Leicester: InterVarsity, 4th edn, 1994), pp. 1260–76 (1261).

138 It is not altogether clear what the precise role of the powers in Colossians was. Some scholars have speculated that the Colossian error taught that the spiritual powers controlled access to heaven and so needed to be placated by asceticism in order to gain heavenly entry. See, e.g., Lincoln, *Paradise*, pp. 114–20; O'Brien, *Colossians*, p. xxxiii; Aletti, *Colossiens*, pp. 211–13. In this view, the spiritual powers of the Colossian error served as the mediators rather than Christ.

139 In opposition to the view of the Colossian error in which the spiritual powers serve as the mediators for heavenly ascent, Andrew J. Bandstra argues that the primary problem of the Colossian heresy was that there was no need for a mediator whatsoever and so as a result, no need for Christ, 'Colossian Errorists', especially pp. 332–33, 343. In Bandstra's view, the role of the angels or spiritual powers in the Colossian error was to give instructions for the ascetic practices which were required to gain heavenly visions and participation in the heavenly worship. In this view, the angels, or spiritual powers, were not divine mediators, Bandstra, 'Colossian Errorists', p. 339. Bandstra's hypothesis that there was no need for a mediator in the Colossian heresy, which in general has not been well received, may indeed be correct but it is doubtful that such a belief served as a 'polemic', as Bandstra also contends.

it is quite possible that we might find in the letter of Ephesians some associations and connections with the Jewish mystical teaching of Colossians. We now turn our attention to Eph. 2.6 and its surrounding context to investigate whether Jewish merkabah mysticism or the Jewish mystical heresy of Colossians can illumine the heavenly status granted to believers.

6. *Examination of Ephesians 2.6 in the Light of Jewish Mysticism*

Following our examinations of Jewish mysticism in Second Temple Jewish literature, mystical thought in the life and writings of Paul, and the Jewish mystical heresy in Colossians 2, we now turn our attention to Eph. 2.6 and its surrounding context. In this section, our purpose is to investigate the relationship between Jewish mysticism and the heavenly status granted to believers in Eph. 2.6. In this examination we will investigate: (1) conceptual comparisons between Jewish mysticism and Eph. 2.6 and its wider context; (2) exegetical, linguistic, and conceptual links between Eph. 2.6 and Paul's teaching on and address of the Colossian error; (3) contextual clues in Ephesians 2 for a possible implicit polemic against Judaizers. We turn our attention now to these tasks.

a. Conceptual comparison of Jewish mysticism and Ephesians 2.6 and its larger context

As stated above, our first task is to examine possible conceptual links between Ephesians 2 and Jewish mystical thought. Since the discovery of the Dead Sea Scrolls, a number of scholars have noted possible parallels, similar themes, and similar terminology between the Qumran manuscripts and the New Testament letter of Ephesians.[140] In fact, Timothy Lim contends that, of all the letters in the Pauline corpus, 'Ephesians shows the greatest proportion of Qumranic terminology and

140 See, e.g., Franz Mussner, 'Contributions Made by Qumran to the Understanding of the Epistle to the Ephesians', *Paul and Qumran* (ed. Jerome Murphy-O'Connor, OP; London: Geoffrey Chapman, 1968), pp. 159–78; Kuhn, 'Epistle', pp. 115–31; Pierre Benoit, 'Qumran and the New Testament', *Paul and Qumran* (ed. Jerome Murphy-O'Connor, OP; London: Geoffrey Chapman, 1968), pp. 1–30, (16–17); Timothy H. Lim, 'Paul, Letters of', *Encyclopedia of the Dead Sea Scrolls* 2, pp. 638–41 (638); Bertil Gärtner, *The Temple and the Community in Qumran and the New Testament: A Comparative Study in the Temple Symbolism of the Qumran Texts and the New Testament* (SNTSMS 1; Cambridge: Cambridge University Press, 1965), pp. 60–66; Nils Alstrup Dahl, 'Ephesians and Qumran', *Studies in Ephesians: Introductory Questions, Text- & Edition-Critical Issues, Interpretation of Texts and Themes* (ed. David Hellholm, Vemund Blomkvist, and Tord Fornberg; WUNT 131; Tübingen: Mohr Siebeck, 2000), pp. 107–44; Lincoln, 'Re-Examination', pp. 473, 475; Lincoln, *Paradise*, pp. 149–52, 165–67; S. F. Noll, 'Qumran and Paul', *DPL*, pp. 777–83 (778); Vermes, *Introduction*, p. 40.

ideas'.[141] In particular, some scholars have argued for possible parallels between Ephesians 2 and the Qumran texts 1QH 11, Hymn 10 and 1QH 19, Hymn 21.[142]

> **1QH 11, Hymn 10** I thank Thee, O Lord, for Thou has redeemed my soul from the Pit, and from the hell of Abaddon. Thou hast raised me up to everlasting height. I walk on limitless level ground, and I know there is hope for him whom Thou hast shaped from dust for the everlasting Council. Thou hast cleansed a perverse spirit of great sin that it may stand with the host of the Holy Ones, and that it may enter into community with the congregation of the Sons of Heaven. Thou hast allotted to man an everlasting destiny amidst the spirits of knowledge, that he may praise Thy Name in a common rejoicing and recount Thy marvels before all Thy works. (Vermes)

> **1QH 19, Hymn 21** In thy wrath are all chastisements, but in Thy goodness is much forgiveness and Thy mercy is towards the sons of Thy goodwill. For thou hast made known to them the counsel of Thy truth, and hast taught them Thy marvelous mysteries. For the sake of Thy glory, Thou has purified man of sin that he may be one [with] the children of Thy truth and partake of the lot of Thy Holy Ones; that bodies gnawed by worms may be raised from the dust to the counsel [of Thy truth], and that the perverse spirit (may be lifted) to the understanding [which comes from Thee]; that he may stand before Thee with the everlasting host and with [Thy] spirits [of holiness], to be renewed together with all the living and to rejoice together with them that know. (Vermes)

141 Lim, 'Paul', p. 638, though Lim considers Ephesians to be deutero-Pauline.

142 Franz Mussner, 'Contributions', pp. 159–78, and A. T. Lincoln who follows Mussner in 'Re-Examination', p. 473, and *Paradise*, pp. 149–50. The Qumran text 1QS 11.3-10 is also similar in theme and language to the two texts cited above. Finally, see also 4Q 491, fragment 11. For discussions of 4Q 491, fragment 11, see Morton Smith, 'Ascent to the Heavens and Deification in 4QM^{a}', *Archaeology and History in the Dead Sea Scrolls: The New York University Conference in Memory of Yigael Yadin* (ed. Lawrence H. Schiffman; JSPSup, 8/American Schools of Oriental Research/Journal for the Study of the Old Testament Monograph Series, 2; Sheffield: Sheffield Academic Press, 1990), pp. 181–88; John J. Collins, 'A Throne in the Heavens: Apotheosis in Pre-Christian Judaism', *Death, Ecstasy, and Other Worldly Journeys* (ed. John J. Collins and Michael Fishbane; Albany: State University of New York Press, 1995), pp. 43–58; Martin G. Abegg, 'Who Ascended to Heaven? 4Q491, 4Q427, and the Teacher of Righteousness', *Eschatology, Messianism, and the Dead Sea Scrolls* (ed. Craig A. Evans and Peter W. Flint; Studies in the Dead Sea Scrolls and Related Literature 1; Grand Rapids: Eerdmans, 1997), pp. 61–73. In 4Q 491, fragment 11, an unknown speaker proclaims that he has 'a throne of strength in the congregation of the "gods"' (Vermes) and that he dwells in heaven. The identity of the speaker is probably a person and suggestions include the Teacher of Righteousness, a person speaking on behalf of the teacher, or another teacher within the Qumran community. Though there are some evident similarities between this text and Eph. 2.6, one notable difference is that the experience of the speaker in 4Q 491, fragment 11 seems to be unique and therefore not an experience of the community at large.

In *The Cultic Setting of Realized Eschatology in Early Christianity*,[143] David Aune reviews some important discoveries in Heinz-Wolfgang Kuhn's Heidelberg's book *Enderwartung und gegenwärtiges Heil: Untersuchungen zu den Gemeindeliedern von Qumran*.[144] On the basis of these two Qumran texts, Kuhn lists five eschatological acts which are appropriated in the present age by members of the Qumran community: (1) resurrection; (2) new creation; (3) communion with angels; (4) deliverance from the final power of the realm of death; (5) proleptic eschatological transference to heaven.[145] On the basis of Kuhn's exegesis of these two Qumran texts, we find parallels to all of these eschatological acts in Ephesians 2.

1 *Resurrection*: In Eph. 2.5-6 God 'made us alive together with Christ (συνεζωοποίησεν τῷ Χριστῷ) ... and raised us up (συνήγειρεν) with Him'.
2 *New Creation*: In Eph. 2.10 believers are God's workmanship, created in Christ Jesus (κτισθέντες ἐν Χριστῷ Ἰησοῦ) for good works. Additionally, in Eph. 2.15, Christ '[abolishes] in His flesh the enmity ... so that in Himself He might make (or create [κτίσῃ]) the two into one new man'.
3 *Communion with angels*: Ephesians 2.19 reads that 'you are no longer strangers and aliens, but you are fellow citizens with the saints (τῶν ἁγίων), and are of God's household'. A number of scholars have argued for understanding ἁγίων here as a reference to angels. This interpretation, however, is inconsistent with Paul's usage in Ephesians and throughout the Pauline corpus where ἅγιοι refers to believers;[146] however, since the expression συμπολῖται τῶν ἁγίων καὶ οἰκεῖοι τοῦ θεοῦ most likely refers to the saints as 'fellow citizens with the redeemed of all ages',[147] then, while we do not find a reference to communion with angels in 2.19, it is probable that a participation in the heavenly community is in view.[148]
4 *Deliverance from the final power of the realm of death*: In Eph. 2.1 Paul describes the former plight of believers as dead in their sins and trespasses; however, in Eph. 2.5-6 God has made them alive with Christ and raised them up with him. Paul continues to develop this image of believers' deliverance with his statement that they have been saved (ἐστε σεσῳσμένοι) by grace through faith (2.8).
5 *Proleptic eschatological transference to heaven*: God has seated believers in the heavenlies in Christ Jesus (2.6).

143 David Edward Aune, *The Cultic Setting of Realized Eschatology in Early Christianity* (NovTSup 28; Leiden: Brill, 1972).

144 Heinz Wolfgang Kuhn, *Enderwartung und gegenwärtiges Heil: Untersuchungen zu den Gemeindeliedern von Qumran* (SUNT 4; Göttingen: Vandenhoeck & Ruprecht, 1966). As cited in Aune, *Cultic Setting*, pp. 31–33.

145 As cited in Aune, *Cultic Setting*, pp. 31–33.

146 Cf. Hoehner, *Ephesians*, pp. 392–93; O'Brien, *Ephesians*, p. 211; Lincoln, *Ephesians*, pp. 150–51; Turner, 'Mission', p. 145.

147 Hoehner, *Ephesians*, p. 396; see also Hoehner's full discussion, *Ephesians*, pp. 392–96.

148 Cf. O'Brien, *Ephesians*, p. 211.

In similar fashion, Franz Mussner also identifies the bond between the community and Heaven within the Qumran writings[149] and writes that the Qumran manuscripts greatly clarify Eph. 2.18-22 and Eph. 2.5-6.[150] In Eph. 2.18-22 the community of the church, which includes both Jews and Gentiles, has 'access to the Father'.[151] In Eph. 2.5-6 those who are united to Christ join him in the heavenly realms just as the members of the Qumran community are united with the sons of heaven.[152] Mussner notes possible parallels between what God has accomplished for believers in Eph. 2.5-6 and what God has done for the Qumran community in 1QH 11, Hymn 10.[153] God has made believers alive (συνεζωποίησεν), has raised them (συνήγειρεν), and has seated them (συνεκάθισεν) with Christ in the heavenlies. In the Qumran text, God has redeemed the sinner's soul from the pit and has made him rise to everlasting heights so that he might enter into the fellowship of the heavenly assembly.[154]

In addition to the similarities between Ephesians and these two Qumran texts, we can also identify some common themes from our study of Jewish merkabah mysticism and Ephesians 2:

1 *Heavenly journey*: Though there is no heavenly journey for the redeemed in Ephesians, believers are granted a heavenly status (Eph. 2.6). In Eph. 4.10 Christ has ascended above all the heavens.
2 *Ascent to God's throne in the highest heaven*: In Eph. 2.6 believers have been raised up with Christ and have been seated with him in the heavenlies. Christ has ascended above all the heavens (Eph. 4.10) and is seated at the right hand of God in the heavenlies (Eph. 1.20).
3 *Early Jewish mysticism as throne mysticism*: Within the Pauline corpus outside Ephesians, Paul draws upon common themes in merkabah mysticism and writes that Christ is the image of God (εἰκὼν τοῦ θεοῦ) (2 Cor. 4.4), that the glory of God is found in the face of Christ (2 Cor. 4.6), and that Christ is the image of the invisible God (εἰκὼν τοῦ θεοῦ τοῦ ἀοράτου). In a clear allusion to Psalm 110, Paul writes in Eph. 1.20 that the one whom he had previously described as the image and glory of God is enthroned and seated at the right hand of God in the heavenlies.
4 *Depiction of a heavenly Temple*: Though in Ephesians we do not find an exact parallel to the apocalyptic descriptions of the heavenly Temple, Paul does portray the church as a holy Temple in the Lord (ναὸν ἅγιον ἐν κυρίῳ) and as the dwelling place of God in the Spirit (κατοικητήριον τοῦ θεοῦ ἐν πνεύματι) (2.19-22). Additionally, the description of believers as συμπολῖ ται τῶν ἁγίων καὶ οἰκεῖοι τοῦ θεοῦ (2.19) has led many commentators

149 Mussner, 'Contributions', p. 164.
150 Mussner, 'Contributions', pp. 166–67.
151 Mussner, 'Contributions', p. 166.
152 Mussner, 'Contributions', pp. 166–67; see 1QS 11.7-8; 1QH 3.19-22; 1QH 11.8-14.
153 Mussner, 'Contributions', p. 167.
154 Mussner, 'Contributions', p. 167; cf. p. 175.

to conclude that Eph. 2.19-22 is indeed a reference to the church as an eschatological heavenly Temple of God.

5 *A special relationship between God's throne of Glory and other heavenly thrones; the throne as a place of honour that is promised for the righteous*: In Eph. 2.6 Paul can portray believers as enthroned with Christ and as in the heavenlies with Christ precisely because of the special relationship which believers have with Christ – that of union with him (ἐν Χριστῷ Ἰησοῦ) (Eph. 2.5-6).

From our analysis of 1QH 11, Hymn 10, 1QH 19, Hymn 21, and common themes of merkabah mysticism, we note quite a number of conceptual and thematic similarities with Eph. 2.5-6 and the larger context of Ephesians. What are we to make of these possible conceptual similarities and associations? Though he acknowledges that there is no direct dependence of Ephesians on the Qumran manuscripts, Mussner has argued, however, that the thematic association of ideas between the two leads to the conclusion that 'the thematic material of Eph has its roots in a tradition that is also represented at Qumran'.[155] It seems at times Lincoln has also understood the parallels with Qumran to be the result of some sort of influence[156] while at other times he writes that the realized eschatological language of Eph. 2.5-6 was a development of his teaching in Colossians which would also serve as a safeguard against the Hellenistic syncretism of Asia Minor.[157] In our view, there are two primary reasons for the thematic similarities between the Qumran manuscripts and the realized eschatology of Ephesians: (1) a similar hermeneutic in which the community is understood as the Temple of God; (2) the similarities between Eph. 2.5-6 and Col. 2.12-13 and 3.1-4, namely that Paul wrote Ephesians 2 with some of the same concerns as he had in mind when he addressed the Colossian heresy. We will now examine the first of these reasons but, as stated above, we will discuss the similarities between Eph. 2.5-6 and Colossians in the next section.

In the Old Testament, the Temple represented the dwelling place of God on earth and so also the place where God could be met. In our study of merkabah mysticism above, we noted that the instability of the Second Temple led to the apocalyptic notion that it was necessary to ascend to the heavenly Temple in order to access God and to understand his ways. While the notion of heavenly ascent is not well attested in the Qumran manuscripts, the perversion of the Second Temple similarly led the Dead Sea community to break from the Temple, albeit in an altogether different fashion. Since the Qumran community deemed the Second Temple and its priesthood to be corrupt, it located the Temple

155 Mussner, 'Contributions', p. 178; cf. p. 173.

156 Lincoln, 'Re-Examination', p. 473; *Paradise*, pp. 149–52.

157 Lincoln, *Paradise*, pp. 135–40.

or the dwelling place of God within the actual Qumran community.[158] This doctrine sheds great light on the Qumran texts discussed above which describe the communion between the Dead Sea community and the heavenly community (4Q405 20 ii, 21-2; 1QH 11, Hymn 10; 1QH 19, Hymn 21; 1QS 11.3-10).

As noted above, some scholars have observed similarities and have drawn parallels between the heavenly status of the Qumran community and Ephesians 2. It is our contention that some of these thematic associations can be accounted for on the basis of a similar hermeneutic – the identification of the community as the Temple.[159] In Eph. 2.19-22 Paul also describes the church or the community of believers as the Temple and as the dwelling place of God in the Spirit. As a result, when we compare these passages, what we find is that this common identification of the community as the Temple accounts for many of the conceptual similarities identified above. Upon close inspection, however, it becomes clear that Paul's understanding of the church as the Temple[160] is quite different from the Qumran understanding. Whereas the basis for Qumran's identification of the community as the Temple was the wickedness and corruption of the Second Temple and its priesthood, the basis for Paul's identification of the church as the Temple was specifically centred on Christ. Whereas during Jesus's life early Christian theology and Christology identified Jesus as the Temple (cf. Mt. 12.6; Mk 14.58; Jn 2.19-21), after his death and resurrection, early Christian theology identified believers as the dwelling place of God in the Holy Spirit (cf. Jn 14.23; 1 Cor. 3.16-17; 6.19; 2 Cor. 6.16; Eph. 2.19-22; 1 Pet. 2.4-5).[161] It seems likely that Paul drew upon this early Christian tradition and affirmed first, Christ as the Temple, and then, subsequently, the believers in whom Christ dwelt through his Spirit as the Temple.[162] Moreover, the absolute exclusion of the

158 See especially the excellent discussion of Rowland, *Open Heaven*, pp. 116–20. Rowland discusses three primary texts (1QH 11, Hymn 10; 1QH 19, Hymn 21; 1QS 11.3-10), which we have also cited and discussed above, and concludes that as a result of the Qumran community's separation from the Temple, the members of the community viewed themselves as linked with the heavenly world and as the true Temple in which the heavenly world was connected to mankind. See also Newsom, *Songs*, pp. 5–21, 38–58; Newsom, 'Songs', p. 889; Gary A. Anderson, 'Worship, Qumran Sect', *Encyclopedia of the Dead Sea Scrolls* 2, pp. 991–96, especially 991–94.

159 Cf. Mussner, 'Contributions', p. 173. Bertil Gärtner also notes the close connection between Eph. 2.18-22 and Qumran, *Temple*, pp. 60–66.

160 In addition to Eph. 2.19-22, cf. also 1 Cor. 3.16-17; 6.19; 2 Cor. 6.16.

161 For a more thorough discussion of the metaphor of Temple in early Christian theology, see O'Brien, 'Church', pp. 98–105.

162 Cf. also Sigurd Grindheim who contends that 'the early Christian identification of the believers and the temple seems to owe more to exegesis of the OT than to a direct dependence on the Qumran community', 'What the OT Prophets Did Not Know: The Mystery of the Church in Eph 3,2–13', *Bib* 84 (2003), pp. 531–53 (543, note 45).

Gentiles from the Qumran temple community stands in stark contrast to the New Testament temple community which consists of both Jews and Gentiles.[163] As a result, while the identification of the community as the Temple both in Qumran and Paul accounts for some of their thematic similarities, the different justifications for their understandings demonstrate that it is not necessary to account for the similarities on the basis of dependence or a continuity of tradition.[164] In order to account for additional similarities between Eph. 2.6 and Jewish mysticism, we must turn to a comparison of Eph. 2.5-6 with Colossians.

b. Exegetical, theological, and linguistic links between Ephesians 2.6 and the Colossian heresy

For our purposes, it is significant that Paul's direct teaching and warning against the Colossian heresy (Col. 2.16-23) is bound by two passages, Col. 2.12-13 and Col. 3.1-4, which demonstrate theological, conceptual, and linguistic parallels with Eph. 2.5-6. For the careful reader, the numerous linguistic and theological parallels between Col. 2.12-13 and Eph. 1.19-20 and Eph. 2.5-6 are evident. In Eph. 1.19-20 it is the working of God's mighty strength which raised Christ (ἐγείρας) from the dead (ἐκ νεκρῶν). In Eph. 2.5-6 Paul also writes that, though believers were previously dead in their sins (νεκροὺς τοῖς παραπτώμασιν; cf. Col. 2.13, νεκροὺς ὄντας [ἐν] τοῖς παραπτώμασιν), God has now made them alive together with Christ (συνεζωοποίησεν τῷ Χριστῷ; cf. 2.13, συνεζωοποίησεν σὺν αὐτῷ) and raised them up with Christ (συνήγειρεν; cf Col 2.12, συνηγέρθητε). In both Colossians and Ephesians, Paul writes that these wonderful blessings for those 'in Christ' are the result of God's gracious activity in Christ and are appropriated through faith (Col. 2.12, διὰ τῆς πίστεως; Eph. 2.8, διὰ πίστεως) in him.

In Col. 3.1-4 we once again find both linguistic and conceptual parallels with Eph. 1.20 and 2.6. In Col. 3.1 Paul links an ethical and theological exhortation to a theological doctrine about believers. He has stated previously that believers have been raised with Christ (Col. 2.12). Now Paul implores his readers, as a result of their already being raised up with Christ, to seek the things above (τὰ ἄνω), where Christ is seated at the right hand of God (cf. Eph. 1.20). Paul continues this exhortation and urges his readers to set their minds on the things above (τὰ ἄνω) rather than the things on the earth (τὰ ἐπὶ τῆς γῆς) (3.2). In Col. 3.3 Paul once again picks up the theme of 'dying with Christ' (cf.

163 Cf. Grindheim, 'OT Prophets', p. 543; Aletti, *Éphésiens*, pp. 34–36.

164 In his examination of the similar themes between Qumran and Ephesians, Nils Alstrup Dahl concludes that there is a common literary milieu and shared ideology, but yet also a significant new influence for Paul in the person of Christ, 'Ephesians and Qumran', pp. 107–44. In our estimation, Paul's views of Christ as the Temple and of believers' union with Christ account for the thematic similarities without having to understand the Qumran literature and Ephesians as sharing a common literary milieu and ideology.

Col. 2.12, συνταφέντες αὐτῷ ἐν τῷ βαπτισμῷ; Rom. 6.3-11) and writes that the result of believers' 'dying with Christ' is that their life is now hidden with Christ in God. In his analysis, Lincoln regards Col. 3.1-4 as a reference to believers' incorporation into Christ's resurrection and exaltation.[165] In his comparison of Col. 3.1-4 and Eph. 2.6, Lincoln continues and writes, 'In fact Ephesians 2.6 only makes explicit what is implicit in Colossians 3.1ff where the believer is to seek τὰ ἄνω because Christ is above and the believer's life is hid with Christ in God.'[166] As a result, there is a clear conceptual link between Col. 3.1-4 where believers are hidden with Christ and Eph. 2.6 where believers are raised up and seated with Christ in the heavenlies.

As discussed above, Col. 2.12-13 and Col. 3.1-4 represent Paul's teaching and exhortations in response to the Colossian error which he addresses directly in 2.16-23. New Testament scholars have long agreed that the principal means of Paul's addressing of the Colossian heresy is Christology (cf. 1.15-20). In Col. 2.9-10 Paul writes that all the fullness (πλήρωμα) of the Deity dwells in Christ, and then writes that believers have been made complete (πεπληρωμένοι) in Christ. With his Christology and his description of believers who are united to Christ, Paul communicates to his readers that there is no reason, and that it is indeed futile, to resort to asceticism and visionary practices in order to gain access to the presence of God. God's presence and fullness are already revealed in Christ and believers have been made complete in him. In addition, those 'in Christ' have also been made alive in him and have been raised up with him (2.12-13). After Paul directly addresses the Colossian heresy (2.16-23), which we have identified above as a Jewish mystical asceticism, he writes in Col. 3.1-4 that believers, as a result of their incorporation into Christ, share in his resurrection and exaltation. In 3.1-4 Paul desires for his readers to recognize and to know that their relationship to Christ and their union with him serve as the basis for their access to God. Additionally, Lincoln has correctly noted that Paul's exhortation for the Colossians to seek the things above (3.1-2) was the very thing that the errorists had obsessed about.[167] What we find then in Col. 2.9-13 and 3.1-4 is that Paul combats the realized eschatology of the errorists both with Christology and a realized eschatology which is focused upon and grounded in Christ.

For our examination of Eph 2.6, the theological, conceptual, and linguistic associations with Col. 2.12-13 and Col. 3.1-4 are significant. To be specific, it seems that Paul's addressing of the Colossian error provided the initial impetus for Paul's writing of Eph 2.5-6. As stated previously, it is our view that Paul wrote Colossians to address the specific

165 Lincoln, *Paradise*, p. 122.

166 Lincoln, *Paradise*, p. 148; cf. Lincoln, 'Re-Examination', pp. 473–74.

167 Lincoln, *Paradise*, pp. 126–27.

challenges of the church in Colossae and then wrote Ephesians as a more general letter and for a wider readership for the churches along the road from Ephesus to Colossae.[168] In light of the Jewish mystical ascetic movement which had infiltrated Colossae, Paul seized the opportunity to address some similar concerns in the letter to the Ephesians, albeit in a more implicit manner and with more general instruction.[169] Just as Col. 3.1-4 serves to demonstrate Christ's supremacy and believers' full access to God through Christ, so Eph. 2.5-6 also clearly communicates that a heavenly status and full access to God is already a reality for those 'in Christ'. The readers of Ephesians need not turn to asceticism, visions, or heavenly ascents in order to access the presence of God and to enter the heavenly throne room since, on account of their relationship to Christ, they are already ἐν τοῖς ἐπουρανίοις. Not only is this understanding consistent with the conceptual and linguistic parallels in Colossians, it is also consistent with the larger context of Ephesians 2. As a result, we now turn our attention to Eph. 2.11-22.

c. Ephesians 2.11-22 and a possible implicit polemic against Judaizers

In his commentary on Ephesians, Andrew Lincoln correctly recognizes that within the context of Ephesians, 2.11-22 stands parallel to 2.1-10.[170] While in 2.1-10 Paul reminds his readers of the salvation and new life which they have received in Christ, in 2.11-22 Paul contrasts Gentiles' former position outside the promises and salvation of Israel with Gentiles' present state as participants in God's blessings to Israel through Christ.[171] With Paul's focus both on Gentiles' new standing before God and new relation to Israel, we find both vertical and horizontal dimensions to the salvation which God has accomplished in Christ. In 2.12 Paul describes the former plight of Gentile believers as separate from Christ, excluded from the commonwealth of Israel, strangers to the covenants of promise, having no hope, and without God in the world; however, because of their new life in Christ, Paul writes that Gentile believers have been brought near by the blood of Christ (2.13). Not only have they been brought near, but Christ, through his death and resurrection, has also broken down the dividing wall between Jew and Gentile and established peace and unity both with

168 Turner, 'Ephesians', p. 1222.

169 A number of commentators have also recognized the connection between Paul's polemic against the Colossian error and the more general instruction in Ephesians which would also implicitly address similar concerns. See Turner, 'Mission and Meaning', pp. 143–48; M. D. Goulder, 'Visionaries of Laodicea' *JSNT* 43 (1991), pp. 15–39; Lincoln, *Paradise*, pp. 135–40, 148, 166–67, although Lincoln identifies the Colossian philosophy as a Hellenistic syncretism with some Jewish elements.

170 Lincoln, *Ephesians*, p. 131; cf. Andrew T. Lincoln, 'The Church and Israel in Ephesians 2', *CBQ* 49.4 (1987), pp. 605–24 (607).

171 Lincoln, *Ephesians*, p. 131.

God and with each other (2.14-17). As a result, both Jews and Gentiles have access to God in one Spirit through Christ (2.18). Similarly, in 2.19-22 we also find these horizontal and vertical dimensions in Paul's description of the church as God's household and as the Temple of God. While in 2.19 Paul writes that his Gentile readers are no longer strangers and aliens but instead are fellow citizens with the saints (τῶν ἁγίων)[172] and members of God's household, in 2.19-22 he describes the church as the Temple which is the dwelling place of God in the Spirit. As a result, in Paul's description of the church as the Temple and as the dwelling place of God in the Spirit, we find another graphic illustration of the uniting of the heavenly realms and earthly believers.[173]

If our understanding of Eph. 2.5-6 is correct, then Paul's teaching on the horizontal Jew–Gentile relations and believers' vertical relationship to God makes perfect sense within the context of Ephesians 2. Since Gentiles are now heirs of God's promises and fellow citizens with God's people through Christ, they need not resort to Jewish demands or practices to be identified with God's people. Additionally, Paul's instruction serves to remind Jewish Christians in the congregations that now Gentiles are indeed heirs of God's promises and have been brought near through Christ. Thus Christ's reconciliation of Jew and Gentile and his creating them as one new man is a significant step in Christ's ἀνακεφαλαιώσασθαι of all things and serves as another picture of Christ's reconciliation of two earthly hostilities.[174] Finally, Paul's teaching reminds his primarily Gentile but also Jewish readers that both Jews' and Gentiles' access to God is through Christ in the Spirit (2.18) and that both groups were in need of God's reconciliation through Christ's death on the cross (2.16).

In light of our analysis, the themes of Eph. 2.11-22, such as Gentiles' reconciliation with Jews and access to God, make sense in light of Paul's desire to provide a safeguard for the churches in the Lycus Valley against any false teaching such as was encountered in Colossae. It is our view that scholars of Ephesians have by and large overlooked this possible motive for Paul's writing of Eph. 2.11-22. While some scholars have understood this passage as evidence of some sort of division between Jews and

172 As noted above, τῶν ἁγίων should be understood as a reference to believers and the expression συμπολῖται τῶν ἁγίων καὶ οἰκεῖοι τοῦ θεοῦ should be understood as a reference to all of God's redeemed people throughout all ages.

173 See especially the discussion of Lincoln, *Paradise*, pp. 153–54. In our view, the uniting of heaven and earth through the description of the church as the Temple serves as a picture of the ἀνακεφαλαιώσασθαι of all things in heaven and on earth in Christ. For Paul, this uniting of heaven and earth can presently be witnessed and experienced through believers' session with Christ ἐν τοῖς ἐπουρανίοις and through the picture of the church as the Temple of God, though the final consummation of Christ's ἀνακεφαλαιώσασθαι still lies in the future.

174 So Turner, 'Mission', pp. 144–45; cf. O'Brien, *Ephesians*, pp. 200–201.

Gentiles,[175] others have emphasized the general tone of Ephesians and so concluded that the intent of Paul's instruction here was not to address a specific Jew–Gentile issue but simply to communicate the salvation history of which the Gentiles are now a part.[176] Our understanding of these verses would then represent a middle position of sorts between these two views. In his commentary on Ephesians, Lincoln writes:

> It is significant, however, that the writer chooses to help his Gentile readers appreciate the greatness of their salvation by setting it in the context of Israel's former privileges and their own former deficiencies. He does this not only because he is in all probability a Jewish Christian, but also because he wants his readers to be aware that their salvation has not taken place in a vacuum. Salvation has a history, they have a place in that history, and there is a sense in which in experiencing salvation they have entered into the heritage of Israel.[177]

Thus for Lincoln, Paul's purpose in writing Eph. 2.11-22 is to educate his Gentile readers of their great salvation in Christ, the history of that salvation and their place in it, and their new identity in light of Christ's salvific work.[178] If such is the case, could Paul's teaching, in addition to its pedagogical function, not also serve as an implicit warning and safeguard against those who might impose Jewish demands or practices on the church? If believers have been assured of their equal standing along with the Jews and their access to God through Christ, then they would feel no need to succumb to Jewish expectations, practices, and demands.

In his article 'Mission and Meaning in Terms of "Unity" in Ephesians', Max Turner also recognizes the either real or potential threat of a Judaizing group.[179] Turner regards the reference to the Gentiles as 'the uncircumcision' in 2.11 'as a term of derogation' and indicates that such a Judaiazing mission might be present.[180] Paul's first response is to describe this group as the 'so-called circumcision' (ὑπὸ τῆς

175 See the brief discussion of Lincoln, *Ephesians*, pp. 132–34.

176 So Lincoln, *Ephesians*, pp. 132–34; cf. O'Brien, *Ephesians*, pp. 182–85.

177 Lincoln, *Ephesians*, p. 133.

178 Lincoln, *Ephesians*, p. 133. See also Lincoln's discussion in 'Church', pp. 608–609, 618–19.

179 For Turner's discussion, see 'Mission', pp. 138–48. Contra Lincoln who regards the later composition of Ephesians as evidence that there was no Judaizing mission. Lincoln contends that, in contrast to Galatians, the later date and composition of Ephesians indicates that a major shift had occurred in the early church. While Jewish Christians had greater influence when Paul wrote Galatians, the setting of Ephesians reflects a later date when Gentile Christians had the greater influence, Lincoln, 'Church', p. 620. A significant consideration in Lincoln's conclusion is his view that Ephesians is pseudepigraphal and so reflects a date towards the end of the first century when Jerusalem had fallen, Lincoln, 'Church', p. 620.

180 Turner, 'Mission', p. 144.

λεγομένης περιτομῆς) and to recognize the merely physical nature of their circumcision (ἐν σαρκὶ χειροποιήτου) (2.11).[181] Paul's next response, as we have argued above, is to describe both Jew and Gentile believers as a new entity with equal access to God (2.14-18) and as fellow citizens with the saints and members of God's household (2.19).[182] Furthermore, the church, comprised of both Jews and Gentiles, is growing into a holy Temple in the Lord and serves as the dwelling place of God in the Spirit (Eph. 2.20-22).[183] As Turner writes, 'If Jewish and Gentile believers already share this heavenly and eschatological unity, which will one day embrace the cosmos, the judaising mission has no rationale.'[184] Additionally, if these Jewish and Gentile believers comprehend the remarkable implications of their description as the Temple of God in which God dwells by his Spirit, then they will not feel compelled to succumb to a possible Jewish ascetic mysticism which boasts of heavenly visions and participation in the heavenly community. Indeed, they need not feel compelled since they already participate in the heavenly community through Christ.[185]

In light of our understanding of Eph. 2.5-6, such an implicit warning and general safeguard for believers in the Lycus Valley seem appropriate for the setting of Eph. 2.11-22. In the Old Testament, the Temple represented the locus of God's presence on earth and the place where God could be met. As noted above, after the destruction of the Temple and the subsequent instability of the Second Temple, it became necessary in Second Temple Jewish thought to ascend to the throne of God in order to access his presence and to understand his ways. In Colossians 2 we found that such a Jewish mystical trend continued with the Colossian errorists' claims of visions, entering the presence of God, and taking part in the angelic worship. While in Eph. 2.6 Paul writes that believers are already raised up and seated with Christ in the heavenlies, in Eph. 2.19-22 Paul describes believers as the Temple of God, the very locus of God's presence. Thus Paul's description of the church as members of God's household and as the Temple turns any visionary claim by possible Judaizers on its head. Consequently, Paul's readers would clearly understand that believers are linked with the heavenly world through their union with Christ and through the Holy Spirit.

181 Turner, 'Mission', p. 144.

182 Turner, 'Mission', p. 144.

183 O'Brien correctly notes that the two expressions ναὸν ἅγιον ἐν κυρίῳ and κατοικητήριον τοῦ θεοῦ ἐν πνεύματι are 'parallel descriptions of the same thing', *Ephesians*, p. 221; 'Church', p. 103.

184 Tuner, 'Mission', p. 145.

185 Cf. Turner, 'Mission', p. 145; O'Brien, *Ephesians*, p. 221; Lincoln, *Paradise*, pp. 153–54.

7. Summary and Conclusion of Ephesians 2.6 in the Light of Jewish Mysticism

The majority of Ephesians' commentators have noted the general nature and character of the letter, namely that there is no strong or central polemic and that Ephesians by and large consists of general Christian teaching and exhortation.[186] Though there is a general warning in Eph. 4.14 not to be led astray by false doctrine, such an understanding seems consistent with the letter's lack of specific references, lack of major concerns or problems, and the more general theological discourses and exhortations. As a result, to posit a specific setting or polemic for Ephesians seems misguided;[187] however, Andrew Lincoln has cautioned that such an approach can be too extreme and has noted that despite its more general character in comparison with some of Paul's other letters, Ephesians still has clear indications that Paul wrote the letter for a particular audience and shaped its contents to address their specific needs and challenges.[188] Additionally, on account of similar terminology and themes with Colossians, it is quite likely that some of the same concerns which Paul addressed in Colossians are still present within the area of Western Asia Minor.[189] Though it is not the entire background or occasion for the letter, one of the concerns of Ephesians is likely the Jewish ascetic mysticism encountered in Colossae.[190]

186 See, e.g., Lincoln, *Ephesians*, pp. xl, lxxiv, lxxxvi–lxxxvii; Lincoln, *Paradise*, pp. 135–39; Lincoln and Wedderburn, *Theology*, p. 78; Turner, 'Ephesians', pp. 1222–23; O'Brien, *Ephesians*, pp. 49–51; Best, *Ephesians*, pp. 63–75; Hoehner, *Ephesians*, pp. 97–106; Aletti, *Éphésiens*, pp. 13–17.

187 Contra, e.g., Goulder, 'Visionaries'; Derwood C. Smith, 'The Ephesian Heresy and the Origin of the Epistle to the Ephesians', *Ohio Journal of Religious Studies* 5.2 (1977), pp. 78–103; Arnold, *Power and Magic*. For brief discussions of scholars who have argued for a more specific purpose or background for Ephesians, see Lincoln, *Ephesians*, pp. lxxix–lxxxi, and Hoehner, *Ephesians*, pp. 97–106.

188 So Lincoln, *Ephesians*, p. xl, though Lincoln regards Ephesians as pseudepigraphal.

189 Cf. Lincoln, *Ephesians*, p. lxxxii; Lincoln, *Paradise*, pp. 135–39, and to a lesser extent O'Brien, *Ephesians*, pp. 56–58; Turner, 'Ephesians', pp. 1222–25.

190 With our more moderate stance, we disagree with Goulder who contends that the primary purpose or entire background for Ephesians is to counter Jewish apocalyptic visionaries such as those encountered in Colossae, Goulder, 'Visionaries', pp. 15–39, especially pp. 20, 37. Goulder's hypothesis is interesting and, though we can agree with him that one of Paul's concerns in Ephesians was an implicit safeguard and polemic against Jewish mysticism, it is misguided to posit this background for the entire letter. Moreover, Goulder seems to draw more from other Pauline epistles than from the actual text of Ephesians, Goulder fails to recognize the general nature of Ephesians in comparison to other letters in the Pauline corpus, and much of Goulder's primary evidence is late and so must be read back into Ephesians. Much more fanciful than Goulder's hypothesis is Derwood C. Smith's claim that Ephesians was written to refute Gentiles who were first converted to a Philonic type of Judaism before their conversion to Christianity, Smith,

In our examination of Jewish merkabah mysticism and its relation to the heavenly status granted to believers in Eph. 2.6, we noted conceptual parallels from both apocalyptic literature and the Qumran manuscripts. On the one hand, these parallels can be explained on the basis of the identification of the community as the Temple in both Qumran and Paul. On the other hand, the close associations between Eph. 2.5-6 and Col. 2.11-13 and Col. 3.1-4 lead to the conclusion that Paul's addressing of the Jewish ascetic mysticism in Colossians 2-3 is the catalyst for his emphasis of the realized eschatological salvation accomplished in Christ in Eph. 2.5-6. Furthermore, Paul's teaching in Eph. 2.5-6, with its evident conceptual similarities to the realized eschatology of many Qumran texts, also serves as an implicit safeguard against a similar Jewish ascetic mysticism in the wider Asia Minor region. The Colossian false teaching, which we have identified as a Jewish mystical asceticism, involved visions and heavenly ascent to the throne room of God where the visionaries would take part in the angelic worship. The fact that Paul formulated and modelled Eph. 2.5-6 from Col. 2.12-13 and Col. 3.1-4, two passages which form part of Paul's polemic against this false teaching, indicate that it is quite likely that he had this false teaching in mind when he penned Eph. 2.5-6. As a result, Paul writes that those 'in Christ' have been raised up with him and seated with him in the heavenlies (Eph. 2.6). Paul's point would be clear. If anyone desires access to the presence of God and to the divine throne, these are to be found in Christ and are indeed already a reality for believers who are seated in the heavenlies with Christ.[191] Regardless, Paul's teaching in Colossians provided the initial impetus for the development of this cosmic salvation in which believers have been raised up with Christ and seated with him in the heavenlies (Eph. 2.6).[192] This remarkable statement communicates the greatness of believers' salvation accomplished in Christ and also serves as an implicit safeguard against a similar Jewish ascetic mysticism such as was encountered in Colossians. The larger context of Ephesians 2 (vv. 11-22) also indicates a subtle and implicit polemic against a real or possible Judaizing group in Asia Minor. Finally, since there is abundant evidence of Judaism, as well

'Ephesian Heresy'. According to Smith, the members of this group already believed they existed in a heavenly and bodiless state because of their faulty view of baptismal resurrection and ascension. Though there is some evidence for a subtle polemic against a type of Jewish mysticism, there is no evidence that Ephesians was written to counter a specific type of Philonic Jewish-Christian error which regarded its members as already existing in a heavenly and bodiless state.

191 Goulder also notes the polemical force of Eph. 2.6 against a Jewish visionary movement, 'Visionaries', p. 25; cf. Turner who contends that the polemical thrust of Eph. 2.6 is partly against a Judaizing mission, 'Mission', p. 143, note 14.

192 Cf. Lincoln who contends that Colossians was the catalyst for the development of the cosmic salvation and the realized eschatological heavenly dimension in Ephesians, *Ephesians*, p. lxxxii.

as Jewish mystical and apocalyptic thought in the region of Asia Minor, Paul's addressing of these issues in Colossians and Ephesians makes sense in light of the religious milieu of Asia Minor.[193]

Before we proceed to our exegetical sketch of Eph. 2.1-10, we should write a few brief comments concerning one other difficult and interesting subject which pertains to our examination. As we noted above, both Luke's accounts of Paul and Paul's writings testify to the fact that Paul was a visionary and mystic. Presumably the greatest of Paul's visions or mystical experiences is his ascent to the throne of God in 2 Cor. 12.1-4. The latter portion of our examination, however, has focused on Paul's opposition to mystical activities and heavenly ascents. This tension can even be seen through the work of some scholars who focus almost exclusively on the way in which apocalyptic shaped Paul's theology and the work of other scholars who concentrate on Paul's opposition to apocalyptic and mysticism. How are we to reconcile these two seemingly different strands of thought?

193 For evidence of a substantial, thriving, and influential Jewish population in Asia Minor in the first century AD, see Paul R. Trebilco, *Jewish Communities in Asia Minor* (SNTSMS 69; Cambridge: Cambridge University Press, 1991), especially pp. 1–36, 142, 164–65, 189; Sherman E. Johnson, 'Asia Minor and Early Christianity', *Christianity, Judaism, and Other Greco-Roman Cults: Studies for Morton Smith at 60* (ed. Jacob Neusner; SJLA 12; vol. 2, Early Christianity; Leiden: Brill, 1975), pp. 77–145, especially pp. 97–124, 143–45. For our purposes, it is interesting to note Trebilco's conclusions that the Judaism in Asia Minor was not syncretistic (*Jewish Communities*, p. 142), that Jewish communities in Asia Minor interacted with Gentiles more than other places (*Jewish Communities*, pp. 164–65), and that the Jewish communities in Asia Minor were influential enough that Jewish practices could have been adopted by Christian communities (*Jewish Communities*, p. 189). Pierre Benoit has noted that Asia Minor would have been an area in which there was a strong Qumran tradition and influence, 'Qumran', pp. 16–17. For a discussion of both Jewish and Jewish-Christian apocalyptic movements in Asia Minor, see David Frankfurter, 'The Legacy of Jewish Apocalypses in Early Christianity: Regional Trajectories', *The Jewish Apocalyptic Heritage in Early Christianity* (ed. James C. VanderKam and William Adler; CRINT; Section 3, Jewish Traditions in Early Christian Literature 4; Minneapolis: Fortress Press, 1996), pp. 129–200 (129–42). Even within the NT we find similar themes in other books addressed to various churches in Asia Minor, namely 1 Peter (1.3-5, 2.4-5, 3.21-22) and Revelation (chapters 3–4; cf. especially 3.12; 3.21; 4.2). It is certainly possible that these texts also served as general and implicit safeguards or polemics against a Jewish mystical movement. Additionally, we find evident Christian interest in the apocalyptic tradition in *Martyrdom of Isaiah*, *Ascension of Isaiah*, *4 Ezra* 1–2, *Greek Apocalypse of Ezra*, *Vision of Ezra*, *3 Baruch*, the Christian interpolations in *Testament of the Twelve Patriarchs*, *Testament of Isaac*, *Testament of Jacob*, the Christian interpolations in *Testament of Solomon*, and the Christian additions in *Testament of Adam*. For additional evidence of Jewish mysticism in early Christianity, see Philip Alexander's discussion in *The Mystical Texts* (Library of Second Temple Studies 61/Companion to the Qumran Scrolls 7; London: T & T Clark, 2006), pp. 138–43. Alexander concludes that there were many apocalypses and mystical texts with both Jewish and Christian motifs, and that it is often difficult to discern which motifs are Jewish and which ones are Christian, *Mystical Texts*, p. 139.

On the one hand, it seems likely that Paul did not view his mystical experiences as normative for all believers, but rather he believed that his status, role, and position as ἀπόστολος Χριστοῦ Ἰησοῦ privileged him as a recipient of the gospel which he received through ἀποκαλύψεως Ἰησοῦ Χριστοῦ (Gal. 1.11-12). Additionally, though Paul experienced a number of visions and mystical experiences, there is no evidence that he actually sought out such experiences. To this end, some scholars have noted the comparatively passive visionary experiences of Paul in contrast to some of the practices employed to induce visions in many of the apocalypses. In 2 Cor. 12.1-4, for example, Paul's description of his ascent as being 'caught up' (ἁρπαγέντα; ἡρπάγη) to heaven perhaps suggests the passive or involuntary nature of his experience.[194] Additionally, Paul does not list any techniques or ascetic practices necessary for his ascent and his only possible qualification is his description of the visionary as ἄνθρωπος ἐν Χριστῷ.[195] Such a description proves to be highly significant for Paul's opposition to some mystical practices and for his addressing of the Colossian heresy.

In our estimation, it seems that, though Paul experienced numerous visions and even an ascent to heaven, he clearly condemned any such practices which would seek visions or heavenly ascent outside of Christ. As noted above, our view of the Colossian heresy was that a group of Jewish mystics, most likely outside the church, advocated ascetic practices in order to behold visions, ascend to the presence of God, and join in the angelic worship. For Paul, the most significant problem with the Colossian heresy, though by no means the only one, is that Christ was notably absent. As noted above, a number of Ephesians' scholars have observed parallels and similarities between Ephesians and the Qumran manuscripts. How much this tradition on the one hand influenced Paul's thought and on the other hand afforded Paul the opportunity to engage a Jewish mystical heresy we cannot be certain. It is our inclination that, as in Colossians, the similar themes in Ephesians were the result of engaging a Jewish ascetic mystical tradition such as the Colossian heresy; however, the themes and language were also an outworking of Paul's theology of cosmic salvation accomplished in Christ and Paul's view of believers' union with Christ.

194 So also Lincoln, 'Paul', p. 215; Murray J. Harris, *The Second Epistle to the Corinthians: A Commentary on the Greek Text* (NIGTC; Grand Rapids: Eerdmans, 2005), p. 837. Cf. also Schäfer who implies that the ascent might be involuntary, 'New Testament and Hekhalot Literature', pp. 22, 33. Martha Himmelfarb has pointed out, however, that it was also common in other Jewish and Christian ascent accounts for God to bring about the ascent, 'The Practice of Ascent', pp. 123–37.

195 Contra Morray-Jones who claims that the 'merkabah mysticism' context of Paul's vision leads to the probable conclusion that Paul made use of mystical techniques to bring about his ascent, 'Paradise Revisited: Part 2', pp. 283–84.

8. Exegetical Sketch of Ephesians 2.1-10

The purpose of this exegetical sketch of Eph. 2.1-10 is to highlight those issues which are essential for a proper understanding of believers' heavenly session with Christ in Eph. 2.6. We do not attempt here a full exegesis of this passage. Such an endeavour is beyond the scope of this study and detailed exegetical treatments can be found in the numerous commentaries and studies on Ephesians. Rather, as stated above, we will investigate concerns which are important for a proper interpretation of Eph. 2.6 and seek to answer the question of how believers are seated ἐν τοῖς ἐπουρανίοις with Christ.

A careful reading of Eph. 1.15-2.10 demonstrates Paul's portrayal of the intimate relationship between Christ and believers.[196] In Eph. 1.19-20 Paul writes that the same power which God used (ἐνήργησεν) to raise (ἐγείρας) Christ from the dead (ἐκ νεκρῶν) and seat (καθίσας) Christ at his right hand in the heavenlies is also at work (τὴν ἐνέργειαν) in believers. Of particular interest is that soon after writing about Christ's death (1.20), Paul next writes about the 'death' of his readers. In Eph. 2.1 Paul writes that believers were also dead (νεκρούς) but with the qualification τοῖς παραπτώμασιν καὶ ταῖς ἁμαρτίαις (cf. Eph. 2.5). In Eph. 2.2-3 Paul explains what he means by the expression νεκροὺς τοῖς παραπτώμασιν καὶ ταῖς ἁμαρτίαις and elaborates further upon believers' former condition when he writes that they walked according to the course of this world, according to the prince of the power of the air, that they lived in the lusts of their flesh, and that they were children of wrath. Paul's qualification τοῖς παραπτώμασιν καὶ ταῖς ἁμαρτίαις and his subsequent description of believers' former lives clarifies that the type of death which Paul refers to here is a 'spiritual' death.[197]

In Eph. 2.4-5 Paul writes that God, because of his great mercy and love, has made believers, who were formerly dead in their sins (νεκροὺς τοῖς παραπτώμασιν), alive with Christ (συνεζωοποίησεν τῷ Χριστῷ). Since the same power that raised Christ from the dead is at work in believers (1.19-20), it is fitting, though also somewhat surprising, that Paul should write that believers who were dead in their sins have also been made alive with Christ. These verses are strongly reminiscent of and most likely represent a reworking of Col. 2.13, where Paul writes that God has made believers, who were dead in sins (νεκροὺς ὄντας [ἐν]

196 The best treatment of the intimate association between Christ's and believers' exaltation in Eph. 1.20 and Eph. 2.6 is Thomas G. Allen's 'Exaltation and Solidarity with Christ'. Allen writes that the associations between Eph. 1.20-21 and Eph. 2.1-7 '(point) to a real and effective solidarity between Christ and his followers', 'Exaltation', p. 104; cf. O'Brien, *Ephesians*, pp. 154, 166–67.

197 Cf. Caragounis, *Mysterion*, p. 150; O'Brien, *Ephesians*, pp. 156–57; Lincoln, *Ephesians*, pp. 92–93; Best, *Ephesians*, pp. 200–201; Hoehner, *Ephesians*, pp. 307–308.

τοῖς παραπτώμασιν), alive (συνεζωοποίησεν) with Christ.[198] In Eph. 2.6 Paul spells out the implications of believers' having been made alive with Christ when he writes that God has also raised (συνήγειρεν) them up with Christ and seated (συνεκάθισεν) them with Christ ἐν τοῖς ἐπουρανίοις in Christ Jesus (2.6).[199] With this statement, a clear allusion to Eph. 1.20, Paul makes even stronger the close identity between Christ and believers as he applies the same verbs and acts but with the σύν prefix (συνήγειρεν; συνεκάθισεν) to believers as he did to Christ in Eph. 1.20 (ἐγείρας; καθίσας). In Eph. 2.8-9 Paul emphasizes that this great salvation which has been accomplished by Christ is not by works but rather is the gift of God which is received by grace through faith. Whereas believers used to walk (περιεπατήσατε) according to the course of this world and according to the prince of the power of the air, they are now God's workmanship created in Christ Jesus to walk (περιπατήσωμεν) in good works.

From this brief exegetical sketch of Eph. 2.1-10, we can clearly observe Paul's view of the intimate connection between Christ and believers. In his analysis of the passage, Horacio Lona notes a connection between Christology and soteriology and writes, 'So wie Christus nach 1,20 durch die Kraft Gottes von den Toten auferweckt und in den Himmel zur Rechten Gottes versetzt wurde, so wurde der Christ von Gott mit Christus auferweckt und in den Himmel versetzt.'[200] The use of the σύν prefix in Eph. 2.6 with the verbs of Eph. 1.20 also serves to emphasize this close association. Perhaps the strongest indication of this intimate connection between Christ and believers though is Paul's use of the phrase ἐν Χριστῷ Ἰησοῦ. Indeed, 'the phrase ... provides further explanation of how it can be said that what God did for Christ he did at the same time for believers'.[201] Believers have been raised up with Christ and seated with him in the heavenlies ἐν Χριστῷ Ἰησοῦ. The use of this Pauline expression here points not only to Christ as the agent of this salvation, but also to the fact that believers have been incorporated into Christ.[202] This connection between Christology and soteriology and the notion of incorporation into Christ represent what we might term

198 Cf. Rom. 6.8 and 2 Tim. 2.11 where the promise is that believers will live (συζήσομεν) with Christ.

199 It seems best not to understand the verbs συνεζωοποίησεν, συνήγειρεν, and συνεκάθισεν as three separate acts which correspond to the traditional events of resurrection, ascension, and session, O'Brien, *Ephesians*, p. 170, note 67. Rather, it is better to understand the relationship of the three verbs either 'as aspects of the same act of God' (Best, *Ephesians*, pp. 217–18) or with συνήγειρεν and συνεκάθισεν as further explanation of συνεζωοποίησεν (O'Brien, *Ephesians*, p. 170, note 67; Best, *Ephesians*, p. 218).

200 Lona, *Eschatologie*, p. 363. As Allen notes, these correlations demonstrate that what God 'has accomplished in Christ, he has also accomplished for believers', Allen, 'Exaltation', p. 104.

201 Lincoln, *Ephesians*, p. 105.

202 Lincoln, *Ephesians*, p. 105.

a 'historical' aspect to the salvation accomplished in Christ. Since there is solidarity between Christ and believers and since believers have been incorporated into Christ who is ἐν τοῖς ἐπουρανίοις, they can also appropriately be described as ἐν τοῖς ἐπουρανίοις.[203]

The notion of incorporation into Christ also reveals the eschatological character of believers' cosmic salvation in Eph. 2.6.[204] Since Christ, as the representative head of all believers, is ἐν τοῖς ἐπουρανίοις, it is fitting that believers who are incorporated into Christ also reign with him ἐν τοῖς ἐπουρανίοις. Thus we find here a picture of Paul's already/not yet eschatological paradigm. Indeed, the statement that believers have been raised up with Christ and seated with him in the heavenlies 'spells out the implications of the relationship of incorporation in Christ in their most developed form in the Pauline corpus'.[205] In Gal. 3.28, in a statement which could be considered as perplexing as the one in Eph. 2.6, we find another example of Paul's already/not yet eschatological paradigm through the use of the 'in Christ' formula, but with a horizontal emphasis. In Gal. 3.28 Paul writes that there is neither Jew nor Greek, slave nor free man, male nor female, but rather all are one ἐν Χριστῷ Ἰησοῦ. Whereas the eschatological emphasis in Gal. 3.28 is horizontal, in Eph. 2.6 Paul's emphasis is on the vertical implications of

203 See also Lincoln, *Ephesians*, p. 105; Lincoln, *Paradise*, p. 148; Lincoln, 'Re-Examination', pp. 472–74; Lona, *Eschatologie*, p. 298; Bietenhard, *Die himmlische Welt*, p. 211, note 1; Ridderbos, *Paul*, pp. 214, 347; Vos, *Pauline Eschatology*, pp. 37–39; Allen, 'Exaltation', p. 116, note 10; Turner, 'Mission', p. 143, note 14; Best, *Ephesians*, pp. 117, 221–23; O'Brien, *Ephesians*, p. 170; Hoehner, *Ephesians*, pp. 334–35.

204 Paul's statement that believers (on earth) are seated with Christ in the heavenlies is another significant act in God's ἀνακεφαλαιώσασθαι τὰ πάντα ἐν τῷ Χριστῷ, τὰ ἐπὶ τοῖς οὐρανοῖς καὶ τὰ ἐπὶ τῆς γῆς. We previously noted that the union of Jews and Gentiles, two earthly hostilities, was a significant step in God's ἀνακεφαλαιώσασθαι of all things in Christ; however, in Eph. 2.6, it is not merely earthly realities or heavenly realities (such as the powers) which are summed up in Christ, but rather God's eschatological act of bringing together heaven and earth through believers' union with Christ who is seated ἐν τοῖς ἐπουρανίοις. Whereas this eschatological act has been inaugurated by the Christ event, its consummation and complete fulfilment still lie in the future. We also noted above that Paul's vision of the church as the temple of God in Eph. 2.19–22 serves as a similar picture.

205 Lincoln, *Ephesians*, p. 105; cf. Lincoln, *Paradise*, pp. 148, 166–67. We have argued above that the impetus for the realized eschatological language of Eph. 2.5-6 was Paul's addressing of the Colossian heresy in Col. 2.11-13 and Col. 3.1-4. Paul's teaching in Eph. 2.5-6 would subsequently serve as an implicit safeguard against a similar Jewish mystical movement within greater Asia Minor. Goulder ('Visionaries', p. 25) and more moderately Turner ('Mission', p. 143, note 14) also recognize the polemical nature of Eph. 2.5-6 against an actual or possible Jewish visionary movement. A number of other commentators also recognize that Paul utilized the realized eschatological language of Eph. 2.5-6 as some sort of polemic or at least to address a specific situation in the lives of his readers. See, e.g., Lincoln, *Paradise*, pp. 135–40, 148, 166–67; Lincoln, *Ephesians*, pp. 105–109; O'Brien, *Ephesians*, pp. 167, 170–72; G. F. Wessels, 'The Eschatology of Colossians and Ephesians', *Neot* 21 (1987), pp. 183–202, (197–200).

the salvation accomplished in Christ.[206] Though the complete fulfilment of believers' session ἐν τοῖς ἐπουρανίοις still lies in the future, there is nevertheless a realized and experiential aspect to this cosmic salvation.[207] Thus for believers the future expectation of the heavenly world has become present.[208] Moreover, as a result of their union with Christ, believers participate both in Christ's life and reign in heaven.[209]

Though believers' solidarity with Christ and incorporation into Christ shed much light on the heavenly status of believers in Eph. 2.6, this does not fully explain Paul's statement that believers are seated ἐν τοῖς ἐπουρανίοις. A number of scholars have understood the heavenly status granted to earthly believers in Eph. 2.6 as proleptic – that the fulfilment of believers' resurrection and session ἐν τοῖς ἐπουρανίοις is so assured in the future that Paul can speak of it as already having been accomplished.[210] Such an interpretation is certainly plausible and it seems probable that there is a proleptic element to the cosmic salvation Paul describes in Eph. 2.6; however, if a proleptic session with Christ ἐν τοῖς ἐπουρανίοις was all Paul intended, then, in our estimation, it would seem unnecessary for Paul to insert the significant phrase ἐν Χριστῷ Ἰησοῦ. As discussed above, the cosmic salvation accomplished by Christ and believers' session ἐν τοῖς ἐπουρανίοις as a result of their incorporation into Christ entail an experiential component which is already realized in the lives of believers, though its complete fulfilment still lies in the future. In order to answer the question of how believers are presently seated ἐν τοῖς ἐπουρανίοις, we must once again compare the experiences of Christ in Eph. 1.20 with the experiences of believers in Eph. 2.1-6.

In Eph. 1.20 Paul writes that God raised Christ from the dead and seated Christ at his right hand in the heavenlies. At the risk of stating the obvious, Paul here writes of Christ's physical death, physical resurrection, and physical ascension to the right hand of God where Christ is now seated in his heavenly rule. On the other hand, in our brief exegetical sketch, we noted that Paul's description of believers as νεκροὺς τοῖς παραπτώμασιν καὶ ταῖς ἁμαρτίαις (Eph. 2.1; cf. Eph. 2.5) refers not to a physical death but rather to a 'spiritual' death. As a result, when Paul writes in Eph. 2.5-6 that God has made believers alive (συνεζωοποίησεν)

206 So also Christopher Rowland, *Christian Origins: An Account of the Setting and Character of the Most Important Messianic Sect of Judaism* (London: SPCK, 1985), p. 292; Lona, *Eschatologie*, pp. 363–64; Vos, *Pauline Eschatology*, pp. 37–38; Lincoln, 'Re-Examination', pp. 481–83.

207 See also Lincoln, 'Re-Examination', p. 474; Lincoln, *Ephesians*, pp. 108–109; Vos, *Pauline Eschatology*, pp. 37–38; Hoehner, *Ephesians*, p. 336; Wessels, 'Eschatology', pp. 188–90.

208 Vos, *Pauline Eschatology*, p. 38.

209 Lincoln, 'Re-Examination', p. 474.

210 See, e.g., Bruce, *Colossians, Philemon, Ephesians*, p. 287; Caragounis, *Mysterion*, p. 150; Turner, 'Ephesians', p. 1229; Muddiman, *Ephesians*, p. 109.

with Christ, has raised them up with him (συνήγειρεν), and has seated (συνεκάθισεν) them with Christ in the heavenlies, we should expect that, just as believers were not dead in the same way Christ was, so also they were not made alive, nor raised up, nor seated in the heavenlies in the same way Christ was.[211] As Thomas Allen writes, 'The text does not picture a physical resuscitation nor a bodily transportation.'[212] Since believers were not formerly dead and subsequently raised from the dead in the same way as Christ, why should we expect believers to be seated in the heavenlies in the same way as Christ? This seems precisely to be the problem for commentators such as Odeberg and McGough who interpret the heavenlies as the spiritual atmosphere of the church on earth. Such commentators want believers to be seated in the heavenlies in the exact same way as Christ; they deem that impossible, and so they abandon the meaning of the term ἐπουράνιος and spiritualize the heavenlies in Ephesians. Interestingly, by spiritualizing the heavenlies, these commentators still do not solve their exegetical and theological quandaries. They seemingly want an exact analogy between Christ in Eph. 1.20 and believers in Eph. 2.5-6, but it is just as obvious that believers are not made alive and raised up with Christ in the same way in which Christ was. For commentators who spiritualize the heavenlies, these acts should be just as troublesome.

One of the keys for a proper understanding of Eph. 2.5-6 and thus the session of believers ἐν τοῖς ἐπουρανίοις is Paul's use of metaphor.[213] It will have become obvious by now that, though both Christ and believers experience death, resurrection, ascension, and session in the heavenlies in Ephesians, they do not experience these events in the same manner as of yet. Paul's point in Eph. 2.5-6 is that just as God has raised Christ from the dead and seated him in the heavenlies, God has also done these very same things for those who are in Christ spiritually, i.e. Spiritually, in/by the Holy Spirit.[214] We have already noted in Eph. 1.13-14 that believers have been sealed with the Holy Spirit and that the Spirit serves as an ἀρραβών of believers' inheritance. In addition, Geerhardus Vos notes the Holy Spirit's role in resurrection and contends that 'the Spirit is both the instrumental cause of the resurrection-act and the permanent substratum of the resurrection-life'.[215] In other places in

211 See also Allen, 'Exaltation', p. 106; Wessels, 'Eschatology', pp. 188–89; Caragounis, *Mysterion*, p. 150.

212 Allen, 'Exaltation', p. 106.

213 See also Wessels, 'Eschatology', pp. 188–89.

214 So also Allen, 'Exaltation', p. 106; Caragounis, *Mysterion*, p. 150. Lincoln has also drawn attention to the close association between the heavenly world and the spiritual (i.e. of the Holy Spirit) world in 'Re-Examination', p. 470.

215 Geerhardus Vos, 'The Eschatological Aspect of the Pauline Conception of the Spirit', *Biblical and Theological Studies* (New York: Charles Scribner's Sons, 1912), p. 234. See further Vos, 'Eschatological Aspect', pp. 244–45, and Hamilton, *Holy Spirit*, pp. 12–21.

the Pauline corpus, the Spirit's role in both physical and spiritual resurrection is even more clearly identified (cf. Rom. 1.4; 8.2; 8.10-11). In Eph. 2.5-6 the Spirit is not only the instrument of resurrection but also the link between believers on earth and the heavenly realms.[216] Since the same power which God used to raise Christ from the dead and seat him in the heavenlies is at work in believers, God applies these same benefits to those who are united to Christ. These benefits are already realized in the lives of believers as a result of the Spirit (Eph. 1.13-14; 2.18) and as a result of their relationship to Christ (2.6), but they also await their final fulfilment at the consummation (2.7).[217] Thus there is an already/not yet tension to believers' experience of Christ's cosmic salvation, in the role of the Holy Spirit, and in believers' union with Christ.[218] Though at present believers are not raised up and seated in the heavenlies in the same way as Christ, they are nevertheless raised up and seated in the heavenlies in a 'mystical' way through the Holy Spirit. As a result, the expression ἐν τοῖς ἐπουρανίοις does not lose its local significance as a reference to the abode of God; rather, while Christ's session ἐν τοῖς ἐπουρανίοις is at present fully realized, believers at present are seated ἐν τοῖς ἐπουρανίοις through the Holy Spirit and through their union with Christ and yet also await the final fulfilment of this heavenly session in the future.

9. *Conclusions*

In our examination of Eph. 2.6, we sought to answer two primary questions related to Paul's enigmatic and astounding statement that believers have been seated with Christ in the heavenlies: (1) Why might Paul have written this statement/Can we discern a possible motive for Paul to have written this statement? (2) What did Paul mean when he wrote that believers are seated in the heavenlies/How are believers seated in the heavenlies? In reference to the first question, we concluded that Eph. 2.6 served as a subtle and implicit polemic, as well as a general safeguard, against a Jewish ascetic mysticism. Our investigations of

216 So also Lincoln, *Paradise*, pp. 153–54.

217 In his comment on Eph. 2.6, the early church father Jerome noted well both the connection between and eschatological tension of the Holy Spirit and believers' session in the heavenlies when he wrote, 'But it can also be said that just as we have received the *arrhabon* (security) of the Holy Spirit but also his total fullness has not yet followed, so also we sit with Christ and rule, not yet having obtained the perfect sitting in the heavenly places' (Heine).

218 See further Wessels, 'Eschatology', pp. 183–90; Lincoln, 'Re-Examination', pp. 473–74, 481–83; Ridderbos, *Paul*, p. 214; Vos, *Pauline Eschatology*, pp. 37–38; O'Brien, *Ephesians*, pp. 169–72. On the eschatological tension of the Holy Spirit, see Hamilton, *Holy Spirit*, pp. 26–40.

the themes of Jewish merkabah mysticism and several Qumran texts revealed similarities between Jewish mystical thought and the themes of Ephesians 2; however, most telling were the conceptual and linguistic parallels between Col. 2.12-13 and Col. 3.1-4, which represented part of Paul's polemic against a Jewish ascetic mysticism, and Eph. 2.5-6. While some scholars have observed similarities between the Qumran manuscripts and Ephesians 2, they have in turn either done very little to explain the reason for these similarities or have argued for some sort of common tradition between the Qumran manuscripts and the author of Ephesians. Our conclusion, as well as our contribution to this discussion, however, is that these similarities can primarily be accounted for because Paul had concerns about the Jewish mystical ascetic teaching which was so prevalent in Colossae and wrote Eph. 2.6 to provide a general and implicit safeguard against a similar Jewish mystical teaching which also might have been prevalent in the wider region of the Lycus Valley. In addition, our investigation of Eph. 2.11-22 also revealed what is likely a subtle polemic against a possible Judaizing movement.

In reference to the second question, we explored the meaning of Eph. 2.6 and concluded that the context of Ephesians 2 is critical for a proper understanding of how believers are seated in the heavenlies with Christ. Since it is obvious that Paul refers to a spiritual death in Eph. 2.1-5, as opposed to the physical death of Christ in Eph. 1.20, we should similarly not expect believers to be raised up and seated in the heavenlies physically but rather spiritually (i.e. by or through the Holy Spirit). Such an understanding is consistent with both Paul's 'already/not yet' eschatological paradigm and Paul's view on the role of the Holy Spirit in this eschatological tension. While at present believers have been raised up and seated with Christ in the heavenlies through the Holy Spirit and as a result of their union with Christ, they still look forward to the future consummation and completion of these acts in the future. Since New Testament scholars by and large have not attempted to address the question of what Paul meant in his statement that believers have been seated in the heavenlies, but have instead chosen to focus on other issues, our discussion of this question has shed more light on Paul's enigmatic statement and so proved to be a contribution to the field of New Testament studies.

Chapter 8

Exegetical and Conceptual Analysis of Ephesians 3.1-13

1. *Introduction and the Apocalyptic Background to 'Mystery'*

In Eph. 3.1-13 Paul begins his intercessory prayer when he writes τούτου χάριν but then abruptly changes thought in order to emphasize his role in the revelation of God's mystery in the gospel. In the process, Paul reveals a significant aspect of the mystery of Christ, calls attention to the role of the church in the revelation of God's mystery, and reiterates the full access to God which believers have in Christ. We have previously noted some of the similarities between Paul's writings and various motifs in Jewish apocalyptic literature. In this passage, Paul draws upon the apocalyptic themes of 'mystery' and 'revelation' in his presentation of the gospel of Christ. These themes are by no means peripheral to the thought of Ephesians but rather are closely related to the ἀνακεφαλαιώσασθαι of all things in Christ (Eph. 1.9-10).[1] To this end, Peter O'Brien writes that Eph. 3.9-10 is 'the key passage which focuses on the grand design of God's salvation-historical plan'.[2] In our examination, we will focus our attention on the revelation of mysteries within apocalyptic literature[3] and then subsequently the revelation of the mystery of Christ in Eph. 3.1-13.

In his monumental study *The Open Heaven*, Christopher Rowland argues that the essence of apocalyptic is 'the revelation of the divine mysteries through visions or some other form of immediate disclosure of heavenly truths'.[4] As previously noted, the instability of the Second

1 O'Brien, *Ephesians*, p. 63.

2 O'Brien, *Ephesians*, p. 63.

3 On the Old Testament, apocalyptic, and Judaism as the proper background for Paul's conception of 'mystery', see Caragounis, *Mysterion*, pp. 22–34, 121–35; Bockmuehl, *Revelation and Mystery*; Grindheim, 'OT Prophets', especially pp. 533–34; Hoehner, *Ephesians*, pp. 428–34; Lincoln, *Ephesians*, pp. 30–31; Best, *Ephesians*, pp. 134–38; O'Brien, *Ephesians*, pp. 108–15.

4 Rowland, *Open Heaven*, p. 70. Similarly, Rowland also contends 'that the presupposition of apocalyptic is its interest in that which is secret', *Open Heaven*, p. 445. See further Rowland's excellent discussion of the revelation of Divine mysteries as an essential component of apocalyptic, *Open Heaven*, pp. 9–22.

Temple and Israel's post-exilic adversities led to a theological mood where the transcendence of God dominated Jewish thought. As a result, indirect means of revelation were often eschewed for direct and authoritative revelations about God and his purposes.[5] Rowland writes, 'Thus the key to the whole movement is that God reveals his mysteries directly to man and thereby gives them knowledge of the true nature of reality so that they may organize their lives accordingly.'[6] The disclosure of the divine will and the heavenly mysteries occur in a variety of means including heavenly ascents, dreams, and both angelic and divine pronouncements.[7] In Dan. 2.28 we read that 'there is a God in heaven who reveals mysteries' (ἔστι θεὸς ἐν οὐρανῷ ἀνακαλύπτων μυστήρια).[8] Though there is no ascent to heaven, we still note an explicit connection between God in heaven and the revelation of mysteries. Furthermore, we also find in Dan. 2.28 a connection between the revelation of mysteries and eschatological fulfilment as Nebuchadnezzar's visions are descriptive of events which will take place ἐπ' ἐσχάτων τῶν ἡμερῶν.[9] In *3 Baruch* an angel of the Lord promises to disclose mysteries to Baruch (chapter 1). Of particular significance is an account in *2 Enoch* in which Enoch, after he ascends to heaven and sees the Lord enthroned (*2 Enoch* 22), subsequently has the secrets of heaven revealed to him (*2 Enoch* 22-33). Similarly, *1 En.* 71.3-4, *1 Enoch* 72–82, *Apocalypse of Abraham* 18–32, and Revelation 4–5 are all examples of the revelation of divine or heavenly secrets to the seer.[10] In his analysis, Christopher Rowland summarizes well this relationship between heaven and the revelation of divine mysteries when he writes: 'In both cases there is reflected the belief that the secrets of the universe are in some sense stored up in heaven. Heaven is a kind of repository of the whole spectrum of human history which can be glimpsed by the elect.'[11]

5 Rowland, *Open Heaven*, p. 11.

6 Rowland, *Open Heaven*, p. 11. Rowland also notes that apocalyptic, as a means to divine knowledge of revelations, was often utilized to support a particular way of life, *Open Heaven*, p. 123.

7 Rowland, *Open Heaven*, pp. 70–72. On the exegetical and esoteric nature of apocalyptic, see Ithamar Gruewald, *From Apocalypticism to Gnosticism*, pp. 55–59. Gruenwald writes, 'The esoteric dimension of Apocalypticism, then, lies in its relationship to the revelation of the divine word in Scripture. Apocalypticism reveals those layers of thought and expression that assumedly have not been revealed in an explicit way in Scripture', p. 59.

8 Cf. Dan. 2.47.

9 See further the discussion of Caragounis, *Mysterion*, pp. 123–26.

10 See Rowland's discussion, *Open Heaven*, pp. 55–56. The heavenly secrets which are revealed are often varied and include cosmogony, astronomy, and knowledge of human history or future. In addition to the passages listed above, though it cannot be strictly categorized as an apocalypse, we could also include the divine revelations concerning God's goodness and justice given by an angel in *Jubilees*.

11 Rowland, *Open Heaven*, p. 56. Cf. Newsom who also notes the explicit connection between heaven and the revelation of mysteries in the Qumran literature when she writes that 'heaven is, above all, the place of God's presence and rule, as well as the place

In Eph. 3.1-13 it seems likely that Paul draws upon this apocalyptic concept of the revelation of divine mysteries.[12] In this particular passage, we observe three levels of the revelation of the mystery of Christ: (1) God's revelation to Paul (as well as to the other apostles and prophets of Christ) (vv. 1-5); (2) Paul's revelation of this mystery to the Gentiles through his writings (vv. 3-6) and his preaching of Christ (vv. 7-9); (3) the church's disclosing of the mystery to the rulers and authorities ἐν τοῖς ἐπουρανίοις[13] (v. 10). We will examine each of these in turn.

2. *God's Revelation to Paul*

We have already noted the significance of Paul's mystical background in his visions, revelation from God, and his ascent to heaven. Such revelations from the Lord shaped both his understanding of the gospel and his proclamation of Christ. In Eph. 3.3-4 we see once again Paul's assertion that the mystery was made known (ἐγνωρίσθη) to him κατὰ ἀποκάλυψιν with the result that he now has insight into the mystery of Christ.[14] As is often the case in apocalyptic, the revelation of this mystery has an eschatological perspective[15] as it was not made known (ἐγνωρίσθη) in other generations as it has now been revealed (ἀπεκαλύφθη) to Christ's apostles and prophets in the Spirit (v. 5).[16] With

of the holy angels who serve God and have knowledge of truth and mysteries', Newsom, 'Heaven', pp. 338–39.

12 Ephesians 3.1-13 is not the only passage in Ephesians where such themes appear; cf. Eph. 1.8-10 and Eph. 1.17-18. See also Col. 1.23-29 which most likely served as the source for Eph. 3.1-13.

13 We will argue below that, like Eph. 1.21 and Eph. 6.12, the ἀρχαί and ἐξουσίαι in Eph. 3.10 refer to personal, evil, and spiritual powers. As we have previously noted, the presence of evil powers ἐν τοῖς ἐπουρανίοις is one of the troublesome issues for scholars of Ephesians and has contributed to the predominant interpretation in which the heavenlies are spiritualized; however, since it is not until Eph. 6.12 that the ἀρχαί and ἐξουσίαι in the heavenlies are explicitly described as evil, we will reserve our discussion of this complex and intriguing topic for our examination of Eph. 6.12.

14 It would be misguided to conclude, however, that Paul viewed the mystery of Christ as his innovation. See O'Brien's discussion of Paul's use of the OT Scriptures which promised beforehand the basis for the gospel and the mystery of Christ (Rom. 1.2; 3.21; 15.8-12; Gal. 3.8), *Ephesians*, pp. 231–32.

15 Cf. Col. 1.26-27; Rom. 11.25-26; 16.25-26; Dan. 2.27-47. In *Apocalyptic and Merkavah Mysticism*, Ithamar Gruenwald discusses the relationship between the revelation of divine secrets and the days of eschatological fulfilment in apocalyptic literature. He writes, 'The apocalypticists, who lived in the deep conviction that the days of the eschatological fulfilment were close at hand, believed that whatever had been concealed from man, because of the injustice that reigned in the world, could now be released for the knowledge and benefit of the just ...', Gruenwald, *Apocalyptic and Merkavah Mysticism*, p. 12. See Gruenwald's discussion, *Apocalyptic and Merkavah Mysticism*, pp. 12–13.

16 Cf. Mt. 13.10-11, Mk 4.10-11, and Lk. 8.9-10 where the disciples of Christ are granted to know the mysteries of God's Kingdom.

this statement, Paul clarifies both the recipients and the means of this divine revelation, though for Paul ἐν πνεύματι excludes neither visions nor ascents.

In Eph. 3.1-5 Paul appears to draw upon the categories of apocalyptic in order to establish his authority and role as a recipient of God's revelation through Christ. In similar fashion to the apocalypticists, Paul proclaims that he, along with the apostles and prophets, is privy to the revelation of God's mystery through Christ. In our previous study, we noted the importance of visions and even an ascent to heaven for Paul's theology and his understanding of the gospel. Here in Ephesians, Paul proclaims that he received this knowledge κατὰ ἀποκάλυψιν and ἐν πνεύματι. While the seers in apocalyptic utilized their visionary experiences for a particular theological agenda,[17] Paul here seems to do likewise in advancing his understanding of the mystery of Christ. What does seem evident is that Paul sees himself (as well as the other apostles and prophets) as a final authority of sorts on the revelation of God's mystery through Christ. In this sense, Paul does not allow for additional or alternative revelations of God or Christ for his readers. Nowhere is this communicated more strongly than in Gal. 1.6-9 when Paul writes that even an angel from heaven may not preach an alternative gospel.[18]

From our studies of Col. 2.11-3.4 and Ephesians 2, we concluded that it is likely that a Jewish mystical teaching served as the impetus for Paul's statement in Eph. 2.6 that believers have been raised up with Christ and have been seated with him ἐν τοῖς ἐπουρανίοις. Though we cannot be certain, it is possible that there is a similar motivation for Paul in Eph. 3.1-13. Just as Paul opposed the Jewish mystical practice of ascent, perhaps Eph. 3.1-13, in addition to emphasizing Paul's role in the revelation of the mystery of Christ, also serves as an implicit safeguard against those who would claim additional or alternative revelations from God which they would have received in their visions. Thus it would be clear to Paul's readers that God's revelation of the mystery of Christ is not from angels, visions, or heavenly ascents. It is rather God's revelation to Paul, the apostles, and the prophets.[19] Furthermore, God has already made known to believers τὸ μυστήριον τοῦ θελήματος αὐτοῦ in Christ (Eph. 1.9) and it is actually the church

17 Here we make no claim as to the actual authenticity of the visionary experiences within apocalyptic. As previously noted, the theological agenda of the apocalyptic visionaries was often an attempt to defend God's goodness and/or justice in circumstances which were characterized by evil and/or injustice.

18 We will demonstrate below that the Pauline 'mystery' is rightly understood as the mystery of Christ. On the connection between the mystery and the gospel, see Rom. 16.26. O'Brien also rightly recognizes this connection between 'mystery' and 'gospel' when he compares Eph. 3.3 with Gal. 1.12, 15-16, *Ephesians*, p. 230.

19 Cf. Col. 1.25–27 where the mystery has now been revealed to God's saints (τοῖς ἁγίοις αὐτοῦ).

which is God's instrument of revelation as ἡ πολυποίκιλος σοφία τοῦ θεοῦ is made known to the heavenly powers (Eph. 3.10).[20] While it remains a possibility that these verses represent a safeguard or subtle polemic against a Jewish mystical error, it is evident that Paul draws upon the apocalyptic concepts of 'mystery' and 'revelation' in his formulation of Eph. 3.1-13. Regardless, Eph. 3.1-13 demonstrates to Paul's readers that God's mystery in Christ has now been revealed to Paul (as well as the other apostles and prophets) and subsequently to all believers (Eph. 1.9; 3.2-9).

3. Paul's Revelation of the Mystery through his Writings (vv. 3-6) and his Preaching of Christ to the Gentiles (vv. 7-9) (the Content of the Mystery)

Before we proceed to examine Paul's disclosure of the mystery of Christ, we should first provide a broad overview of 'mystery' in Paul and the mystery of Christ in Eph. 3.1-13. In a broad sense, 'mystery' in Paul refers 'to the revelation of what was previously hidden but has now been disclosed by God'.[21] In Eph. 3.1-13, as in a number of other places in the Pauline corpus (Rom. 11.25; 16.25-26; 1 Cor. 1.18-2.16; Col. 1.25-27), the mystery of Christ is connected with the inclusion of Gentiles in the promises of God through Christ (3.6).[22] In other passages, 'mystery' is more general and refers to the mysteries of God, Christ, or the gospel (1 Cor. 4.1; Eph. 1.9-10; 6.19; Col. 2.2; 4.3).[23] O'Brien correctly notes that the starting point for understanding the Pauline 'mystery' is Christ and that 'there are not a number of "mysteries" with limited applications, but one supreme "mystery" with a number of applications'.[24] That being noted, a great number of these applications of the mystery of Christ in Paul are in fact associated with the salvation of Gentiles and their acceptance before God along with the Jews. As a result, in Ephesians 3 we can rightly identify the mystery of Christ as 'the complete union

20 Cf. Turner who also recognizes the possibility that Eph. 3.6-10 implicitly addresses a Jewish mysticism such as was encountered in Colossians, 'Mission', pp. 146–48. We will explore this notion in more detail below.

21 O'Brien, *Ephesians*, p. 109.

22 Here the Gentiles are fellow heirs (συγκληρονόμα), fellow members of the body (σύσσωμα), and fellow partakers (συμμέτοχα) of the promise in Christ Jesus through the gospel.

23 In addition to the passages listed above, 1 Cor. 15.51 describes the mystery of the final resurrection, Eph. 5.31-32 depicts marriage as a metaphor for the mystery of Christ and the church, and the pastorals refer to the mystery of faith (1 Tim. 3.9) and the mystery of godliness (1 Tim. 3.16). In 1 Cor. 13.2, 1 Cor. 14.2, and 2 Thess. 2.7, the usage of 'mystery' is general rather than technical.

24 O'Brien, *Ephesians*, p. 110. O'Brien warns that it is misguided to conclude that the equal footing of Gentiles with Jews is the sole content of the mystery of Christ in Paul.

of Jews and Gentiles with each other through the union of both with Christ. It is this double union, with Christ and with each other, which is the substance of the "mystery".'[25] Since the central theme of Ephesians is 'the uniting of all things in heaven and earth in Christ', a natural outworking of this ἀνακεφαλαιώσασθαι is the union of Jews and Gentiles through Christ.[26]

We observed above that the first line of revelation in Eph. 3.1-13 is God's revelation of the mystery of Christ to Paul. The second is Paul's disclosing of this mystery to the church through two means – his writings and his preaching the riches of Christ to the Gentiles. In Eph. 3.3-4 Paul makes clear that his letters demonstrate his insight into the mystery of Christ. Though we cannot be certain of how much Paul actually reveals, the implication of v. 4 is that Paul's letters do indeed contain some revelation of this mystery. This supposition is confirmed in 3.6 when we read what is at least a portion of the mystery's content – that the Gentiles are fellow sharers of God's blessings, fellow members of God's people, and fellow sharers of the promise in Christ Jesus through the gospel. As a result, Paul's statement in Eph. 3.6 proves to be an actual description of the mystery of Christ revealed to Paul and yet also serves as exhortation for both Jew and Gentile readers.[27] For his Gentile readers, which represent Paul's primary audience in the letter of Ephesians, this doctrine once again serves to demonstrate that in Christ they are sharers in God's promises. They need not resort to Jewish customs or traditions in order to partake in the promises of God or to have access to God (3.12). For his Jewish Christian readers,[28] this doctrine emphasizes the gracious activity of God to include the Gentiles in the promises of God. They must realize that both Jews' and Gentiles' acceptance before God and access to him is through union with Christ (ἐν ᾧ) and through faith in Christ (διὰ τῆς πίστεως αὐτοῦ) (3.12).

In addition to his writings, Paul also views his call from God (vv. 7-8) to preach Christ to the Gentiles (v. 8) as a disclosing of the mystery of Christ. We read in Eph. 3.8-9 that Paul's commission is to preach Christ to the Gentiles (v. 8) and to bring to light (φωτίσαι) the mystery

25 O'Brien here quotes Stott, *The Message of Ephesians*, p. 117. As cited in O'Brien, *Ephesians*, p. 236. Cf. Bockmuehl, *Revelation and Mystery*, pp. 201–203; Grindheim, 'OT Prophets', pp. 531–33; Turner, 'Mission', pp. 145–48; Harris, 'Reconsidered', p. 78; Lincoln, *Ephesians*, pp. 174–89; Best, *Ephesians*, pp. 299–327; Hoehner, *Ephesians*, pp. 433–34. See further Seyoon Kim's discussion of the revelation of the gospel, the mystery of Christ, and unity of Jews and Gentiles in *Origin*, pp. 67–99.

26 So O'Brien, *Ephesians*, pp. 110, 247–48, and Turner, 'Mission', especially pp. 144–48.

27 Thus Eph. 3.1-13 also demonstrates that Jew and Gentile relations, both within the church and outside the church, may have been one of Paul's concerns when he wrote the letter of Ephesians.

28 Though Paul's primary audience was Gentiles (cf. 2.11; 3.1), there were no doubt some Jewish Christians within the congregations of Asia Minor.

(μυστηρίου) which has been hidden in God (v. 9). Consequently, the very act of Paul's preaching Christ to the Gentiles serves as a testimony of God's gracious activity to the Gentiles and as a disclosure of the mystery of Christ. This act of Paul's preaching to the Gentiles makes clear that they too can share in God's promises through Christ. Jewish Christians must also recognize this preaching of Christ to the Gentiles and Gentiles' acceptance before God as the eschatological disclosure of God's mystery which was previously hidden but is now revealed (vv. 5-9). This revelation of God's mystery is 'in accordance with the eternal purpose which He carried out in Christ Jesus our Lord' (v. 11).

4. The Church's Revelation of the Mystery to the Rulers and Authorities ἐν τοῖς ἐπουρανίοις

In Eph. 3.10 we note the third and final level of revelation in Eph. 3.1-13 with Paul's surprising statement that it is actually the church which makes known God's mystery in Christ (the manifold wisdom of God)[29] to the spiritual powers in the heavenlies. Within apocalyptic, there are numerous passages in which angels are privy to various divine mysteries and perhaps even serve as God's agents to reveal these divine mysteries to a visionary.[30] On the other hand, we also find passages where heavenly mysteries are not revealed to both good and evil angels. For example, in *2 En.* 24.3, whereas God reveals to Enoch the secrets of creation, God states that he did not reveal these secrets to his angels.[31] One other noteworthy passage is *1 En.* 16.2-3 which reads, 'And so to the Watchers on whose behalf you have been sent to intercede – who were formerly in heaven – (say to them), "You were (once) in heaven, but not all the mysteries (of heaven) are open to you, and you (only) know the rejected mysteries."' In this passage from *1 Enoch*, we note some similarities with Eph. 3.10 as various heavenly mysteries are not revealed to the evil spiritual powers who were once located in heaven.

In Eph. 3.9-10 the result of the disclosing of the mystery of Christ (3.9) is that the manifold wisdom of God might now in turn be made known (γνωρισθῇ) to the rulers and the authorities ἐν τοῖς ἐπουρανίοις

29 That ἡ πολυποίκιλος σοφία τοῦ θεοῦ should be identified as the mystery of Christ is seen in the connection between vv. 9–10. Paul's preaching brings to light (φωτίσαι) the administration of the mystery (ἡ οἰκονομία τοῦ μυστηρίου) with the result that the manifold wisdom of God is made known to the rulers and authorities. Cf. Lincoln, *Ephesians*, p. 185, and Best, *Ephesians*, p. 324, who also note the connection between the manifold wisdom of God in 3.10 and mystery in 3.9.

30 This proves to be true in the case of both good (*Jub.* 4.21; *1 En.* 71.3-4; *1 Enoch* 72–81; *2 Enoch* 22–33; *3 Baruch* 1–17) and rebellious angels (*1 Enoch* 8–10; *1 Enoch* 69).

31 The reference in *2 En.* 24.3 is to the righteous angels of God; cf. *2 En.* 40.3 and the NT text 1 Pet. 1.12.

through the church (3.10). In our examination of Eph. 1.15-23, we noted that the ἀρχαί, ἐξουσίαι and other related terms both in Ephesians and in the rest of the Pauline corpus are personal, spiritual (or supernatural), and evil powers.[32] Since the ἀρχαί and ἐξουσίαι in Eph. 1.21 are references to God's enemies and since it is certain that the ἀρχαί and ἐξουσίαι in Eph. 6.12 are evil, it is also best to understand the ἀρχαί and ἐξουσίαι in Eph. 3.10 as personal, spiritual, and evil powers.[33] The church,[34] as the instrument of God's revelation, bears witness through its very existence to the union of Jews and Gentiles and so reveals God's wisdom and mystery in Christ to the spiritual powers in the heavenlies.[35] The Gentiles' sharing in the promises of God along with the Jews through faith bears witness both to Christ's power over the rulers and authorities[36] and God's mysterious work of salvation in Christ since 'the powers cannot hinder the advance of the gospel to Gentiles or their incorporation, along with Jews, into the body of Christ'.[37] Thus, through the revelation of God's mystery in Christ, Paul demonstrates to his readers that the spiritual powers have been stripped of both their powers to accuse and to lead the nations astray.[38] Moreover, Paul's reversal of roles in which the church reveals the mystery of God to the spiritual powers might also serve as an implicit safeguard and polemic against those who would claim to have received revelations as a result of their heavenly visions.[39] As a result, Paul's readers would realize that

32 See our brief discussion in chapter 6, the exegetical, conceptual, and lexical analysis of Eph. 1.15-23.

33 Contra Turner who believes the references are to 'the *whole* host of heavenly beings' ('Mission', p. 146; emphasis Turner's) and include both evil powers and God's angels ('Ephesians', p. 1234). The use of these terms in other NT passages as enemies of God (1 Cor. 15.24-25; Col. 2.15) provides further evidence and confirmation that they refer to evil powers.

34 Here we once again take τῆς ἐκκλησίας as a reference to the universal church. Contra O'Brien who insists the term refers to 'the heavenly gathering that is assembled around Christ *and* as a local congregation of Christians...', *Ephesians*, p. 246. Emphasis O'Brien's.

35 So Arnold, *Power and Magic*, p. 63; O'Brien, *Ephesians*, p. 246; Bockmuehl, *Revelation and Mystery*, p. 203; Lincoln, *Ephesians*, pp. 186–87; Best, *Ephesians*, p. 325.

36 Thus the church is 'a tangible reminder that their authority has been decisively broken and that all things are to be subject to Christ', Lincoln, *Paradise*, p. 155; cf. O'Brien, *Ephesians*, p. 63.

37 O'Brien, *Ephesians*, p. 247.

38 Accusation and deception are the two primary ways in which the evil spiritual powers operate in the OT and Jewish literature. We will explore further the nature and role of the powers in Ephesians in our excursus on the spiritual powers in Ephesians.

39 Once again, from the parallels with Colossians, such an interpretation is a possibility. For example, O'Brien notes that the background to the expression ἐν πάσῃ σοφίᾳ in Colossians (1.9; 1.28; 3.16) should be understood against the false teaching infiltrating the community, O'Brien, *Ephesians*, p. 108, note 88. While the false teaching in Colossae only has what should probably be understood as the 'appearance of wisdom' (λόγον μὲν ἔχοντα

they need not turn to visionary practices to receive revelations from God since God has already made known to believers the mystery of his will in Christ. Indeed, those in Christ should not turn to such visionary practices since they are actually God's instrument for revealing the mystery of Christ to the spiritual powers in the heavenlies.

5. *Conclusion*

In Eph. 3.1-13 Paul draws upon the apocalyptic themes of 'mystery' and 'revelation' in his presentation of the gospel of Christ. In our examination of this passage, we detected three means of God's revelation of the mystery of Christ – God's revelation to Paul, Paul's disclosure to the Gentiles, and the church's revelation to the rulers and authorities. Additionally, we observed how each of these three levels of revelation quite possibly represents another subtle and implicit polemic against a Judaizing movement, in particular a Jewish mysticism. Through the mystery of the gospel of Christ, the powers are stripped of their abilities both to accuse God's people and lead the nations astray. As a result, both Jew and Gentile believers have received full access to God through Christ and they need not resort to visionary practices either to access the presence of God or to receive revelations from God. Moreover, it is the church which reveals the mystery and power of the gospel to the spiritual powers through the union of Jews and Gentiles in Christ. Consequently, our examination of Eph. 3.1-13 also confirms our argument that one of Paul's concerns in Ephesians was to address a possible Jewish mystical movement such as was encountered in Colossae, albeit in a more implicit, subtle, and general manner.

σοφίας) (Col. 2.23), in Christ are πάντες οἱ θησαυροὶ τῆς σοφίας καὶ γνώσεως ἀπόκρυφοι, O'Brien, *Ephesians*, p. 108, note 88. The expression ἐν πάσῃ σοφίᾳ also appears in Eph. 1.8 in close association with the mystery of Christ and the ἀνακεφαλαιώσασθαι of all things in Christ (Eph. 1.9-10). In Eph. 1.17 Paul prays that God might grant his readers πνεῦμα σοφίας καὶ ἀποκαλύψεως ἐν ἐπιγνώσει of Christ. In Eph. 3.10 Paul writes that ἡ πολυποίκιλος σοφία τοῦ θεοῦ is made known to the rulers and authorities in the heavenlies through the church. Whereas in Colossians Christ is the source of all wisdom and knowledge, in Ephesians the riches of God's grace in Christ have been lavished on believers in all wisdom and insight (Eph. 1.7-8). What is more, it is actually the church, not the heavenly powers, which reveal ἡ πολυποίκιλος σοφία τοῦ θεοῦ (Eph. 3.10). Since Christ has lavished all wisdom and insight on believers and since it is the church which is actually God's instrument of revelation, believers need not turn to heavenly visions for their source of revelation. See also Turner's discussion of Eph. 3.6-10 as an implicit negation of a Jewish mysticism such as was encountered in Colossians, 'Mission', pp. 146–48. Turner contends that Eph. 3.10 'represents the peak of Paul's subtle polemic' against a Jewish mysticism since it reverses the opponents' agenda by making the church the instrument of God's revelation to the spiritual powers in the heavenlies, 'Mission', pp. 147–48.

Chapter 9

Exegetical and Conceptual Analysis of Ephesians 6.12

1. *Introduction*

By and large, the passages in Ephesians which we have examined with the expression ἐν τοῖς ἐπουρανίοις have emphasized the 'already' pole of Pauline eschatology.[1] In Eph. 1.3 believers are blessed with every spiritual blessing in the heavenlies. Ephesians 1.15-23 speaks of Christ's ascension to God's right hand and his present reign over all of his enemies. Believers are raised up with Christ and seated with him in the heavenlies in Eph. 2.6. In Eph. 3.1-13 the eschatological revelation of the mystery of Christ emphasizes the 'already' aspect in Pauline thought. However, when we arrive at Eph. 6.10-20, we encounter a completely different emphasis – the 'not yet' pole or perspective of Pauline eschatology[2] – when we read that believers are engaged in a battle against the spiritual forces of evil ἐν τοῖς ἐπουρανίοις.[3]

1 Of course, we could identify some exceptions to this statement. The 'already' act of raising up believers and seating them with Christ ἐν τοῖς ἐπουρανίοις in 2.6 is tempered by the future fulfilment in 2.7. Additionally, the presence of the rulers and authorities ἐν τοῖς ἐπουρανίοις in 3.10 emphasizes the 'not yet' pole.

2 O'Brien, *Ephesians*, p. 33. No doubt this contrast within these passages which contain the expression ἐν τοῖς ἐπουρανίοις can be at least partially attributed to the rough division of Ephesians into the didactic section of chapters 1–3 and the paraenetic section of chapters 4–6. For discussions of the already/not yet paradigm in Eph. 6.10-20, see Lincoln, 'Re-Examination', pp. 475–76, 479–80; Lincoln, *Ephesians*, pp. 438, 442–43; O'Brien, *Ephesians*, pp. 458–59, 464–65.

3 Many scholars find in Eph. 6.10-20 a parallel with the battle and military symbolism of the War Scroll from Qumran; see, e.g., Vermes, *Introduction*, p. 40. Others note the importance of the War Scroll for the background of Eph. 6.10–20 but also note differences between the two texts; see, e.g., Lincoln, *Paradise*, p. 165; Lincoln, *Ephesians*, pp. 437–38; Lincoln, 'Re-Examination', p. 475; Best, *Ephesians*, p. 586. In *The Complete Dead Sea Scrolls in English*, Vermes writes that the War Scroll 'should not be mistaken for a manual of military warfare pure and simple. It is a theological writing, and the war of which it treats symbolizes the eternal struggle between the spirits of Light and Darkness', Vermes, *Complete Dead Sea Scrolls*, p. 163. Though Vermes here makes a valid point, it is still nonetheless evident that, though the battle involved both good and evil angels, the weapons and the battle in the War Scroll were explicitly not spiritual but rather physical (1QM 1.4-15; 1QM 11.1; 1QM 11.16–12.5; 1QM 17.10-15; 1QM

From the very outset of Eph. 6.10-20, Paul exhorts his readers to 'be strong in the Lord and in the strength of His might' (6.10).[4] At the beginning of v. 11, Paul further elaborates on how believers are to stand firm – by putting on the full armour of God. Next, we discover the reason for these two exhortations – so that believers 'will be able to stand firm against the schemes of the devil' (6.11b). In v. 12 Paul elaborates on the nature of this conflict and writes that believers' battle is not against αἷμα καὶ σάρκα, but rather πρὸς τὰς ἀρχάς, πρὸς τὰς ἐξουσίας, πρὸς τοὺς κοσμοκράτορας τοῦ σκότους τούτου, πρὸς τὰ πνευματικὰ τῆς πονηρίας ἐν τοῖς ἐπουρανίοις. As in Eph. 1.21, the list of evil powers in Eph. 6.12 is not comprehensive and does not represent a complex angelology or demonology with various orders and ranks.[5] In line with the other appearances in Ephesians, the expression ἐν τοῖς ἐπουρανίοις in Eph. 6.12 should be understood as a local reference. Additionally, Ernst Percy correctly notes, 'Zweitens ist zu beachten, dass ἐν τοῖς ἐπουρανίοις 6,12 nicht als das Gebiet, innerhalb dessen der Gläubige mit den bösen Geistermächten kämpft, erwähnt wird, sondern als der

18.1-7). Consequently, it is our contention that the War Scroll is not a parallel to and did not serve as the background for the spiritual battle of Eph. 6.10-20 which is explicitly not against αἷμα καὶ σάρκα (Eph. 6.12). For others who argue similarly, see Arnold, *Power and Magic*, pp. 109–10; Kehl, 'Erniedrigung', pp. 380–81, 389; Thorsten Moritz, *A Profound Mystery: The Use of the Old Testament in Ephesians* (NovTSup 85; Leiden: E. J. Brill, 1996), pp. 186–87. Is it possible that, just as Eph. 2.6 served as an implicit polemic and response to Jewish mystical thought, Eph. 6.12 also served a similar function for those who might have been influenced by the Qumran notion of a physical battle with the Romans (or Kittim)? This seems to be the suggestion and implication of Kehl, 'Erniedrigung', pp. 380–81, 389, and perhaps this matter is worthy of further research. The primary background for Eph. 6.10-20 is the OT book of Isaiah, especially chapters 11, 52, and 59. For additional support and thorough discussions of the view that Isaiah is the primary background for Eph. 6.10-20, see Moritz, *Profound Mystery*, pp. 178–212; O'Brien, *Ephesians*, pp. 456–82; Thielman, 'Ephesians', pp. 830–33; Arnold, *Power and Magic*, pp. 108–109; Page, *Powers*, p. 187; Turner, 'Ephesians', pp. 1242–44.

4 Here Paul employs a number of synonyms for 'strength' to emphasize his point. The expression ἐν τῷ κράτει τῆς ἰσχύος αὐτοῦ calls to mind the expression κατὰ τὴν ἐνέργειαν τοῦ κράτους τῆς ἰσχύος αὐτοῦ in 1.19 and so reminds his readers to appropriate this power that is already at work in them. Whether ἐνδυναμοῦσθε is taken as a passive or a middle is of little consequence, but our preference is for the passive (rendering the translation 'be strengthened in the Lord') since the source for believers' strength is from the Lord rather than themselves; cf. O'Brien, *Ephesians*, pp. 460–61; Hoehner, *Ephesians*, p. 820; Lincoln, *Ephesians*, p. 441; Best, *Ephesians*, p. 590; Turner, 'Ephesians', p. 1243.

5 See further O'Brien, *Ephesians*, pp. 467–68; Page, *Powers of Evil*, pp. 246–48; Lincoln, *Ephesians*, pp. 444–45. The expression τὰ πνευματικὰ τῆς πονηρίας should be understood as a general and comprehensive term for all evil spiritual powers; cf. Lincoln, *Ephesians*, pp. 444–45; O'Brien, *Ephesians*, p. 467; Hoehner, *Ephesians*, p. 828. For a detailed discussion of the terms τὰς ἀρχάς, τὰς ἐξουσίας, and τοὺς κοσμοκράτορας τοῦ σκότους τούτου, see Hoehner, *Ephesians*, pp. 276–77, 826–29. We will discuss the background and function of the spiritual powers in more detail in our excursus on the spiritual powers in Ephesians.

Wohnort derjenigen Mächte, gegen die der Gläubige zu kämpfen hat.'[6] Ephesians 6.13 reiterates the exhortations of 6.11 and once again urges the readers to take up the armour of God so they can resist in the evil day and stand firm. The urgent need to stand firm against the devil, the present battle with the spiritual forces of evil, and the presence of the evil spiritual powers ἐν τοῖς ἐπουρανίοις all serve to highlight the fact that there still remains a future fulfilment of God's salvation in Christ for believers.

A number of recent commentators have convincingly demonstrated the importance of Eph. 6.10-20 within the thought and flow of Ephesians.[7] The passage represents the conclusion of the paraenesis and so serves to reinforce the previous exhortations, yet also in places recapitulates the entire letter's themes and terminology.[8] The structure of the passage can be divided into three basic sections: (1) vv. 10-13 (exhortation to be strong in the Lord and to put on the armour of God); (2) vv. 14-17 (the armour to put on); (3) vv. 18-20 (the need for prayer). Within these verses, there are of course numerous issues and themes which we could explore.[9] However, as previously noted, it is not our intention merely to rehash commentaries or previous studies. Rather, we will focus our attention on the issue which we believe has been the most troubling and significant for understanding the heavenlies in Ephesians – the notion of evil spiritual powers in heaven (or in the heavens).

2. *Evil Spiritual Powers ἐν τοῖς ἐπουρανίοις in Ephesians 6.12*

We have previously observed that the heavenly status granted to believers in Eph. 2.6 has led scholars to spiritualize the heavenlies in Ephesians. In Eph. 6.12 we find the second main impetus for spiritualizing the heavenlies – the fact that the spiritual forces of evil reside ἐν τοῖς ἐπουρανίοις. Since the time of the church fathers, this statement has perplexed commentators and, as a result, led to a variety of ways to address or understand this perplexing statement in Eph. 6.12. While

6 Percy, *Probleme*, p. 182, note 7; cf. Lincoln ('Re-Examination', p. 475) and Harris ('Reconsidered', p. 86) who also follow Percy.

7 See now O'Brien, *Ephesians*, pp. 456–60. O'Brien argues that 'the paragraph ... serves as the climax of the letter as a whole, bringing it to a conclusion', p. 457; cf. Lincoln, *Ephesians*, p. 432; Turner, 'Ephesians', p. 1242. Lincoln also draws some loose comparisons between Eph. 6.10–20 and the *peroratio*, a rhetorical function in classical literature, *Ephesians*, pp. 432–34, 438.

8 O'Brien, *Ephesians*, pp. 458–60. See further Lincoln, *Ephesians*, pp. 432–33, 438–41.

9 E.g. grammatical and exegetical issues, the notion of heavenly warfare in Qumran and apocalyptic, the armour of God and its connection with OT and other Jewish literature, and the terminology for the spiritual forces of evil, just to name a few. Readers can consult the numerous commentaries on Ephesians for discussions of these issues.

some early commentators such as Basil, Jerome, and Origen take ἐν τοῖς ἐπουρανίοις as a reference to the sky or air,[10] others such as Chrysostom and Theodore of Mopsuestia take the preposition ἐν in a referential sense and conclude that believers' struggle with the spiritual forces of evil is *about* heavenly things (as opposed to earthly ones).[11] The motivation for this non-local interpretation of Chrysostom and Theodore is almost certainly a desire to keep the spiritual forces of evil out of heaven. Moreover, some ancient witnesses such as P^{46} and Didymus of Alexandria completely omit ἐν τοῖς ἐπουρανίοις from 6.12. Andrew Lincoln reasons that the motivation for this omission was 'quite probably because the copyist could not conceive of such an explicit reference to wicked powers in heaven'.[12] Finally, a theological objection to the notion of evil powers in the heavenlies may have accounted for the appearance of the sparsely attested alternative reading ἐν τοῖς ὑπουρανίοις.[13]

The thought of evil powers in heaven has similarly led modern scholars and commentators to make sense of this difficulty. Since some of the ancient alternatives no longer seem viable,[14] the most common course of action has been to spiritualize the heavenlies and define them as the spiritual atmosphere of the church on earth;[15] however, as we have decisively demonstrated, such an understanding of the expression ἐν τοῖς ἐπουρανίοις is equally as untenable as the early Christian alternatives since there is no lexical basis for this understanding of the term ἐπουράνιος. Consequently, we must conclude that Eph. 6.12 does indeed portray the location of the spiritual forces of evil as in the heavens. As a result, it is our purpose in this chapter to investigate the notion of evil powers in the heavens.

10 See both Origen's comment on Eph. 6.12 and Jerome's comment on Eph. 6.12. As cited in Heine, *Commentaries*, pp. 257–58. See also Lash, 'Devils', p. 163.

11 Lash, 'Devils', p. 163. Chrysostom and Theodore take ἐν as equivalent to ὑπέρ and περί correspondingly. My emphasis above.

12 Lincoln, 'Re-Examination', p. 475, note 2; cf. Harris, 'Reconsidered', p. 86, note 46.

13 So Lash who implies that a Manichean theological agenda may have led to this alternative reading, 'Devils', p. 171.

14 Recent textual criticism has ruled out the possibilities of omitting ἐν τοῖς ἐπουρανίοις from Eph. 6.12 or altering the expression to ἐν τοῖς ὑπουρανίοις. Similarly, recent critical studies on the heavenlies in Ephesians have demonstrated that the expression ἐν τοῖς ἐπουρανίοις is a formula and must have the same meaning in all of its appearances, i.e. a local one. See our history of interpretation for further discussion. Here we do not rule out Basil, Origen, and Jerome's understanding that ἐν τοῖς ἐπουρανίοις might be a reference to the 'sky' or 'air'.

15 See especially Odeberg and McGough. See further our excursus on the influence of Odeberg's view in chapter 2, the history of interpretation of the heavenlies.

3. Biblical Examples

Though they are few, there are some passages in the Old Testament which portray evil powers in heaven. Perhaps the clearest and most famous example is Job 1.6-7 which records that the sons of God (LXX οἱ ἄγγελοι τοῦ θεοῦ) came to present themselves before the Lord and Satan came with them (v. 6). Since they came before the presence of the Lord, the implication of Job 1.6-7 is that the angels and Satan were in heaven. In response to the Lord's question, Satan says that he has come from roaming around on the earth (v. 7). The significance of this passage is that it clearly portrays Satan as having access both to heaven and to earth. Similarly, in Zech. 3.1 an angel shows Zechariah a vision of Joshua the high priest standing before the angel of the Lord with Satan there to accuse Joshua.

When we arrive at the New Testament, what we find is a fulfilment or continuation of sorts of the above examples. While in the Old Testament the most explicit examples of evil powers in heaven are descriptions of Satan before God in heaven in an accusing role, the New Testament primarily speaks of Satan's being cast out of heaven. For example, in Lk. 10.17-19, Jesus's depiction of Satan's casting out of heaven coincides with the success of the disciples' ministry, Christ's authority over his enemies, and the demons' subjection to the power of Christ. Additionally, in Rev. 12.7-13 we read of warfare in heaven with the result that Satan and his angels are cast out of heaven. The implications of Satan's removal from heaven in Rev. 12.7-13 are that Christ has complete authority over both earth and heaven and that Satan can no longer accuse the 'brethren' (ἀδελφοί). While in the Old Testament Satan's place in heaven seems to be of a more permanent nature and with the ability to accuse, the New Testament portrays Satan's access to heaven as temporary and without the ability to accuse.[16]

When we compare these Old and New Testament texts with Paul's portrayal of the evil powers in Ephesians, we find both continuity and discontinuity. On the one hand, Lk. 10.17-19 and Rev. 12.7-13, similarly to Eph. 1.20-23, also depict Christ's authority over his enemies and all spiritual powers. The authority which Christ has over these evil spiritual powers, demonstrated in his present reign at the right hand of God 'above' all of them in Eph. 1.21, also insinuates that since these powers are subject to Christ, they can no longer accuse believers (cf. Eph. 2.1-10; Col. 2.13-14). On the other hand, apart from Eph. 6.12, we find no New Testament parallel in which evil spiritual powers seemingly have a permanent place in heaven. Whereas several Old

16 This is also the general view of Bietenhard who notes that in the NT Satan still has access to heaven but his access is not permanent and he can no longer accuse, *Die himmlische Welt*, pp. 211–14. See also the discussion of Schoonhoven, *Wrath*, pp. 44–53.

Testament passages clearly describe Satan's access to and activity in heaven, the New Testament passages describe Satan and his angels' removal from heaven. Consequently, the description of evil powers in the heavenlies in Eph. 6.12 is unique to the New Testament.[17] Before we proceed to our analysis of Jewish and Christian texts outside Scripture, we will examine one Old Testament text which is somewhat ambiguous in its portrayal of evil powers in heaven.

4. Daniel 10 as an Ambiguous Passage

In Daniel 10 we find a picture of both good and evil spiritual powers at work in the world. Daniel has a vision in which an angel of the Lord comes to him and explains that the prince of the kingdom of Persia withstood him for twenty-one days (v. 13). Michael came to this angel's aid with the result that the angel was able to visit Daniel (v. 13). Similarly, vv. 20-21 also depict the struggle between good and evil angelic powers. Though it is not explicitly stated, the implication of Daniel 10 is that these spirit powers have access to and are operative in both heaven and earth.[18]

In his excellent discussion of Daniel 10 and the Jewish notion of angelic rulers over the nations in *The Open Heaven*, Christopher Rowland makes several salient points.[19] First, Rowland writes that the context makes it clear that these princes, along with Michael, are not human kings but rather angels or spiritual powers. Second, he notes that a significant theme within Jewish thought is that the nations have angelic representatives.[20] For example, in LXX Deut. 32.8 we read that the Lord divided the nations according to the number of the angels of God. Additionally, in *Jub*. 15.31-32 we read,

> And he sanctified it (Israel), and gathered it from among all the children of men; for there are many nations and many peoples, and all are his (God's) and over all hath he placed spirits in authority to lead them astray from him. But over Israel he did not appoint any angel or spirit, for he alone is their ruler ...[21]

17 See further the discussion of Bietenhard, *Die himmlische Welt*, pp. 211–14. Bietenhard similarly notes that Eph. 6.12 is the only place in the NT where evil powers are in heaven, *Die himmlische Welt*, p. 212, note 1.

18 This also seems to be the opinion of Lincoln, *Paradise*, p. 154, and Rowland, *Open Heaven*, pp. 89–92.

19 Rowland, *Open Heaven*, pp. 89–92. For what follows in our discussion of Daniel 10, I am indebted to Rowland, *Open Heaven*, pp. 89–92.

20 Rowland points to Daniel 10, LXX Deut. 32.8, and *Jub*. 15.31–32, *Open Heaven*, pp. 89–90.

21 As cited in Rowland, *Open Heaven*, pp. 89–90. Translation by Rowland.

These angelic powers often abuse their power (*1 Enoch* 89), lead the nations astray from God (*Jub.* 15.30-31), and account for the temporary prosperity of the nations of the world and the suffering of Israel. Thus a belief in the interrelatedness of earthly and heavenly realities develops so that the dominance or fall of a heavenly power is reflected in the dominance or fall of its earthly counterpart. Though God had granted these angelic powers authority, Israel looked forward to the day when God would bring victory for his people on earth. This earthly reality would be accompanied by God's corresponding victory over the spirit powers in heaven. Rowland writes, 'We thus have a picture here of God, as it were, voluntarily surrendering his sovereignty to lesser divine beings for a period, until the time comes for the final vindication of God's ways in earth and heaven.'[22]

Though there are no direct allusions to Daniel 10 in Ephesians, we do find places where Paul draws upon several of these Jewish themes to demonstrate their fulfilment in Christ. Certainly the themes of heavenly and spiritual warfare, though not identical, are present in both Daniel 10 and Ephesians 6. Whereas in Daniel the battle is between good and evil angelic powers, in Ephesians Paul emphasizes believers' role in this cosmic struggle with the evil spiritual powers. Additionally, Paul clearly portrays Christ as having won the decisive victory over the evil spiritual powers (Eph. 1.20-23) and as having inaugurated the time of God's vindication which results in the final restoration of heaven and earth (Eph. 1.10). The implications for the readers of Ephesians are two-fold. First, since these angelic powers no longer rule the cosmos and the nations of the world, the ἔθνη (i.e. nations or Gentiles) are free to submit to God's rule (Eph. 2.4-10; 3.1-13) and so become members of God's household through Christ (Eph. 2.11-22; 3.1-13). Second, believers do not need to fear or to submit to these angelic powers, since, as a result of their union with Christ, these powers can no longer accuse or condemn believers who now fight from a position of strength and victory (Eph. 1.20-23; 2.4-10; 3.1-13; 6.10-20).

5. *The Place of Punishment in the Heavens*

In apocalyptic literature, perhaps the most common description of evil spiritual powers in the heavens is the depiction of hell, or the place of punishment, as located in one of the heavens. In *2 Enoch* 7 the second heaven is the place of punishment for angels who turned away from the Lord.[23] Similarly, *2 Enoch* 18 locates the Grigori, or the Watchers who

22 Rowland, *Open Heaven*, p. 91.

23 Contrast this with later descriptions of hell as subterranean in *2 Enoch* 18 and *2 En.* 40.12. F. I. Andersen correctly notes the difficulty in harmonizing the evil and Satan

turned away from the Lord, in the fifth heaven.[24] Though the text of *2 Enoch* 10 is somewhat ambiguous, it is possible that the third heaven, in addition to being the location of Paradise, is also the location of rebellious angels who practise sin on the earth. In *Questions of Ezra*, we discover that the four lower heavens are characterized by evil and that the location of hell is in the third heaven or sphere (*Ques. Ezra* 1.19-21).[25] Similar to *2 Enoch*, the Greek version of *3 Baruch* describes the lower heavens as the prison or place of punishment for sinners and evil angels. While the first heaven is reserved for those who built the tower against God (*3 Baruch* 2), the second heaven is the location of those who plotted to build the tower and who forced others to build it (*3 Baruch* 3). Finally, the location of Satan and Hades is in the third heaven (*3 Baruch* 4).[26]

There are also some ambiguous examples from *1 Enoch*. *First Enoch* 18.11-14 speaks of 'a place without the heavenly firmament above it or earthly foundation under it or water ... prison house for the stars and powers of heaven' (Isaac). Similarly, *1 Enoch* 21 locates the stars of heaven and the prison of angels in a place that seems to be neither heaven nor earth. Though these descriptions do not clearly communicate that the place of imprisonment is in heaven, they nevertheless do describe the stars of heaven and the powers of heaven as evil spiritual forces.[27] It is consistent with both biblical and ancient thought to speak of stars as in or as part of 'the heavens' (e.g. Gen. 1.16-17; 15.5; 22.17; 26.4; Mt. 24.29; Mk 13.25; 1 Cor. 15.40-41).

passages in *2 Enoch*, *OTP* 1, pp. 154–55, note d. Though it is evident that the cosmology of *2 Enoch* is not entirely consistent, a possible harmonization of these passages is possible if the location of hell in the second heaven is only temporary, Andersen, *OTP* 1, pp. 11–12, note i. See also Andersen's note on *2 En.* 40.12 where he writes that the longer manuscripts allow for the possibility that the location of this 'subterranean' hell is in one of the heavens, *OTP* 1, pp. 154–55, note j.

24 Contrast this with *1 En.* 14.5 and *Jub.* 5.5–10 where the place of punishment for the watchers is inside the earth. Additionally, in *Jubilees* some of the spirits of the watchers remained on the earth subject to Satan (chapter 10). See the discussion of Wintermute, 'Introduction', p. 47.

25 In *Questions of Ezra* the lower heavens also serve as the temporary place of sinners who are imprisoned by demons, Recension B ch. 5. See M. E. Stone's brief discussion of the cosmology of *Questions of Ezra* in 'Introduction to Questions of Ezra', *OTP* 1, pp. 591–95 (591–94).

26 In the Greek version, the fourth heaven serves as the resting place of the righteous (*3 Baruch* 10) and also the beginning of the upper, good heavens. On the other hand, the locations of hell and the resting place for the righteous are not located in the first four heavens in the Slavonic version. See the discussion of H. E. Gaylord Jr in 'Introduction to 3 (Greek Apocalypse of) Baruch', *OTP* 1, pp. 653–61, especially pp. 656–57.

27 Cf. *1 En.* 90.21-24.

We find no precise analogy in Ephesians with the apocalyptic notion that the place of punishment for evil angelic powers is in the heavens. Indeed, there is nothing in either the New Testament or the Old Testament which would directly attest to this apocalyptic view. Second Peter 2.4 and Jude 6 both speak of angels who sinned and are now imprisoned but these texts do not make any claim as to the location of their imprisonment. Thus, for our purposes, perhaps what is most significant from this analysis is that it was not uncommon in Jewish thought for evil to be associated with heaven in some way. From these texts, we have observed that the lower heavens were often associated with evil and were also routinely identified as the place of punishment for sinners or angels who turned away from the Lord.

6. Non-Biblical Examples of Evil Powers in Heaven

The majority of the non-biblical examples of evil powers in the heavens are dependent in some way upon the examples in Scripture. In *Jub.* 17.16, which is reminiscent of the story of Job, Satan (the Prince Mastema) comes before God and urges God to test Abraham by sacrificing his son Isaac. The implication here is that, like the Old Testament account of Job, Satan has access to the presence of God in heaven and utilizes his access to accuse or encourage temptation of God's people. In *2 En.* 29.3-5 Satan and his angels are cast 'from the height' with the result that they are now 'flying around the air'.[28] Similarly, in the Latin text of *Life of Adam and Eve* (*Vita*), Satan and his angels are cast out of the heavens and onto the earth (12.1-2; 16.1). We have already encountered two New Testament examples (Lk. 10.17-19 and Rev. 12.7-13) which also speak of Satan's casting out of heaven. *First Enoch* 40.7 speaks of impious angels who are prohibited from entering the presence of the Lord so that they cannot accuse those on the earth. This verse seems to draw upon the Old Testament notion of Satan's accusing role and yet also demonstrates an affinity with the New Testament notion of Satan and his angels being cast out of heaven.[29] Finally, in *Apoc. Zeph.* 3.5-9 we read of the angels of the accuser who sit at the gate of heaven and write down the sins of men. In this passage, we find evil angelic powers who seemingly have access to heaven and who also assist Satan in his accusing role as depicted in the Old Testament.

28 In his notes on *2 En.* 29.3-5, F. I. Andersen writes that these verses might represent a Christian interpolation, Andersen, *OTP* 1, p. 149, notes i and j.

29 The considerations of date and composition for the Similitudes are most complex and there is no general agreement among scholars on these issues. As a result, we make no claim for any sort of dependence of *1 En.* 40.7 on the NT or, on the other hand, the NT on *1 En.* 40.7.

In addition to the passages above which exhibit close affinities with the Old and New Testaments, we also find examples in apocalyptic literature which associate the lower heavens with evil or darkness. Though they are not explicitly described as evil, the lower heavens in *Testament of Levi* are associated with darkness and God's judgement (chapters 2–3). In his notes on *Testament of Levi* 2–3, H. C. Kee writes that 'the pervasion of the lower heaven by darkness is a common feature in apocalyptic literature'.[30] We have already noted above that the location of hell in *Questions of Ezra* is in the third heaven. In addition, we also find that the four lower heavens in this book are associated with evil, sin, terror, quarrels, and wars (*Ques. Ezra* 1.19-21). For our purposes, the primary significance of these passages from *Testament of Levi* and *Questions of Ezra* is that the association of the lower heavens with evil, sin, or darkness was common within some strands of Jewish thought.

Perhaps the most extensive treatment of evil angelic powers is found in *Testament of Solomon*. When we consider the significance of the Testament of Solomon for our investigation of Ephesians, we must be cautious in any conclusions we draw since scholars generally date *Testament of Solomon* late and argue that the book is dependent upon the New Testament. Indeed, there are passages where the testament is almost certainly dependent upon Ephesians.[31] In his introduction to *Testament of Solomon*, D. C. Duling assigns a date somewhere between the first and third century AD.[32] However, Duling does note that whether we date the testament early or late, 'there is general agreement that much of the testament reflects first-century Judaism in Palestine'.[33] There is also disagreement over the authorship of this work and it is possible that it was either Jewish with Christian editing or the product of a Greek-speaking Christian.[34] Although the date of *Testament of Solomon* is late, it is nevertheless of some value for New Testament studies since the work reflects both Jewish and Christian thought from around the turn of the century.

There are two major contributions from *Testament of Solomon* for our examination of evil powers in heaven and the cosmology of Ephesians. First, in reference to cosmology, it is clear that *Testament*

30 Kee, *OTP* 1, p. 789, note 3a. Kee points to *2 En.* 5.1, *1 En.* 60.17-18, and *Jub.* 37.1-10 as additional texts which describe wintry elements associated with God's judgement.

31 See, e.g., *T. Sol.* 8.2 and 18.2 which speak of the κοσμοκράτορες τοῦ σκότους. Many scholars regard this reference as dependent upon τοὺς κοσμοκράτορας τοῦ σκότους in Eph. 6.12.

32 D. C. Duling, 'Introduction to Testament of Solomon', *OTP* 1, pp. 935–59 (940–43).

33 Duling, 'Introduction', p. 942.

34 Duling, 'Introduction', pp. 943–44.

of Solomon is clearly tripartite with the heavens above, the earth in the middle, and hell below the earth.[35] Within the testament, there are numerous references to the spirits of the air, of the earth, and under the earth (Greek title; 18.3; 22.1). The significance of these cosmological divisions is not in number since the cosmology of Ephesians is clearly bipartite, but rather in the titles given to the divisions. In Eph. 2.2 there is a reference to Satan as τὸν ἄρχοντα τῆς ἐξουσίας τοῦ ἀέρος. The fact that *Testament of Solomon* utilizes 'air' to refer to the heavenly regions possibly sheds light on its use in Ephesians. As a result, Eph. 3.10 and Eph. 6.12 might not be the only references to evil powers in the heavenly regions in Ephesians. Therefore, our understanding of evil powers in heaven and the cosmology of Ephesians must also take into account the activity of Satan as τὸν ἄρχοντα τῆς ἐξουσίας τοῦ ἀέρος (Eph. 2.2).[36]

Second, *Testament of Solomon* clearly portrays demons as having access to both heaven and earth. In chapter 1, we read of the demon Ornias's perverse activities on the earth. In 2.3 Ornias says to Solomon, 'Sometimes I become a creature with wings (flying) up to the heavenly regions' (Duling). Similarly, in 20.12-15 demons who cause destruction on earth can also fly up to the firmament, fly among the stars, and even hear decisions from God.[37] Within the New Testament, it is not uncommon to read of the activities of Satan and demons on the earth. What has been so problematic for scholars of Ephesians is that these evil powers are active in the heavenlies. In *Testament of Solomon*, we find that evil spiritual powers have access both to earth and the heavenly regions. In addition to these examples from *Testament of Solomon*, the composite work *Ascension of Isaiah*, which is widely believed to have both Jewish and Christian origins, locates the home of Satan and his hosts in the firmament which is below the seven heavens (4.1-3; 7.9-12).[38]

Our examination of evil powers in the heavens in various Jewish and Christian texts outside the Old and New Testaments leads to a similar conclusion as our examination of the heavens as the place of punishment. We once again observe that in several strands of Jewish and Christian thought it was not uncommon to speak of evil powers in heaven (*Jub.* 17.16; *Apoc. Zeph.* 3.5-9; *T. Sol.* 2.3; 20.12-15). In *Testament of Solomon*, there are examples of demons which have access both to earth and to the heavenly regions. There are texts which draw upon the Old Testament notion of evil powers as accusing agents

35 See Duling's discussion, 'Introduction', p. 952.

36 See further H. Bietenhard's brief discussion of ἀήρ in H. Bietenhard, 'Demon, Air, Cast Out', *NIDNTT* 1, pp. 449–53, especially pp. 449–50.

37 In *Testament of Solomon*, the world-rulers of darkness (κοσμοκράτορες τοῦ σκότους) are also described as stars in heaven (chapter 8).

38 Evil also characterizes the firmament in *Ascension of Isaiah* (7.9-12; 10.28-31; 11.23).

in heaven (*Apoc. Zeph.* 3.5-9) and there are also passages which demonstrate affinities with the New Testament theme of Satan and his angels having been cast out of heaven (*2 En.* 29.3-5; *LAE* 12.1-2; 16.1). Interestingly, *1 En.* 40.7 exhibits both of these characteristics as the impious angels are prohibited from entering the presence of the Lord so they cannot accuse those on the earth. *Jubilees* 17.16 alludes to the Old Testament theme of Satan as tempter or deceiver. In Jewish thought, it was also common to associate the lower heavens with sin, evil, darkness, and God's judgement (*Testament of Levi* 2–3; *Ques. Ezra* 1.19-21). In *Ascension of Isaiah*, the firmament, or the region below the seven heavens, is the abode of Satan and the evil powers. In Ephesians the location of the evil spiritual powers is also in the heavens; however, Christ's reign over the spiritual powers and believers' union with Christ assure believers that these powers can no longer accuse and can no longer ultimately lead the nations astray from God. Additionally, the location of the evil powers in the lower heavens in several apocalyptic texts allows for the possibility that the evil powers in Ephesians might also be located in the lower heavens.

7. Conclusions

The purpose of our examination of Eph. 6.12 was to investigate the notion of evil powers in heaven. While there are some previous studies with very general discussions on the notion of evil or evil powers in heaven, this subject is one which by and large has received relatively little attention in biblical studies. In the light of this, our examination represents a thorough analysis of the notion of evil powers in heaven in the Old Testament, the New Testament, and Second Temple Jewish texts including apocalyptic literature and the Qumran manuscripts. Moreover, we also examined the significance of these Old Testament, New Testament, and Second Temple Jewish texts for a proper understanding of both Eph. 6.12 and Eph 6.12 in relation to the rest of the New Testament. From our investigation of evil powers in the heavens, we note three common themes which appear frequently in Jewish and Christian texts which shed light on the presence of evil powers ἐν τοῖς ἐπουρανίοις in Ephesians. First, it is not uncommon for evil powers to have access to or to be located in the heavens. The degree to which these Jewish and Christian texts should inform our understanding of Eph. 6.12 is open to debate. Nevertheless, they should steer us away from the conclusion that the notion of evil spiritual powers in the heavens is incomprehensible.[39] Such a conclusion has led to the

39 For additional discussions of evil powers and the realm of darkness in heaven, see Rowland, *Open Heaven*, pp. 92–93; Schoonhoven, *Wrath*, especially pp. 40–66; Bietenhard, *Die himmlische Welt*, pp. 205–21.

various exegetical fallacies detailed above, namely understanding the expression ἐν τοῖς ἐπουρανίοις in a purely referential sense rather than local or spiritualizing the heavenlies so that they become the spiritual atmosphere of the church on earth.

Second, when the evil powers are portrayed as having access to the presence of God, their typical functions are to tempt, deceive, lead astray, or accuse God's people. The New Testament alludes to all of these themes and demonstrates that because of Christ and his authority over the evil powers, they can no longer accuse (Rev. 12.7-13) and can no longer completely deceive the nations or prevent the nations from taking part in God's salvation in Christ. Though Ephesians is the only New Testament book which explicitly states that the evil powers are located in the heavens, its description of Christ's authority and rule over the heavenly powers (Eph. 1.20-21), its description of the powers' inability to prevent the nations from submitting to God (Ephesians 2; 3.1-13), and its description of the great salvation accomplished in Christ (Eph. 2.4-10) are all consistent with the other New Testament accounts which depict Satan and the evil powers as cast out of heaven. In this sense, there is not a great difference between the passages which portray Satan and his evil powers as cast out of heaven (Lk. 10.17-19; Rev. 12.7-13) and Eph. 3.10 and 6.12.

Third, the lower heavens are often the location of the evil powers and are also at times associated with sin, darkness, perversion, or rebellion. In Ephesians the description of Christ's exaltation as 'above' the spiritual powers (Eph. 1.20-21), the description of the evil spiritual powers ἐν τοῖς ἐπουρανίοις (6.12), and Satan's description as 'the prince of the power of the air' (2.2) allow for the possibility that the spiritual forces of evil ἐν τοῖς ἐπουρανίοις in Eph. 6.12 are also associated with or located in the lower heavens.[40] We will explore this possibility in more detail in our discussion of the cosmology of Ephesians.

40 Cf. also Jean Daniélou, *The Theology of Jewish Christianity* (ed. and trans. John A. Baker; The Development of Christian Doctrine Before the Council of Nicaea 1; London: Darton, Longman & Todd, 1964), pp. 174, 190; Schnackenburg, *Ephesians*, pp. 77, 273; Turner 'Ephesians', p. 1243; Bietenhard, *NIDNTT* 2, p.193; U. Schoenborn, 'Οὐρανός', *Exegetical Dictionary of the New Testament* 2, pp. 543–47 (546). Additionally, as noted above, the church fathers Basil, Jerome, and Origen understand the expression ἐν τοῖς ἐπουρανίοις in Eph. 6.12 as a reference to 'the sky' or 'the air'.

Chapter 10

Excurses Related to 'the Heavenlies' in Ephesians

1. The Cosmology of Ephesians

In much the same fashion as the heavenlies, the cosmology of Ephesians has similarly perplexed commentators, and as a result, there has been little agreement on various cosmological issues in the letter. Though there has not been universal agreement, the general consensus among most recent commentators is that the cosmology of Ephesians is bipartite or two-tiered, and so composed of the heavens and the earth (cf. 1.10; 3.15; 4.9-10).[1] In our estimation, the references to the heavens and the earth in Eph. 1.10, 3.15, and 4.9-10 provide sufficient evidence that this basic two-tiered structure accurately reflects the cosmology of Ephesians.[2] Beyond this, there have been few attempts to discern the cosmology of Ephesians or harmonize its teachings on the basic structure of heaven and earth. As a result, this excursus serves as a contribution to New Testament studies through our examination of some generally overlooked cosmological issues in Ephesians. In our analysis, we will investigate three primary issues which are significant for the cosmology of Ephesians. First, we will examine the larger Pauline corpus for possible evidence for a general Pauline cosmology. Second, we will examine the references to οὐρανός and ἐπουράνιος in Ephesians for their significance within the cosmology of Ephesians. Third, we will investigate the notion of a plurality of heavens in Ephesians and offer some brief thoughts on the implications of our analysis in light of other New Testament references.

1 See, e.g., Lincoln, 'Re-Examination', pp. 479–80; Lincoln, *Ephesians*, pp. 20, 34; Best, *Ephesians*, pp. 118, 384; O'Brien, *Ephesians*, pp. 60, 112, 294–97; Robert L. Foster, 'Reoriented to the Cosmos: Cosmology and Theology in Ephesians through Philemon', *Cosmology and New Testament Theology* (ed. Jonathan T. Pennington and Sean M. McDonough; Library of New Testament Studies 355; New York: T & T Clark, 2008), pp. 107–24 (110); Harris, 'Reconsidered', pp. 83–84. The basis for a three-tiered cosmology of Ephesians is dependent upon a tripartite understanding of Eph. 4.9-10 where Christ descended εἰς τὰ κατώτερα μέρη τῆς γῆς. Those who argue for a tripartite cosmology understand τῆς γῆς as a partitive genitive; however, we take τῆς γῆς as a genitive of apposition which further defines τὰ κατώτερα μέρη. For a discussion of Eph. 4.9-10 and the various interpretive issues, see Lincoln, *Ephesians*, pp. 244–48.

2 See the references cited above.

a. Cosmology in Paul outside Ephesians

Within this section, we will address two basic cosmological issues within the larger Pauline corpus. First, we will investigate whether there is evidence of a consistent cosmological view in Paul, namely whether the cosmos is bipartite and composed of the heavens and earth, or whether it is tripartite and so composed of the heavens, the earth, and a place designated as 'under the earth'. Second, we will investigate the questions of whether Paul believed in a plurality of heavens and, if so, whether he believed in a specific number of heavens.

Of the eleven passages (including Ephesians) which refer to the makeup of the cosmos in Paul, eight are clearly bipartite with the heaven(s) above and the earth below (1 Cor. 8.5; 1 Cor. 15.40-49; 2 Cor. 5.1-2; Eph. 1.10; Eph. 3.15; Col. 1.16, 20; Col. 3.1-2; Phil. 3.19-20). The three remaining passages, Rom. 10.6-7, Phil. 2.10, and Eph. 4.9-10, are more ambiguous and so allow for the possibility of a tripartite view of the cosmos. We have already briefly discussed Eph. 4.9-10 and concluded that the reference to τὰ κατώτερα [μέρη] τῆς γῆς should be understood as a genitive of apposition and is consistent with the bipartite cosmology of Ephesians. In our study of the term ἐπουράνιος in the New Testament, we also concluded that the references to ἐπουρανίων καὶ ἐπιγείων καὶ καταχθονίων in Phil. 2.10 do not represent a developed or specific Pauline cosmology. The reasons for this are that Paul most likely incorporated an already existent hymn and that these three categories in Phil. 2.10 were also commonly utilized in antiquity to communicate universality. In Rom. 10.6-7 Paul alludes to Deut. 30.11-14 and writes:

> [6] But the righteousness based on faith speaks as follows: 'DO NOT SAY IN YOUR HEART, "WHO WILL ASCEND INTO HEAVEN (εἰς τὸν οὐρανόν)?" (that is, to bring Christ down), [7]or "WHO WILL DESCEND INTO THE ABYSS (εἰς τὴν ἄβυσσον)?" (that is, to bring Christ up from the dead).'

Though the contrast between the abyss, or the realm of the dead, and heaven in Rom. 10.6-7 could be representative of a tripartite cosmology, there are also good reasons for not understanding these verses as representative of a developed Pauline cosmology. First, it seems that the references to the 'abyss' (Rom. 10.7) and the 'sea' (Deut. 30.13) were interchangeable within Jewish thought.[3] In fact, three other Jewish passages which also allude to Deut. 30.11-14 all contrast 'heaven' with the 'sea' (Bar. 3.29-30; Philo, *De Posteritate Caini* 84–85; *Targum Neofiti* on Deuteronomy 30).[4] Second, Leon Morris recognizes that 'in

3 See further Douglas J. Moo, *The Epistle to the Romans* (NICNT; Grand Rapids: Eerdmans, 1996), pp. 655–56; Leon Morris, *The Epistle to the Romans* (Grand Rapids: Eerdmans, 1988), p. 383.

4 For a comparison of Deut. 30.11-14, Bar. 3.29-30, Philo, *De Posteritate Caini*

these two verses Paul is using expressions that had become proverbial for what is impossible'.[5] Third, to focus too exclusively on the cosmological implications of the abyss in Rom. 10.7 would be at the expense of missing Paul's primary theological point – that Christ has already been resurrected and any attempt or desire to descend into the 'abyss' would be foolish.[6] Consequently, it is by no means evident that Paul's intent in Rom. 10.6-7 was to depict a tripartite cosmology.

Of particular interest is the fact that in Scripture we find a number of different cosmologies. In addition to the cosmological divisions of Phil. 2.10 and Rom. 10.6-7, Rev. 5.13 refers to 'heaven', 'earth', 'under the earth', and 'under the sea' while Exod. 20.4 refers to 'heaven', 'earth', and 'water beneath the earth'. It is quite possible that the areas referred to as 'the abyss', 'under the earth', 'under the sea', and 'water beneath the earth' were conceived of as actually part of the earth.[7] Therefore, the references to 'under the earth' in Phil. 2.10 and 'the abyss' in Rom. 10.7 may not be representative of a tripartite cosmology but rather would further represent that which is on the earth and so be included within τὰ ἐπίγεια. As a result, it is possible and perhaps even likely that Paul conceived of the basic divisions of the cosmos as 'the heavens' above and 'the earth' below in a bipartite structure.[8] Though the evidence is somewhat ambiguous, we regard this view as the most consistent with the references to the cosmos in the Pauline corpus. For our purposes, however, the issue of whether Paul conceived of a bipartite or tripartite cosmology is of little consequence. What is of considerable significance, however, is the question of whether or not Paul conceived of a specific number of heavens.

Of all the references to οὐρανός and ἐπουράνιος (when used in a local sense) in Paul, eleven refer to a single heaven (Rom. 1.18; Rom. 10.6; 1 Cor. 8.5; 1 Cor. 15.47; 2 Cor. 5.2; Gal. 1.8; Col. 1.23; Col. 4.1; 1 Thess. 1.10; 1 Thess. 4.16; 2 Thess. 1.7) and fifteen refer to a plurality

84–85, and *Targum Neofiti* on Deuteronomy 30 with Rom. 10.6-8, see James D. G. Dunn, *Romans 9–16* (WBC 38B; Dallas: Word Books, 1988), p. 604. Morris also notes that 'the abyss' in LXX Ps. 106.26 is utilized as the translation for 'the sea' in Ps. 107.26, *Romans*, p. 383, note 30.

5 Morris, *Romans*, p. 383.

6 See further Morris, *Romans*, pp. 383–84; Moo, *Romans*, pp. 655–56; Dunn, *Romans*, pp. 614–15; Brendan Byrne, *Romans* (SP 6; Collegeville, MN: The Liturgical Press, 1996), p. 318.

7 This is essentially the argument and conclusion of Pennington in *Heaven and Earth*. See further Pennington's discussion of the cosmology of the OT, Second Temple Jewish literature, and Matthew in *Heaven and Earth*, pp. 169–216.

8 Contra Joel White who contends that Paul believed in a tripartite universe, Joel White, 'Paul's Cosmology: The Witness of Romans, 1 and 2 Corinthians, and Galatians', *Cosmology and New Testament Theology* (ed. Jonathan T. Pennington and Sean M. McDonough; Library of New Testament Studies 355; New York: T & T Clark, 2008), pp. 90–106 (93–94).

of heavens (2 Cor. 5.1; 2 Cor 12.2;[9] Eph. 1.3; Eph. 1.10; Eph. 1.20; Eph. 2.6; Eph. 3.10; Eph. 3.15; Eph. 4.10; Eph. 6.9; Eph. 6.12; Phil. 3.20; Col. 1.5; Col. 1.16; Col. 1.20). However, since the writers of the New Testament commonly utilized the plural of οὐρανός to reflect the Hebrew plural שָׁמַיִם, we cannot draw any significant conclusions from the plural use of οὐρανός or ἐπουράνιος.[10] As a result, for the questions of whether Paul conceived of a plurality of heavens and a specific number of heavens, we must turn our attention to 2 Cor. 12.1-4 where Paul recounts his ecstatic experience in which he was caught up (ἁρπαγέντα) to the third heaven. We have previously examined 2 Cor. 12.1-4 for its significance within the mystical thought and life of Paul. For our present purposes, our task is to determine the significance of the third heaven. In his *Die himmlische Welt im Urchristentum und Spätjudentum*, Hans Bietenhard provides an accurate and helpful structure of the passage:

a. οἶδα ἄνθρωπον ἐν Χριστῷ πρὸ ἐτῶν δεκατεσσάρων
b. εἴτε ἐν σώματι οὐκ οἶδα, εἴτε ἐκτὸς τοῦ σώματος οὐκ οἶδα, ὁ θεὸς οἶδεν
c. ἁρπαγέντα τὸν τοιοῦτον ἕως τρίτου οὐρανοῦ
α. καὶ οἶδα τὸν τοιοῦτον ἄνθρωπον
β. εἴτε ἐν σώματι εἴτε χωρὶς τοῦ σώματος οὐκ οἶδα, ὁ θεὸς οἶδεν
γ. ὅτι ἡρπάγη εἰς τὸν παράδεισον καὶ ἤκουσεν ἄρρητα ῥήματα ἃ οὐκ ἐξὸν ἀνθρώπῳ λαλῆσαι.[11]

Bietenhard recognizes in 2 Cor. 12.1-4 a parallel structure in which line a corresponds to line α, line b corresponds to line β, and line c corresponds to line γ.[12] On the basis of this parallelism, Bietenhard writes, 'Die Parallelität in der sprachlichen Form weist auf ein und dasselbe Erlebnis hin. Von da aus dürfen wir aber auch schließen, daß in c und γ dasselbe gemeint ist: dem dritten Himmel entspricht das Paradies, das Paradies ist im dritten Himmel.'[13] In agreement with Bietenhard, we understand 2 Cor. 12.1-4 as a reference to one experience with parallel terminology wherein the third heaven is identified as Paradise.[14]

9 In 2 Cor. 12.2 the reference is to the singular 'third heaven' (τρίτου οὐρανοῦ), but the fact that there is a 'third heaven' implies a plurality of heavens.

10 Second Corinthians 5.1-2 demonstrates the interchangeability of the singular and plural forms of οὐρανός with the use of ἐν τοῖς οὐρανοῖς in v. 1 and ἐξ οὐρανοῦ in v. 2.

11 Bietenhard, *Die himmlische Welt*, p. 164.

12 Bietenhard, *Die himmlische Welt*, p. 164.

13 Bietenhard, *Die himmlische Welt*, p. 164; cf. Lincoln, 'Paul', p. 211; Lincoln, *Paradise*, p. 77.

14 See further Harris, *2 Corinthians*, pp. 840–45; Craig S. Keener, *1–2 Corinthians* (New Cambridge Bible Commentary; Cambridge: Cambridge University Press, 2005), p. 239; Jan Lambrecht, *Second Corinthians* (SP 8; Collegeville, MN: The Liturgical Press, 1999), p. 201; Morray-Jones, 'Paradise Revisited: Part 2', p. 278. Contra Rowland who concludes that 2 Cor. 12.1-4 refers to one experience with two definite or distinct parts. As

Though, on the basis of the parallel structure, we have identified the third heaven with Paradise, we have not yet determined the significance of this heaven in this passage or in the thought of Paul. In his analysis, Andrew Lincoln also identifies the third heaven with Paradise and compares 2 Cor. 12.1-4 with *2 Enoch* 8 and *Apocalypse of Moses* (37.5; 40.1) which also place Paradise in the third heaven.[15] As a result of this comparison, Lincoln concludes it is likely in 2 Cor. 12.1-4 that Paul merely adopts the terminology and cosmological views of his time.[16] Moreover, since Paul adopts the terminology and cosmological views of his time, it is not possible to determine on the basis of 2 Cor. 12.1-4 how many heavens Paul actually conceived of.[17] Lincoln provides a helpful caution that we should not too readily identify Paul's account of his ascent to heaven in 2 Cor. 12.1-4 with the elaborate heavenly ascents and numbering of the heavens in apocalyptic. However, it is our view that Paul here did indeed have a specific number of heavens in mind and that the references to the third heaven and Paradise are of more significance than Lincoln suggests.

In his discussion of 2 Cor. 12.1-4, Rowland concludes that the reference to Paradise represents what is likely the highest heaven. In arriving at this conclusion, Rowland notes that in apocalyptic, it is only at the highest point or in the presence of God that the visionary is revealed divine secrets (*1 En.* 71.3-4; *2 Enoch* 22ff).[18] Thus the revelation of the ἄρρητα ῥήματα to Paul in Paradise (which we have demonstrated is also the third heaven) indicates that it is to be identified with the presence of God.[19] Moreover, the identification of Paradise with the presence of God is consistent with the other New Testament texts concerning Paradise (Lk. 23.43; Rev. 2.7; Rev. 22.1-3).[20] As a result,

a result, Rowland does not identify the third heaven with Paradise but rather concludes that the third heaven was a part of Paul's heavenly journey before he reached Paradise, *Open Heaven*, pp. 381–82. In his discussion, however, Rowland does correctly dismiss the notion that Paul here refers to two separate experiences in the two parts of the structure, p. 381.

15 Lincoln, *Paradise*, p. 79; Lincoln, 'Paul', p. 213. See also Bietenhard who similarly compares Paul's location of Paradise in the third heaven with *2 Enoch*, *Die himmlische Welt*, p. 166. In contrast to Lincoln, however, Bietenhard thinks it is likely that, because of the comparison with *2 Enoch*, Paul also conceived of seven heavens, *Die himmlische Welt*, p. 166.

16 Lincoln, 'Paul', p. 213; cf. Lincoln, *Paradise*, p. 79.

17 Lincoln, *Paradise*, p. 79; Lincoln, 'Paul', p. 213; cf. Joel White who also cautions that Paul's ascent to the third heaven in 2 Corinthians 12 might not represent the apocalyptic notion of a stratified heaven since Paul might have simply borrowed the language of visions and heavenly ascents, White, 'Paul's Cosmology', pp. 93–94.

18 Rowland, *Open Heaven*, pp. 381–83.

19 Contra Bietenhard who considers the connection between 2 Cor. 12.1-4 and *2 Enoch* to be so strong that the most likely conclusion is that Paul conceived of seven heavens, *Die himmlische Welt*, p. 166.

20 Rowland notes that both Rev. 22.1-3 and *Life of Adam and Eve* 25 also identify Paradise with the presence of God, *Open Heaven*, pp. 382–83.

it is our view that Paul conceived of the third heaven as the highest heaven and also referred to this heaven as Paradise in order to identify it with the presence of God.[21] Furthermore, it is quite possible and indeed probable that Paul adopted the very general and undeveloped Old Testament view of the heavens. Within this unsophisticated view and Paul's basic Old Testament framework, the heavens could refer to the sky, the firmament, or the presence of God.[22] Thus, in 2 Cor. 12.1-4, Paul utilized the terminology of 'third heaven' and 'Paradise' to communicate that he ascended to the very presence of God.

b. Οὐρανός and 'Επουράνιος in the cosmology of Ephesians

As noted above, the basic cosmological structure of Ephesians is bipartite with the heavens above and the earth below. In this section, we will focus on Paul's teaching on the heavens in Ephesians through an examination of the relationship between ἐν οὐρανοῖς and ἐν τοῖς ἐπουρανίοις. As we have stated on a number of occasions, the fact that the heavenlies in Ephesians have proved to be perplexing and troublesome for commentators has led to a number of different understandings and interpretations. In addition to the heavenly status granted to believers (2.6) and the presence of evil powers in the heavenlies (6.12), another significant interpretive issue which has troubled and perplexed commentators is the relationship between the phrases ἐν (τοῖς) οὐρανοῖς and ἐν τοῖς ἐπουρανίοις in Ephesians. In our examinations of ἐπουράνιος in both biblical and non-biblical sources, we concluded that the terms οὐρανός and ἐπουράνιος are synonymous and that it is erroneous to posit a major distinction in meaning between them; however, we must also address the question of whether there is some sort of minor distinction wherein both terms retain their usual meanings as references to that which is spatially distinct from the earth, but yet also refer to different parts of 'the heavens'.

The reference to Christ's ascension ὑπεράνω πάντων τῶν οὐρανῶν in Eph. 4.10 is interesting in light of the fact that the explicit location after Christ's ascension in Eph. 1.20 is ἐν τοῖς ἐπουρανίοις (cf. also ἐν οὐρανοῖς in Eph. 6.9). Rather than positing a distinction in meaning between

21 So also Harris, *2 Corinthians*, p. 840; Keener, *1–2 Corinthians*, p. 239; Lambrecht, *2 Corinthians*, p. 201; Philip Edgcumbe Hughes, *Paul's Second Epistle to the Corinthians* (NICNT; Grand Rapids: Eerdmans, 1962), pp. 432–34; Morray-Jones, 'Paradise Revisited: Part 2', p. 278; J. F. Maile, 'Heaven, Heavenlies, Paradise', *DPL*, pp. 381–83 (382). Contra Gooder who contends that Paul's account in 2 Corinthians 12 is a failed ascent wherein Paul did not ascend to the presence of God, *Only the Third Heaven?*, pp. 190–211.

22 See further Schoonhoven, *Wrath*, pp. 8–9, 64; Hughes, *2 Corinthians*, pp. 432–34; Keener, *1–2 Corinthians*, p. 239; Daniélou, *Theology*, p. 174. See also our brief discussion of the meaning and references of 'heaven' or 'the heavens' at the end of chapter 4, the NT study of ἐπουράνιος.

οὐρανός and ἐπουράνιος in Ephesians, however, it is best to understand the description of Christ's ascent ὑπεράνω πάντων τῶν οὐρανῶν in Eph. 4.10 as an emphasis of Christ's sovereignty and supreme exaltation. A common theme in the Old Testament is that the heavens cannot contain God (1 Kgs 8.27; 2 Chron. 2.6; 2 Chron. 6.18). In Eph. 4.10 Paul applies that same theme to Christ and his exaltation.[23] This interpretation is also consistent with similar uses of οὐρανός in Hebrews where Christ is depicted as ὑψηλότερος τῶν οὐρανῶν in 7.26, but yet explicitly ἐν τοῖς οὐρανοῖς in 8.1.[24]

In *The Ephesian Mysterion*, Chrys C. Caragounis argues that the heavenlies overlap with οὐρανός but are not completely identical with it. Whereas οὐρανός consists of the layers from the air to God's throne, the heavenlies only consist of the higher heavenly levels from the realm of the cosmic forces to God's throne.[25] Caragounis's only justification for this decision seems to be that the heavenlies are bound up with the salvation events.[26] Robert Foster advocates an even more interesting proposal when he writes that Paul distinguishes between the heavenly places (ἐν τοῖς ἐπουρανίοις) and the κόσμος which is made up of the heavens (τοῖς οὐρανοῖς) and the earth.[27] Foster writes:

> Thus, Paul's cosmology reflects two important realities: the heavenly places and the universe, with the universe divided further into the heavens and the earth. The basic distinction between the heavenly places and the universe is that the universe came into existence some time after the heavenly places.[28]

Although the implications of Foster's proposal are not altogether clear, it is possible that the heavens (τοῖς οὐρανοῖς) would refer to the visible, created heavens whereas the heavenlies (ἐν τοῖς ἐπουρανίοις) would possibly refer to the upper portion where God and Christ reside.

As alluded to above, we do not believe there is any justification in Ephesians for such minor distinctions between these two expressions. From our examination of ἐπουράνιος in both biblical and non-biblical sources, we also observed that there was no difference in meaning between the terms οὐρανός and ἐπουράνιος, except of course in regard

23 See the brief discussion of Lincoln, *Ephesians*, p. 248. Lincoln also notes the 'paradoxical language' in Ephesians to describe Christ's exaltation and present location, *Ephesians*, p. 248.

24 Cf. also Caragounis, *Mysterion*, pp. 151–52.

25 Caragounis, *Mysterion*, p. 152. As we have noted above, what appears to be problematic for Caragounis is the appearance of two different local expressions for heaven (ἐν οὐρανοῖς and ἐν τοῖς ἐπουρανίοις) in the same letter and even in close proximity to each other. With his minor distinction, Caragounis appears to address this conundrum.

26 Caragounis, *Mysterion*, p. 152.

27 Foster, 'Reoriented', pp. 108–12, especially p. 111.

28 Foster, 'Reoriented', p. 111.

to their functions as a noun and an adjective. Moreover, we also noted that various authors often chose to vary their terms for heaven for what seemed to be merely stylistic purposes.[29] Based on the evidence within Ephesians and the evidence outside the letter, we contend that Paul utilized the expressions ἐν οὐρανοῖς and ἐν τοῖς ἐπουρανίοις in Ephesians synonymously. As a result, it is misguided to assign different cosmological significance to these two local expressions for heaven.

c. A plurality of heavens in Ephesians?

In this section, we will investigate whether there is evidence for a plurality of heavens within the cosmology of Ephesians. A careful reading of Ephesians reveals that all of the references to οὐρανός and ἐπουράνιος are plural. Whether these plural references were of some significance to Paul or whether they were merely representative of the Hebrew שָׁמַיִם is open to debate. In *The Wrath of Heaven*, Schoonhoven correctly identifies the Old Testament as the proper source for Paul's view of heaven and writes that Paul was not concerned about a specific number of heavens, a typical concern within apocalyptic and Rabbinic thought.[30] In his discussion of Eph. 4.10, Lincoln concedes that Paul appears to indicate a plurality of heavens but also doubts that Paul has a specific number in mind.[31] Moreover, Paul's point in Eph. 4.10 is not to give cosmological teaching but rather to demonstrate Christ's superiority.[32] In his article on the heavenlies, Harris allows for the possibility that the plural use of οὐρανός is of some significance.[33] O'Brien believes that the background for the plurality of heavens in Ephesians is the Old Testament and Jewish notion of several 'heavens' but writes that

29 See, e.g., Sextus Empiricus, *Against the Astrologers* 5.43-45a, Philo, *Legum Allegoria* Book III LVIII.162–168, and *Testament of Job* 32–36 which possibly alternates between the same local expressions for heaven as Ephesians (ἐν οὐρανοῖς and ἐν τοῖς ἐπουρανίοις).

30 Schoonhoven, *Wrath*, p. 64; cf. Lincoln, 'Re-Examination', pp. 479–80.

31 Lincoln, *Paradise*, p. 158. Lincoln also connects the plurality of heavens in Eph. 4.10 with 2 Corinthians 12. In both passages, Lincoln does not believe Paul conceives of a specific number of heavens.

32 Lincoln, *Paradise*, p. 158.

33 Harris, 'Reconsidered', pp. 75–76, 81. However, it also appears that one of Harris's concerns in regard to the plural usage of οὐρανός is to understand the plural τῶν οὐρανῶν in Eph. 4.10 as 'a metaphor of simple replacement in which the "powers" of 1.21, who are subjugated to Christ, are replaced in 4.10 by a reference to the locus of their dwelling', 'Reconsidered', p. 84. Harris writes that this would also correspond to τὰ ἐπὶ τοῖς οὐρανοῖς in 1.10, 'Reconsidered', p. 84, note 41. We do not find Harris's argument and interpretation compelling. As we have briefly discussed above, the reference to Christ's ascent above the heavens reflects the OT notion of the heavens' inability to contain God. Additionally, the ἀνακεφαλαιώσασθαι of all things in Eph. 1.10 includes, but is also more comprehensive than, Christ's victory over the powers. Consequently, we believe it is improper to substitute the 'powers' for the 'heavens' in Eph. 1.10 and 4.10.

the significance of the imagery is metaphorical rather than literal.[34] Finally, Caragounis contends there is no doubt that there is a plurality of heavens in Ephesians but also writes it is not possible to know the number.[35]

In agreement with Schoonhoven and Lincoln, we contend that the proper background for Paul's conception of 'the heavens' in Ephesians is the Old Testament. In light of this, we also agree that there is nothing which suggests that Paul was overly concerned with apocalyptic or Rabbinic speculations about the number of heavens in Ephesians.[36] However, from our exegesis and discussion of 2 Cor. 12.1-4, we concluded that the terminology of 'Paradise' and 'third heaven' was indeed of significance to Paul since these terms represented Paul's ascent to the very presence of God. In this sense, Paul does conceive of a specific number of heavens, though this is not necessarily Paul's motivation for the plural usage or the force of his thought in Ephesians. As noted above, within Paul's basic Old Testament framework, 'heaven' could refer to the atmosphere (Ps. 147.8; Mt. 6.26), the firmament (Gen. 1.7, 14), or the dwelling place of God (Ps. 2.4; Mt. 6.9) and it is probable that these three basic Old Testament divisions comprised Paul's view of heaven. Such a view is also consistent with the unsophisticated and undeveloped doctrine of the heavens as found in the Old Testament and need not be dependent upon apocalyptic or Rabbinic speculations.[37]

Though we have argued that the general Old Testament framework is Paul's background for his view of heaven, we must still determine whether there is any significance in the plural usage of οὐρανός and ἐπουράνιος in Ephesians. Whether Paul intended this plural usage to reflect his view of three heavens or whether it was merely a reflection of the Hebrew שָׁמַיִם is impossible to establish with any certainty; however, as noted above, Christ's ascent ὑπεράνω πάντων τῶν οὐρανῶν in Eph. 4.10 at least allows for the possibility and perhaps even implies that Paul conceived of a plurality of heavens in Ephesians. One of the critical exegetical issues for this question is the usage of the preposition ὑπεράνω in Eph. 1.21. In Ephesians we read that both Christ (1.20) and the spiritual forces of evil (6.12) are located ἐν τοῖς ἐπουρανίοις, yet we

34 O'Brien, *Ephesians*, pp. 96–97.

35 Caragounis, *Mysterion*, p. 151. See also Adela Yarbro Collins who believes the references in Ephesians are consistent with a plurality of heavens, Adela Yarbro Collins, 'The Seven Heavens in Jewish and Christian Apocalypses', *Death, Ecstasy, and Other Worldly Journeys* (ed. John J. Collins and Michael Fishbane; Albany: State University of New York Press, 1995), pp. 59–93 (68).

36 Schoonhoven, *Wrath*, p. 64; cf. Lincoln, 'Re-Examination', pp. 479–80.

37 Schoonhoven also recognizes that though Paul was not concerned with apocalyptic or Rabbinic speculations about the number of heavens, he did adopt the basic OT view that heaven could refer to the atmosphere, the firmament, or the dwelling place of God, *Wrath*, p. 64.

also read that Christ is above (ὑπεράνω) these powers. The preposition ὑπεράνω which can mean 'above' or 'far above'[38] is often utilized in a purely spatial sense to denote the location of someone or something over another (e.g. Neh. 12.38-39; Jon. 4.6; Heb. 9.5). On the other hand, the term can also be utilized in a metaphorical sense to communicate power, authority, and/or superiority (e.g. Deut. 26.19; 28.1; Eph. 4.10). In light of Christ's description in 1.20 at the right hand of God and the usage of ὑπεράνω in 4.10, it seems that Paul primarily had in mind the latter sense when he wrote in 1.20-21 that Christ is ὑπεράνω the evil spiritual powers.[39]

It does remain a possibility, however, that Paul also intended a spatial distinction in his description of Christ ὑπεράνω the evil spiritual powers. Within later Jewish thought, 'the air' was often considered the location of demons or evil spiritual powers (*2 En.* 29.3-5; *Asc. Isa.* 4.1-3; 7.9-12; 10.28-31; 11.23; *T. Sol.* 2.3; 18.3; 20.12-15).[40] Thus the reference to Satan as τὸν ἄρχοντα τῆς ἐξουσίας τοῦ ἀέρος in Eph. 2.2 is consistent with these texts which depict evil powers in the lower heavens, the firmament, or the air. Moreover, since the descriptions of Satan in 'the air' (2.2) and the evil spiritual powers in the heavenlies (6.12) refer to the same general location,[41] it is possible and perhaps even likely that Paul's description of the evil powers in the heavenlies in Eph. 6.12 is consistent with the notion in Jewish thought that evil powers inhabited the lower heavens.[42] As a result, though Paul adopted the basic Old Testament understanding of heaven, he also, in all probability, drew upon later Jewish thought and conceived of the evil powers as dwelling

38 See Hoehner's discussion of ὑπεράνω in which he demonstrates that though it is possible for the term to carry the meaning 'far above', the usual meaning of ὑπεράνω is 'above', Hoehner, *Ephesians*, p. 276.

39 See Best's discussion where he also recognizes the difficulty of whether to understand the term ὑπεράνω in a literal or metaphorical sense, *Ephesians*, p. 172.

40 See further Bietenhard, *NIDNTT* 1, pp. 449, 451; Daniélou, *Theology*, pp. 174, 190; Lincoln, *Ephesians*, p. 96; Turner, 'Ephesians', p. 1229.

41 So also Lincoln, 'Re-Examination', pp. 475–76, note 4; Lincoln, *Paradise*, p. 165; Lincoln, *Ephesians*, pp. 95–96; O'Brien, *Ephesians*, p. 160; Page, *Powers*, p. 186; Daniélou, *Theology*, p. 174; Schnackenburg, *Ephesians*, p. 273; Bietenhard, *NIDNTT* 1, p. 449; Origen; Jerome. It is likely that Paul describes Satan's activity as in 'the air' in order to emphasize Satan's proximity to the earth for influencing mankind while the location of the heavenlies for the evil spiritual powers depicts their supernatural character, Lincoln, 'Re-Examination', pp. 475–76. Moreover, if there is any distinction, 'it could be that the "air" indicates the lower reaches of the heavenly realms', Lincoln, *Ephesians*, p. 96. The lower reaches would represent the heavenly realm(s) which the evil spiritual powers inhabit.

42 Cf. Daniélou, *Theology*, pp. 174, 190; Schnackenburg, *Ephesians*, pp. 77, 273; Turner 'Ephesians', p. 1243; Bietenhard, *NIDNTT* 2, p. 193; Schoenborn, *EDNT* 2, p. 546. Additionally, as previously noted, the church fathers Basil, Jerome, and Origen understand the expression ἐν τοῖς ἐπουρανίοις in Eph. 6.12 as a reference to 'the sky' or 'the air'.

in 'the air' or the lower heavens. Whereas he would have located the evil powers in the lower heavens, Paul would have located the abode of God in the highest heaven.[43] In such a scenario, the preposition ὑπεράνω might also carry a spatial dimension.[44]

From our examination of 2 Cor. 12.1-4, we concluded that Paul most likely adopted the basic Old Testament understanding of heaven which could refer to the sky, the firmament, or the abode of God. In this sense, Paul did believe in a plurality of heavens, though these 'levels' were by no means clearly defined in the Old Testament. There is also some justification for the view that Paul utilized the plural of οὐρανός and ἐπουράνιος in Ephesians to communicate a plurality of heavens. Regardless of their location, it is evident in Ephesians that Christ has authority and power over the evil spiritual powers (1.20-23). In light of Christ's authority and power, it also seems likely that Paul did not conceive of these evil powers, though they are described as ἐν τοῖς ἐπουρανίοις, as having permanent access to the presence of God. In this sense, the depiction of the evil spiritual powers in Ephesians is consistent with other New Testament descriptions of Satan and his angels as having been cast out of heaven and as no longer having the ability to accuse (Lk. 10.17-19; Rev. 12.7-13). Thus, in Ephesians and in the whole of the New Testament, the evil spiritual powers' access to heaven is most likely confined to the lower heavens while any access to the presence of God would be of a more temporary rather than permanent nature and without the ability to accuse.[45]

2. *Why* ἐν οὐρανοῖς *and* ἐν τοῖς ἐπουρανίοις *in Ephesians?*

In this excursus, we will address and attempt to answer the difficult question of why Paul chose to vary his terminology for local expressions of heaven in Ephesians. Throughout this book, we have maintained that the expressions ἐν οὐρανοῖς and ἐν τοῖς ἐπουρανίοις in Ephesians are properly understood as synonymous. We have rejected the interpretations of commentators such as Odeberg and McGough who posit

43 Cf. Caragounis who notes that God's throne would be at the highest spot in the highest heaven, *Mysterion*, p. 151.

44 Cf. Schnackenburg, *Ephesians*, pp. 77, 273; however, Schnackenburg also at times downplays the spatial significance of this language for 'a spiritual sense', *Ephesians*, p. 51. O'Brien (*Ephesians*, p. 141, note 201) and Caragounis (*Mysterion*, p. 151) also seem to allow for this possibility.

45 This is also the general argument of Bietenhard in *Die himmlische Welt*, pp. 211–14. See also the discussion of Schoonhoven, *Wrath*, pp. 44–53. Schoonhoven recognizes that Satan and the evil powers have been cast out of the heavenly court so that they can no longer accuse, *Wrath*, pp. 44–53; however, Schoonhoven believes that the evil powers are operative in every sphere, even in the dwelling place of God, *Wrath*, p. 65.

a major distinction in meaning between these expressions and who, consequently, define the heavenlies as the spiritual life of the church on earth. Similarly, we have also rejected views with minor distinctions in meaning wherein the expressions refer to different levels or concepts of heaven.[46] Finally, commentators such as Lincoln, Caragounis, and Lona have drawn a literary distinction of sorts between these two expressions.[47] While such interpretations cannot be entirely dismissed, they are also not without their difficulties.[48]

The fact that Paul utilized synonymously these two different local expressions for heaven leads to the question of why he opted to vary his terminology at all. One plausible suggestion for this dilemma is that Paul preferred to utilize the noun οὐρανός in his contrast with the noun γῆ.[49] In his analysis of the heavenlies Ernst Percy writes:

> Auch der Umstand, dass der Ausdruck ἐν τοῖς ἐπουρανίοις zum Unterschied von ἐν τοῖς οὐρανοῖς nicht mit dem entsprechenden Gegensatz, d.h. in diesem Falle ἐν τοῖς ἐπιγειοις, verbunden wird, sondern dass es statt dessen 1,10 und 3,15 heisst ἐπὶ bzw. ἐν (τοῖς) οὐρανοῖς καὶ ἐπι (τῆς) γῆς (Odeberg a.a.O. S. 8 f.), berechtigt nicht zu der erwähnten Distinktion zwischen den beiden Ausdrücken in bezug auf ihren Sinn: der Gegensatz ἐν (τοῖς) οὐρανοῖς καὶ ἐπι (τῆς) γῆς ist ja eine stehende Formel, was dagegen nicht mit ἐν τοῖς ἐπουρανίοις καὶ ἐν τοῖς ἐπιγείοις der Fall ist.[50]

It does indeed seem that the general preference for Paul (and other Greek writers) was to follow a general pattern of contrasting the noun οὐρανός with the noun γῆ and the adjectives ἐπουράνιος/οὐράνιος with the adjective ἐπίγειος. Examples of this pattern include 1 Cor. 8.5; 15.40-49; Eph. 1.10; 3.15; 4.10; Col. 1.16, 20.[51] It is also striking that the adjective ἐπίγειος appears only seven times in all of Scripture (Jn 3.12; 1 Cor. 15.40 [2x]; 2 Cor. 5.1; Phil. 2.10; Phil. 3.19; Jas 3.15) and its usage in these references is never in a local sense. It also seems

46 See the discussions of Caragounis and Foster in our excursus on the cosmology of Ephesians.

47 Lincoln's view is that in Ephesians, while οὐρανός is utilized for a broad range of meanings including the eschatological, ἐν τοῖς ἐπουρανίοις is employed specifically in an eschatological perspective, 'Re-Examination', p. 479. Caragounis writes that the heavenlies are bound up with the salvation events, *Mysterion*, p. 152. Lona believes that the expression ἐν τοῖς ἐπουρανίοις is utilized in statements about the church or community, *Eschatologie*, p. 298.

48 See chapter 2, the history of interpretation of the heavenlies, for discussions and critiques of Lincoln's, Caragounis's, and Lona's views.

49 So Percy, *Probleme*, p. 182, note 7.

50 Percy, *Probleme*, p. 182, note 7. On the basis of this theory, Percy also concludes that the meanings of the expressions ἐν (τοῖς) οὐρανοῖς and ἐν τοῖς ἐπουρανίοις are the same, *Probleme*, p. 182, note 7. Cf. Lincoln who follows Percy in, 'Re-Examination', p. 478.

51 Possible exceptions include 2 Cor. 5.1 and Phil. 3.19-20.

evident, as Percy implies, that the preference for describing an earthly location was to utilize the phrase ἐπὶ (τῆς) γῆς and that the usual contrast to this phrase was ἐν (τοῖς) οὐρανοῖς.[52] Consequently, it is plausible that Paul originally penned the formulaic and liturgical ἐν τοῖς ἐπουρανίοις in Eph. 1.3 and continued to utilize this expression throughout the letter except when there was a contrast with the earth (1.10; 3.15; 4.10).[53] The implicit contrast with the earth in Eph. 6.9[54] would also have led Paul to utilize ἐν οὐρανοῖς on this occasion.

In addition to Percy's suggestion, we have argued that it is also possible that Paul simply chose to vary his terminology for stylistic purposes. There is precedent for our argument from *Testament of Job* (32–36), Sextus Empiricus (*Against the Astrologers* 5.43-45a), and Philo (*Legum Allogoria* Book III LVIII.162–168). The fact that *Testament of Job* quite possibly alternates between the very same local expressions for heaven as those in Ephesians (ἐν οὐρανοῖς and ἐν τοῖς ἐπουρανίοις) with no difference in meaning is particularly revealing. As a result, it is possible that in Ephesians Paul simply chose to vary his terminology for heaven for stylistic purposes.

3. Evil Spiritual Powers in Ephesians and in the Larger Pauline Corpus

In this excursus, we will demonstrate that the proper background for Paul's view of the powers is the Old Testament and Second Temple Judaism. Though a number of previous scholars have also made this general claim, our primary contribution in this excursus will be to develop more fully this argument and demonstrate its validity within the context of Ephesians. As we have noted on a number of occasions, the ἀρχαί, ἐξουσίαι and other related terms in Ephesians and in the larger Pauline corpus are personal, spiritual, and evil powers.[55] The background[56] of these powers is to be located more generally in the Old

52 See, e.g., 1 Cor. 8.5; Eph. 1.10; 3.15; 4.10; Col. 1.16, 20; Rev. 5.3; 5.13. We should note here that 2 Cor. 5.1 and Phil. 3.19-20 both contrast ἐπίγειος with ἐν (τοῖς) οὐρανοῖς; however, Percy's hypothesis is still plausible since the usage of ἐπίγειος is not local and since we do not find a local use of ἐπουράνιος in contrast with the earth.

53 Though they are genitive clauses, the usage of τὰ κατώτερα μέρη τῆς γῆς and ὑπεράνω πάντων τῶν οὐρανῶν in 4.9-10 is still local.

54 The implicit contrast is with masters/lords κατὰ σάρκα (i.e. on the earth) (6.5) and the Master/Lord ἐν οὐρανοῖς (6.9).

55 See our discussions of Eph. 1.15-23, Eph. 3.1-13, and Eph. 6.12.

56 Here we use the term 'background' very loosely. As we will observe, the most extensive angelologies are found in *2 Enoch* and *Testament of Adam*. The issue of dating for *2 Enoch* is most complex as various scholars argue for a pre-Christian origin to a Middle Ages composition. The general consensus is that *2 Enoch* has a long and complicated history of compilation and editing. For a discussion of date, composition, and

Testament and Jewish literature but, more specifically, in apocalyptic literature. The most elaborate list of the various ranks of angels is found in *2 Enoch* 20 where the seventh heaven is the location of (1) archangels; (2) incorporeal forces; (3) dominions; (4) origins; (5) authorities; (6) cherubim; (7) seraphim; (8) thrones; (9) regiments; (10) shining *otanim* stations. *Testament of Adam* 4 also includes an elaborate list of nine groups of angels according to their hierarchy: (1) Angels (lowest); (2) Archangels; (3) Archons; (4) Authorities; (5) Powers; (6) Dominions; (7) Thrones; (8) Cherubim; (9) Seraphim.[57] In *Testament of Levi*, though they are not identified as particular classes or ranks, the spirits of Beliar are located in the second heaven. On the other hand, seemingly located in the highest heaven with the Great Glory are the archangels, thrones, and authorities (*T. Levi* 3.8).[58] From these various lists, the terms origins (ἀρχαί), authorities (ἐξουσίαι), incorporeal forces (δυνάμεις), dominions (κυριότητες), thrones (θρόνοι), and angels (ἄγγελοι) are all terms which also appear in the Pauline corpus in varying lists to refer to spiritual powers (Rom. 8.38; 1 Cor. 15.24; Eph. 1.21; 3.10; 6.12; Col. 1.16; 2.10; 2.15).[59]

Of particular interest is the fact that in the apocalyptic texts, in contrast to their usage in the Pauline corpus, these powers (i.e. ἀρχαί, ἐξουσίαι and other related terms) are not enemies of the Lord but are rather angels who serve and worship the Lord.[60] Most commentators gloss over this divergence and offer no real explanation for the significant difference in the usage of these terms.[61] One common explanation for the apparent disparity is that Jewish theology included a belief in angels who controlled the world and human

the editorial process of *2 Enoch*, see Andersen, 'Introduction', pp. 92–98. Additionally, *Testament of Adam*, which was almost certainly written after the books of the NT, is assigned a date from the second to fifth century AD. In his introduction to *Testament of Adam*, S. E. Robinson believes the work to be Jewish with Christian additions and assigns a date in the third century AD, S. E. Robinson, 'Introduction to Testament of Adam', *OTP* 2, pp. 989–92 (989–90). As a result of the possible late and ambiguous dates for the composition of *2 Enoch* and *Testament of Adam*, we make no argument for any sort of dependence of these works on Ephesians or Ephesians on these works.

57 Robinson notes that 'the most fully developed doctrine in the Testament of Adam is its angelology', Robinson, 'Introduction', p. 991. See Robinson's brief discussion of this angelology, 'Introduction', p. 991.

58 Cf. also *1 En.* 61.10.

59 See also 1 Cor. 2.6-8 for an ambiguous usage of ἀρχόντων which would correspond to the archons of *Testament of Adam* 4. We do not list above the references for 'angels' since Paul uses the term for both good and evil angels.

60 In the Pauline corpus, the only term which refers to good angels is ἄγγελοι, though Paul also speaks of evil ἄγγελοι (e.g. 2 Cor. 12.7).

61 The fact that these terms refer to good angels in these Jewish and apocalyptic texts is no doubt part of Carr's justification for his argument that the ἀρχαί, ἐξουσίαι, and related terms in Paul all refer to the good and pure angelic host of God. See Carr, *Angels*.

events and that these angels had both good and evil counterparts.[62] The major problem with this view is that much of the argument is only by assertion and there is little evidence to support it. Pierre Benoit correctly notes that the Pauline terminology for the powers 'does not find in these (apocalyptic) writings the usage which would completely explain its provenance'.[63]

A better and more cautious approach, though not entirely unrelated, is to understand the background for Paul's view of the powers within the context of Old Testament and Jewish thought.[64] As we noted in our examination of Eph. 6.12, there was a widespread Old Testament and Jewish belief that God had delegated authority over the various nations of the world to angels (LXX Deut. 32.8); however, these angels often abused their power (*1 Enoch* 89), led the nations astray from God (*Jub.* 15.30-31), and became hostile to God. As a result, we find a depiction of the struggle between good and evil angelic powers as the rulers of various nations in Daniel 10.13, 20-21.[65] Though there is no direct link between the Jewish usage of these terms and Paul's usage, there is nevertheless a conceptual link between the rebellion of the angelic authorities and Paul's appropriation of these governmental terms which were often utilized to refer to various spiritual powers.[66]

In various places throughout this examination, we have also noted that the primary ways in which Satan and the evil powers wage war on God's people and the nations of the world are through leading astray (Dan. 10.13, 20-21; *Jub.* 15.30-31; 2 Cor. 11.14), accusing (Zech. 3.1; *1 En.* 40.7; *Apoc. Zeph.* 3.5-9), and various means of temptation (Job; *Jub.* 17.16; 1 Cor. 7.5).[67] In the letter of Ephesians, and throughout the larger Pauline corpus, Paul draws upon and alludes to these Old Testament and Jewish themes in order to demonstrate Christ's authority over Satan and the evil powers.[68] In Eph. 1.20-21 we read of Christ's

62 See, e.g., Arnold who writes, 'While all three texts refer to the angelic hierarchy surrounding God's throne, the Jews believed the same hierarchy existed in the kingdom of evil', *Powers of Darkness*, p. 90.

63 Benoit, 'Pauline Angelology', p. 9.

64 So also Lincoln, *Ephesians*, pp. 62–65; Gombis, 'Ephesians 2', p. 409; Best, *Ephesians*, p. 175; Benoit, 'Pauline Angelology'.

65 For discussions of the Jewish notion of angelic rulers over the nations, see Rowland, *Open Heaven*, pp. 89–92; Benoit, 'Pauline Angelology', especially pp. 5–16; Arnold, *Powers of Darkness*, pp. 62–65.

66 See also Benoit, 'Pauline Angelology', pp. 5–16.

67 See also Schoonhoven's discussion of some of these themes in *Wrath*, pp. 44–53.

68 Thus our understanding of the powers is in contradistinction to Clinton Arnold's view that Paul's readers lived in fear of the evil spirits and cosmic powers which were believed to control and dominate mankind, Arnold, *Power and Magic*; Arnold, 'Ephesians', pp. 246–47. Cf. Gombis who also critiques Arnold's view, Gombis,

exaltation at the right hand of God and his present reign over the evil powers and all his enemies. In Ephesians 2 we read of the great salvation accomplished in Christ for believers. As Timothy Gombis has pointed out, many commentators struggle to identify the close relationship between these two passages in Ephesians.[69] If we read Ephesians 2 in light of Christ's victory over the powers, we can clearly identify some similar themes between Christ's defeat of the powers and the Old Testament and Jewish view of the powers we described above.[70]

First, we notice the contrast between believers' former way of life when they walked κατὰ τὸν ἄρχοντα τῆς ἐξουσίας τοῦ ἀέρος (2.2) and their present life in Christ as a result of God's mercy (2.4-10). Since Satan's authority completely to deceive the nations has been broken in Christ, we note a transfer of dominion or a transfer of authority from Satan to Christ (cf. Col. 1.13-14).[71] Perhaps Paul makes this theme even more explicit when he writes in Eph. 2.11-22 that Gentile believers, who were formerly separate from Christ, have been brought near through Christ and have become members of God's household.

Second, since the great salvation accomplished in Christ is by grace through faith (2.8-9), Christ has also stripped the powers of their ability to accuse God's people. While this theme is more subtle in Ephesians, it is made explicit in Paul's description of salvation in Col. 2.10-15. In Col. 2.10-15 Paul ties together Christ's headship over the powers (Col. 2.10), the salvation accomplished in Christ (Col. 2.11-14), Christ's disarming of the powers (Col. 2.15), and the impossibility of accusing believers (2.14) through Christ's work in which Christ cancelled out the χειρόγραφον.[72] Additionally, in Eph. 2.2-10 the salvation accomplished in Christ, which believers receive through the gracious act of God, also demonstrates that there is no longer a certificate of debts for believers and that the powers can no longer accuse.[73] In Eph. 2.6 Paul demonstrates the extent to which believers share in Christ's reign over and freedom from the accusing powers when he writes that they have been raised up and seated with Christ in the heavenlies.[74]

In Eph. 3.1-13 the revelation of God's mystery that τὰ ἔθνη are συγκληρονόμα καὶ σύσσωμα καὶ συμμέτοχα of the promise in Christ also

'Ephesians 2', p. 409, note 13.

69 Gombis, 'Ephesians 2', pp. 403–405.

70 Though we are not convinced by all aspects of his thesis in 'Ephesians 2', Gombis's argument that Ephesians 2 should be read in the light of Christ's victory over the powers sheds much light on Paul's view of the powers and Paul's description of the salvation accomplished in Christ in Ephesians 2.

71 See also Paul's commission from God to preach to the Gentiles in Acts 26.16-18.

72 For a discussion of χειρόγραφον, see O'Brien, *Colossians*, pp. 124–26.

73 Cf. Rom. 8.33-39.

74 Turner also notes the polemical force of Eph. 2.6 against the powers who accuse in 'Mission', p. 143, note 14.

serves to emphasize that Satan's power over the nations has been broken. The evil powers can no longer completely deceive the nations since the nations now also share in the promises of Israel. Moreover, Paul's statement in 3.10 that it is actually the church which reveals the mystery to the rulers and the authorities in the heavenlies reverses what were often the typical Jewish roles, as the spiritual powers were often perceived in Jewish thought to be instrumental in some way in the revelation of mysteries.[75] In Eph. 6.10-20 we read of believers' battle with the spiritual forces of evil and believers' need to stand firm against the schemes of the devil. In 6.12 Paul reveals the spiritual character of this battle when he writes that it is not against αἷμα καὶ σάρκα. He further emphasizes the character of the battle with his description of the armour of God. Believers are to adorn themselves with the belt of truth, the breastplate of righteousness, the gospel of peace, the shield of faith, the helmet of salvation, and the sword of the Spirit. Such weapons are appropriate for standing firm against the devil and the evil powers which surely desire to lead astray, condemn, and tempt believers. Paul's request for prayer so that the gospel would go forth (6.19-20) further confirms Satan's and the powers' schemes to lead astray and condemn.

In light of our understanding of the Colossian heresy and in light of our argument that a subtle and implicit polemic against a form of Jewish mysticism contributed to Paul's formulation of Eph. 2.6, we must also investigate what role, if any, the powers played in receiving visions and participating in heavenly ascents. For those who identify the Colossian heresy with Jewish mystical thought, the view that the powers had to be placated in order to participate in the heavenly visions is quite prevalent.[76] In support of this view, it is evident that angels and intermediaries often play an important role in heavenly ascent and the revelation of mysteries in many apocalypses.[77] While such a view is certainly plausible, the text of Colossians nowhere explicitly confirms that the powers play such a prominent role in the revelation of heavenly visions. In our view, it is just as likely that the powers, rather than mediators, are messengers or servants who simply give the instructions or requirements for participation in the heavenly visions.[78] Whatever the case, Paul alludes to the accusing and deceiving tactics of the evil powers in Colossians (2.8-15). Thus Paul reminds his readers that, since Christ has triumphed over the powers, the certificate of debt for believers has been cancelled and there is no reason to submit to the legalistic practices and ascetic demands of the powers. Moreover, since believers are already raised up with Christ

75 See Gruenwald, *From Apocalypticism to Gnosticism*, p. 7.

76 See, e.g., Lincoln, *Paradise*, pp. 111–12; O'Brien, *Colossians*, pp. 131–32, 143; Sappington, *Revelation and Redemption*, pp. 222.

77 See the discussion of Gruenwald, *From Apocalypticism to Gnosticism*, p. 7.

78 Bandstra, 'Errorists', pp. 335, 339.

and hidden with him in God (3.1-4), they need not adhere to the ascetic practices of the Jewish mystical group in order to have access to the presence of God.

Chapter 11

Conclusion

The expression ἐν τοῖς ἐπουρανίοις is indeed one of the most intriguing phrases in all of Scripture. There is certainly no other location in the Old or New Testament which serves as the locus of God's presence, the place of Christ's exaltation at God's right hand, the location of earthly believers, and the abode of the evil spiritual powers. What has proved to be the most troublesome and enigmatic for scholars of Ephesians are that earthly believers are seated ἐν τοῖς ἐπουρανίοις (Eph. 2.6) and that the evil spiritual powers also find their abode ἐν τοῖς ἐπουρανίοις (Eph. 6.12). The difficulty and apparent implausibility of these two statements have consequently led scholars to interpret the expression in a variety of ways. In *The View of the Universe in the Epistle to the Ephesians*, Hugo Odeberg argues that the heavenlies describe 'the whole of the Spiritual Reality, the Divine World, including not only the heavens but also the spiritual life, in which the Church partakes in its earthly conditions'.[1] Though it has found an array of critics, Odeberg's understanding, or a similar form of it, has nevertheless proved to be the most prevalent interpretation in New Testament studies over the last seventy-five years. In our examination, however, we have demonstrated that Odeberg's interpretation is both flawed and untenable, that there is no basis for a distinction between the expressions ἐν τοῖς ἐπουρανίοις and ἐν (τοῖς) οὐρανοῖς, and that these variant local expressions for 'heaven' are actually synonymous.

Since the evidence from Greek sources, Jewish sources, the Apostolic Fathers, the Septuagint, and the New Testament supports our position that the expressions ἐν τοῖς ἐπουρανίοις and ἐν (τοῖς) οὐρανοῖς are synonymous and always refer to that which is spatially distinct from the earth, our task was to investigate the heavenlies in Ephesians and, in particular, the difficult statements of Eph. 2.6 and Eph. 6.12, in order to shed light on these interpretive challenges. In our examination of Eph. 2.6, we concluded that a subtle polemic and implicit safeguard against a form of Jewish mystical thought provided the motivation and impetus for Paul to pen his astounding statement that believers have been seated ἐν τοῖς ἐπουρανίοις with Christ. Furthermore, Paul's

1 Odeberg, *View*, p. 12.

doctrine of believers' union with Christ and incorporation into Christ provided Paul with the necessary theological paradigm to formulate his view of this cosmic salvation in Christ. Finally, the Holy Spirit's role in Paul's eschatological paradigm demonstrates how believers, though they remain physically on the earth, also find their existence in heaven with Christ. In our examination of Eph. 6.12, we observed that it was not uncommon in Jewish thought for evil powers to be located in or associated with the heavens. Moreover, we concluded that, though evil powers are operative in the heavens in Ephesians, as a result of Christ's victory, these evil powers can no longer accuse believers or completely lead astray the nations. From the evidence in Jewish literature and in Ephesians, it is also possible that the lower heavens serve as the location of the evil powers in Eph. 6.12.

Our hope and expectation is that this book serves as the most comprehensive examination of the heavenlies in Ephesians. Our lexical analysis of the term ἐπουράνιος sheds much light on its use in a variety of sources and also demonstrates the close relationship between the terms ἐπουράνιος and οὐρανός. Our examinations of Eph. 2.6 in the light of Jewish mysticism and the presence of evil powers in the heavenlies in Eph. 6.12 highlight comparatively overlooked areas of scholarship in studies of Ephesians. It is our hope that these examinations serve to advance the discussions and understandings of these difficult verses. Finally, it is also our hope that the exegetical and conceptual analyses of Eph. 1.3-14, Eph. 1.15-23, Eph. 2.1-10, Eph. 3.1-13, and Eph. 6.10-20, as well as our excurses of the cosmology of Ephesians and the evil powers in Ephesians, provide a contribution for studies in Ephesians and also in the larger field of the New Testament.

Appendix

Definition and Clarification of Synonymy

Throughout this book, we have maintained that the terms ἐπουράνιος and οὐρανός/οὐράνιος, as well as the expressions ἐν τοῖς ἐπουρανίοις and ἐν (τοῖς) οὐρανοῖς, are synonymous. Here we will define more sharply and clarify our claim that these terms and expressions are synonymous. First, as we stated in the methodological section of our examination of ἐπουράνιος outside the New Testament, one obvious difference between the terms ἐπουράνιος and οὐρανός is that the former is an adjective while the latter is a noun. In this sense, we would not assert that the two terms are synonymous since one means 'heavenly' while the other means 'heaven'. When we make the claim that the terms ἐπουράνιος and οὐρανός/οὐράνιος are synonymous, what we mean is that they are synonymous in respect to the locations they represent. The implication of this is that the expressions ἐν τοῖς ἐπουρανίοις and ἐν (τοῖς) οὐρανοῖς, when both are local as in Ephesians, are synonymous. Additionally, we can further clarify our argument with our assertion that the adjectives ἐπουράνιος and οὐράνιος are synonymous.

In *Linguistics and Biblical Interpretation*, Peter Cotterell and Max Turner provide a helpful distinction between the 'sense' and 'reference' of a word's meaning.[1] While 'word sense' is 'how that word (or expression) relates in meaning to other words or expressions in the language',[2] the 'reference' 'is the *thing in the world which is intentionally signified by that word or expression*'.[3] Cotterell and Turner also note the dangers either of confusing word sense and reference or of not distinguishing between word sense and reference.[4] Furthermore, Cotterell and Turner emphasize that while partial synonymy is quite common, '*absolute synonymy* hardly ever occurs (for there is little point in a language retaining two words with exactly the same range of sense, connotations, habitual collocations, and social register)'.[5] A common

1 For a full discussion, see Cotterell and Turner, *Linguistics*, pp. 77–187.

2 Cotterell and Turner, *Linguistics*, pp. 77–78; cf. pp. 139–75.

3 Cotterell and Turner, *Linguistics*, p. 84; cf. pp. 82–90. Emphasis Cotterell and Turner's.

4 See especially Cotterell and Turner's discussion entitled 'A Clarifying Note on Synonymy' in *Linguistics*, pp. 159–61.

5 Cotterell and Turner, *Linguistics*, p. 159. Cotterell and Turner note that though

error, even in academic literature, is the tendency to label terms 'synonyms' or 'synonymous' when they actually only refer to the same thing.[6] One poignant example of this confusion of lexical categories is demonstrated by the fact that Margaret Thatcher in 1988 could have been identified as 'the leader of the Conservative Party' or 'the prime minister'.[7] While these expressions clearly refer to the same person (i.e. Margaret Thatcher), they certainly carry different senses and so are not synonymous.[8]

In *Language, Meaning and Context*, John Lyons also contends that 'absolute synonymy' between terms or expressions is 'extremely rare' and writes that terms or expressions must be identical in meaning (not merely similar) to be considered synonymous.[9] Additionally, Lyons gives three guidelines to distinguish between partial synonymy and absolute synonymy:

1 Synonyms are *fully* synonymous if, and only if, *all their meanings* are identical.
2 Synonyms are *totally* synonymous if, and only if, they are synonymous *in all contexts.*
3 Synonyms are *completely* synonymous if, and only if, they are identical *on all (relevant) dimensions of meaning.*[10]

According to Lyons, though there is a sense in which partial synonyms can be considered synonymous, for terms or expressions to be considered absolute synonyms, they must meet all three of these criteria and so be fully, totally, and completely synonymous.[11]

lexemes might be synonymous in one or even several senses and so exhibit partial synonymy, it is highly unlikely that they will be synonymous in all of their senses, *Linguistics*, p. 159.

6 Cotterell and Turner, *Linguistics*, p. 159.

7 Cotterell and Turner, *Linguistics*, p. 161.

8 Cotterell and Turner, *Linguistics*, p. 161; cf. Cotterell and Turner's example of 'faith', 'word', and 'truth', which have mistakenly been identified as 'synonymous' when the terms are actually only used interchangeably to refer to 'the gospel' in various New Testament passages, *Linguistics*, pp. 160–61. See further Cotterell and Turner's excursus on κεφαλή for an additional example of how two terms can have the same referent but different sense, *Linguistics*, pp. 141–45.

9 John Lyons, *Language, Meaning and Context* (Fontana Linguistics; London: Fontana Paperbacks, 1981), p. 50. For Lyons's full discussion, see *Language*, pp. 50–55. The same material and an almost identical discussion, word for word in most places, can also be found in John Lyons's updated and expanded volume *Linguistic Semantics: An Introduction* (Cambridge: Cambridge University Press, 1995), pp. 60–65. See further Lyons, *Language*, pp. 75–97, and Lyons, *Linguistic Semantics*, pp. 102–30.

10 Lyons, *Language*, pp. 50–51.

11 Lyons, *Language*, p. 51. For examples of how two partial synonyms are not absolutely synonymous according to each guideline, see Lyons, *Language*, pp. 51–55.

After reviewing the precise definitions of synonymy from Peter Cotterell and Max Turner's *Linguistics and Biblical Interpretation* and John Lyons's *Language, Meaning and Context*, we are now able to define more sharply our claim that the terms ἐπουράνιος and οὐράνιος are synonymous. In reference to John Lyons's precise definition of synonymy in *Language, Meaning and Context*, we contend that the terms ἐπουράνιος and οὐράνιος are 'fully', 'totally', and 'completely' synonymous and are thus 'absolute synonyms'. From our examination of the primary material and from our consultation of various lexicons, we maintain that all of their meanings are identical, that they are synonymous in all contexts, and that they are identical on all relevant dimensions of meaning. In reference to Cotterell and Turner's work on lexical synonymy, we contend that the terms ἐπουράνιος and οὐράνιος are synonymous in both 'sense' and 'reference'. We have maintained throughout this book that ἐπουράνιος and οὐράνιος (in addition to the noun οὐρανός) all refer to that which is spatially distinct from the earth. Here we also contend that there is also no distinction in 'sense' between ἐπουράνιος and οὐράνιος. Indeed, it is difficult to discern how there could even be a distinction in 'sense' between these terms unless perhaps one is inclined to accept Caragounis's suggestion that ἐπουράνιος (or the heavenlies in Ephesians) only consists of the higher heavenly levels from the realm of the cosmic forces to God's throne.[12]

Though Lyons, and Cotterell and Turner have convincingly demonstrated that absolute synonymy is very rare, it seems that the terms ἐπουράνιος and οὐράνιος do indeed represent one of these very rare instances of absolute synonymy between two lexemes.[13] As we noted above, this conclusion is consistent with our examination of the primary material[14] and also with the numerous lexicons which we have consulted.[15] With such an understanding, the prefix 'ἐπ-' in ἐπουράνιος does not mean 'upon' nor does it refer to the higher reaches of 'heaven'. If the prefix 'ἐπ-' carries any force, it merely denotes 'at' or 'in', rendering the

12 Caragounis, *Mysterion*, p. 152. It is significant to note that Caragounis's argument for this understanding of ἐπουράνιος seemingly only applies to Ephesians.

13 Since ἐπουράνιος and οὐράνιος are absolute synonyms, the implication is that the expressions ἐν τοῖς ἐπουρανίοις, when used as a local substantive such as in Ephesians, and ἐν (τοῖς) οὐρανοῖς are also synonymous.

14 See especially our examinations of Sextus Empiricus, *Against the Astrologers* 5.43–45a; Philo, *Legum Allegoria*, Book III LVIII.162–168; Philo, *De Gigantibus* 62; *Testament of Job* 32–36.

15 See e.g. Traub, *TDNT* 5, pp. 536–42; Bietenhard, *NIDNTT* 2, pp. 184–96; O. Michel, 'ἐπουράνιος', *EDNT* 2, pp. 46–47; Schoenborn, *EDNT* 2, pp. 543–47, especially p. 547; BDAG, pp. 388, 737–39; Johannes P. Louw and Eugene A. Nida (eds), *Greek English Lexicon of the New Testament Based on Semantic Domains* (2 vols; New York: United Bible Societies, 1988), vol. 1, pp. 3–4, entries 1.8 ('ἐπουράνιος, ον') and 1.12 ('οὐράνιος, ον; ἐπουράνιος, ον'). There is no distinction in meaning between ἐπουράνιος and οὐράνιος in any of these lexicons or theological dictionaries.

definition 'in heaven' or 'heavenly' for the term ἐπουράνιος, which is the same basic meaning of the term οὐράνιος.[16] Whether this was always the case we cannot be certain but from the time of Homer's eighth-century-BC Greek until the composition of the New Testament documents and beyond, there is no discernible difference in meaning between the terms ἐπουράνιος and οὐράνιος.[17] In general, the New Testament preference between these two adjectives is ἐπουράνιος but it is difficult to discern whether or not this preference was the result of extra-biblical usage.[18]

16 See also Traub, *TDNT* 5, p. 538.

17 There is also no distinction in the meanings of ἐπουράνιος and οὐράνιος in modern Greek.

18 See Bietenhard, *NIDNTT* 2, p. 192, and Schoenborn, *EDNT* 2, p. 547.

Bibliography

Abbott, T. K., *The Epistles to the Ephesians, and to the Colossians* (International Critical Commentary; Edinburgh: T & T Clark, 1897).

Abegg, Martin G., 'Who Ascended to Heaven? 4Q491, 4Q427, and the Teacher of Righteousness', in *Eschatology, Messianism, and the Dead Sea Scrolls* (ed. Craig A. Evans and Peter W. Flint; Studies in the Dead Sea Scrolls and Related Literature 1; Grand Rapids: Eerdmans, 1997), pp. 61–73.

Aletti, Jean-Noël, *Saint Paul Épitre aux Colossiens: Introduction, traduction et commentaire* (Études Bibliques New Series 20; Paris: J Gabalda, 1993).

———, *Saint Paul Épître aux Éphésiens: Introduction, traduction et commentaire* (Études Bibliques New Series 42; Paris: J. Gabalda, 2001).

———, *Saint Paul Épître aux Philippiens: Introduction, traduction et commentaire* (Études Bibliques New Series 55; Paris: J. Gabalda, 2005).

Alexander, Patrick H., John F. Kutsko, James D. Ernest, Shirley A. Decker-Lucke, and David L. Petersen (eds), *The SBL Handbook of Style: For Ancient Near Eastern, Biblical and, Early Christian Studies* (Peabody, MA: Hendrickson, 1999).

Alexander, Philip, *The Mystical Texts* (Library of Second Temple Studies 61/Companion to the Qumran Scrolls 7; London: T & T Clark, 2006).

Allen, Thomas G., 'Exaltation and Solidarity with Christ: Ephesians 1.20 and 2.6', *Journal for the Study of the New Testament* 28 (1986), pp. 103–20.

Andersen, F. I., 'Introduction to 2 (Slavonic Apocalypse of) Enoch', in vol. 1 of *The Old Testament Pseudepigrapha* (ed. James H. Charlesworth; 2 vols; London: Darton, Longman & Todd, 1983), pp. 91–100.

Anderson, Gary A., 'Worship, Qumran Sect', in vol. 2 of *Encyclopedia of the Dead Sea Scrolls* (ed. Lawrence H. Schiffman and James C. VanderKam; 2 vols; Oxford: Oxford University Press, 2000), pp. 991–96.

Arnold, Clinton E., 'The "Exorcism" of Ephesians 6.12 in Recent Research: A Critique of Wesley Carr's View of the Role of Evil

Powers in First-Century AD Belief', *Journal for the Study of the New Testament* 30 (1987), pp. 71–87.

———, *Ephesians: Power and Magic: The Concept of Power in Ephesians in Light of its Historical Setting* (Cambridge: Cambridge University Press, 1989).

———, *Powers of Darkness: Principalities and Powers in Paul's Letters* (Downers Grove, IL: InterVarsity, 1992).

———, 'Ephesians, Letter to the', in *Dictionary of Paul and His Letters* (ed. Gerald F. Hawthorne, Ralph P. Martin, and Daniel G. Reid; Downers Grove, IL: InterVarsity, 1993), pp. 238–49.

Attridge, Harold W., *The Epistle to the Hebrews: A Commentary on the Epistle to the Hebrews* (Hermeneia; Philadelphia: Fortress Press, 1989).

Aune, David Edward, *The Cultic Setting of Realized Eschatology in Early Christianity* (Supplements to Novum Testamentum 28; Leiden: Brill, 1972).

Balz, Horst and Gerhard Schneider (eds), *Exegetical Dictionary of the New Testament* (trans. James W. Thompson and John W. Medendorp; 3 vols; Grand Rapids: Eerdmans, 1990–93).

Bandstra, Andrew J., 'Did the Colossian Errorists Need a Mediator?', in *New Dimensions in New Testament Study* (ed. Richard N. Longenecker and Merrill C. Tenney; Grand Rapids: Zondervan, 1974), pp. 329–43.

Barrett, C. K., *A Commentary on the First Epistle to the Corinthians* (Black's New Testament Commentaries; London: A & C Black, 2nd edn, 1971).

———, *The Gospel According to St. John: An Introduction with Commentary and Notes on the Greek Text* (London: SPCK, 2nd edn, 1978).

Barth, Markus, *Ephesians: Introduction, Translation, and Commentary* (Anchor Bible 34–34A; 2 vols; Garden City: Doubleday, 1974).

Bate, H. N. (ed.), *The Sibylline Oracles: Books III–V* (trans. H. N. Bate; New York: MacMillan, 1918).

Bauer, W., F. W. Danker, W. F. Arndt, and F. W. Gingrich, *Greek–English Lexicon of the New Testament and Other Early Christian Literature* (Chicago, 3rd edn, 1999).

Beasley-Murray, George R., *John* (Word Biblical Commentary 36; Nashville: Thomas Nelson, 2nd edn, 1999).

Benoit, Pierre, 'Qumran and the New Testament', in *Paul and Qumran: Studies in New Testament Exegesis* (ed. Jerome Murphy-O'Connor; London: Geoffrey Chapman, 1968), pp. 1–30.

———, 'Pauline Angelology and Demonology: Reflexions on the Designations of the Heavenly Powers and on the Origin of Angelic Evil According to Paul', *Religious Studies Bulletin* 3.1 (1983), pp. 1–18.

Best, Ernest, 'Ephesians 1.1', in *Essays on Ephesians* (Edinburgh: T & T Clark, 1997), pp. 1–16.

———, 'Ephesians 1.1 Again', in *Essays on Ephesians* (Edinburgh: T & T Clark, 1997), pp. 17–24.

———, 'Who Used Whom? The Relationship of Ephesians and Colossians', *New Testament Studies* 43 (1997), pp. 72–96.

———, *A Critical and Exegetical Commentary on Ephesians* (New International Critical Commentary; London: T & T Clark, 1998).

Bietenhard, H., *Die himmlische Welt im Urchristentum und Spätjudentum* (Wissenschaftliche Untersuchungen zum Neuen Testament 2; Tübingen: J. C. B. Mohr, 1951).

———, 'Demon, Air, Cast Out', in *New International Dictionary of New Testament Theology* (ed. Colin Brown; 4 vols; Carlisle: Paternoster, rev. edn, 1986), pp. 449–53.

———, 'Heaven, Ascend, Above', in *New International Dictionary of New Testament Theology* (ed. Colin Brown; 4 vols; Carlisle: Paternoster, rev. edn, 1986), vol. 2, pp. 184–96.

Bockmuehl, Markus N. A., *Revelation and Mystery in Ancient Judaism and Pauline Christianity* (Wissenschaftliche Untersuchungen zum Neuen Testament, Second Series 36; Tübingen: J. C. B. Mohr, 1990).

———, *The Epistle to the Philippians* (Black's New Testament Commentaries; London: Hendrickson, 1998).

Boismard, M.-É., *L' Énigme de la letter aux Éphésiens* (Études Bibliques New Series 39; Paris: J. Gabalda, 1999).

Bratcher, Robert G. and Eugene A. Nida, *A Translator's Handbook on Paul's Letter to the Ephesians* (New York: United Bible Societies, 1982).

Brock, S. P. (ed.), *Testamentum Iobi* (Pseudepigrapha Veteris Testamenti Graece 2; Leiden: Brill, 1967).

Brown, Colin (ed.), *New International Dictionary of New Testament Theology* (4 vols; Carlisle: Paternoster, rev. edn, 1986).

Brown, Raymond E., *The Churches the Apostles Left Behind* (New York: Paulist; London: Geoffrey Chapman, 1984).

Bruce, F. F., *Paul: Apostle of the Free Spirit* (Exeter: Paternoster, 1977).

———, *The Epistles to the Colossians, to Philemon, and to the Ephesians* (New International Commentary on the New Testament; Grand Rapids: Eerdmans, 1984).

———, *The Epistle to the Hebrews* (New International Commentary on the New Testament; Grand Rapids: Eerdmans, rev. edn, 1990).

Byrne, Brendan, *Romans* (Sacra Pagina Series 6; Collegeville, MN: The Liturgical Press, 1996).

Caird, G. B., *Paul's Letters from Prison* (New Clarendon Bible: New Testament; Oxford: Oxford University Press, 1976).

Caragounis, Chrys C., *The Ephesian Mysterion: Meaning and Content* (Coniectanea Biblica, New Testament Series 8; Lund: Gleerup, 1977).

Cargal, Timothy B., 'Seated in the Heavenlies: Cosmic Mediators in the Mysteries of Mithras and the Letter to the Ephesians', *Society of Biblical Literature Seminar Papers* 33 (1994), pp. 804–21.

Carr, Wesley, *Angels and Principalities: The Background, Meaning and Development of the Pauline Phrase hai Arahai kai hai Exousiai* (Society for New Testament Studies Monograph Series 42; Cambridge: Cambridge University Press, 1981).

Carson, D. A., *The Gospel According to John* (Pillar New Testament Commentary; Leicester: InterVarsity, 1991).

Charles, R. H., *The Greek Versions of the Testaments of the Twelve Patriarchs* (Oxford: Clarendon Press, 1908).

Charlesworth, James H., 'Introduction for the General Reader', in *The Old Testament Pseudepigrapha* (ed. James H. Charlesworth; 2 vols; London: Darton, Longman & Todd, 1983), vol. 1, pp. xxi–xxxiv.

——— (ed.), *The Old Testament Pseudepigrapha* (2 vols; London: Darton, Longman & Todd, 1983–85).

———, *The Old Testament Pseudepigrapha and the New Testament: Prolegomena for the Study of Christian Origins* (Society for New Testament Studies Monograph Series 54; Cambridge: Cambridge University Press, 1985).

Clemens, John S., 'Note on the Phrase ἐν τοῖς ἐπουρανίοις', *The Expository Times* 2 (1891), p. 140.

Collins, Adela Yarbro, 'The Seven Heavens in Jewish and Christian Apocalypses', in *Death, Ecstasy, and Other Worldly Journeys* (ed. John J. Collins and Michael Fishbane; Albany: State University of New York Press, 1995), pp. 59–93.

Collins, John J., *The Apocalyptic Imagination: An Introduction to the Jewish Matrix of Christianity* (New York: Crossroad, 1984).

———, 'Was the Dead Sea Sect an Apocalyptic Movement?', in *Archaeology and History in the Dead Sea Scrolls: The New York University Conference in Memory of Yigael Yadin* (ed. Lawrence H. Schiffman; Journal for the Study of the Pseudepigrapha Supplement Series 8/American Schools of Oriental Resarch/Journal for the Study of the Old Testament Monograph Series 2; Sheffield: Sheffield Academic Press, 1990), pp. 25–51.

———, 'A Throne in the Heavens: Apotheosis in Pre-Christian Judaism', in *Death, Ecstasy, and Other Worldly Journeys* (ed. John J. Collins and Michael Fishbane; Albany: State University of New York Press, 1995), pp. 43–58.

Collins, Raymond F., *First Corinthians* (Sacra Pagina Series 7; Collegeville, MN: The Liturgical Press, 1999).

Conzelmann, H., *Der Brief an die Epheser*. (Das Neue Testament Deutsch; Göttingen: Vandenhoeck and Ruprecht, 11th edn, 1968).

Cotterell, Peter and Max Turner, *Linguistics and Biblical Interpretation* (Downers Grove, IL: InterVarsity, 1989).

Dahl, Nils Alstrup, 'Benediction and Congratulation', in *Studies in Ephesians: Introductory Questions, Text- & Edition-Critical Issues, Interpretation of Texts and Themes* (ed. David Hellholm, Vemund Blomkvist, and Tord Fornberg; Wissenschaftliche Untersuchungen zum Neuen Testament 131; Tübingen: Mohr Siebeck, 2000), pp. 279–314.

———, 'Ephesians and Qumran', in *Studies in Ephesians: Introductory Questions, Text- & Edition-Critical Issues, Interpretation of Texts and Themes* (ed. David Hellholm, Vemund Blomkvist, and Tord Fornberg; Wissenschaftliche Untersuchungen zum Neuen Testament 131; Tübingen: Mohr Siebeck, 2000), pp. 107–44.

———, 'Das Proömium des Epheserbriefes', in *Studies in Ephesians: Introductory Questions, Text- & Edition-Critical Issues, Interpretation of Texts and Themes* (ed. David Hellholm, Vemund Blomkvist, and Tord Fornberg; Wissenschaftliche Untersuchungen zum Neuen Testament 131; Tübingen: Mohr Siebeck, 2000), pp. 315–34.

Daniélou, Jean, *The Theology of Jewish Christianity* (ed. and trans. John A. Baker; The Development of Christian Doctrine Before the Council of Nicaea 1; London: Darton, Longman & Todd, 1964).

Dean-Otting, Mary, *Heavenly Journeys: A Study of the Motif in Hellenistic Jewish Literature* (Judentum und Umwelt 8; Bern: Peter Lang, 1984).

Deissmann, Adolf, *Light from the Ancient East: The New Testament Illustrated by Recently Discovered Texts of the Graeco-Roman World* (trans. R. M. Strachan; London: Hodder and Stoughton, 1910).

Duling, D. C., 'Introduction to Testament of Solomon', in vol. 1 of *The Old Testament Pseudepigrapha* (ed. James H. Charlesworth; 2 vols; London: Darton, Longman & Todd, 1983), pp. 935–59.

Dunn, James D. G., 'The Problem of Pseudonymity', in *The Living Word* (Philadelphia: Fortress Press, 1987), pp. 65–85.

———, *Romans 9–16* (Word Biblical Commentary 38B; Dallas: Word Books, 1988).

Ellingworth, Paul, *The Epistle to the Hebrews: A Commentary on the Greek Text* (New International Greek Testament Commentary; Grand Rapids: Eerdmans, 1993).

Ellis, E. Earle, 'Paul and His Opponents: Trends in the Research', in *Christianity, Judaism and Other Greco-Roman Cults: Studies for Morton Smith at 60* (ed. Jacob Neusner; vol. 1, New Testament; Studies in Judaism in Late Antiquity 12; Leiden: Brill, 1975), pp. 264–98.

Eskola, Timo, *Messiah and the Throne: Jewish Merkabah Mysticism and Early Christian Exaltation Discourse* (Wissenschaftliche Untersuchungen zum Neuen Testament; Second Series 142; Tübingen: Mohr Siebeck, 2001).

Evans, Craig A., 'The Colossian Mystics', *Biblica* 63 (1982), pp. 188–205.

Fee, Gordon D., *The First Epistle to the Corinthians* (New International Commentary on the New Testament; Grand Rapids: Eerdmans, 1987).

Foster, Robert L., 'Reoriented to the Cosmos: Cosmology and Theology in Ephesians through Philemon', in *Cosmology and New Testament Theology* (ed. Jonathan T. Pennington and Sean M. McDonough; Library of New Testament Studies 355; New York: T & T Clark, 2008), pp. 107–24.

Foulkes, Francis, *The Letter of Paul to the Ephesians: An Introduction and Commentary* (The Tyndale New Testament Commentaries; Leicester: InterVarsity, 1989).

Fowl, Stephen E., *Philippians* (Two Horizons New Testament Commentary; Grand Rapids: Eerdmans, 2005).

Francis, Fred O., 'The Background of Embateuein (Col. 2.18) in Legal Papyri and Oracle Inscriptions', in *Conflict at Colossae: A Problem in the Interpretation of Early Christianity Illustrated by Modern Studies* (ed. and trans. Fred O. Francis and Wayne A. Meeks; Missoula, MT: Society of Biblical Literature and Scholars Press, 1975), pp. 197–207.

———, 'Humility and Angelic Worship in Col. 2.18', in *Conflict at Colossae: A Problem in the Interpretation of Early Christianity Illustrated by Modern Studies* (ed. and trans. Fred O. Francis and Wayne A. Meeks; Missoula, MT: Society of Biblical Literature and Scholars Press, 1975), pp. 163–95.

Frankfurter, David, 'The Legacy of Jewish Apocalypses in Early Christianity: Regional Trajectories', in *The Jewish Apocalyptic Heritage in Early Christianity* (ed. James C. VanderKam and William Adler; Compendia Rerum Iudaicarum ad Novum Testamentum; Section 3, Jewish Traditions in Early Christian Literature 4; Minneapolis: Fortress Press, 1996), pp. 129–200.

Gärtner, Bertil, *The Temple and the Community in Qumran and the New Testament: A Comparative Study in the Temple Symbolism of the Qumran Texts and the New Testament* (Society for New Testament Studies Monograph Series 1; Cambridge: Cambridge University Press, 1965).

Gaylord Jr, H. E., 'Introduction to 3 (Greek Apocalypse of) Baruch', vol. 1 of *The Old Testament Pseudepigrapha*; ed. James H. Charlesworth; 2 vols; London: Darton, Longman & Todd, 1983), pp. 653–61.

Gibbs, John G., *Creation and Redemption: A Study in Pauline Theology* (Leiden: Brill, 1971).

Gnilka, Joachim, *Der Epheserbrief* (Herders Theologischer Kommentar zum Neuen Testament 10:2; Freiburg: Herder, 1971).

Gombis, Timothy G., 'Ephesians 2 as a Narrative of Divine Warfare' *Journal for the Study of the New Testament* 26.4 (2004), pp. 403–18.

Gooder, Paula R., *Only the Third Heaven?: 2 Corinthians 12.1-10 and Heavenly Ascent* (Library of New Testament Studies 313; London: T & T Clark, 2006).

Goodspeed, Edgar J., *The Meaning of Ephesians* (Chicago: The University of Chicago Press, 1933).

Goulder, Michael D., 'The Visionaries of Laodicea', *Journal for the Study of the New Testament* 43 (1991), pp. 15–39.

———, 'Vision and Knowledge', *Journal for the Study of the New Testament* 56 (1994), pp. 53–71.

The Greek Bucolic Poets (trans. J. M. Edmonds; Loeb Classical Library; London: William Heinemann, 1928).

Grindheim, Sigurd, 'What the OT Prophets Did Not Know: The Mystery of the Church in Eph. 3,2–13', *Biblica* 84 (2003), pp. 531–53.

Gruenwald, Ithamar, *Apocalyptic and Merkavah Mysticism* (Arbeiten zur Geschichte des Antiken Judentums und des Urchristentums 14; Leiden: Brill, 1980).

———, *From Apocalypticism to Gnosticism: Studies in Apocalypticism, Merkavah Mysticism and Gnosticism* (Beiträge zur Erforschung des Alten Testaments und des Antiken Judentums 14; Frankfurt am Main: Peter Lang, 1988).

Gunther, John J., *St Paul's Opponents and Their Background: A Study of Apocalyptic and Jewish Sectarian Teachings* (Supplements to Novum Testamentum 35; Leiden: Brill, 1973).

Guthrie, Donald, *The Pastoral Epistles: An Introduction and Commentary* (Tyndale New Testament Commentaries. Leicester: InterVarsity, 2nd edn, 1990).

Hamilton, Neill Q., *The Holy Spirit and Eschatology in Paul* (Scottish Journal of Theology Occasional Papers 6; Edinburgh: Oliver and Boyd, 1957).

Hanson, Anthony Tyrell, *The New Testament Interpretation of Scripture* (London: SPCK, 1980).

Harris, Murray J., *Raised Immortal: Resurrection and Immortality in the New Testament* (London: Marshall, Morgan & Scott, 1983).

———, *The Second Epistle to the Corinthians: A Commentary on the Greek Text* (New International Greek Testament Commentary; Grand Rapids: Eerdmans, 2005).

Harris III, W. Hall, '"The Heavenlies" Reconsidered: *Οὐρανός* and Ἐπουράνιος in Ephesians', *Bibliotheca Sacra* 148.589 (1991), pp. 72–89.

Hawthorne, Gerald F., *Philippians* (Word Biblical Commentary 43; Waco: Word Books, 1983).

Hays, Richard B., *First Corinthians* (Interpretation: A Bible Commentary for Teaching and Preaching; Louisville: John Knox Press, 1997).

Heil, John Paul, *Ephesians: Empowerment to Walk in Love for the Unity of All in Christ* (Studies in Biblical Literature 13; Atlanta: Society of Biblical Literature, 2007).

Heine, Ronald E., *The Commentaries of Origen and Jerome on St Paul's Epistle to the Ephesians* (Oxford Early Christian Studies; Oxford: Oxford University Press, 2002).

Hengel, Martin, '"Sit at My Right Hand!" The Enthronement of Christ at the Right Hand of God and Psalm 110:1', in *Studies in Early Christology* (Edinburgh: T & T Clark, 1995), pp. 119–225.

Hermetica (ed. and trans. Walter Scott; 4 vols; Oxford: Oxford University Press, 1924–36).

Himmelfarb, Martha, 'Apocalyptic Ascent and the Heavenly Temple', in *Society of Biblical Literature Seminar Papers 1987* (ed. Kent Harold Richards; Atlanta: Scholars Press, 1987), pp. 210–17.

———, *Ascent to Heaven in Jewish and Christian Apocalypses* (Oxford: Oxford University Press, 1993).

———, 'The Practice of Ascent in the Ancient Mediterranean World', in *Death, Ecstasy, and Other Worldly Journeys* (ed. John J. Collins and Michael Fishbane; Albany: State University of New York Press, 1995), pp. 123–37.

Hoehner, Harold W., *Ephesians: An Exegetical Commentary* (Grand Rapids: Baker, 2002).

Holmes, Michael E. (ed.), *The Apostolic Fathers: Greek Texts and English Translations* (Grand Rapids: Baker Books, 3rd edn, 1999). Updated edition of *The Apostolic Fathers: Greek Texts and English Translations of Their Writings* (ed. and trans. J. B. Lightfoot and J. R. Harmer; ed. and rev. Michael W. Holmes; Grand Rapids: Baker Books, 2nd edn, 1992). Updated edition of Lightfoot, J. B., *The Apostolic Fathers: Revised Texts with Short Introductions and English Translations* (ed. and completed by J. R. Harmer; London: Macmillan, 1891).

Homer, *Odyssey* (trans. A. T. Murray; Loeb Classical Library; 2 vols; Cambridge: Harvard University Press, 1960).

———, *Iliad* (trans. A. T. Murray; Loeb Classical Library; 2 vols; Cambridge: Harvard University Press, 2nd edn, 1999).

Hooker, Morna D., 'Were there False Teachers in Colossae?', in *Christ and Spirit in the New Testament: In Honor of Charles Francis Digby Moule* (ed. Barnabas Lindars and Stephen S. Smalley; Cambridge: Cambridge University Press, 1973), pp. 315–31.

Hughes, Philip Edgcumbe, *Paul's Second Epistle to the Corinthians* (New International Commentary on the New Testament; Grand Rapids: Eerdmans, 1962).

Hurtado, Larry W., *One God, One Lord: Early Christian Devotion and Ancient Jewish Monotheism* (Edinburgh: T & T Clark, 2nd edn, 1998).

Isaac, E., 'Introduction to 1 (Ethiopic Apocalypse of) Enoch', in vol. 1 of *The Old Testament Pseudepigrapha* (ed. James H. Charlesworth; 2 vols; London: Darton, Longman & Todd, 1983), pp. 5–12.

Johnson, Luke Timothy, *The Writings of the New Testament: An Interpretation* (Minneapolis: Fortress Press, rev. edn, 1999).

———, *Hebrews: A Commentary* (New Testament Library; Louisville: Westminster John Knox Press, 2006).

Johnson, Sherman E., 'Asia Minor and Early Christianity', in *Christianity, Judaism and Other Greco-Roman Cults: Studies for Morton Smith at 60* (ed. Jacob Neusner; vol. 2, Early Christianity. Studies in Judaism in Late Antiquity 12; Leiden: Brill, 1975), pp. 77–145.

Kasemann, E., 'Epheserbrief', in *Die Religion in Geschichte und Gegenwart: Handwörterbuch für Theologie und Religionswissenschaft* (ed. Kurt Galling; 7 vols; Tübingen: J. C. B. Mohr, 3rd edn, 1957–65), vol. 2, pp. 518–19.

Kee, H. C., 'Introduction to Testaments of the Twelve Patriarchs', in vol. 1 of *The Old Testament Pseudepigrapha* (ed. James H. Charlesworth; 2 vols; London: Darton, Longman & Todd, 1983), pp. 775–81.

Keener, Craig S., *The Gospel of John: A Commentary* (vol. 1; Peabody, MA: Hendrickson, 2003).

———, *1–2 Corinthians* (New Cambridge Bible Commentary; Cambridge: Cambridge University Press, 2005).

Kehl, N. von, 'Erniedrigung und Erhöhung in Qumran und Kolossä', *Zeitschrift für Katholische Theologie* 91 (1969), pp. 364–94.

Kim, Seyoon, *The Origin of Paul's Gospel* (Wissenschaftliche Untersuchungen zum Neuen Testament; Second Series 4; Tübingen: J. C. B. Mohr, 1981).

Kittel, Gerhard and Gerhard Friedrich (eds), *Theological Dictionary of the New Testament* (trans. Geoffrey. W. Bromiley; 10 vols; Grand Rapids: Eerdmans, 1964–76).

Knight III, George W., *The Pastoral Epistles: A Commentary on the Greek Text* (New International Greek Testament Commentary; Grand Rapids: Eerdmans, 1992).

Knox, Wilfred L., *St. Paul and the Church of the Gentiles* (Cambridge: Cambridge University Press, 1939).

Kraft, Robert A. et al. (eds), *The Testament of Job: According to the SV Text* (Greek text and English translation ed. Robert A. Kraft et al.; Pseudepigrapha Series, Society of Biblical Literature 4/Texts and Translations, Society of Biblical Literature 5; Missoula, MT: Society of Biblical Literature and Scholars Press, 1974).

Kreitzer, Larry J., '"Crude Language" and "Shameful Things Done in Secret" (Ephesians 5.4, 12): Allusions to the Cult of Demeter/ Cybele in Hierapolis?', *Journal for the Study of the New Testament* 71 (1998), pp. 51–77.

———, 'The Plutonium of Hierapolis and the Descent of Christ into the "Lowermost Parts of the Earth" (Ephesians 4.9)', *Biblica* 79 (1998), pp. 381–93.

Kuhn, Heinz Wolfgang, *Enderwartung und gegenwärtiges Heil: Untersuchungen zu den Gemeindeliedern von Qurmran* (Studien zur Umwelt des Neuen Testaments 4; Göttingen: Vandenhoeck & Ruprecht, 1966).

Kuhn, Karl Georg, 'Der Epheserbrief im Lichte der Qumrantexte', *New Testament Studies* 7 (1960–61), pp. 334–46.

———, 'The Epistle to the Ephesians in the Light of the Qumran Texts', in *Paul and Qumran: Studies in New Testament Exegesis* (ed. Jerome Murphy-O'Connor; London: Geoffrey Chapman, 1968), pp. 115–31.

Kümmel, Werner Georg, *Introduction to the New Testament* (trans. Howard Clark Kee; Nashville: Abingdon, 17th edn, 1975).

Lambrecht, Jan, *Second Corinthians* (Sacra Pagina Series 8; Collegeville, MN: The Liturgical Press, 1999).

Lane, William L., *Hebrews* (Word Biblical Commentary 47a–b; 2 vols; Nashville: Thomas Nelson, 1991).

Lash, Christopher J. A., 'Where Do Devils Live?: A Problem in the Textual Criticism of Ephesians 6.12', *Vigiliae Christianae* 30 (1976), pp. 161–74.

Lemmer, H. R., 'Reciprocity between Eschatology and Pneuma in Ephesians 1.3–14', *Neotestamentica* 21 (1987), pp. 159–82.

Liddell, H. G., R. Scott, and H. S. Jones, *A Greek–English Lexicon* (with revised supplement; Oxford: Clarendon Press, 9th edn, 1996).

Lightfoot, Joseph Barber, *Saint Paul's Epistle to the Philippians* (London: Macmillan, 1881).

———, *Notes on Epistles of St. Paul from Unpublished Commentaries* (London: Macmillan, 1895).

Lim, Timothy H., 'Paul, Letters of', in vol. 2 of *Encyclopedia of the Dead Sea Scrolls* (ed. Lawrence H. Schiffman and James C. VanderKam; 2 vols; Oxford: Oxford University Press, 2000), pp. 638–41.

Lincoln, Andrew T., 'A Re-Examination of "The Heavenlies" in Ephesians', *New Testament Studies* 19 (1973), pp. 468–83.

———, '"Paul the Visionary": The Setting and Significance of the Rapture to Paradise in 2 Corinthians 12.1-10', *New Testament Studies* 25 (1979), pp. 204–20.

———, *Paradise Now and Not Yet: Studies in the Role of the Heavenly Dimension in Paul's Thought with Special Reference to his*

Eschatology (Society for New Testament Studies Monograph Series 43; Cambridge: Cambridge University Press, 1981).

———, 'The Use of the OT in Ephesians', *Journal for the Study of the New Testament* 14 (1982), pp. 16–57.

———, 'The Church and Israel in Ephesians 2', *Catholic Biblical Quarterly* 49.4 (1987), pp. 605–24.

———, *Ephesians* (Word Biblical Commentary 42; Nashville: Thomas Nelson, 1990).

———, *The Gospel According to Saint John* (Black's New Testament Commentaries; London: Hendrickson, 2005).

Lincoln, Andrew T. and A. J. M. Wedderburn, *The Theology of the Later Pauline Letters* (New Testament Theology; Cambridge: Cambridge University Press, 1993).

Lona, Horacio E., *Die Eschatologie im Kolosser- und Epheserbrief* (Forschung zur Bibel 48; Würzburg: Echter, 1984).

Louw, Johannes P. and Eugene A. Nida (eds), *Greek English Lexicon of the New Testament Based on Semantic Domains* (2 vols; New York: United Bible Societies, 1988).

Lucian (trans. M. D. Macleod; vol. 7; Loeb Classical Library; London: William Heinemann, 1961).

Lyonnet, Stanislas, 'Paul's Adversaries in Colossae', in *Conflict at Colossae: A Problem in the Interpretation of Early Christianity Illustrated by Modern Studies* (ed. and trans. Fred O. Francis and Wayne A. Meeks; Missoula, MT: Society of Biblical Literature and Scholars, 1975), pp. 147–61.

Lyons, John, *Language, Meaning and Context* (Fontana Linguistics; London: Fontana Paperbacks, 1981).

———, *Linguistic Semantics: An Introduction* (Cambridge: Cambridge University Press, 1995).

MacDonald, Margaret Y., *Colossians and Ephesians* (Sacra Pagina 17; Collegeville, MN: The Liturgical Press, 2000).

McGough, Michael Everett, 'An Investigation of Ἐπουράνιος in Ephesians' (unpublished doctoral dissertation; New Orleans Baptist Theological Seminary, 1987).

Maile, J. F., 'Heaven, Heavenlies, Paradise', in *Dictionary of Paul and His Letters* (ed. Gerald F. Hawthorne, Ralph P. Martin, and Daniel G. Reid; Downers Grove, IL: InterVarsity, 1993), pp. 381–83.

Marshall, I. Howard, *A Critical and Exegetical Commentary on the Pastoral Epistles* (International Critical Commentary on the Holy Scriptures of the Old and New Testaments; Edinburgh: T & T Clark, 1999).

Martin, Ralph P., *Carmen Christi: Philippians ii. 5-11 in Recent Interpretation and in the Setting of Early Christian Worship* (Grand Rapids: Eerdmans, rev. edn, 1983).

———, *The Epistle of Paul to the Philippians: An Introduction and Commentary* (The Tyndale New Testament Commentaries 11; Leicester: InterVarsity, 2nd edn, 1987).

———, *Ephesians, Colossians, and Philemon* (Interpretation: A Bible Commentary for Teaching and Preaching; Atlanta: John Knox Press, 1991).

Metzger, Bruce, 'Paul's Vision of the Church: A Study of the Ephesian Letter', *Theology Today* 6.1 (1949), pp. 49–63.

———, *A Textual Commentary on the Greek New Testament* (Stuttgart: Deutsche Bibelgesellschaft, 2nd edn, 1994).

Michel, O., 'ἐπουράνιος', in *Exegetical Dictionary of the New Testament* (ed. Horst Balz and Gerhard Schneider; trans. James W. Thompson and John W. Medendorp; 3 vols; Grand Rapids: Eerdmans, 1990–93), vol. 2, pp. 46–47.

Mitton, C. Leslie, *Ephesians* (New Century Bible; London: Marshall, Morgan & Scott, 1976).

Moo, Douglas J., *The Epistle to the Romans* (New International Commentary on the New Testament; Grand Rapids: Eerdmans, 1996).

Moritz, Thorsten, *A Profound Mystery: The Use of the Old Testament in Ephesians* (Supplements to Novum Testamentum 85; Leiden: E. J. Brill, 1996).

Morray-Jones, C. R. A., 'Paradise Revisited (2 Cor. 12.1-12): The Jewish Mystical Background of Paul's Apostolate: Part 1: The Jewish Sources', *Harvard Theological Review* 86.2 (1993), pp. 177–217.

———, 'Paradise Revisited (2 Cor. 12.1-12): The Jewish Mystical Background of Paul's Apostolate: Part 2: Paul's Heavenly Ascent and Its Significance', *Harvard Theological Review* 86.3 (1993), pp. 265–92.

Morris, Leon, *The First Epistle of Paul to the Corinthians: An Introduction and Commentary* (Tyndale New Testament Commentaries 7; Leicester: InterVarsity, 2nd edn, 1985).

———, *The Epistle to the Romans* (Grand Rapids: Eerdmans, 1988).

———, *Expository Reflections on the Letter to the Ephesians* (Grand Rapids: Baker Books, 1994).

Moule, H. C. G., *The Epistle to the Philippians* (Cambridge Bible for Schools and Colleges; Cambridge: Cambridge University Press, 1923).

Moulton, James Hope and George Milliagan, *The Vocabulary of the Greek Testament: Illustrated from the Papyri and Other Non-Literary Sources* (London: Hodder and Stoughton, rev.edn, 1952).

Mounce, William D., *Pastoral Epistles* (Word Biblical Commentary 46; Nashville: Thomas Nelson, 2000).

Muddiman, John, *A Commentary on the Epistle to the Ephesians* (Black's New Testament Commentaries; London: Continuum, 2001).

Mussner, Franz, 'Contributions Made by Qumran to the Understanding of the Epistle to the Ephesians', in *Paul and Qumran: Studies in New Testament Exegesis* (ed. Jerome Murphy-O'Connor; London: Geoffrey Chapman, 1968), pp. 159–78.

———, *Der Brief an die Epheser* (Ökumenischer Taschenbuchkommentar zum Neuen Testament 10; Gütersloh: Gütersloher Verlagshaus, 1982).

Newsom, Carol A., *Songs of the Sabbath Sacrifice: A Critical Edition* (Harvard Semitic Studies 27; Atlanta: Scholars Press, 1985).

———, 'Heaven', in *Encyclopedia of the Dead Sea Scrolls* (ed. Lawrence H. Schiffman and James C. VanderKam; 2 vols; Oxford: Oxford University Press, 2000), vol. 1, pp. 338–40.

———, 'Songs of the Sabbath Sacrifice', in *Encyclopedia of the Dead Sea Scrolls* (ed. Lawrence H. Schiffman and James C. VanderKam; 2 vols; Oxford: Oxford University Press, 2000), vol. 2, pp. 887–89.

Nickelsburg, George W. E., *Jewish Literature Between the Bible and the Mishnah: A Historical and Literary Introduction* (Philadelphia: Fortress Press, 1981).

Noll, S. F., 'Qumran and Paul', in *Dictionary of Paul and His Letters* (ed. Gerald F. Hawthorne, Ralph P. Martin, and Daniel G. Reid; Downers Grove, IL: InterVarsity, 1993), pp. 777–83.

O'Brien, Peter T., 'Ephesians I: An Unusual Introduction to a New Testament Letter', *New Testament Studies* 25.4 (1979), pp. 504–16.

———, *Colossians, Philemon* (Word Biblical Commentary 44; Nashville: Thomas Nelson, 1982).

———, 'Principalities and Powers: Opponents of the Church', in *Biblical Interpretation and the Church: Text and Context* (ed. D. A. Carson; Exeter: Paternoster, 1984), pp. 110–50.

———, 'The Church as a Heavenly and Eschatological Entity', in *The Church in the Bible and the World: An International Study* (ed. D. A. Carson; Exeter: Paternoster, 1987), pp. 88–119, 307–11.

———, *The Epistle to the Philippians: A Commentary on the Greek Text* (New International Greek Testament Commentary; Grand Rapids: Eerdmans, 1991).

———, 'Colossians' in *New Bible Commentary* (ed. D. A. Carson, R. T. France, J. A. Motyer, and G. J. Wenham; Leicester: InterVarsity, 4th edn, 1994), pp. 1260–76.

———, *The Letter to the Ephesians* (Pillar New Testament Commentary; Grand Rapids: Eerdmans, 1999).

Odeberg, Hugo, *The View of the Universe in the Epistle to the Ephesians* (Lund: Gleerup, 1934).

Oracula Sibyllina (ed. Aloisius Rzach; Prague: F. Tempsky, 1891).

Page, Sydney H. T., *Powers of Evil: A Biblical Study of Satan and Demons* (Grand Rapids: Baker Books, 1995).

Patzia, Arthur G., *Ephesians, Colossians, and Philemon* (New International Biblical Commentary 10; Peabody, MA: Hendrickson, 1990).
Penner, Erwin, 'The Enthronement of Christ in Ephesians', *Direction* 12.3 (1983), pp. 12–19.
Pennington, Jonathan T., *Heaven and Earth in the Gospel of Matthew* (Supplements to Novum Testamentum 126; Leiden: Brill, 2007).
Percy, Ernst, *Die Probleme der Kolosser-und Epheserbriefe* (Acta Regiae Societatis Humaniorum Litterarum Lundensis 39; Lund: Gleerup, 1946).
Philo (trans. F. H. Colson and G. H. Whitaker; Loeb Classical Library; 10 vols; London: William Heinemann, 1929–1962).
Plato: With an English Translation (trans. Harold North Fowler; Loeb Classical Library; vol. 1; London: William Heinemann, 1960).
Pope, R. Martin, 'Studies in Pauline Vocabulary: Of the Heavenly Places', *The Expository Times* 23 (1912), pp. 365–68.
Quintus Smyrnaeus, *The Fall of Troy/Quintus Smyrnaeus* (trans. Arthur S. Way; Loeb Classical Library; London: William Heinemann, 1913).
Ridderbos, Hermann, *Paul: An Outline of His Theology* (trans. J. R. de Witt; Grand Rapids: Eerdmans, 1975).
Roberts, J. H., 'Jewish Mystical Experience in the Early Christian Era as Background to Understanding Colossians', *Neotestamentica* 32.1 (1998), pp. 161–89.
Robinson, J. Armitage, *St. Paul's Epistle to the Ephesians* (London: James Clarke, 1904).
Robinson, S. E., 'Introduction to Testament of Adam', in vol. 1 of *The Old Testament Pseudepigrapha* (ed. James H. Charlesworth; 2 vols; London: Darton, Longman & Todd, 1983), pp. 989–92.
Rowland, Christopher, *The Open Heaven: A Study of Apocalyptic in Judaism and Early Christianity* (London: SPCK, 1982).
———, 'Apocalyptic Visions and the Exaltation of Christ in the Letter to the Colossians', *Journal for the Study of the New Testament* 19 (1983), pp. 73–83.
———, *Christian Origins: An Account of the Setting and Character of the Most Important Messianic Sect of Judaism* (London: SPCK, 1985).
Sanders, Jack T., 'Hymnic Elements in Ephesians 1–3', *Zeitschrift für die Neutestamentamentliche Wissenschaft* 56 (1965), pp. 214–32.
Sappington, Thomas J., *Revelation and Redemption at Colossae* (Journal for the Study of the New Testament Supplement Series 53; Sheffield: Sheffield Academic Press, 1991).
Saunders, Ernest W., 'The Colossian Heresy and Qumran Theology', in *Studies in the History and Text of the New Testament* (ed. Boyd L. Daniels and M. Jack Suggs; Studies and Documents 29; Salt Lake City: University of Utah Press, 1967), pp. 133–45.

Schäfer, Peter, 'New Testament and Hekhalot Literature: The Journey into Heaven in Paul and in Merkavah Mysticism', *Journal of Jewish Studies* 35.1 (1984), pp. 19–35.

Schlier, Heinrich, *Der Brief an die Epheser: ein Kommentar* (Düsseldorf: Patmos, 1957).

———, *Principalities and Powers in the New Testament* (Quaestiones Disputatae 3; New York: Herder and Herder, 1961).

Schnackenburg, Rudolf, *Ephesians: A Commentary* (trans. Helen Heron; Edinburgh: T & T Clark, 1991).

Schoenborn, U., οὐρανός', in *Exegetical Dictionary of the New Testament* (ed. Horst Balz and Gerhard Schneider; trans. James W. Thompson and John W. Medendorp; 3 vols; Grand Rapids: Eerdmans, 1990–1993), vol. 2, pp. 543–47.

Scholem, Gershom G., *Major Trends in Jewish Mysticism* (New York: Schocken Books, 3rd edn, 1954).

———, *Jewish Gnosticism, Merkabah Mysticism, and Talmudic Tradition* (New York: The Jewish Theological Seminary of America, 1960).

Schoonhoven, Calvin R., *The Wrath of Heaven* (Grand Rapids: Eerdmans, 1966).

Schrage, Wolfgang, *Der erste Brief an die Korinther* (Evangelisch-Katholischer Kommentar zum Neuen Testament 7/4; 4 vols; Düsseldorf: Benziger, 2001).

Scott, James M., 'Throne-Chariot Mysticism in Qumran and in Paul', in *Eschatology, Messianism, and the Dead Sea Scrolls* (ed. Craig A. Evans and Peter W. Flint; Studies in the Dead Sea Scrolls and Related Literature 1; Grand Rapids: Eerdmans, 1997), pp. 101–19.

Segal, Alan F., *Two Powers in Heaven: Early Rabbinic Reports about Christianity and Gnosticism* (Studies in Judaism in Late Antiquity 25; Leiden: Brill, 1977).

———, 'Heavenly Ascent in Hellenistic Judaism, Early Christianity and their Environment', in *Aufstieg und Niedergang der Römischen Welt: Geschichte und Kultur Roms im Spiegel der neueren Forschung* 23.2 (ed. H. Temporini and W. Haase; Part 2, *Principat*, 23.2; Berlin: Walter de Gruyter, 1980), pp. 1333–94.

———, *Paul the Convert* (New Haven: Yale University Press, 1990).

Sextus Empiricus (trans. R. G. Bury; Loeb Classical Library; vol. 4; London: William Heinemann, 1949).

Silva, Moisés, *Philippians* (Baker Exegetical Commentary on the New Testament; Grand Rapids: Baker Academic, 2nd edn, 2005).

Simon, Ulrich, *Heaven in the Christian Tradition* (London: Wyman and Sons, 1958).

Smith, Derwood C., 'The Ephesian Heresy and the Origin of the Epistle to the Ephesians', *Ohio Journal of Religious Studies* 5.2 (1977), pp. 78–103.

Smith, Ian K., *Heavenly Perspective: A Study of the Apostle Paul's Response to a Jewish Mystical Movement at Colossae* (Library of New Testament Studies 326; London: T & T Clark, 2006).

Smith, Morton. 'Ascent to the Heavens and Deification in 4QM[a]', in *Archaeology and History in the Dead Sea Scrolls: The New York University Conference in Memory of Yigael Yadin* (ed. Lawrence H. Schiffman; Journal for the Study of the Pseudepigrapha Supplement Series 8/American Schools of Oriental Research/ Journal for the Study of the Old Testament Monograph Series 2; Sheffield: Sheffield Academic Press, 1990), pp. 181–88.

Snodgrass, Klyne, *Ephesians* (NIV Application Commentary; Grand Rapids: Zondervan, 1996).

Spittler, R. P., 'Introduction to Testament of Job', in *The Old Testament Pseudepigrapha* (ed. James H. Charlesworth; 2 vols; London: Darton, Longman & Todd, 1983), vol. 1, pp. 829–38.

Stone, M. E., 'Introduction to Questions of Ezra', in *The Old Testament Pseudepigrapha* (ed. James H. Charlesworth; 2 vols; London: Darton, Longman & Todd, 1983), vol. 1, pp. 591–95.

Stott, John R. W., *The Message of Ephesians: God's New Society* (The Bible Speaks Today; Leicester: InterVarsity, 1979).

Talbert, Charles H., *Ephesians and Colossians* (Paideia Commentaries on the New Testament; Grand Rapids: Baker Academic, 2007).

The Testament of Abraham: The Greek Recensions (trans. Michael E. Stone; Pseudepigrapha Series, Society of Biblical Literature 2/Texts and Translations, Society of Biblical Literature 2; Missoula, MT: Society of Biblical Literature, 1972).

Thielman, Frank S., 'Ephesians', in *Commentary on the New Testament Use of the Old Testament* (ed. G. K. Beale and D. A. Carson; Grand Rapids: Baker Academic, 2007), pp. 813–33.

Thiselton, Anthony C., *The First Epistle to the Corinthians: A Commentary on the Greek Text* (New International Greek Testament Commentary; Grand Rapids: Eerdmans, 2000).

Thurston, Bonnie B. and Judith M. Ryan, *Reading Colossians, Ephesians, and 2 Thessalonians: A Literary and Theological Commentary* (Reading the New Testament Series; New York: Crossroad, 1995).

———, *Philippians and Philemon* (Sacra Pagina Series 10; Collegeville, MN: The Liturgical Press, 2005).

Towner, Philip H., *The Letters to Timothy and Titus* (New International Commentary on the New Testament; Grand Rapids: Eerdmans, 2006).

Traub, H., ὀὐρανός, οὐράνιος, ἐπουράνιος, οὐρανόθεν', in *Theological Dictionary of the New Testament* (ed. Gerhard Kittel and Gerhard Friedrich; 10 vols; Grand Rapids: Eerdmans, 1964–1976), vol. 5, pp. 497–543.

Trebilco, Paul R., *Jewish Communities in Asia Minor* (Society for the New Testament Studies Monograph Series 69; Cambridge: Cambridge University Press, 1991).

Turner, Max, 'Ephesians', in *New Bible Commentary* (ed. D. A. Carson, R. T. France, J. A. Motyer, and G. J. Wenham; Leicester: InterVarsity, 4th edn, 1994), pp. 1222–44.

———, 'Mission and Meaning in Terms of "Unity" in Ephesians', in *Mission and Meaning: Essays Presented to Peter Cotterell* (ed. Anthony Billington, Tony Lane, and Max Turner; Carlisle, United Kingdom: Paternoster, 1995), pp. 138–66.

van Roon, A., *The Authenticity of Ephesians* (Supplements to Novum Testamentum 39; Leiden: Brill, 1974).

Vermes, Geza, *The Complete Dead Sea Scrolls in English* (London: Allen Lane/The Penguin Press, 1997).

———, *An Introduction to the Complete Dead Sea Scrolls* (London: SCM Press, 1999).

Vos, Geerhardus, 'The Eschatological Aspect of the Pauline Conception of the Spirit', in *Biblical and Theological Studies* (New York: Charles Scribner's Sons, 1912), pp. 209–59.

———, *The Pauline Eschatology* (Princeton: Princeton University Press, 1930).

Wallace, Daniel B., *Greek Grammar Beyond the Basics: An Exegetical Syntax of the New Testament* (Grand Rapids: Zondervan, 1996).

Wessels, G. F., 'The Eschatology of Colossians and Ephesians', *Neotestamentica* 21 (1987), pp. 183–202.

White, Joel, 'Paul's Cosmology: The Witness of Romans, 1 and 2 Corinthians, and Galatians', in *Cosmology and New Testament Theology* (ed. Jonathan T. Pennington and Sean M. McDonough; Library of New Testament Studies 355; New York: T & T Clark, 2008), pp. 90–106.

Wink, Walter, *Naming the Powers: The Language of Power in the New Testament* (Philadelphia: Fortress Press, 1984).

Wintermute, O. S., 'Introduction to Jubilees', in *The Old Testament Pseudepigrapha* (ed. James H. Charlesworth; 2 vols; London: Darton, Longman & Todd, 1985), vol. 2, pp. 35–51.

Witherington III, Ben, *The Letters to Philemon, the Colossians, and the Ephesians: A Socio-Rhetorical Commentary on the Captivity Epistles* (Grand Rapids: Eerdmans, 2007).

Yamauchi, Edwin, 'Qumran and Colosse', *Bibliotheca Sacra* 121 (1964), pp. 141–52.

Zerwick, Max and Mary Grosvenor, *A Grammatical Analysis of the Greek New Testament* (vol. II, Epistles – Apocalypse; Rome: Biblical Institute Press, 1979).

Index of Ancient Sources

Old Testament

Index of Modern Authors